EDMUND BURKE AND THE INVENTION OF MODERN CONSERVATISM, 1830–1914

OXFORD HISTORICAL MONOGRAPHS

The *Oxford Historical Monographs* series publishes some of the best Oxford University doctoral theses on historical topics, especially those likely to engage the interest of a broad academic readership.

Editors

P. CLAVIN J. DARWIN J. INNES
J. MCDOUGALL D. PARROTT S. A. SMITH
B. WARD-PERKINS J. L. WATTS W. WHYTE

Edmund Burke and the Invention of Modern Conservatism, 1830–1914

An Intellectual History

EMILY JONES

OXFORD
UNIVERSITY PRESS

Great Clarendon Street, Oxford, OX2 6DP,
United Kingdom

Oxford University Press is a department of the University of Oxford.
It furthers the University's objective of excellence in research, scholarship,
and education by publishing worldwide. Oxford is a registered trade mark of
Oxford University Press in the UK and in certain other countries

© Emily Jones 2017

The moral rights of the author have been asserted

First Edition published in 2017

Impression: 5

All rights reserved. No part of this publication may be reproduced, stored in
a retrieval system, or transmitted, in any form or by any means, without the
prior permission in writing of Oxford University Press, or as expressly permitted
by law, by licence or under terms agreed with the appropriate reprographics
rights organization. Enquiries concerning reproduction outside the scope of the
above should be sent to the Rights Department, Oxford University Press, at the
address above

You must not circulate this work in any other form
and you must impose this same condition on any acquirer

Published in the United States of America by Oxford University Press
198 Madison Avenue, New York, NY 10016, United States of America

British Library Cataloguing in Publication Data
Data available

Library of Congress Control Number: 2016952216

ISBN 978-0-19-879942-9

Printed in Great Britain by
CPI Group (UK) Ltd, Croydon, CR0 4YY

Links to third party websites are provided by Oxford in good faith and
for information only. Oxford disclaims any responsibility for the materials
contained in any third party website referenced in this work.

Acknowledgements

This book would have been impossible to write without the financial support provided by the Arts and Humanities Research Council, the University of Oxford History Faculty Lothian Studentship, and Exeter College, Oxford. I am also thankful to Pembroke College, Cambridge, for electing me as their Mark Kaplanoff Research Fellow; it was here that the final manuscript was completed. The fact that it could be written at all, however, is thanks to the remarkable staff of both the John Radcliffe Hospital in Oxford and the Clatterbridge Cancer Centre. I am eternally grateful, in particular, to Allyson Parry, Stana Bojanic, and Brian Haylock.

The intellectual problem at the heart of this monograph initially piqued my interest as an undergraduate, but solving this problem has taken me through three cities that I have had the pleasure to call home: Manchester, Oxford, and Cambridge. From the moment I walked into his office as an undergraduate at Manchester, Stuart Jones has been a constant source of advice and encouragement. I am incredibly indebted to all of the historians who have quizzed and conversed with me since; and I would like to thank, in particular, Richard Bourke, Jane Garnett, Christina de Bellaigue, and Faramerz Dabhoiwala. This book is clearer and more rigorous thanks to the excellent counsel of my DPhil examiners, Philip Williamson and Simon Skinner, as well as OUP's anonymous reader.

I owe a special debt, however, to my supervisor, Peter Ghosh. Peter's enthusiasm for my project—not to mention a shared desire to write properly historical intellectual history—was apparent from the start; a real 'ditto to Mr Burke' moment which I hope was mutual in some small part. My work, and not least this book, has been infinitely improved thanks to his scholarly engagement, conceptual rigour, and passion for stylistic clarity. It has been a pleasure and a privilege to work with a historian who combines fearless criticism with such great humour and generosity. I am forever thankful for his support, encouragement, and friendship over the last five years.

My thanks must also go to the staff at the Bodleian Library, Oxford (especially the Upper Reading Room), the British Library, Cambridge University Library, and the archivists at Trinity and King's Colleges, Cambridge. I am particularly grateful to the Master and Fellows of Trinity College, Cambridge for permission to cite material from the J. R. M. Butler Papers, and to the Master of King's College, Cambridge for permission to use copyrighted material from the J. M. Keynes Papers.

In the process of turning my thesis into this book, I have also incurred debts to both the Oxford Historical Monographs committee and those at OUP who have been invaluable guides. I must thank, in particular, John Watts, Cathryn Steele, Brian North, and OUP's anonymous reader for their assistance and encouragement.

My final thanks are, of course, to my friends and family. In Oxford I found that rarest of things: the greatest friend and intellectual ally in all things nineteenth century, and much else besides. I have never enjoyed history so much as when I'm with James Kirby, with whom many of the thoughts and arguments detailed here were first thrashed out, expanded, and refined. James also provided perspective, moral support, laughter, and cups of tea when I needed them most, as did many other friends: I also send my thanks to the Maximum Laughs Crew, the Female Leaders of the Free World, and everyone else—you know who you are; to Joe Wright, who achieved the unthinkable and learnt to read my mind; and, lastly, to my parents, for their endless love and support.

Contents

List of Abbreviations	ix
1. Introduction	1
The Life and Afterlife of Edmund Burke	2
Writing the History of a Tradition	8
A Brief Literary History	11
2. Constitutional Politics, *c*.1830–1880	16
English Constitutionalism	20
Whigs and Liberals	28
Tories and Conservatives	34
Church and State	43
Conclusion	52
3. Irishness, National Character, and the Interpretation of Political Thought, *c*.1830–1914	56
Wisdom	59
Passion	68
Madness	73
Conclusion	79
4. Critical Recovery, *c*.1860–1880	81
Intellectual Context	87
Critical Problems	92
Critical Recovery: Thought	95
Critical Recovery: Character	107
Conclusion	112
5. Irish Home Rule, *c*.1886–1893	114
Burke Before the Kite	117
The Gladstonian Argument	122
Opposition: Liberal Unionists and Conservatives	135
History and Party Identity	144
Conclusion	153
6. The New Conservatism, *c*.1885–1914	156
The Political Context	157
The Intellectual Context	160
The Political Philosophy of Edmund Burke	163

Political Conservatism	177
Conclusion	194

7. Learning Conservatism: Burke in Education, *c*.1880–1914   197
    At School   201
    At University   210
    Autodidacticism   219
    Conclusion   226

8. Epilogue   228

Bibliography   233
Index   265

List of Abbreviations

BM	*Blackwood's Magazine*
CR	*Contemporary Review*
DR	*Dublin Review*
EHR	*English Historical Review*
EJPT	*European Journal of Political Theory*
ER	*Edinburgh Review*
FR	*Fortnightly Review*
HEI	*History of European Ideas*
HJ	*Historical Journal*
HPT	*History of Political Thought*
ICS	*Indian Civil Service*
JBS	*Journal of British Studies*
JHI	*Journal of the History of Ideas*
NC	*Nineteenth Century*
NR	*National Review*
ODNB	*Oxford Dictionary of National Biography*
QR	*Quarterly Review*
SR	*Saturday Review*
TCD	*Trinity College, Dublin*
TRHS	*Transactions of the Royal Historical Society*
VS	*Victorian Studies*
WR	*Westminster Review*
WSEB	*Writings and Speeches of Edmund Burke*

1
Introduction

> There was an honest Irishman, a great favourite among them, who used to entertain them with raree-shows, and to exhibit a magic lantern to the children on winter evenings. He had gone quite mad upon this subject. Sometimes he would call out in the middle of the street, 'Take care of that corner, neighbours; for the love of Heaven, keep clear of that post, there is a patent steel-trap concealed thereabouts.' Sometimes he would be disturbed by frightful dreams; then he would get up at dead of night, open his window and cry 'fire,' till the parish was roused, and the engines sent for. The pulpit of the Parish of St George seemed likely to fall; I believe that the only reason was that the parson had grown too fat and heavy; but nothing would persuade this honest man but that it was a scheme of the people at St Dennis's, and that they had sawed through the pillars in order to break the rector's neck. Once he went about with a knife in his pocket, and told all the persons whom he met that it had been sharpened by the knife-grinder of the next parish to cut their throats
>
> Thomas Babington Macaulay, 1824[1]

Today, the ideological centrality of Macaulay's knife-wielder, Edmund Burke, to C/conservatism as either an intellectual (small 'c') or political (capital 'C') tradition is beyond dispute.[2] Burke's distinctive brand of organic, historic conservatism—usually summarized as a belief in the organic nature of society and politics (hence a dislike of 'mechanical' abstract theory when applied to practical politics); reverence for history and tradition; and respect for religion, property, and order—has been internationally influential in both academic analysis and in a more concrete political sense. An ordinary student encounter with Burke in any context outside an empirical discussion of eighteenth-century Britain finds him presented as the 'founder of conservatism', focusing in particular on

---

[1] T. B. Macaulay, 'Some Account of a Great Lawsuit Between the Parishes of St Dennis and St George in the Water' [1824], *Lays of Ancient Rome, Essays and Poems* (1910), 307.
[2] For intellectual and stylistic clarity, 'Conservative' is used to indicate party political affiliation, whereas 'conservative' denotes the intellectual tradition. Where both terms are applicable 'C/conservative' is employed.

his impassioned critique of the French Revolution, *Reflections on the Revolution in France* (1790). But this apparently neat intellectual and political legacy is in fact modern; the product of a long historical process which gradually but decisively distilled Burke's work (an assortment of writings, letters, and speeches) into an ever-convenient political philosophy of conservatism—a body of thought which is deeply connected to British Conservatism. The purpose of this book is to ascertain exactly when and how 'Burkean conservatism' was first shaped into a powerful intellectual and political force in Britain. For this reason, it portrays both the historical development of Burke's reputation and also a significant strand in the broader political and intellectual tradition of C/conservatism. In doing so, my aim has been to provide a much more precise idea of how political traditions are constructed, as well as how they adapt and evolve in changing circumstances and contexts—be they political, intellectual, cultural, or otherwise.

THE LIFE AND AFTERLIFE OF EDMUND BURKE

Before the invention of Burkean conservatism there was of course a 'historical Burke'. Born in Dublin in 1730, the son of a Catholic mother and a converted Anglican father, Burke established his literary reputation through publications such as *Vindication of Natural Society* (1756), a pastiche of Bolingbroke, and the aesthetic philosophical treatise *On the Origins of the Sublime and Beautiful* (1757), before entering parliament in 1765. Upon securing a seat, Burke worked under the patronage of the Whig grandee Lord Rockingham, and his most celebrated contributions to political issues of the time include his *Thoughts on the Cause of the Present Discontents* (1770), which attacked royal prerogative and defended party government, and his speeches on the American crisis (1774–5). Burke earned a reputation as a great rhetorician, a promoter of Whig principles, and a reformer of perceived abuses: the position of Catholics, the slave trade, political economy, and the alleged corruption of the Governor-General of India, Warren Hastings. Yet he had opposed parliamentary reform from at least the early 1780s (in sharp contrast to his friend and prominent Whig Charles James Fox), and Burke's political status went into decline following the death of his patron, Rockingham, in 1782. When the French Revolution broke out in 1789 Burke was quick to judge it a disaster at a time when almost all his contemporaries were rejoicing at the downfall of a rotten *ancien régime*. As Revolution turned to Terror, however, Burke was praised as prophetic by former opponents, including George III, though his intense obsession with the Revolution caused both his friends and detractors concern. By the time of his retirement in 1794, and his death in 1797, Burke's irascible temper and uncompromising belief in the terrible danger that the Revolution posed to mankind—and more specifically to Britain—had split the Whigs and left him with few close allies. In the years that followed many of Burke's supporters were reconciled with Fox following the creation of the Ministry of All the Talents in 1806, and his key political protégés French Lawrence and William Windham died in 1809 and 1810, respectively.

This historical picture contrasts vividly with the received view of Burke we encounter today. Unsurprisingly, therefore, his reception history has already attracted the attention of a number of writers, who divide into three groups. The first group of writers consists of scholars of Burke as either an individual thinker or historical figure. They include, most centrally, the American conservatives of the mid-twentieth century, such as Russell Kirk and Peter Stanlis, for whom Burke—the critic of British taxation of the American colonies—became a magnificent defensive weapon against encroaching 'Jacobinical' Cold War Communism.[3] 'In any practical sense,' Kirk stated, 'Burke is the founder of our conservatism.' He provided 'the true school of conservative principle'.[4] At the same time, Burke's fiery demands for Catholic relief and belief in the religious basis of society proved attractive for conservative Catholics such as Stanlis and Francis Canavan, who sought to reinvent Burke not only as a conservative, but as a proponent of natural law who could be utilized in the battle with 'liberalism'.[5] The natural law interpretation was one of the more contentious aspects of Burke's American conservative appropriation, as Drew Maciag shows in *Edmund Burke in America*, but other 'conservatives' such as Peter Viereck and Gertrude Himmelfarb were still happy to invoke *Reflections* as canonical ammunition against 'liberal reform'.[6]

This predominantly American school of writers condemned an earlier set of nineteenth- and early twentieth-century British and Irish authors, who had presented Burke as a 'positivist' and a 'utilitarian'. The Liberals John Morley, Leslie and James Fitzjames Stephen, W. E. H. Lecky, and even the Idealist philosopher John MacCunn were targeted especially, and their work is summarily dismissed for not demonstrating a 'correct

---

[3] Russell Kirk, *The Conservative Mind* (1954), 13–64, *passim*; Peter Stanlis, *Edmund Burke and the Natural Law* (1958), 249–50.
[4] Kirk, *The Conservative Mind*, 15–16.
[5] Francis Canavan, *The Political Reason of Edmund Burke* (1960), ix, 189–94; *Edmund Burke: Prescription and Providence* (1987), 178–9; *The Political Economy of Edmund Burke* (1995), 175–6.
[6] Drew Maciag, *Edmund Burke in America: The Contested Career of the Father of Modern Conservatism* (2013), 196–9, 204, 213, 224–8.

understanding' of Burke's thought.[7] Later scholars have followed suit, and a similar verdict can be found in more recent studies, including those of Drew Maciag, Isaac Kramnick, F. P. Lock, and Clara Gandy.[8] The 'dominant interpretation of Burke' advanced by writers like Leslie Stephen and Morley, according to James Coniff and Michel Fuchs, placed him as a forerunner of Benthamite utilitarianism—defined as promoting the greatest happiness of the greatest number, and the value of expediency in politics.[9] From these examples, it is concluded that interpreting Burke as a utilitarian was 'the British standard' for the next eighty years.[10] A very neat target was thus constructed for Burke's conservative advocates whose lodestar was natural law. A reassessment of these 'liberal utilitarian' writers will be offered in Chapter 4, but for now it is crucial to note that accounts of Burke's reception history which overlook the work of the pre-1914 writers sideline a crucial period in Burke's critical recovery. Nor should it be forgotten that much of this work was published, read, and reviewed in North America, and it too performed a key role in the history and development of Anglophone conservatism as a body of thought. The mid-twentieth century was a truly seminal moment in Burke's reception history—what Maciag calls the 'Burkean moment' when he was first widely recognized as a conservative in America.[11] Yet Burke's transformation into a conservative was not (as Maciag holds) 'mostly an American undertaking': as we shall see, it had in fact been brought about by British writers and the workings of British politics half a century earlier.[12]

---

[7] Stanlis, *Burke and the Natural Law*, xi, 4, 29–34; 'Edmund Burke in the Twentieth Century' in Stanlis, ed., *The Relevance of Edmund Burke* (1964), 49–50; Canavan, *Political Reason of Edmund Burke*, 3.

[8] Maciag, *Burke in America*, 109; David Dwan and Christopher Insole, 'Introduction', in Dwan and Insole, eds., *The Cambridge Companion to Edmund Burke* (2012), 7, 13 n.3; Stephen H. Browne, *Edmund Burke and the Discourse of Virtue* (1993), 101; F. P. Lock, *Burke's Reflections on the Revolution in France* (1985), 94–5; Clara Ingram Gandy, 'A Bibliographical Survey of Writings on Edmund Burke, 1945–75', *British Studies Monitor*, 8 (1978), 3–21, 4; Isaac Kramnick, *The Rage of Edmund Burke: Portrait of an Ambivalent Conservative* (1977), 41, 46.

[9] James Coniff, *The Useful Cobbler: Edmund Burke and the Politics of Progress* (1994), 1; Michel Fuchs, *Edmund Burke, Ireland, and the Fashioning of the Self* (1996), 5, 9.

[10] Dennis O'Keeffe, *Edmund Burke* (2010), 94.

[11] Maciag, *Burke in America*, 206.

[12] Ibid., 166. See also Emily Jones, 'Drew Maciag: Edmund Burke in America', *History*, 99 (Apr. 2014), 399–41. A recent MA thesis, taking Hansard as its principal source, has also approached this problem: Hannah Z. Sidney, 'Inventing Burke: Edmund Burke and the Conservative Party, 1790–1918', City University of New York, 2014. Although necessarily limited in scope and depth, Sidney very reasonably concludes that Burke was not constructed as a Conservative until the twentieth century. That said, the framework lacks conceptual rigour: hence Hugh Cecil is positioned rather simplistically as the chief agent of such a shift in 1912; the individual who '[gave] voice to an undifferentiated mass of emotion' (p. 71).

This brings us to a second school of thought: histories and theories of British or Anglophone C/conservatism more broadly conceived. One important consequence of the canonization of Burke as the 'founder of conservatism' has been to identify likenesses between Burke and other 'C/conservative' politicians, authors, intellectuals, and so on—usually traced backwards through a series of concepts such as dislike of applying theory to politics, a preference for gradual reform, or reverence for tradition and more elite forms of government—who seem to fit the bill. But those who go looking for such things can find them almost anywhere: hence on this principle almost anyone can be 'Burkean' because, in this type of analysis, perceived similarities take precedence over the actual, historical, political categorizations of individual figures, or indeed what they thought about Burke.[13] As a result Burke has been linked with a wide variety of figures who are now deemed to be Burkean. Indeed, many of the nineteenth-century Liberals (later Liberal Unionists) who appear in this book, such as Matthew Arnold, J. F. Stephen, and W. E. H. Lecky, have also been portrayed as 'conservatives' according to modern conceptions of democracy and religion in historical scholarship.[14] This 'conservative' political philosophy has been further linked, as Frank O'Gorman claims, to British party politics: Burke's thought 'made Conservatism possible and paved the way for its ultimate expression in the decades after his death'.[15]

A final group of commentators consists of intellectual historians of the nineteenth century whose primary focus is neither Burke nor C/conservatism but who cast an oblique light on him nonetheless. In these accounts, Burke is usually portrayed extremely positively: he was a 'universal hero' whose influence can be traced through a number of key intellectual figures, as above.[16] John Burrow in particular sees 'a kind of diffused Burkeanism' penetrating the whole of nineteenth-century

---

[13] See, for example, Iain Hampsher-Monk, 'Edmund Burke in the Tory World', in Jeremy Black, ed., *The Tory World* (2016), 91–2; Corey Robin, *The Reactionary Mind: Conservatism from Edmund Burke to Sarah Palin* (2011), 34, 42, *passim*; Ted Honderich, *Conservatism: Burke, Nozick, Bush, Blair?* (2005), 1, 8, *passim*; Frank O'Gorman, *British Conservatism from Burke to Thatcher* (1986), xiii, 12–24, *passim*. For a good popular example, see Anne McElvoy, 'Conservatism: The Grand Tour' (BBC Radio 4, Sept. 2013).

[14] B. E. Lippincott, *Victorian Critics of Democracy* (1938), 102, 106–7, 212–13; Kirk, *The Conservative Mind*, 267–86; O'Gorman, *British Conservatism*, 37–9; Andrew Vincent, *Modern Political Ideologies* (2010), 61.

[15] Frank O'Gorman, *Edmund Burke: His Political Philosophy* (1973), 11, 145–6. See also Robert Eccleshall, *English Conservatism since the Restoration* (1990), 3, 10, 18, 39–43, 80–2, 203–6, 214–16; Jesse Norman, *Edmund Burke: Philosopher, Politician, Prophet* (2013), 282.

[16] H. S. Jones, *Victorian Political Thought* (2000), 68. See also Matthew Arnold, *Edmund Burke on Irish Affairs*, ed. C. C. O'Brien (1988), xxxii; Kirk, *The Conservative Mind*, 166–8.

thought, providing a 'hidden' presence in the 'intellectual stock' of Liberals as well as Tories whenever they referenced 'their favourite image for constitutional change as the repairs and piecemeal additions to an inherited mansion, and...for tradition as a major part of political wisdom'.[17] What Burrow believes to be 'Burkeanism', however, is an exceptionally loose definition which implies no more than an evolutionary constitutionalism. 'Reading Stubbs', he states in *A History of Histories*, 'often seems like witnessing the scholarly illustration and historical elaboration of the thought of Edmund Burke: such slow, accumulative growth and constant adaptation was a sign of life.'[18] This makes the usefulness of Burkean or Burkeanism as an analytical tool questionable. As we will see (Chapter 2, 'English Constitutionalism'), this kind of constitutionalism was far too widespread and diffuse to be traced back to Burke alone. Burrow therefore provides a less explicitly partisan reading, but one which nonetheless binds very diverse figures—from Macaulay to F. W. Maitland—together under a Burkean canopy.

Thus we reach a historiographical conundrum. How could Burke have been at one and the same time a universally admired organic, historic constitutionalist, a partisan Conservative, and a 'positivist-utilitarian-liberal'? In *That Noble Science of Politics*, Burrow (alongside Stefan Collini and Donald Winch) notes quite rightly that Burke did not achieve immediate canonical status as a conservative organicist in Britain.[19] Furthermore the seminal work of James Sack offers a convincing account of why Burke was overlooked by Tories before 1830 by focusing mainly on his problematic Irish and Catholic connections.[20] So according to the existing scholarship, Burke was either moulded into a C/conservative idol almost immediately after this date, or after 1945. In suggesting otherwise, it is essential to refute the notion that the best way to chart this historical

---

[17] Stefan Collini, Donald Winch, and John Burrow, *That Noble Science of Politics: A Study in Nineteenth-Century Intellectual History* (1983), 20. See also, for example, John Burrow, *Whigs and Liberals: Continuity and Change in English Political Thought* (1988), 9–10, *passim*; *A Liberal Descent: Victorian Historians and the English Past* (1983), 2, 131; Stefan Collini, *Public Moralists: Political Thought and Intellectual Life in Britain, 1860–1930* (1991), 293; Julia Stapleton, *Englishness and the Study of Politics: The Social and Political Thought of Ernest Barker* (2006), 51–2. Both Collini and Stapleton see a 'diffused Burkeanism' in A. V. Dicey.
[18] John Burrow, *A History of Histories: Epics, Chronicles, Romances and Inquiries from Herodotus and Thucydides to the Twentieth Century* (London, 2007), 410. See also Anthony Brundage and Richard A. Cosgrove, *The Great Tradition: Constitutional History and National Identity in Britain and the United States, 1870–1960* (2007); Jones, *Victorian Political Thought*, 55.
[19] Collini, Winch, and Burrow, *Noble Science of Politics*, 20.
[20] J. J. Sack, 'The Memory of Pitt and the Memory of Burke: English Conservatism Confronts its Past, 1806–1829', *HJ*, 30 (1987), 623–40.

change is to look for what *we* see as Burkean in past thought. If we measure Burkeanism by cautious reformism or mistrust of democracy—stock features of nineteenth-century political commentary, Liberal as well as Conservative—our goalposts are pitched widely indeed. Intellectual history should offer the reader more than perceived resemblances based on an a priori agenda. This book does not attempt to trace the purported influence of Burke through echoes, or through past figures who appear to match our modern definition of Burkean.[21] Rather, it asks how Burke was actually portrayed and analysed through a variety of mediums, and shows how and why this development occurred. Only by letting go of Burkean and its present-day connotations will we gain a compelling account of Burke's shifting reputation as well as the reimagining of C/conservatism in Britain.

One final point to note relates to the continental European appropriation of Burke. This was significantly different: more Catholic, more theoretical, and far less concerned (if at all) with defects in his personal history.[22] Continental readers were much better equipped to read Burke—particularly *Reflections*—without the direct experience of Burke as a bad-tempered Irishman serving as a Whig in a British parliament. This provided a degree of malleability even in the early nineteenth century that was not possible in Britain. That is not to say that British and Irish readers were wholly unaware of (in particular) German and French scholarship on Burke, but that readings of Burke in Britain were shaped far more by indigenous concerns and issues. This was due to a variety of factors: most significantly, the self-satisfaction engendered by the unique British Constitution had created a widespread aversion to abstract and universalist political theorizing and its application to practical politics. This was particularly true in England, where there was little interest in systematizing Burke's works until the end of the century, and even then the influence of British Idealism—inspired in part by German scholarship—is obvious. This book tells the story of Burke's British and Irish reception history. In doing so, it demonstrates that the moment when it becomes possible for Irish Burke, one-time Rockingham Whig, to be adopted by a British (and especially English) audience as a seminal 'political philosopher' of C/conservatism is an absolutely pivotal moment. This is the moment when he first occupies a central canonical position in British

---

[21] As in Maciag, *Burke in America*, 33–46, 122–8.
[22] J. A. Green, 'Friedrich Gentz's Translation of Burke's Reflections', *HJ*, 57 (Sept. 2014), 639–59; 'Edmund Burke's German Readers at the End of Enlightenment, 1790–1815', PhD thesis, University of Cambridge, 2017; Rod Preece, 'Edmund Burke and his European Reception', *The Eighteenth Century*, 21 (1980), 255–73; H. Ben-Israel, *English Historians on the French Revolution* (1968), 118.

thought, and (so to speak) lays the foundations of his 'C/conservatism'. And though we will not trace the later reception of these interpretations across the Atlantic, there can be no doubt that the transformation of Burke into a C/conservative in Britain occurred long before the outbreak of the Cold War.

WRITING THE HISTORY OF A TRADITION

The central question to be answered, therefore, is that of how Burke, the Irish–British Whig politician, was moulded into his modern designation of the 'founder of conservatism'—or, as Dwan and Insole put it, 'Disneyland Burke'.[23] A satisfactory account requires an analysis of the critical themes that did most to transform his reputation; not a narrative history of everything that was said about Burke in the nineteenth century, nor a series of selections of statements made by distinguished Victorians and Edwardians. Another central premise underlying this study is that it is essential to distinguish between *literary* and *political* utterances about Burke, as for example in the case of his purported 'genius'. This is an elementary necessity when examining a notoriously eloquent political writer frequently praised for his prose style. When one does distinguish between literary admiration and political or political–philosophical commentary, it becomes much easier to think about how penetrating a stated 'influence' is, for example, in Macaulay, Gladstone, and Disraeli—to name a few of the more well-known historical actors who have been linked with Burke in the past. It also requires a qualitative rather than quantitative account: all texts are not equal in terms of intellectual significance and cultural dissemination. A simple word search for 'Burke', or even 'Edmund Burke', in digitized books and journals is fraught with problems from the start: Burke was referred to not as 'Edmund Burke' but 'Mr. Burke' for much of the century, and (when his title was dropped) column inches were filled with advertisements for both his work and that of his namesakes—grave-robbers and peerage guides included.

This leads us to sources. I have given far greater prominence to public, published, and printed discussion which reached a wide audience compared to unpublished, archival material. Of primary consideration are the major texts and articles which were either exclusively focused on Burke, or allocated him a central role. But my scope is broader: this book also takes in more popular political texts and speeches, *Hansard*, histories, memoirs,

---

[23] Dwan and Insole, 'Introduction', in *Companion to Edmund Burke*, 13.

periodical articles, reviews, teaching material, all of which must be fitted alongside the more major publications of familiar political and intellectual figures in a properly contextual history of political thought. This is something more than the history of political thought in its usual sense, however, since the object of study is not only Burke, but the development of Burkean conservatism. Here, the importance of reading, reviewing, debate, and education in establishing and maturing political ideas is seen as crucial. I wish to bridge the gap between the traditionally more conceptual history of political thought, focused on canonical thinkers and themes, and the history of the making of political traditions, in this case Conservatism. The time span is a relatively long one, but, as with any period of intellectual history, even the bookmarking dates—1830 to 1914—do not indicate a precise beginning or cut-off point. Still, the boundaries are significant: firstly, the beginning of a new era of political and constitutional history following Catholic emancipation and the 1832 Reform Act; and, secondly, the firm establishment of Burke as a C/conservative thinker following another period of constitutional crisis between 1909 and 1914.

The idea of a 'political tradition' is employed here in a specific sense. Rather than attempting to prove that Conservatives created (or have always had) an overarching 'ideology'—a limiting term which connotes a relatively rigid system of beliefs—the term 'political tradition' is employed. Indeed, a broadly focused label of this kind is necessary in a period of popular politics. Having said this, I do not rely uncritically on the existing literature on 'traditions': the idea of there being a 'British Political Tradition' draws on the foundational work of W. H. Greenleaf, among others, and later work on this topic has generally been carried out in politics departments, rather than by historians.[24] Exceptions to this rule include studies of invented national traditions by historians from Eric Hobsbawm to Paul Readman, all of whom look beyond the 'Westminster Model' to the histories of sport, historical pageantry, and so on.[25] I agree with Hobsbawm, that studying 'invented traditions' is essential because they reveal the 'symptoms' and 'indicators' of developments which are otherwise difficult for historians to identify.[26]

Unfortunately, however, very little historical work has been done which attempts to historicize ideological and/or party political, as opposed to

---

[24] W. H. Greenleaf, *The British Political Tradition* (1983); Mark Bevir, 'On Tradition', *Humanitas*, 8 (2000), 28–53; Matthew Hall, *Political Traditions and UK Politics* (2011).

[25] Eric Hobsbawm and Terence Ranger, eds., *The Invention of Tradition* (1983); Paul Readman, 'The Place of the Past in English Culture, *c.*1890–1914', *Past and Present*, 186 (2005), 147–99. See also Collini, *Public Moralists*, ch. 9; Jose Harris, *Private Lives, Public Spirit: A Social History of Britain, 1870–1914* (1993), 33.

[26] Hobsbawm, 'Introduction', in Hobsbawm and Ranger, *Invention of Tradition*, 12.

national, traditions. As a result, an interpretative structure of modern 'conservatism' and 'liberalism' is often imposed onto nineteenth-century Britain, which tends to link figures who look superficially more similar than they actually were. If we define 'political tradition', first of all, as a series of inherited beliefs—for instance on the constitution, political genealogies, partisan hero-worship, and so on—that can be adapted as contexts and circumstances change, as in Mark Bevir's 'radical historicist' reading,[27] this then provides a broad conceptual framework for thinking about the ways in which political identities are altered and realigned. Properly historicized political traditions are not just a means to 'complicate' our understanding of past thought: they offer a tool which helps us to understand the ways in which ideas are adapted; how principles and histories are altered in order to legitimate political action or rhetorical intervention; and how different strands of a broad-based political tradition such as Conservatism are picked up and put down accordingly.[28] Extending our knowledge of the changing reputation of Burke and the invention of Burkean C/conservatism is the fundamental base for comprehending our definitions of Burke, Conservatism, and conservatism today.

Within the complex networks of political tradition, original thinkers occupy an important space and so, paradoxical as it may seem, the reception history of canonical political thinkers can provide a starting point. Stefan Collini's work on the late Victorian reception of J. S. Mill, the 'universal hero' in accounts of nineteenth-century liberalism, suggests a preliminary framework, detailing four key stages that political thinkers pass through (not necessarily in order) on the road to becoming a canonized 'classic'. The first is when a thinker is still seen as relevant to contemporary issues, and invoked accordingly. The second is reached when living writers and politicians are seen as 'disciples' continuing to apply their principles. In a third phase an author becomes an 'authority' who, at certain key moments, becomes a focus for alignment, for or against. The fourth and final stage is the moment when the figure becomes a 'classic', unanimously admired but of little or no contemporary political use.[29] Most canonical thinkers, Collini argues, pass through the first two stages. However, the point at which the writer makes the transition to the third—when it becomes 'in

---

[27] Mark Bevir, 'A History of Modern Pluralism', in Bevir, ed., *Modern Pluralism: Anglo-American Exchanges since 1880* (2012), 8–9; *The Making of British Socialism* (2011), 12; Robert Adcock, Mark Bevir, and Shannon C. Stimson, 'A History of Political Science: How? What? Why?' in Adcock et al., eds., *Modern Political Science: Anglo American Exchanges since 1880* (2007), 2–8.
[28] On this final point, see Jon Lawrence, 'Class and Gender in the Making of Urban Toryism', *EHR*, 428 (1993), 634.
[29] Collini, *Public Moralists*, 318.

everyone's interest, no matter what their political allegiance' to attempt to appropriate or establish their position in relation to that thinker—is of central interest for the historian of national traditions, as it is a much rarer phenomenon.[30] By drawing on more popular sources—obituaries, memoirs, and periodical articles—Collini's study is suggestive of a method by which the intellectual historian may bridge the gap between canonical thinkers and more popular political traditions.

Burke provides an interesting application and critique of Collini's model. Firstly, as will be demonstrated in Chapters 2 and 3 (on Burke's constitutionalism and Irishness, respectively), he had few disciples—political or intellectual—in the years after his death, and different parts of his work were upheld and rejected by quite different political parties and actors. The point at which he reached stage three occurs, as Chapter 5 illustrates, during the debates on Irish Home Rule from 1885. But though Burke had achieved 'classical' status by the end of our study, he is still utilized by politicians and intellectuals to this day—albeit with less fervour than during the 1880s, 1910s, or 1950s America. So this framework can provide only a skeleton. In order to secure Burke's position at the head of a C/conservative tradition, four essential conditions must be met: firstly, cross-party agreement that Burke was an important political thinker with a distinctive body of political thought is needed (Chapter 4); secondly, this body of thought is deemed to be internally consistent and best interpreted as 'C/conservative' (Chapter 6, 'The Political Philosophy of Edmund Burke'); thirdly, that this is then used enthusiastically by a considerable number of political Conservatives who identify themselves as Burke's intellectual heirs (Chapter 6, 'Political Conservatism'); and, finally, it is disseminated at a broad level (most notably through schools and universities) thereby creating a firmly established tradition (Chapter 7). This is the specific framework which will guide my analysis. In this way, the work and reading habits of more obscure authors, journalists, teachers, and learners can be placed centre stage as the major protagonists in the history of the reputation of a classic, canonical political thinker—and in the invention of the broader tradition of Burkean C/conservatism.

A BRIEF LITERARY HISTORY

Before we begin, an overview of the publication history of both Burke and his major commentators is necessary. It is particularly important to outline

---

[30] Ibid., 319.

the availability of Burke's works and correspondence, as well as the publication of cheaper editions and abridgements of his work, because the first posthumous edition of Burke's collected works suffered from mismanagement.[31] Though Burke had promoted and published his own speeches during his lifetime, his executors French Laurence and, after Laurence's death in 1809, Walker King were slow to bring out his *Works* (from 1803)—the last of the sixteen volumes only appearing in 1827, thirty years after his death. There were reissues of the complete collected works throughout the nineteenth century, but the classic edition of Burke was Bohn's nine-volume *Works of the Rt. Hon. Edmund Burke* (1854 and later reprints), which included the fifth edition of James Prior's *Memoir of the Life and Character of the Rt. Hon. Edmund Burke* (1824; enlarged in 1826) as the ninth and final volume.[32] In addition, four volumes of Burke's *Correspondence* appeared in 1844, although many of his letters remained inaccessible until 1948.[33] Abridged editions of Burke's works then became more widely available in the second half of the century. The most critically acclaimed was Oxford's three-volume Clarendon edition, which was edited and introduced by the historian Edward John Payne, published between 1874 and 1878, and went through several later reissues.[34]

The abridged editions consisted of what were seen to be Burke's most important writings and speeches. These were, typically, the *Thoughts on the Cause of the Present Discontents* (1770), the speeches on the American colonies (1774–5), and *Reflections on the Revolution in France* (1790). Slightly less popular were the speeches and letters regarding his Bristol constituency (1774–80) and his other French writings such as the *Appeal from the New to the Old Whigs* (1791) and the *Letters on a Regicide Peace* from the mid-1790s. Earlier works such as his *Vindication of Natural Society* (1756) and *On the Sublime and Beautiful* (1757), as well as the Indian writings and speeches, including those on the impeachment of Warren Hastings (1788–95)—which Burke himself saw as the most important work of his career—and the economical treatise *Thoughts and Details on Scarcity* (1795; posthumously published in 1800), were usually excluded from the 'selected works'. As printing technologies advanced towards the

---

[31] T. W. Copeland, 'The Reputation of Edmund Burke', *JBS*, 1 (1962), 78.

[32] *The Works of the Rt. Hon. Edmund Burke*, ed. H. G. Bohn (1854). There were other editions by Bell's: *The Works of the Rt. Hon. Edmund Burke*, 6 vols (1868–72; and later reprints); J. C. Nimmo: *The Works of the Rt. Hon. Edmund Burke*, 12 vols (1887); and Oxford University Press: *The Works of the Rt. Hon. Edmund Burke*, eds. H. Wills and F. W. Rafferty, 6 vols (1906–7).

[33] *Correspondence of the Rt. Hon. Edmund Burke*, eds. C. W. W. Fitzwilliam and R. Bourke, 4 vols (1844).

[34] *Burke: Select Works*, ed. E. J. Payne, 3 vols (1874–8; and later reprints).

end of the century, it became possible to publish ever cheaper editions, and copies of his key texts were included in popular reading series such as J. M. Dent's Everyman's Classics as well as in specially commissioned school textbooks. Burke's Irish writings were presented in an easily accessible form by Matthew Arnold in 1881, although as we will see this did not mean he could not be cited as an authority on Irish affairs, from Catholic relief to disestablishment of the Irish Church, earlier in the century.[35]

Burke's principal biographers, meanwhile, provided the cornerstones of Burke scholarship in the nineteenth century and were thus indispensable as tools or quarries with which to mould public perceptions.[36] An 'official' biography never surfaced, and so the potential for interpretation was vast. Beginning with the virtually unknown James Prior (1790–1869), his *Memoir of the Life and Character of the Rt. Hon. Edmund Burke* (1824/1826) totalled over 1,100 pages and ran through five editions.[37] Prior is in every respect an obscure figure. What can be said is that he was a Protestant Irishman, born in Co. Antrim, who saw wartime service as a ship's surgeon between 1810 and 1815. After the peace, Prior settled down to a successful shore-based career in the naval hospital service, leading to a knighthood in 1858. This left him time to write and he became a successful man of letters, who was elected to the Athenaeum in 1830, producing two major biographies of eighteenth-century Irishmen: the *Life* of Burke as well as Goldsmith (1837).[38] Coming from such a background, Prior believed himself to be impartial as regards British politics, though he still aligned himself on the pro-Catholic side with men such as Canning and John Wilson Croker. His relatively successful biography can be contrasted with that of another Irishman, George Croly (1780–1860). A staunch Anglican Tory and clergyman, Croly's *Memoir of the Rt. Hon. Edmund Burke* (serialized in *Blackwood's* in the 1830s, and published in 1840) was far less reputable—its impact and longevity were, as we will see, comparatively short-lived due to his failure to incorporate Burke's Catholic writings and connections.[39]

---

[35] Edmund Burke, *Irish Affairs*, ed. Matthew Arnold (1881).
[36] Copeland, 'Reputation of Edmund Burke', 80–1; W. T. Laprade, 'Edmund Burke: An Adventure in Reputation', *Journal of Modern History*, 32 (1960), 327–32.
[37] Two earlier (and discredited) biographies were produced following his death: Charles M'Cormick, *Memoirs of the Rt. Hon. Edmund Burke; or, an Impartial Review of his Private Life, His Publick Conduct, his Speeches in Parliament, &c.* (1797); Robert Bisset, *The Life of Edmund Burke, Comprehending an Impartial Account of his Literary and Political Efforts and a Sketch of the Conduct and Character of his most Eminent Associates, Coadjutors, and Opponents* (1798).
[38] L. Lunney, 'Prior, Sir James', in J. Mcguire and J. Quinn, eds., *Dictionary of Irish Biography: From the Earliest Times to the Year 2002* (2009).
[39] George Croly, *A Memoir of the Rt. Hon. Edmund Burke* (1840).

Burke's next major biographer, Thomas Macknight (1829–99), was an Englishman. And yet, after studying medicine at King's College, London (1849–51) where he came under the influence of the Christian Socialist F. D. Maurice, Macknight spent the second half of his life in Ireland as the editor of the Belfast *Northern Whig* newspaper. His *History of the Life and Times of Edmund Burke* (1858–60) was an 1,800-page epic and the sum of eight years' work.[40] Previously, Macknight had published, anonymously, a hostile biography of Disraeli which praised the then Peelite Gladstone.[41] Macknight was a Liberal and a Peelite, though as a devout Anglican and a student of Maurice he also saw established churches as symbols of the moral bonds holding a nation together; Irish disestablishment was a circumstantial exception. Macknight's debt to Burke was equal if not greater than his debt to Maurice: he named his first son Edmund in 1860, and his newspaper editorials made copious references to Burke. After publishing a *Life of Bolingbroke* (1863), Macknight's unsuccessful marriage caused him to relocate to Belfast in 1866, but his deep Protestant faith prevented divorce and remarriage.[42] Even when he died in 1899, Macknight was revising the *Life of Burke*, preparing an annotated edition of Burke's works, and finishing a history of political progress in the nineteenth century which began with the death of Burke in 1797.[43]

Burke's most notable nineteenth-century biographer was the Blackburn-born John Morley (1838–1923). Morley was known first as the editor of the *Fortnightly Review*, the author of numerous studies on political thinkers and the influential *On Compromise* (1874), who then became a Liberal MP and cabinet minister. He followed the work of Prior and Macknight with *Edmund Burke: a Historical Study* (1867) and *Burke* (1879) for the 'English Men of Letters' series.[44] In comparison to Macknight, Morley appears as a very different sort of Liberal. The son of an Evangelical Anglican surgeon, Morley attended Lincoln College, Oxford, but was forced to leave with only a pass degree after his loss of religious faith resulted in total financial and emotional severance from his family. During the 1860s, he struggled to establish himself as a writer and absorbed the teachings of Auguste Comte. Already acquainted with Mill and a confirmed believer in social evolution, by 1870 Morley had exchanged Positivism for Mill's more individualistic

---

[40] Thomas Macknight, *History of the Life and Times of Edmund Burke* (1858–60).
[41] [Thomas Macknight], *The Rt. Hon. Benjamin Disraeli: A Literary and Political Biography* (1854).
[42] Thomas Macknight, *Life of Lord Bolingbroke* (1863); Marie-Louise Legg, 'Macknight, Thomas', *ODNB* (2004).
[43] Thomas Macknight, *Political Progress of the Nineteenth Century*, ed. C. C. Osborne (1905).
[44] John Morley, *Edmund Burke: A Historical Study* (1867); *Burke* (1879).

teachings. He was certainly an 'advanced' Liberal—yet one who held Burke in the highest regard as a political thinker.

The major critical analyses of Burke's thought that followed these biography–histories were noticeably more philosophical. These included that by John MacCunn (1846–1929), Professor of Philosophy at the University of Liverpool, who published *The Political Philosophy of Burke* in 1913.[45] All of these authors and their texts, in addition to the other writers, politicians, and educators also detailed in the following chapters, contributed to shaping Burke's reputation. What this outline of prominent Burke scholarship provides for now, however, is a preliminary indication of the changes which Burke's legacy was to undergo. The remainder of this book is devoted to telling this story.

---

[45] John MacCunn, *The Political Philosophy of Burke* (1913).

2
Constitutional Politics, *c.*1830–1880

[T]hough Burke lives, we meet with no Burkites.
Henry Sidgwick, 1877[1]

Throughout the nineteenth-century, the English, or British, Constitution occupied a central position in politics and thought at all levels.[2] It was celebrated and upheld across the political spectrum; the stage upon which players and parties acted out their various dramas. This ranged from explicit discussion in theory and politics, to less articulate expressions; from the review culture of Walter Bagehot's *The English Constitution* (1867) and widely diffused histories by Macaulay and Henry Hallam, to Josephine Butler's proclamation in 1871, in reference to the Contagious Diseases Acts, that freeborn Englishmen (and women) could simply *feel* what was 'unconstitutional', without reference to any literary theory of the constitution.[3] The relatively peaceful political experience of Britain in contrast to her continental contemporaries was seen to be a unique product of her historical mixed 'parliamentary' constitution, consisting of King, Lords, and Commons. These institutions had developed gradually over time, along with specific privileges or freedoms—from Magna Carta to the Bill of Rights. 'English constitutionalism' (English and British

---

[1] Henry Sidgwick, 'Bentham and Benthamism in Politics and Ethics' [1877], *Miscellaneous Essays and Addresses* (1904), 136. See also J. Sack, *From Jacobite to Conservative: Reaction and Orthodoxy in Britain, c.1760–1832*, 95.

[2] Robert Saunders, 'Parliament and People: the British Constitution in the Long Nineteenth Century', *Journal of Modern European History*, 6 (2008), 72–87; J. P. Parry, *The Politics of Patriotism: English Liberty, National Identity, and Europe, 1830–1886* (2006), ch. 1; Peter Mandler, *The English National Character: The History of an Idea from Edmund Burke to Tony Blair* (2006), 9–15, *passim*; Edmund Rogers, '1688 and 1888: Victorian Society and the Bicentenary of the Glorious Revolution', *JBS*, 50 (2011), 892–916; James Kirby, *Historians and the Church of England: Religion and Historical Scholarship, 1870–1920* (2016), ch. 5; Angus Hawkins, *Victorian Political Culture: 'Habits of Heart and Mind'* (2015), ch. 1.

[3] H. Hallam, *Constitutional History of England, from the Accession of Henry VII to the Death of George II* (1827); T. B. Macaulay, *History of England, from the Accession of James II* (1858–61); Walter Bagehot, *The English Constitution* (1867); Josephine Butler, *The Constitution Violated* (1871), 2. Butler quotes Burke on parliamentary authority at p. 124.

were terms which were used interchangeably[4]) provided a consensual meeting-house: the political argument lay not between supporters and opponents of the constitution, but in how it should be interpreted, developed, and/or preserved.[5] There were, of course, struggles between differing interpretations of the constitution, but the institutions themselves were supported wholeheartedly. Hence men and women from across the political spectrum—from Chartists and female suffragists to 'die-hard' Tories—found within it a source of legitimating authority for their various schemes and proposals. This is an obvious place to begin our story: with an assessment of Burke's place within this distinctive and hegemonic constitutional tradition.

Political interpretations of the constitution can be divided into two main approaches. On the one hand is the Whig—later Liberal—vision of the constitution. In this view, the constitution is the focus of reforming attention; their rallying cry being the Foxite slogan 'civil and religious liberty'. As one, somewhat disenchanted, Whig pamphleteer observed in 1837: 'We loved our party because we identified it with the preservation and improvement of the British constitution.'[6] Whatever nuances may be detected between Whigs and Liberals, in considering the constitution as a progressive entity the continuities are clear: in 1855 Bagehot noted that while 'The first wish of the Whig is to retain the constitution; the second—and it is of almost equal strength—is to improve it.'[7] Even in 1917, John Morley, the 'advanced' Liberal writer and MP, could still happily stress Liberal intellectual continuity via the constitution; describing men like himself as 'root-and-branch men'—seventeenth-century reformers—who had opposed the modern (Conservative) upholders of the creed of 'Church and Queen'.[8] Though the constitution was said to balance political power between the Commons, Lords, and Crown, it was, as Lord John Russell wrote, towards the welfare of the people (and therefore the popular element) that the Whigs looked for their guiding light: this was 'the end and object of all government' and so, Russell explained, 'one must be ready to interfere with prerogative which they think improper to the wants of the country'.[9] Whereas in the eighteenth

---

[4] For consistency, in this chapter I follow the majority of my sources in using 'English'.
[5] Burrow, *Liberal Descent*, 48.
[6] [Anon.], 'The Constitution as it is or Democracy?' (1837), 23.
[7] Walter Bagehot, 'The First Edinburgh Reviewers' [1855], *Literary Studies: Volume One* (1920), 15.
[8] John Morley, *Recollections* (1917), i. 107. See also J. P. Parry, *Democracy and Religion: Gladstone and the Liberal Party, 1867–1875* (1986), 16.
[9] Lord John Russell, *An Essay on the History of the English Government and Constitution: from the Reign of Henry VII to the Present Time*, 2nd edn (1823), 180–1. For Russell as a

century 'improper prerogative' had been located in the crown, the exact programme of reforms of course changed over time and prerogative might take on a broader meaning; but strengthening the popular element of the constitution and trimming the privileges of the established church were fairly constant themes throughout. Preserving the constitution (and therefore the 'rights of the freeborn Englishman') must necessarily involve adapting it to fit new political and religious circumstances. This would, in turn, have the beneficial consequence of reducing the threat of revolutionary upset.

Tories and Conservatives, on the other hand, honoured the 'Constitution in Church and State'—testifying to their equally deep-rooted constitutional identity. Tories were not intrinsically opposed to all reform but, as Canning stated at Liverpool in 1820, 'I am not sent to parliament to inquire into the question, whether a democracy or monarchy be the best. My lot is cast under the British monarchy.'[10] Historically, their principal concern was adhesion to the established church and the royal prerogative, and the defence of landed property; and while the application of such principles would alter dramatically in practice, this more hierarchical strand of constitutionalism was maintained conceptually throughout the nineteenth century. Support for the crown and the established church did not mean that Tories did not, or could not, market themselves as the true representatives of the nation or suggest potential reforms: unlike 'factional' Whiggism, the crown (and, indeed, the Anglican clergy) were portrayed as standing above party interests, and so it was their Tory defenders who were best equipped to represent the nation. A classic statement of this is Disraeli's *Vindication of the English Constitution* (1835).[11] Although—unlike 'Whig'—'Tory' remained a mainstream political label alongside 'Conservative', there were moments when it seemed that the discursive transition from Toryism to Conservatism would not be a smooth one. Both Disraeli and the journalist Thomas Edwin Kebbel (1826–1917), for instance, abhorred Peel's move towards 'Conservatism' initially.[12] Yet despite his initial worries that 'Conservatism' merely entailed yielding to

---

reformer post-1832 see Robert Saunders, *Democracy and the Vote in British Politics, 1848–1867: The Making of the Second Reform Act* (2011), 38–48.

[10] George Canning, '18 March 1820', *Speeches of the Rt. Hon. George Canning delivered on Public Occasions in Liverpool* (1825), 324.

[11] Benjamin Disraeli, *Vindication of the English Constitution, in a Letter to a Noble and Learned Lord* (1835); H. S. Jones, 'The Idea of the National in Victorian Political Thought', *EJPT*, 5 (2006), 12–21; Georgios Varouxakis, '"Patriotism", "Cosmopolitanism", and "Humanity" in Victorian Political Thought', ibid., 100–18.

[12] T. E. Kebbel, 'Sir Robert Peel' [1862], *Essays upon History and Politics* (1864), 290–1; Benjamin Disraeli, *Coningsby; or, the New Generation* (1844), bk. 2, ch. 5.

Whig measures, by 1886 Kebbel was able to look back and confidently assert: 'In its defence of the Monarchy, the Church, and the territorial Constitution of this country, the Tory party has never faltered.'[13] Even Peel had suggested, in his *Memoirs*, that his reforms succeeded in promoting 'loyalty to the Throne and confidence in the justice of Parliament'.[14] For Tories and Conservatives alike, it was clear that maintaining the constitution required not only negative defence or reaction but active participation based on conceptions of political principle.[15]

In turning to Burke, the first question to be asked is whether this pre-Union Irishman was considered to be an English constitutionalist. On the one hand, Burke, or the idea of what was 'Burkean', has become synonymous in the historiography of nineteenth-century Britain with a bipartisan developmental constitutional approach.[16] Indeed, Burke's adulation of the institutions of state was often expressed with an often unrivalled enthusiasm. This eloquence gave rise to frequent citations of his account of constitutional development, and praise for his statements on key aspects of parliamentary government. And yet, it was by no means easy to make use of this literary and theoretical resource for party political purposes. This was because Burke's enthusiasm could be turned against him: it was seen to house a passion and a rigidity that revealed Burke as both un-English and unconstitutional. In particular, Burke was seen to have upheld the 'strange dogma', epitomized in his *Reflections on the Revolution in France* (1790), that the Whig settlement of 1688–9 was too sacred to be altered. This refusal to budge on the issue of parliamentary reform was increasingly seen to be inconsistent with his account of the historical and flexible nature of British constitutional development which was a cornerstone of its longevity and success.

In considering Burke's constitutionalism this chapter focuses in particular on his account of the developmental nature of the constitution, and on his elucidation of significant concepts of parliamentary government, such as political representation and the role of Members of Parliament and of political parties. It then moves from these general issues to more specific ones, and assesses how Whigs and Liberals and, subsequently, Tories and Conservatives approached Burke from a partisan point of view. The final

---

[13] T. E. Kebbel,, *A History of Toryism, from the Accession of Mr. Pitt in Power in 1783, to the Death of Lord Beaconsfield in 1881* (1886), 408. See also Kebbel, 'Mr. Disraeli' [1860], in *Essays upon History and Politics*, 396; C. H. Sharman, 'Twelve Reasons Why I am a Conservative' (1887).

[14] Quoted in Saunders, *Democracy and the Vote*, 58.

[15] See, for example, R. Dudley Baxter, 'English Parties and Conservatism' (1870), 57–8, 75–6.

[16] Burrow, *Liberal Descent*, 2, 131; *Whigs and Liberals*, 14–15, 68, 106, 112, 138–9.

section considers Burke's place within debates on the relationship of church and state, and the ways in which this impacted discussions of his political thought and identity. In doing so, fundamental problems with Burke's constitutional reputation are highlighted,[17] both in general and party political terms, which prevented his legacy from attaching itself (or, rather, being attached) to any particular political or intellectual tradition in the early to mid-nineteenth century prior to *c.*1880.

ENGLISH CONSTITUTIONALISM

To many commentators past and present, Burke is the English constitutionalist par excellence. As the classicist and political writer George Cornewall Lewis (1803–63) explained: 'To understand the nature of the English Constitution, and appreciate its results, the student must have traced its origin and watched its growth... The progressive character of the English Constitution... is, in fact, its excellence, and [it is this] which accounts for its length of life.'[18] In this context Burke had certainly done his historical research, and was seen to have drunk deeply from its findings. This was displayed most obviously in *Reflections*, in which he contrasted events in France with the Glorious Revolution of 1688, but also in lesser-known earlier writings such as his *Abridgement of English History* (1757–*c.*63).[19] In Burke's hands, the history of the English Constitution became an unsurpassed history of gradual reformation; the slow intertwining of law with liberty. He came to be seen as one of the most eloquent commentators on the historical development of Britain's unique constitution, in addition to being one of its most ferocious defenders. The study of Burke, so the popular Anglican writer Robert Montgomery (1807–55) claimed in 1853, taught readers 'to venerate with increasing reverence THE BRITISH CONSTITUTION'.[20] But praise given to Burke's writings on the constitution was met with qualifications, and it is these qualifications that increasingly placed him in an uncomfortable and somewhat contradictory constitutional position in a post-1832 political environment.

---

[17] Chapter 3 will examine Burke's corresponding extra-constitutional reputation.
[18] George Cornewall Lewis, *Essays on the Administrations of Great Britain, from 1783 to 1830* (1864), vi.
[19] The Convention after the Revolution (from 29 Jan.) and the Bill of Rights (passed in Feb.) occurred in 1688 in the old style calendar, but from 1752 the new style calendar—in which 1 Jan. marked a new calendar year—dated the constitutional settlement as 1689. Burke's commentators, however, generally still referred to the old style '1688' and, for consistency, I have followed their lead.
[20] Robert Montgomery, *Edmund Burke: being First Principles selected from his Writings, with an Introductory Essay* (1853), xxvi.

On the positive side was Burke's adulation for the institutions of state. One anonymous pamphleteer had emphasized in 1826 that Burke's 'first and last care was the British Constitution which he considered the perfection of human wisdom'.[21] The constitution, or his particular reading of it, was considered to have steered all of his intellectual and parliamentary pursuits. The Regius Professor of Modern History at Cambridge, William Smyth (1765–1849), proclaimed in 1841 that Burke 'cannot be too much your study if you mean either to understand or to maintain against its various enemies, open and concealed, designing and mistaken, the singular constitution of this fortunate island'.[22] Smyth, a Holland House Whig, was also the son of an Irish banker with links to the French emigration of the 1790s through J. L. Mallet, and had made the unusual move of writing and delivering some of the first lectures on the French Revolution.[23] In 1872 another historian, the Liberal J. R. Green (1837–83), explained that Burke's specific conception of the constitution was important *because* it was historical. Burke 'looks for the true explanation of our present forms of government to the tradition and progress of the past, and for the mould of our political life to the shape assumed by the earliest English society'.[24] Burke's connection with the notion of continuous historical growth and its use as an explanation for how 'successful' constitutions come into existence was generally supported across the political spectrum in opposition to the mechanical philosophy of 'paper constitutions' as presented in the works of Jeremy Bentham and the French, particularly Sieyès and Rousseau. Burke was seen to have identified a degree of mysticism in the constitution, but also a historicism which could not be taught a priori because each country developed along its own, unique path.[25]

The greatest benefit of evolutionary constitutional development had been the growth of a peculiar, native, conception of liberty. This meant the 'rights of the freeborn Englishman' which had been acquired gradually over time, and enshrined in law as privileges, in contrast to the abstract French Revolutionary 'rights of man'. Men and women stood for the preservation of their national institutions because their development throughout history had coincided with the flowering of English liberties.

---

[21] [Anon.], *Junius Proved to be Burke, with an Outline of his Biography* (1826), 63.
[22] William Smyth, *Lectures on Modern History* (1840), 580.
[23] William Smyth, *Lectures on History: On the French Revolution* (1840). See also Ben-Israel, *English Historians on the French Revolution*, ch. 5.
[24] [J. R. Green], 'Freeman's Growth of the English Constitution', *SR* (4 May 1872), 574.
[25] [J. F. Stephen], 'Edmund Burke', *SR* (10 Apr. 1858), 373; 'Burke on the English Constitution', *SR* (28 Dec. 1867), 815–17.

This in turn produced a distinctive national character. Englishmen were 'fit for liberty', unlike the French in 1789; the English could exercise self-restraint, and understood that liberty did not equal license. The Irish Tory George Croly explained at the opening of his *Memoir* of Burke that the English have, 'by nature', a 'gravity of mind, which tends to save them from political rashness... They alone, of all European nations, have been qualified to build up that last and noblest labour of utility and virtue, a free Constitution.'[26] This sentiment was repeated across the political spectrum, especially following the wave of revolutions which swept across Europe in 1848 but left Britain unscathed.[27] Even at the close of the century, Mandell Creighton (1843–1901), the historian and Anglican bishop, noted in his Romanes Lecture that 'The Englishman has never learned to conceive of himself as... having an inalienable right to do, or be, exactly what suits him best, without regard to the legal or moral rights of others.' Instead, he took with him 'a notion of liberty which is associated with duty and justice; and this is the secret of his success as a civilizing agent'.[28] Burke enters the discussion as an eloquent exponent of this uniquely British union of liberty with order: a 'manly, moral, regulated liberty'.[29] His constitutional conception of liberty may have been a 'negative' one, but it was never set apart from 'order'.[30] This combination of liberty and 'order' was, to contemporaries, noticeably lacking in the more savage Celts and the licentious French, and thus they exhibited a harmful form of 'excessive liberty'.[31] Burke's conception of liberty could, therefore, be convincingly linked with that of his adopted country.

The English Constitution was not only free and historically unique, but parliamentary. Hence Burke's writings on parliamentary government were recurring themes in nineteenth-century commentaries, too. He was, firstly, frequently cited as the origin of modern parliamentary parties and his writings were seen to have initiated the widespread acceptance of political parties as a necessity of British parliamentary government,

---

[26] Croly, *A Memoir of Burke*, i. 1. See also Michael Mitchie, *An Enlightenment Tory in Victorian Scotland: The Career of Sir Archibald Alison* (1997), 142–3, 150.

[27] For example, John Austin, *A Plea For the Constitution* (1859), xi; E. S. Creasy, *The Rise and Progress of the English Constitution*, 3rd edn (1856), 391; Thomas Erskine May, *Democracy in Europe: A History* (1877), i. viii. See also J. P. Parry, 'The Impact of Napoleon III on British Politics, 1851–1880', *TRHS*, 11 (2001), 175; Georgios Varouxakis, *Victorian Political Thought on France and the French* (2002), 2, 79; Saunders, *Democracy and the Vote*, 6.

[28] Mandell Creighton, *The English National Character* (1896), 32.

[29] For example, *Reflections on the Revolution in France*, ed. J. C. D. Clark (2001), 181–3.

[30] James Prior, *Memoir of the Life and Character of the Rt. Hon. Edmund Burke*, 2nd edn (1826), ii. 42; Arthur Hobhouse, 'Liberals and the New Conservatism' (1880), 10–11; Elizabeth van Dedem Lecky, *A Memoir of the Rt. Hon. W. E. H. Lecky* (1909), 307–8; W. Monypenny and G. Buckle, *Life of Benjamin Disraeli* (1910–20), iii. 25.

[31] [Anon.], 'The Orange Prosecutions', *SR* (14 Sept. 1867), 334.

particularly after 1832 when for the first time Westminster politics became efficient two-party politics. In *Thoughts on the Cause of the Present Discontents* (1770), Burke had famously promoted the value of political parties and defined a party as 'a body of men united for promoting by their joint endeavours the national interest upon some particular principle in which they are all agreed'.[32] 'The general defence of political connexion, indeed,' for Lord John Russell—a man who stood in a clear line of descent from Fox—in 1823, 'may be left where Mr. Burke has placed it. There can be nothing more striking, or more sound, than his writings on this subject.'[33] It was also accepted that since parties were by definition expressions of partial opinion, the idea of party implied the necessity of compromise in the practical conduct of politics. The idea of 'compromise', in turn, was seen to reflect a sort of national pragmatism which had helped to ensure the positive development of British institutions.[34] To the electoral reformer Thomas Hare (1806–91), whose *Election of Representatives* (1859) is saturated with references to Burke, it was this necessity of compromise, 'the exigencies under which something of every individual or every combined will, is yielded to the general concord', that regulated and harmonized 'all the business of domestic and social, as well as political, life, wherever that harmony is happily established'.[35] As groups of individuals working towards common goals, parties were portrayed as an extension of moderate constitutional government and thus had a positive stabilizing effect on politics and society.

However, while the post-1832 political world brought about the hegemony of party, party politics did not cease to be a contested constitutional topic. Questions were still raised as to whether parties were an *essential* component of the constitution: were they damaging? Could they eventually be superseded? And, if so, with what? Tories, as the traditional defenders of royal prerogative, were somewhat less accustomed to the defence of party government. Thus, in his *Memoir of Burke* (1840), George Croly declared with heavy irony that

---

[32] *Writings and Speeches of Edmund Burke* [*WSEB*], eds. Paul Langford and Leslie Mitchell, 8 vols (1981–2000), ii. 317.
[33] Lord John Russell, *Essay on the History of the English Government*, 179. See also Charles Cooper, *Upon Party* (1850).
[34] [J. F. Stephen], 'Burke on Popular Representation', *SR* (23 Sept. 1865), 394–6; John Morley, *On Compromise* (1874), 20.
[35] Thomas Hare, *The Election of Representatives, Parliamentary and Municipal*, 3rd edn (1865), 21. Hare issued a 4th edition in 1874 to accommodate the secret ballot, but the Burke references remain untouched. For another Conservative suggestion for electoral reform post-1832 in a more popular pamphlet form, see [Anon.], *Scheme for a Reform of Parliament, by an Ex-MP and a Tory* (1858).

Party would be essential, if it were essential to the British Constitution to give life to a body of men bound together by the single object of seizing on power; sacrificing all individual principle to the general purposes of ambition; and openly declaring all means, however false and dishonourable, to be justified by their use in carrying the party into power.[36]

Political parties, in this reading, were a cover for moral corruption. They also set 'factional' Whig interests above those of the nation as a whole. Likewise, T. E. Kebbel criticized Burke in 1860 for mistaking an accident for something essential. To Kebbel, 'Burke was afraid that the discouragement of party would give too much power to the crown, just as Bolingbroke had feared that the encouragement of party would give too much power to this minister. Both were equally mistaken.' In Burke's case this was because, in promoting political parties, he had 'given to his party a Republican creed'.[37] Like Croly, Kebbel suggested that political parties were not an essential part of the constitution, yet he does so as a partisan in favour of royal prerogative. Hence Burke's views on party government, though seen as foundational, were still far less popular with mid-nineteenth century Tory-Conservatives.

Political parties were by definition sectional rather than national: Whig-Liberals and Tory-Conservatives both used the rhetoric of 'national parties', but each saw the other as representative of different interests, whether it be the welfare of the people; the aristocracy; the 'Venetian Oligarchy'; or the crown. There were concerns that party 'feeling' governed the decisions of men who followed powerful and/or popular leaders, yet there remained higher bases of action and principle than these superficial ties: did not a legislator have duties that transcended party politics, as for instance to the oppressed and suffering of the realm? Hence another important portion of Burke's personal history was his decision to split from his party. In doing so he sacrificed the Whig party's future electoral success over a cause he saw as a mortal threat to his adopted country: the French Revolution.[38] Though conflicting and contradictory, personal independence *and* party loyalty were both considered to be important virtues for a political actor to embody.

Another persistent theme in nineteenth-century political writing on Burke, therefore, is the tug-of-war between the two figures of the 'representative delegate' and the 'independent deliberator'. There was general agreement with Burke's original proposition regarding the relationship between a Member of Parliament and his constituents, as set out to the

---

[36] Croly, *A Memoir of Burke*, ii. 203.
[37] Kebbel, 'Edmund Burke' [1860], *Essays upon History and Politics*, 177.
[38] Lord John Russell, *Essay on the History of the English Government*, 179.

electors of Bristol in 1774. Here, famously, he had stated that parliament itself is a national institution and, moreover, that MPs should not be mere delegates of their constituents; representatives owed them the exercise of independent judgement. In literature which was chiefly concerned with the issue of the representation of communities, therefore, the example of Burke's relations with the electors of Bristol between 1774 and 1780 was of paramount importance. This was not simply a use of Burke's theory of representation but invocation of Burke as a practical historical example. Burke had famously lost his seat for Bristol due to his support for Irish free trade and the relief of Roman Catholics. He was then returned for the pocket borough of Malton, and so this became a popular example to demonstrate that liberal sentiments could be supported by an antiquated constitution. To the Conservative historian Lord Mahon (1805–75), a celebrant of the Pittite tradition, in 1853, it was 'With the noblest public spirit [that] Burke gave his zealous support to these proposals [i.e. free trade and Catholic relief], though directly against the wishes and instructions of his constituents at Bristol.'[39] Commentary of this kind often veiled concerns about the ability and accuracy of popular judgements, regardless of the reforms to the constitution enacted from 1832 onwards. In 1858, for example, Burke's most enthusiastic biographer Thomas Macknight (1829–99) sneered at the foolishness of the Bristol electors acting from self-interest: Burke lost his seat because 'he had refused to court the electors by servile adulation, because he had endeavoured to establish a free trade between England and Ireland, because he had striven to do justice to the debtor, and because... he had laboured to emancipate the Catholic'.[40] There was a consensus derived from this episode, as one pamphleteer explained, that an MP should never represent the wishes of his constituents against the welfare of others, the wider community, and 'general reason' itself.[41] (Though, essentially, 'reason' here was to be equated with the wisdom of hindsight as defined by the author.)

As with discussions on party, ideas of representation were inevitably bound up with the relationship between the nation and the independence of politicians. The very concept of representation itself seemed ludicrous to some. In his proposals for a form of proportional representation, for instance, Thomas Hare considered the problem of diverse urban areas: 'An electoral community formed of thousands of persons, including every

---

[39] Lord Mahon, *History of England from the Peace of Utrecht to the Peace of Versailles, 1713–83* (1853), vii. 146.
[40] Macknight, *Life and Times of Edmund Burke*, ii. 392.
[41] [C. Thompson], 'Observations upon Parliamentary Pledges by Candidates to their Constituents' (1837), 23.

diversity of thought, intelligence, education, and feeling, is driven together, and told, what, if it were not a precept of the constitution, would be a cruel irony, to elect a *representative*.'[42] Hare's proposals for representative reform were inspired by Burke and, in a review of 1860, the Christian Socialist F. D. Maurice was delighted to find that Hare's work was sustained 'by the weighty words of Burke'.[43] The academic lawyer Sheldon Amos (1835–86), in his constitutional writings, put this idea in more digestible, if prosaic form. He stated that

> the earliest, and certainly the most discriminating and philosophic, attempt to exhibit in a systematic shape the kind of reconciliation that ought to be effected between the relations of a Member to his constituents and his relations to the country at large, if the true genius of the English Constitution is to be strictly conformed to, is to be found in Mr. Burke's speech at Bristol.[44]

Amos cited Burke's speech on this occasion as a transitional moment in ideas of representation and delegacy, in which they moved from a less sophisticated to a more 'advanced' stage of political development.[45] The degree to which the lip service paid to high-minded 'Burkean' conceptions of national representation was enacted in practice by MPs is of course debatable. As a rhetorical ideal, however, it was paramount.

Despite these various forms of praise, Burke's view of 'a constitution fully formed and mature' was vulnerable. In particular, his notion of the 1688 constitution as a grand climacteric—the end of constitutional progress—began to look dated to the post-1832 generation, and even more so following the Reform Act of 1867. As J. R. Green noted in his bestselling *A Short History of the English People* (1874), Burke saw the Glorious Revolution of 1688 as the fated close of a great era of national progress which had moved on 'from precedent to precedent'.[46] But Burke's notion of 'closure' did not fit with either the mythical or actual history of the English Constitution. Echoing the sentiments of Cornwall Lewis quoted earlier, George Brodrick (1831–1903), in his contribution to the 1867 *Essays on Reform*, stressed that

> If the stability of our own Constitution has been the marvel of modern times, it is chiefly because it has grown with the growth, strengthened with the strength, and expanded with the expansive energies of the English people.

---

[42] Hare, *Election of Representatives*, 246.
[43] Quoted in F. D. Parsons, *Thomas Hare and Political Representation in Victorian Britain* (2009), 89.
[44] Sheldon Amos, *Fifty Years of the English Constitution, 1830–1880* (1880), 50.
[45] Ibid., 47–52.
[46] J. R. Green, *A Short History of the English People* (1874), 776.

Let it once be stereotyped into a permanent form, and prove itself incapable of further development, and it will lose that which is the essential principle of its life.[47]

Like Green, Thomas Erskine May's *Constitutional History*—which went through fourteen editions between 1861 and 1912, undisturbed by May's death in 1886—was clear in its assertion that Burke was a reformer (of abuses, of economics), but he had never supported any form of parliamentary reform.[48] It was evident, however, that the constitution had continued to grow and progress as it had always done since the birth of the nation. Why then, as Burke seemed to think, would it have suddenly stopped doing so? Constitutional writers such as Amos and E. S. Creasy (1812–78), both of whom also wrote well-known histories and guides to the constitution, argued that Burke held a 'strange dogma', epitomized in *Reflections*, that the Whig settlement of 1688–9 was to be held in sacred reverence, and the constitution noted for its continuous growth thereby became a stationary construction that could be applied to any country, or any age.[49] Burke's notion that 'our ancestors, at the Revolution of 1688, bound, and had a right to bind, both themselves and their posterity to perpetual adherence to the exact order of things then established' was anathema to many English constitutionalists: Burke had misunderstood the historical flexibility of English developments which were a cornerstone of its longevity and success.[50]

So although Burke's historical constitutionalism would later become increasingly linked with notions of organic growth (see Chapter 6), it is important to differentiate here between two types of organic change. While Burke was becoming associated with an organic, historical approach to constitutional development, meaning the continuous growth of the organism itself, this is conceptually distinct from the radical conception of organic change. In this latter conception the organs of the constitution (i.e. the organism itself) were altered at an elemental level, and this represented a much more fundamental or revolutionary change. Thus, in contrast to his more general modern image as a piecemeal reformer (as in the former conception), Burke was in fact portrayed as the opposite of an organic reformer in the latter sense, i.e. as a rigid opponent of elemental, organic constitutional change.

---

[47] George C. Brodrick, 'The Utilitarian Argument Against Reform', *Essays on Reform* (1867), 25.
[48] Thomas Erskine May, *The Constitutional History of England: From the Accession of George the Third* (1912 edn), i. 270.
[49] E. S. Creasy, *The Text-Book of the Constitution: Magna Charta, the Petition of Right, and the Bill of Rights* (1848), 2; *The Rise and Progress of the English Constitution*, 4th edn (1858), 2.
[50] Ibid.; Sheldon Amos, *The Science of Politics*, 2nd edn (1883), 124.

While Burke was seen to promote English, or British, constitutionalism and parliamentary government through eloquent speeches and writings, this was only within limits. He did not invent English constitutionalism; nor were all references to developmental constitutional change a result of the direct influence of Burke; nor was Burke unique in suggesting the English Constitution was the result of historically acquired freedoms.[51] Despite the evident similarity of Macaulay's argument in favour of the 1832 Reform Act—'Reform, that you may preserve'—to Burke's proclamation, in *Reflections*, that 'even when I changed, it should be to preserve'[52] we must be careful when drawing this seemingly neat line of intellectual influence from one to the other based on an echo. There is no historical evidence to suggest that Macaulay was directly referencing Burke here rather than a larger body of well-known developmental constitutional thought, in order to construct a logical rhetorical argument exploiting the predispositions and prejudices of his audience.[53] But while Burke was not the originator of English conservative constitutionalism, he was a notoriously eloquent advocate for it. This eloquence was the aspect of Burke's constitutional thought which appealed to both parties, not least during the reform debates. So although Macaulay did not invoke Burke in his speech (as he did elsewhere[54]), others explicitly summoned him to add authority and literary flair to their speeches. However, in the aftermath of the reform debates (as we shall see), Burke's refusal to budge from the 1688 settlement—a stance which seemed obsolete after 1832—was far less appealing as a guide to modern politics. Yet this was by no means the full extent of Burke's commentary on constitutional and parliamentary government. Now we must consider how the two opposing parties— defined by their particular interpretation of the constitution—appealed to Burke, and whether they could make complete sense of him.

WHIGS AND LIBERALS

While Burke's *Reflections* remained his most famous work, a kind of anti-French totem, his *Thoughts on the Cause of the Present Discontents* (1770)

---

[51] Joanna Innes, '"Reform" in English Public Life', in Arthur Burns and Joanna Innes, eds., *Rethinking the Age of Reform: Britain 1780–1850* (2003), 89; R. J. Smith, *The Gothic Bequest: Medieval Institutions in British Thought, 1688–1863* (1987).
[52] *WSEB*, viii. 72, 292.
[53] T. B. Macaulay, 'Speech on the Reform Bill' [2 Mar. 1831], in *Speeches of T. B. Macaulay* (1853), 25.
[54] Macaulay never produced his planned essay on Burke. However, for his more scattered remarks see pp. 1, 30, 32, 72, 74 in this volume.

was also read with serious interest by influential sections of the political elite well into the next century. *Present Discontents*, an attack on the crown and the influence of the 'King's Friends', was consciously framed by Burke so as to provide the Whig party with a political creed: to outline the benefit of party, and the duties of the politician connecting the political thinker and the political actor. For Russell, in 1823, it served as

> one of the few standard works on the science of government which the world possesses... It rendered a service to this country scarcely less essential, by instilling into the minds of all young politicians, who at that time were greatly increasing in number throughout the country, those wise and beneficial principles which their Whig ancestors had practised, but which the old intriguers of that day had entirely forgotten.[55]

A decade later, Arthur Hallam (1811–33), of *In Memoriam* fame, in his contribution on Burke to the *Gallery of Portraits* (1833–7)—a production of the Society for the Diffusion of Useful Knowledge—stated that *Present Discontents* 'has been termed the Whig Manual, and certainly contains the ablest exposition ever given of the principles held by that party for a long series of years'.[56] Hallam himself had received a six-volume edition of Burke's works from Gladstone on leaving Eton in 1827.[57] Yet, with *Reflections*, Burke had caused a schism within the Whig party that remained unforgiveable for many. In splitting from the Foxites over the French Revolution, Burke—who had provided such a vital service to his party in earlier periods—was blamed for destroying any hope of political success for the decades which followed. For many of his Whig and Liberal admirers, an easy way of dealing with his apostasy was simply to insist that Burke had gone mad, thus invalidating his writings on France. The question of Burke's madness was a debate which began early and continued throughout the period. The answer one gave solved the conundrum—which Lord Acton would later describe as a great problem of modern history[58]—of whether his later writings on France were consistent with his earlier, much admired work. To Henry Brougham, Burke's

> theoretical view of the constitution in those days was as different [as could be] from the high monarchical tone of his latter writings. The King was then 'the representative of the people... and although government certainly is an

---

[55] Lord John Russell, *Essay on the History of the English Government*, 229–30.
[56] A. H. Hallam, 'Burke', *Gallery of Portraits; with memoirs* (1833–7), iii. 35. See also [Anon.], 'The Decline and Fall of Whiggery', *Fraser's Magazine* (Oct. 1864), 397.
[57] John Morley, *Life of Gladstone* (1903), i. 42.
[58] Lord Acton, 'Inaugural Lecture on the Study of History' [1895]; [Anon.], *Lord Acton's Lectures on Modern History*, ER (Apr. 1907), 48. This theme is examined in more detail in Chapter 3, 'Madness', in this volume.

institution of divine authority, yet its forms, and the persons who administer it, all originate from the people.' And then comes that immortal passage so often cited, and which ought to be blazoned in letters of fire over the porch of the Commons' House, illustrating the doctrine it sets out with, that 'their representatives are a control *for* the people, and not *upon* the people; and that the virtue, spirit, and essence of a House of Commons consist in its being the express image of the feelings of the nation.'[59]

Brougham illustrates the admiration which the constitutional views expressed in *Present Discontents* garnered among his contemporaries, but he also reveals how the Whigs were unable and/or unwilling to comprehend and sympathize with his writings on French affairs.[60] Hence Macaulay's argument, in 1832, that 'the violence of the democratic party in France made Burke a Tory'.[61] This division would become a cause of much of the more substantial writing on Burke in the nineteenth century and beyond. The most explicit defence of Burke against his Whig detractors—and specifically *Edinburgh Review* contributors, such as Brougham and Francis Jeffrey—can be found in the closing pages of Thomas Macknight's enormous biography (1858–60): 'Burke was spoken of by the Whig writers as a clever man indeed, whose inconsistency was undeniable, who had introduced into political affairs a philosophical tone... but whose views, especially in his later life, were most unsound, and whose conduct in breaking up the Whig party was of course most unjustifiable.'[62] It was a reputation which was to be underlined well into the 1860s in high-profile works such as the third Lord Holland's *Memoirs of the Whig Party* (1852–4), Russell's *Life of Charles James Fox* (1859–66), and the universalist Liberal Henry Buckle's philosophical history: the *History of Civilization in England* (1857–61).[63]

This was not, however, a wholly original view, as it had been disseminated by earlier Radical writers. The two Burkes, William Hazlitt had contended, 'are not the same person, but opposite persons—not opposite persons only, but deadly enemies'. Typically, in Hazlitt's case, this was not simply a political attack but a personal one: Burke 'was at once a coward, a

---

[59] Henry Brougham, 'Mr. Burke', *Historical Sketches of Statesmen who flourished in the Time of George III; to which are added, remarks on party* (1845), i. 196–7.
[60] See also Thomas Moore, *Life of the Rt. Hon. Richard Sheridan*, 3rd edn (1825), ii. 98.
[61] T. B. Macaulay, 'Burleigh and his Times' [1832], *Critical and Historical Essays* (1907), i. 84.
[62] Macknight, *Life and Times of Edmund Burke*, iii. 748.
[63] Chapter 3 in this volume, 'Madness'; H. R. V. Holland, *Memoirs of the Whig Party*, ed. H. E. Holland [1802] (1852–4), i. 4–14; Lord John Russell, *Life and Times of Charles James Fox* (1859–66), iii. 122–6; H. T. Buckle, *History of Civilization in England* (1857–61), i. 424–32. Cf. Cornewall Lewis, *Essays on the Administrations of Great Britain*, 124.

liar, and a slave'.⁶⁴ William Cobbett's *Political Register* was similarly critical in 1816:

> How amusing it is to hear the world disputing and wrangling about the motives, and principles, and opinions of *Burke*! He had no notions, no principles, no opinions of his own, when he wrote his famous work... He was a poor, needy dependent of a Borough-monger, to serve whom, and please whom, he wrote; and for no other purpose whatever... And yet, how many people read this man's writings as if they flowed from his *own mind*.⁶⁵

Less refined radicals had been content to charge Burke with gross hypocrisy and corruption. In 1821, the Radical reformer John Wade (1788–1875) stated bluntly that Burke 'became a violent Tory; from the advocate of popular rights he became the partisan of the Court; he denounced Reformers as traitors; concession as incipient rebellion.' The reason for this change of heart was, as Cobbett had insisted, neither honourable nor philosophical: he was motivated purely by financial incentive. Burke was 'well-paid for Whiggism. His Toryism was an equally profitable calling. His two pensions were estimated [to be] worth 40,000*l*.'⁶⁶ In this reading, Burke becomes nothing but a selfish opportunist, whose only principle is his remunerative support of a paying oligarchy. His political principles are, by implication, not genuine convictions but simply the means to subsistence.⁶⁷ These previous suggestions are significant as they had surprising resonance and it is crucial to note that at this early date Burke was not uniformly admired as a political thinker who held a clearly defined political philosophy, or even genuine principles.

It was also unclear to contemporaries whether Burke was a consistent friend of liberty, or its enemy. On the one hand, he was the prophet of civil and religious liberties which came to fruition in the nineteenth century: Catholic relief, political economy, free trade, and slave trade reform. In addition, he had opposed American taxation in the 1770s and argued in favour of conciliation, not to mention his declamations against Warren Hastings, the Governor-General of British India, which

---

⁶⁴ William Hazlitt, 'Character of Burke' [1817], *Political Essays* (1819), 264–5.
⁶⁵ William Cobbett, *Political Register* (8 June 1816), quoted in Raymond Williams, 'The Organic Society', in D. E. Ritchie, ed., *Edmund Burke: Appraisals and Applications* (1990), 158.
⁶⁶ John Wade, *A Political Dictionary... Vocabulary of Corruption* (1821), s.v. 'Burke', 10–12. For a later example, see [Anon.], 'The Inherent Evils of all State Governments Demonstrated; being a reprint of Edmund Burke's celebrated Essay entitled "A Vindication of Natural Society" with notes' (1858).
⁶⁷ For a similar sentiment from a later Whig source, see George Wingrove Cooke, *A History of Party, from the Rise of Whig and Tory Factions in the Reign of Charles II to the Passing of the Reform Bill* (1836–7), iii. 378–9.

were famously celebrated by Macaulay.[68] Yet during the French Revolution Burke had (according to his adversaries) opposed liberty (or *liberté*)— a reading which was presumably employed in order to discredit Burke as fundamentally strange, anti-Whig, and even un-English, without discrediting his earlier work. The *New Monthly* noted in 1858 that few public men had had better reason to exclaim 'Save me from my friends!'[69] To Radicals, however, this deception had a deeper, unprincipled, root: it merely 'suited Burke, as an orator, occasionally to eulogize liberty', but 'he never was its friend'.[70] A line was drawn between style and substance. In time, later Liberal apologists of Burke such as Thomas Macknight, W. E. H. Lecky, and John Morley would explain Burke's French writings by elaborating his conception of liberty in more specific terms: it was not only 'real' rather than abstract liberty, but an example of the idea of constitutional freedom with order and moderation as discussed above. Thus the naturalist E. A. Pankhurst explained, in 1886, that for Burke it was essential that freedom itself must be limited in order to be possessed: hence when the 'worshippers' of the French Revolution 'spoke of RIGHTS' Burke 'insisted on DUTY', and 'when they cried out for LIBERTY, he declared that its very existence implied RESTRAINT'.[71] Until then, however, for Whigs, Liberals, and Radicals, there was a sense that Burke's appeal for the liberty of the clerics and aristocrats of a corrupt *ancien régime* had been radically misguided.

Finally, and significantly, Burke was retrospectively blamed by Whigs and Liberals for delaying the 1832 Reform Act. According to prominent Whigs such as Russell, his alleged apostasy over the French Revolution was cited as an indirect cause of this; that is, by splitting the party, he had consigned the Whigs to a much lengthier period of opposition than would otherwise have occurred.[72] It was argued, furthermore, that Burke's ideas and writings were used as an intellectual bulwark against the act. Gladstone would write, in 1865, that the 'anti-populist' teachings of 'Burke and Canning misled many on that subject [parliamentary reform], and they misled me'.[73] In truth, Burke had been a quotable authority on both sides during the reform debates. Evidence from *Hansard*

---

[68] See T. B. Macaulay, 'Warren Hastings' [1841], *Critical and Historical Essays*, i. 550–649. For more on Burke and Warren Hastings, see pp. 219–20 in this volume.
[69] 'Macknight's Life and Times of Burke', *New Monthly Magazine* (Apr. 1858), 428.
[70] T. B. H. Oldfield, *The Representative History of Great Britain and Ireland* (1816), i. vii.
[71] E. A. Pankhurst, *Edmund Burke: A Study of his Life and Character* (1886), 54.
[72] Lord John Russell, *Life and Times of Charles James Fox*, iii. 23, 253.
[73] Morley, *Life of Gladstone*, i. 70; W. E Gladstone, 'Gladstone to G. W. E. Russell, 13 Oct. 1884', *Correspondence on Church and Religion of W. E. Gladstone*, ed. D. C. Lathbury (1910), ii. 326.

demonstrates that he was referenced in both Whig and Tory arguments, including speeches by Russell and Croker.[74] The use of Burke in parliamentary speeches reflected the tenor of the commentary already discussed: for opponents of reform, he was a key example of a notable politician who had gained entry to parliament via a pocket borough,[75] and his conception of representation was praised as one in which all interests were recognized within the existing constitutional framework, though this was—at an electoral level—relatively exclusive.[76] This latter argument—from a speech by Sir John Walsh (1798–1881)—provided a way to dispute the necessity of the Reform Bill by using a Whig critic of parliamentary reform: Burke was 'one of the leading members of the Whig party' when he outlined his view of representation (before the French Revolution and 'the changes of Mr. Burke's political principles'). So Burke the Whig was rhetorically useful to anti-reform Tories as well as in his more familiar guise as an opponent of all things 'revolutionary'.[77]

In the case of the Whig reformers in parliament, however, Burke's pre-Revolutionary writings were put to other uses. In one of the more abstract speeches in favour of the Reform Bill, James Mackintosh—who was intellectually reconciled with Burke after his 1791 attack on the *Reflections*, *Vindiciae Gallicae*—cited Burke's 1775 speech on conciliation with America which argued, in regard to American discontent with British rule, that the people have no interest in disorder, and so when dissent arises it does so for a legitimate reason. To Mackintosh this passage—quoted at great length—provided a way to legitimize the widespread protests for reform both inside and outside of parliament.[78] For Lord Althorp, one of the central architects in the passing of the bill, Burke had indeed provided a model for the defence of party government preferred by Whigs, but he still maintained that his fellow peers should look beyond these factional party interests and towards the broader 'feelings of human nature' in their deliberations.[79] Burke thus provided a sentimental intellectual framework for reformers to draw upon and, over the century, this would become a recurring theme.

---

[74] *Hansard*, 4 Mar. 1831, vol. 3, cc.26–7 (Croker); 9 Mar. 1831, vol. 3, cc.313–15 (Russell).
[75] *Hansard*, 3 Mar. 1831, vol. 2, c.1349 (Peel).
[76] *Hansard*, 4 July 1831, vol. 4, c.660 (Sir John Walsh).
[77] *Hansard*, 6 July 1831, vol. 4 cc.807–8 (Colonel Charles Sidthorp); 12 July 1831, vol. 4 c.1128 (Colonel Edward Connolly); 20 Sept. 1831, vol. 7 cc.228–9 (Viscount Dungannon).
[78] *Hansard*, 4 July 1831, vol. 4, cc.670–95 (Mackintosh).
[79] Ibid., cc.338–9 (Althorp).

These parliamentary debates also help to explain the publication of a small popular book of selections from Burke's works in 1831 entitled *Opinions on Reform*. The compiler was none other than Thomas Haviland Burke, the last male representative of Burke's family.[80] In his introduction Haviland Burke stated that 'The opinions of... Burke' had been 'frequently alluded to in both Houses of Parliament during the debates upon the Reform question'. His purpose in publication, however, was clear: the fact that Burke was cited on a wide range of points during the debates arose from the 'several mistakes' that had been made 'as to what those [Burke's] opinions really were'. These mistakes were due to the fact that 'the volumes in which they [Burke's opinions] are contained' were 'numerous' and 'not generally accessible': it was Haviland Burke's aim, therefore, to correct them.[81] Unfortunately, the reader is not provided with any guidance about how to interpret the texts presented 'correctly'. But while Haviland Burke suggested that support for reform might be found in Burke's oeuvre, the outstanding evidence from the years that followed demonstrates that it became clear to most people that Burke's reformism was limited, and did not include *constitutional* reform. This of course posed a problem for Whig and Liberal supporters of parliamentary reform as a means of extending 'civil and religious liberty'. Hence, by the second-half of the century, Burke was easily positioned as an obstructionist to parliamentary reform by Liberal historians such as Green as well as politicians such as Gladstone. However, as Chapters 5 and 6 outline, this eighteenth-century Whiggish constitutional conservatism, could only achieve real significance as an explanation for Burke's C/conservatism later in the century, when the anti-monarchical elements of *Present Discontents* became correspondingly irrelevant and decontaminated, and when Unionists (Conservative and Liberal) found themselves once again defending the elemental organs of the constitution from 'revolutionary' threats.

TORIES AND CONSERVATIVES

Given his break with the Foxite Whigs over the French Revolution and constitutional reform, it might seem predictable that anti-revolutionary forces would attempt to claim Burke as their own. Yet James Sack has demonstrated the lack of interest in Burke on this side, particularly when compared to Pitt, before 1830—largely because of Burke's Irish heritage

---

[80] Elizabeth R. Lambert, *Edmund Burke of Beaconsfield* (2003), 198 n.53.
[81] Edmund Burke, *Opinions on Reform, by Edmund Burke*, ed. T. H. Burke (1831).

and his sympathies with Indians and Roman Catholics.[82] It is therefore important not to overestimate the influence of the French Revolution on a largely indigenous constitutional tradition, which saw itself as peculiarly English and which felt it had little to learn from France.[83] Of course, Burke did find supporters, but it is significant that this early material is overwhelming generated by Tories and Conservatives who were themselves Irish.[84] This is not to deny the considerable presence Irish Tories had in British life, particularly the periodical press, in the early to mid-nineteenth century. It does suggest, however, that Irish exaltation of Burke was promotional and propagative, rather than representative of British opinion. 'An Irish Tory,' in the unsympathetic words of the Whig historian George Wingrove Cooke (1814–65), 'is an English Tory run mad.'[85] In fact Irish Toryism was distinctive. It reacted to quite different local concerns, and then metamorphosed following the disestablishment of the Irish Church in 1869.[86] Even so, Irish Tories were not a homogeneous group: some, such as James Prior (1790–1869), Burke's first major biographer, were Canningite 'pro-Catholics' and others, such as the *Blackwood's* journalist Croly, were ultra-Protestant defenders of the Anglican church in Ireland. The image they presented of Burke to Britain over this major constitutional issue, therefore, was neither unified nor complete.

The leading figure on the pro-Catholic side was John Wilson Croker (1780–1857), an associate of Peel (until Corn Law repeal in 1846) and an eminent Tory politician in both a Westminster and an Irish context. He was a great admirer of Burke, and went on to declare, in 1847, that Pitt *and* Burke were 'the immortal guides and glory of Conservatism!'[87] It was

[82] J. J. Sack, 'The Memory of Pitt and the Memory of Burke', 623–40. For Burke as a less than representative figure of the 'right' or anti-revolutionary reaction, see J. G. A. Pocock's comments in his edition of *Reflections on the Revolution in France* (1987), xl; Kevin Gilmartin, *Writing Against Revolution: Literary Conservatism in Britain, 1790–1832* (2007), 8–9.

[83] J. J. Sack, *From Jacobite to Conservative: Reaction and Orthodoxy in Britain, c.1760–1832* (1993), 31–3.

[84] J. Prior, *Memoir of the Life and Character of the Rt. Hon. Edmund Burke*, 5th edn (1854); Croly, *A Memoir of Burke*; [William Maginn], 'On the Chances of the Reconstruction of the Tory Party: Sketch of the History of Parties from the Revolution to Burke', *Fraser's Magazine* (Feb. 1833), 223–30.

[85] Wingrove Cooke, *A History of Party*, iii. 506.

[86] For the distinctiveness and demise of Irish Toryism, see Andrews Shields, *The Irish Conservative Party, 1852–1868: Land, Politics, and Religion* (2007), xiv; Joseph Spence, 'The Philosophy of Irish Toryism, 1833–1852', PhD thesis, University of London, 1991, 181–4; Wayne E. Hall, *Dialogues in the Margin: A Study of the Dublin University Magazine* (2000), 207, 231.

[87] J. W. Croker, 'Peel Policy', *QR* (June 1847), 311, quoted in Robert Portsmouth, *John Wilson Croker: Irish Ideas and the Invention of Modern Conservatism, 1800–1835* (2010), 245.

to Croker that Prior, an ally in Irish Toryism and Catholic emancipation, dedicated his *Life* of Burke.[88] In his biography, Prior stated that on points of religious doctrine Burke saw that 'differences of opinion on these points made neither worse subjects, nor worse men'. The age was not then ripe, however, for much liberality of religious feeling: Burke therefore abstained from obtruding his opinions until a more opportune moment.[89] Yet Prior was not attempting to christen Burke as a liberal Tory. On the contrary, he lamented the fact that no English statesman could be anything but a 'party man', and instead promoted Burke as an Irishman, whose Irish identity removed him from a peculiarly English political dualism.[90] Croker also identified his own thought as residing within a distinctively Irish tradition of political thought and read Burke as an Irishman. The full quote from the *Quarterly Review* article just cited reveals this Irish (and pro-Catholic) bias: 'We entreat our friends to ask themselves who were the founders of Maynooth—William Pitt and Edmund Burke, the immortal guides and glory of Conservatism!'[91] (Maynooth College was a state-funded Irish Catholic seminary established in 1795.)[92] Croker's definition of 'Conservative', meanwhile, was essentially 'temperamental' rather than political or constitutional. For Croker, party was simply a consequence of a broad natural division of human minds between those who were more 'experimental' and those who preferred 'stability'.[93]

In a contrasting strategy, the ultra-Protestant side made short-lived efforts to reinterpret the 'Whig manual', *Present Discontents*. The Anglican clergyman and Tory journalist Croly published a series of articles on Burke for *Blackwood's Magazine* in the early 1830s,[94] which were eventually published in book form in 1840. Though Burke on France was his principal subject, he nonetheless attempted to stress an underlying consistency:

---

[88] [James Prior], *The Remonstrance of a Tory to the Right Hon. Robert Peel* (1827). For Prior's use of Burke in criticizing Peel's refusal to serve under Canning, see pp. 6–7, 39, 50–3; Prior, *Life and Character of the Rt. Hon. Edmund Burke*, 5th edn (1854), dedication.

[89] Prior, *Life and Character of the Rt. Hon. Edmund Burke*, 5th edn, 18, 165.

[90] Prior, *Life and Character of the Rt. Hon. Edmund Burke*, 2nd edn, i. xxv, 24, 307.

[91] Croker, 'Peel Policy'; Portsmouth, *Croker*, lx, 245; Sack, *From Jacobite to Conservative*, 72. In addition, Croker's Irish 'brogue' was mocked during parliamentary speeches in the 1830s: see Portsmouth, *Croker*, 158.

[92] For Maynooth's political significance, see Simon Skinner, 'Religion', in David Craig and James Thompson, eds., *Languages of Politics in Nineteenth-Century Britain* (2013), 103–5.

[93] William Thomas, *The Quarrel of Macaulay and Croker: Politics and History in an Age of Reform* (2000), 42, 54–5.

[94] In the mid-1830s, *Blackwood's* circulation stood at around 7,500: David Finkelstein, 'Selling Blackwood's Magazine, 1817–1834', in Robert Morrison and Daniel S. Roberts, eds., *Romanticism and Blackwood's Magazine: 'An Unprecedented Phenomenon'* (2013), 81.

Inconsistency is the favourite topic of the libellers of Burke. But the language which he held in this pamphlet [*Present Discontents*] is the language which he breathed from his expiring tongue—sacred honour for established institutions, hatred of worthless change, and just respect for the natural influence of rank, birth, and property. The change was not in the writer, but in the men. The French Revolution was the boundary-line between the aristocrat of his first day and his last... He as powerfully asserts the superior claim of the first class of the nation to govern the State, in 1770, as he asserted it in the full fury and tempest of 1793.[95]

Even Burke's wisdom, however, had mistaken the 'true hazard of the Constitution; that in contemplating the power of an intriguing Court, he overlooked the tyranny of an irresponsible populace'.[96] But Croly's attempt to shoehorn Burke into an anti-Catholic brand of Toryism was not convincing. In one of his early reviews in the *Rambler*, a young Acton discussed what he saw as Croly's bizarre attempt to derive Tory principles from a Whig politician.[97] The central division of English political parties along constitutional lines made this patching-up appear ludicrous: it was also vulnerable in that it linked Toryism to a violently anti-monarchical text. This point is worth noting: remarkably, it is still possible to trace hostility to *Present Discontents* on this ground as late as 1876. J. S. Brewer (1809–79), the Tory historian and sometime editor of the *Standard*, argued that 'Nobody now... believes in Burke's "Thoughts on the Present Discontents"... No one now thinks that this clever but unscrupulous calumny was anything better than a party invention to conceal the incapacity of the Whigs and their mutual recriminations.'[98] Croly, a fierce Protestant, had also ignored Burke's attitude towards Roman Catholics.[99] Hence Acton demanded that Burke's work on a variety of topics, from Ireland to France, must be read together in order to gain an accurate perception of Burke's thought.[100] Overall then, *pace* Croly, it was still wiser for any Conservatives interested in Burke to focus on his French writing and to stress the inconsistency of his work. The Scottish historian

---

[95] Croly, *A Memoir of Burke*, i. 64.   [96] Ibid., i. 65.
[97] [J. D. Acton], 'History of the Life and Times of Edmund Burke',*Rambler* (Apr. 1858), 268. For a more popular attack on the Tory use of *Reflections* in light of the *Present Discontents*, see Montague Gore, 'Reply to Sir John Walsh's Pamphlet, Entitled "The Present Balance of Parties"' (1832), 46–7.
[98] *QR* (Apr. 1876), re-printed in J. S. Brewer, *English Studies, or Essays: English Literature and History* (1881), 100.
[99] For Croly's anti-Catholicism, see Michael Tomko, *British Romanticism and the Catholic Question: Religion, History and National Identity, 1778–1829* (2011), 50–1; Michael Wheeler, *The Old Enemies: Catholic and Protestant in Nineteenth-Century English Culture* (2006), 139–52.
[100] [Acton], 'Life and Times of Edmund Burke', 269–73.

and Tory Archibald Alison (1792–1867) had realized this in 1837: 'Burke, almost forgotten as a champion of Whig doctrines in the earlier part of his career, stands forth in imperishable lustre as the giant supporter of Conservative principles in the zenith of his intellect.'[101]

In light of these issues, it makes sense to assess the level of interest and admiration Burke inspired in the two best-known Conservative leaders of this period: a rival 'founder of modern Conservatism', Sir Robert Peel, and that exemplary 'Tory Democrat', Benjamin Disraeli. This is a particularly helpful task for our purposes because it demonstrates that the respect and ambivalence expressed towards Burke's life and thought by both men was derived from their personal intellectual and political interests rather than any sense of his inherent 'C/conservatism'. Take Peel: like his long-term correspondent Croker, he had certainly read Burke, and the two of them were early advocates of Burke among a sea of English Tory apathy, since both had had a deep interest in the history of the French Revolution.[102] Peel, like Burke, was terrified that reform would bring about social subversion. That said, he was not a representative man: Peel's perceived hysteria was seen to have lacked the English confidence in the stability of their constitution.[103] As outlined earlier, it was the same fear of constitutional change and (as we will see in Chapter 3) his furious response to the French Revolution that distinguished Burke as an un-English outsider to many later commentators.[104] Still, as Robert Portsmouth points out, whatever Peel got from Burke it was not a rigid adherence to Catholic emancipation: as with Croly, on this key constitutional question they were divided.[105] In 1844, for instance, Peel used a series of quotations, including those from Burke and Henry Grattan (whom he opposed to himself as recognized friends of Catholic relief), as a way of strengthening his own claims in support of the maintenance of the Church of Ireland.[106] But Peel himself acknowledged that when a 'great authority' like Burke was cited in parliament, 'sometimes in the next page, and more frequently in the same, a passage might be found, which, if taken separately, might be relied upon as an authority for opposite doctrines'.[107] So Peel can be

---

[101] Archibald Alison, 'The Athenian Democracy', *BM* [July 1837], reprinted in *Essays Political, Historical, and Miscellaneous* (1850), i. 388.

[102] Portsmouth, *Croker*, 15. See also Brian Young, *The Victorian Eighteenth Century* (2007), 28; Thomas, *Quarrel of Macaulay and Croker*, ch. 6.

[103] Peter Ghosh, 'Gladstone and Peel', in P. Ghosh and L. Goldman, eds., Politics and Culture in Victorian Britain: *Essays in Memory of Colin Matthew* (2006), 50.

[104] Augustine Birrell, 'Edmund Burke', *CR* (July 1886), 41–2.

[105] Portsmouth, *Croker*, 15, 136.

[106] Robert Peel, 'State of Ireland' [23 Feb. 1844], *Speeches of the Late Rt. Hon. Sir Robert Peel* (1853), iv. 335–6. See also his 'Church of Ireland' [7 Apr. 1835], *Speeches*, iii. 115–16.

[107] Robert Peel, 'Parliamentary Reform' [3 Mar. 1831], *Speeches*, ii. 281.

found citing Burke in precisely the same way as he deplored in 1831: Burke was, to him, 'a man of great genius and talents'.[108] But Peel's aloof leadership style was not that of an authentic party politician, and there is no sense that he was attempting intellectually to derive Burke's 'C/conservative' political principles for mass practical inspiration.[109]

Certainly, following Peel's death in 1850, analysts of contemporary political history held divergent opinions regarding his relationship to Burke. For James Burke, a relatively unknown Irish barrister and biographer of the poet Thomas Moore, writing in 1854, Burke differed from Fox, Sheridan, and Grey on the issue of parliamentary reform: 'Burke's policy was, strictly speaking, to preserve the freedom which existed, and not to risk its loss by seeking its extension.' The statesmen of the day whose opinions most resembled Burke's in this respect, he claimed, was Peel.[110] But this Peelite reading of Burke was not uniform in Britain, since Burke was held to have had a very different kind of intellect from Peel. Thus to Walter Bagehot in 1856, writing in the *National Review*, Burke was the opposite of Peel. Here he argued that effective constitutional statesmen should possess common opinions and uncommon abilities: Burke had failed to achieve his objectives in practice precisely because he had been wise too soon.[111] In this way Burke was an imaginative genius, in direct contrast to the more practical Peel, who was a great administrative reformer. There is little sense here that Peel had striven to inject his party with a moderate, reforming conservatism derived from the writings of Burke.

Unlike Peel, Disraeli was—or learned to be—a party politician, and so his views and actions contrast with Peel's. Peel's decision to re-brand Tories as Conservatives had also been met with hostility by Disraeli and his allies, such as Kebbel, and Disraeli would break from Peel and side with the Protectionist rump of the Tory party (though conceding in the early 1850s that the argument for Corn Law repeal had been won).

---

[108] Robert Peel, 'Provision for the Family of Mr. Canning' [13 May 1828], *Speeches*, i. 624.

[109] Ghosh, 'Gladstone and Peel', 47–55. For further criticism of Norman Gash's claim in *Pillars of Government* (1986) that Peel founded 'modern Conservatism', see Portsmouth, *Croker*, 222; Angus Hawkins, '"Parliamentary Government" and Victorian Political Parties c.1830–1880', *EHR*, 104 (1989), 652–4.

[110] *The Speeches of the Rt. Hon. Edmund Burke, with Memoir and Historical Introduction*, ed. James Burke (1854), xxiii. The text was published by the Catholic publisher James Duffy. I have found no evidence that he was a relation of Edmund Burke.

[111] [Walter Bagehot], 'The Character of Sir Robert Peel', *NR* (July 1856), 147. Daniel Ritchie argues that Bagehot admired 'fierce' Burke, though much preferred 'safe' Peel as a political actor: 'Burke's Influence on the Imagination of Walter Bagehot', *Modern Age* (Fall 1989), 324–8. See further, David Craig, 'Statesmanship', in David Craig and James Thompson, eds., *Languages of Politics in Nineteenth-Century Britain* (2013), 48–50.

Despite these differences, this did not mean Disraeli was a straightforward admirer or promoter of Burke. However, the fact that Disraeli took the title earl of Beaconsfield in 1876—Beaconsfield being the location of Burke's former estate, Gregories—has led later historians to extrapolate from this a connection between Burke and Disraeli as another great nineteenth-century Conservative leader.[112] Disraeli's biographer, the Ulster Protestant W. F. Monypenny, for instance, noted how passages in *Vindication of the English Constitution* sound just like Burke, although there is little significant reference to him in the text itself.[113] Writing much later, Jonathan Parry and James Pereiro have also accorded Burke formative influence on Disraeli's thought in the 1830s and 1840s.[114] However, as with Peel, a degree of scepticism is needed when linking Disraeli to Burke, particularly in light of the fact that the canon of 'C/conservatism' was only constructed much later and that, by the time of Monypenny's writing in 1912, Burke had indeed become a C/conservative icon. The particular aspects of Burke's life and thought that Disraeli explicitly admired are therefore worth examining. Though Disraeli left no extended statement or analysis on Burke, it is possible to assess the trail of brief comments on Burke left in his novels, speeches, and letters.

A number of Disraeli's references to Burke, particularly regarding his portrayal of the English Constitution, were glowing. In an 1847 speech at Amersham, for example, Disraeli admired Burke's 'divine effusions' that 'vindicated the social system, and reconciled the authority of law with the liberty of men'.[115] It was here, in his belief in the necessity of unifying liberty with order, that Disraeli too could find reason to laud Burke. Writing to Queen Victoria in 1859, he praised a speech by Edward Bulwer Lytton by claiming that Lytton's 'description of the English constitution, his analysis of Democracy' was 'as rich & more powerful, than Burke'.[116] Yet in a letter to the Liberal MP William Harcourt in 1873 on the career of Pitt, Disraeli contrasted Pitt's Toryism in the early stages—'hostility to borough-mongering, economy, French alliance, and commercial treaties'—to his later, more reprehensible, conduct during the

---

[112] Monypenny and Buckle, *Life of Benjamin Disraeli*, v. 518.
[113] Monypenny and Buckle, *Life of Benjamin Disraeli*, i. 307–8.
[114] J. P. Parry, 'Disraeli and England', *HJ*, 43 (2000), 703, 705; James Pereiro, 'The Reformation and the Principles of the English Constitution in Disraeli's "Young England" Novels', *Bulletin of the John Rylands Library*, 90 (2014), 336–8. At a popular level, Robert Blake's contribution to BBC History Online, 'Disraeli and Gladstone' describes Disraeli's heroic ideal as 'an amalgam of Burke, Bolingbroke and Byron': http://www.bbc.co.uk/history/british/victorians/disraeli_gladstone_01.shtml.
[115] Monypenny and Buckle, *Life of Benjamin Disraeli*, iii. 25.
[116] Benjamin Disraeli, 'Disraeli to Queen Victoria, 22 Mar. 1859', in *Benjamin Disraeli Letters*, eds. M. G. Weibe and Mary S. Millar (2004), vii. 347.

Revolutionary wars. This later stage was 'pure Whiggism; close Parliaments, war with France, national debt and commercial treaties, all prompted and inspired by the arch-Whig trumpeter, Mr. Burke'.[117] Even in these snippets it is possible to see a distinction emerging between general literary and constitutional commentary, and that on the more specific workings of parliamentary politics and party policies.

Disraeli's allusions to Burke in *Sybil* (1845)—his most famous work of the Young England period of the 1830s and 1840s—are similarly revealing. Burke appears as part of a general sweep of the history of English party politics, and there is no particular consideration of Burke as a great C/conservative or Tory thinker, which would have been unthinkable at this date. He is indeed celebrated for his literary skills, and for splitting from the Whigs over the French Revolution, but Burke's defection is explained by personal animosity towards his party: it was his revenge against the Whigs who had refused to recognize his substantial contribution to the development of *Whig* ideas (an implicit reference to *Present Discontents*) rather than a principled defection to the Tories. In the earlier part of his career, Burke 'effected for the whigs what Bolingbroke in a preceding age had done for the tories: he restored the moral existence of the party'. Burke had taught the Whigs 'the ancient principles of their connection, and suffused those principles with all the *delusive* splendour of his imagination'.[118] Yet in refusing Burke high office, the Whigs consequently 'dashed to the ground the rival who had robbed him of his hard-earned greatness; rended in twain the proud oligarchy that had dared to use and to insult him'.[119] Burke's method and style had allowed him to transcend partisanship; but this is something rather different to a party political appropriation. So, despite the chapter beginning with an account of Burke's actions towards his fellow Whigs, Disraeli goes on to pay equal tribute to three other statesmen—concluding by stating that Shelburne, Bolingbroke, and Pitt form together the 'three greatest of English statesmen'.[120] Burke is noticeably absent.

While a significant body of scholarship has already established that Disraeli's brand of Toryism distanced him from Peel, it can also be said that this distanced him politically from Burke. Disraeli held up the age of Pitt as an ideal 'national' system of government, boasting a 'popular monarch' and a 'democratic minister', in the *Vindication of the English*

---

[117] Disraeli, *Disraeli Letters*, ii. 297.
[118] Benjamin Disraeli, *Sybil; or, the Two Nations* (1845), bk. 1, ch. 3, 30. My emphasis.
[119] Ibid., 32. See also [Macknight], *Disraeli: A Literary and Political Biography*, 362–3.
[120] Ibid., 48–9. See also Monypenny and Buckle, *Life of Benjamin Disraeli*, ii. 301–2.

Constitution;[121] but Burke, according to his later comments, had played the role of a wrecking ball. In terms of practical constitutional reform, Disraeli had been a reformer in 1832—he had regretted that the bill had not been 'catholic' enough[122]—and the Second Reform Act of 1867 was of course carried through the Commons by Disraeli. Given the established position on Burke's constitutional reform already outlined, contemporaries such as Thomas Macknight, in his hostile biography of 1854, were not inclined to pair Disraeli's Tory reformism with Burke's constitutional conservatism or his anti-Revolutionary sentiments.[123] Indeed, that Disraeli could comfortably speak of Burke as an 'arch-Whig' in 1873 (seconding Brewer's remarks on *Present Discontents*) is indicative of the continued importance of eighteenth-century constitutional divisions—and thus Pitt and Bolingbroke rather than Burke—to his formative 'Young England' period in the 1830s and 1840s. The low *political* estimate of Burke in *Sybil* is therefore consistent with Disraeli's subsequent comments to Harcourt in 1873, as well as a later novelistic reference to Burke—in *Endymion* (1880)—as a Dionysian 'Maenad' ('the raving ones').[124]

The idea that Disraeli was making a significant bid for Burke's legacy by taking the title of Beaconsfield is therefore somewhat misconceived—although he admired Burke, the move was more an advertisement of his Buckinghamshire roots than an acknowledgement of his status as Burke's political heir. But the title did, of course, create a link between the two politicians through these shared English roots, and this led to sharp criticism of the Conservative leader from at least one corner. To John Morley, a Liberal and the outstanding expositor of Burke and guardian of his legacy in the years c.1867–80, it was

> rather more than one can bear, that the man who entered life as the bravo of the Protectionists, should trick himself out as a successor to the title of the author of the Thoughts on Scarcity... why should the man whose last works in the House of Commons were a plea for the authors of massacre and oppression in Turkey, try to associate his name with the memory of the man who gave fourteen of the best years of his life to punish the oppressor of the

---

[121] Disraeli, *Vindication of the English Constitution*, 173.
[122] Saunders, *Democracy and the Vote*, 70.
[123] [Macknight], *Disraeli: A Literary and Political Biography*, 23, 83, 189–94, *passim*. One of Macknight's reviewers agreed with his insistence on Burke's wisdom, but doubted the internal consistency of both his writing and political action: *The Critic* 'Life of Disraeli' (1 Feb. 1854), 68. Disraeli's later biographer and no great admirer of Burke, J. A. Froude, also attempted to refute Macknight's unfavourable comparison of Disraeli to Burke, but referred only to their literary style; arguing that Disraeli's writing transcended even the 'oriental imagery' of *Reflections* in its 'luxuriance': 'Mr. Disraeli's Letters of Runnymede', *Fraser's Magazine* (Aug. 1874), 266–7.
[124] Benjamin Disraeli, *Endymion* (1880), ch. 12, p. 48.

natives of India? It is excellent, no doubt, to be a wit, to be an epigrammatist, to have the secret of pithy phrase, but what has the artificer of these flashy things to do with the man whose lofty spirit, whose weighty judgement, whose magnanimous aims, whose imperial understanding, gave him such majestic authority over our English speech? How laughable it is![125]

Disraeli had evidently read Burke carefully and thought highly of his 'divine effusions'—yet, as with Peel above, Disraeli was not attempting to extract specific political principles of C/conservatism or Toryism from Burke. What he admired most of all, as he explained to Matthew Arnold in 1864, was Burke's (and others') ability to sustain a career in both literature and politics—to 'do two things at once'—in a manner which Disraeli could not.[126]

CHURCH AND STATE

The English, or British, Constitution was not, of course, purely political and secular: it was a constitution in church and state. The final section of this chapter further explores the use of Burke in explicitly religious debates relating to the position of the established churches of England and Ireland already touched upon, and also how these invocations were intertwined with changing perceptions of Burke's own religious identity—and, most importantly, his perceived connections to Catholicism. This is an elementary concern for historians interested in the construction of political identities in the long nineteenth century primarily because politics was inseparable from religion, and for many the Anglican church had played a key role in securing English constitutional liberty.[127] In order to do so, Burke's links with Catholicism must be outlined as a preliminary, before moving on to consider his function in discussions of church establishment.

It will be clear already that Burke's support of Catholic relief played an important role in shaping his reputation in the early nineteenth century, and was particularly problematic for those Anglican Tories who opposed the dismantling of the privileges of the established church. Though the advent of Catholic emancipation in 1829 began the loosening of institutional constraints against Catholics, they remained subject to

---

[125] John Morley, 'Home and Foreign Affairs', *FR* (Sept. 1876), 408. Morley's specific contribution is discussed more extensively in Chapter 4 in this volume.
[126] Matthew Arnold to his mother (Mary Penrose Arnold), 28 Jan. 1864, *Letters of Matthew Arnold*, ed. Cecil Y. Lang (1996–2002), ii. 270.
[127] Kirby, *Historians and the Church of England*, 78–9, 110–11, 175, 197.

both formal and informal disadvantages. Prejudices were held against Roman Catholics in Britain by all classes and denominations: the restoration of the Catholic hierarchy was seen to threaten the constitution and its most beneficial product—civil and religious liberty. Roman Catholicism represented an unwelcome foreign power within the nation, from both Rome and Ireland, and the loyalty of Catholics to the British monarch over the Pope was a moot point.[128] As a result the constitution in church and state established by the Henrician Reformation and confirmed by the Test Acts of 1672 and 1678 was seen to be endangered by the abolition of these Acts and the admittance of Catholics into public life after 1829.[129] The image of the Irish Catholic also retained a central place in stereotyping the Irish, and Burke was no exception to this rule. During his lifetime, Burke was ridiculed not only for his distinctive Irish brogue, but also as a suspected Jesuit, educated at St Omer—as the voluminous eighteenth-century caricatures of Burke confirm.[130] Though the myth of Burke as a Jesuit priest was in decline by the early to mid-nineteenth century, particularly after 1829, it was still important enough for his early sympathizers, particularly Prior, to reject and disprove.[131] Burke, whose mother and sister were Catholics, was made a kind of political martyr by pro-Catholic Tories, Whigs, and Liberals on the ground that he had been evicted from his seat at Bristol for his support of Catholic relief and Irish free trade.

Understandably then, Burke found many admirers among Catholics and those who criticized the past actions of English statesmen in Ireland. In 1853, following the re-establishment of the Catholic hierarchy in 1850 and the so-called 'Papal Aggression', the *Dublin Review* (a periodical at the apex of Catholic intellectual life) welcomed a reconsideration of Burke's life and writings—including his vision of the constitution:

> in him we could point to one who was a thorough British Statesman in the largest sense of the word, and who yet could and did recognize the principle of Catholicity acting in the fullest harmony with the genius of the British people, and receiving its most complete development in the spirit of the British constitution.[132]

---

[128] Wheeler, *The Old Enemies*, 25–6.
[129] Scott Bennett, 'Catholic Emancipation, the "Quarterly Review", and Britain's Constitutional Revolution', *VS*, 12 (Mar. 1969), 285.
[130] Nicholas K. Robinson, *Edmund Burke: A Life in Caricature* (1996), 48, 83, *passim*.
[131] Prior, *Life and Character of the Rt. Hon. Edmund Burke*, 2nd edn, i. 46.
[132] G. W. Abraham, 'The Works and Correspondence of the Right Hon. Edmund Burke', *DR* (Mar. 1853), 68.

This idea was repeated by (the English) Macknight in 1858. Burke became a 'great philosophic statesman, one of whose most cherished purposes was the emancipation of the Catholics of his native land from the yoke of their Protestant countrymen'.[133] In an 1862 lecture, the Irish Tory Joseph Napier asserted that Bristol 'disgraced itself by rejecting the man who had honoured the constituency by his transcendent talents, his comprehensive knowledge, his consistent integrity, and his manly spirit of independence'.[134] It was a view that filtered into the analyses of many later English Liberal commentators. To the Liberal Augustine Birrell (1850–1933), Burke's 'regard for his Catholic fellow-subjects, his fierce repudiation of the infamies of the Penal Code—whose horrors he did something to mitigate—his respect for antiquity, and his historic sense', were all bolstered by the fact that his 'tenderly loved... mother belonged through life and in death to an ancient and outraged faith'.[135] This kind of sympathetic portrayal was to play an important role in the Home Rule debates, though condemnation of the Penal Code (Liberal or Conservative) in an article published in July of 1886 is perhaps unsurprising—as Burke himself said, few are the friends of departed tyranny.

Some of Burke's Catholic admirers went a step further: it is striking that at the beginning of his career Lord Acton made a notable, if unorthodox, attempt to incorporate (and later to expel) him from a Catholic intellectual tradition. As editor of the *Rambler* from 1858, Acton sought to 're-energize' the Catholic church in England in response to the Ultramontanism of Cardinal Manning, and Burke was one of his instruments here:[136] 'In the writings of his last years (1792–7) whatever was Protestant or partial or revolutionary of 1688 in his political views disappeared, and what remained was a purely Catholic view of political principles and of history.'[137] To contemporary readers this would have had constitutional implications: Seamus Deane—who traces Acton's early determination to incorporate Burke into a Catholic tradition through his manuscript notes, produced roughly between 1858 and 1870—argues that 'Protestant' here refers to the exaltation of the secular state, in contrast to 'Catholic', which sought to develop the autonomy of the church. In these early notes, Acton writes that Burke 'Always prefers Irish Catholics to Irish Protestants.

---

[133] Macknight, *Life and Times of Edmund Burke*, ii. 63.
[134] Joseph Napier, *Edmund Burke: A Lecture, Delivered before the Dublin YMCA* (1862), 57–8.
[135] Birrell, 'Edmund Burke', 27–43, 29.
[136] Seamus Deane, 'Lord Acton and Edmund Burke', *JHI*, 33 (1972), 326; Lord Acton, *Essays on Church and State*, ed. Douglas Woodruff (1952), 12–13.
[137] 16 Feb. 1858, quoted in Francis A. Gasquet, ed., *Lord Acton and His Circle* (1906), 4.

Careful to preserve Catholicism as the main safeguard of Christianity.'[138] His notes from French authors—such as the Comte de Montgaillard (1761–1841), an *émigré* in Britain from 1792, and Charles de Rémusat (1797–1875), a moderate who wrote extensively on English philosophy—implied that Burke was in essence a Catholic and a Protestant only out of expediency, noting the number of Catholics in Burke's immediate family. On an intellectual level too, Acton found that 'Burke's theory [was] supported by the Catholic view of history. What Bossuet says of the divine guidance.' The 'natural followers of Burke' therefore included Adam Müller, K. L. von Haller, Baron d'Eckstein, the 'Romantic School', Schelling, Savigny, and Hegel. Acton was, Deane claims, bringing his two main interests together in Burke: he became the source of the great renaissance of both Catholicism and German historicism in the nineteenth century.[139]

J. B. Robertson (1800–77), a cosmopolitan Englishman and one-time Professor of Modern History and English Literature at Newman's Catholic University at Dublin, also recruited Burke as an advocate of tolerant constitutional politics. Robertson, a Roman Catholic who had previously studied under the French liberal Catholic priest and philosopher Lamennais (1782–1854) and spent much of his life on the continent, stressed the inherently Catholic nature of Burke's thought in his 1868 *Lectures on the Life, Writings, and Times of Edmund Burke*: 'He is still, after the lapse of eighty years, the most catholic-minded of all modern British statesmen.' To Robertson, this was reflected in the Catholic European appreciation of Burke, particularly when compared to the misapprehension or, at least, inadequate appreciation of his political views which prevailed for so long among the more 'constitutional politicians of Protestant England'.[140] Robertson's chief aim appears to be the reintegration of a Catholic element into the British Constitution following the 'interruption' of the Reformation, and the 'disastrous' 1688 Revolution.[141] Like Acton's occasional and sometimes unpublished remarks, this was not a mainstream or representative presentation of Burke, nor of English history. His lectures are strikingly different from British and Anglo-Irish texts on Burke, in that they draw heavily from French and German appropriations of Burke

---

[138] Acton MSS, quoted in Deane, 'Lord Acton and Edmund Burke', 327.

[139] Ibid., 327–8. See also Lord Acton, 'Burke, the Historian', *Essays on Church and State*, 455–6.

[140] J. B. Robertson, *Lectures on the Life, Writings, and Times of Edmund Burke* (1868), xii–xiii. For his earlier, very brief, comments on Burke, see *Public Lectures on Ancient and Modern History, Delivered before the Catholic University of Ireland* (1859), x–xi, 238, 288–9.

[141] Robertson, *Lectures on Burke*, 132–3.

which maintained Burke's Catholicity. Hence, while Robertson's lectures received considerable praise from the Catholic *Dublin Review*, his reading of Burke met with great hostility in the mainstream British press and was dismissed as 'ultramontane'.[142] There were, evidently, limits to Burke's constitutional 'Catholicism'.

To Goldwin Smith (1823–1910), for example, Burke's sympathies for Roman Catholics were not just a question of toleration borne from familial love. To its detriment, Burke's whole constitutional and political thought had been permeated by this Catholic influence. Smith was no supporter of Irish or Indian independence: he was a Liberal Unionist who favoured colonial independence only for Britain's Anglo-Saxon colonies, moving to New York in 1868, and then to Canada in 1871 where he took up residence until his death in 1910. Smith particularly disliked the superstitious element of what he perceived to be the natural state of the Irish-Celtic Catholic, which was elaborated with reference to Burke in 1868:

> His philosophy afforded no firm and lofty ground of immutable faith in things unseen, from which he could form a rational estimate of political systems, as things merely subservient to the higher life of man, venerable only for their utility, not to be altered without good reason, but when there was good reason, to be altered or abolished without superstitious scruple, and destined like all other parts of the outward vesture of humanity to pass away before the end. He did not know that, while many things that are of man are good, nothing is sacred but that which is of God. He was not so much an advocate as a priest of the constitution and its mythical founders; he preached sermons on it as fervent as those of Bossuet, and defended its absurdities by arguments which his piety suggested as strange as ever a Roman friar used in defence of his superstitions. According to him it was ordered by a sort of divine wisdom that Cornwall should have as many members as Scotland, because the representation was thus prevented from being too closely connected with local interests. When the French Revolution got beyond his consecrated type, it forfeited his sympathies, and with a nature so passionate as his, to forfeit sympathy was to incur hatred.[143]

Here Smith transfers the explicitly religious attributes of priest and superstition to more secular objects such as electoral constituencies. Shortly afterwards, in the years following the declaration of papal infallibility in

---

[142] 'Lectures on the Life, Writings, and Times of Edmund Burke', *DR* (Oct. 1868), 563–7; 'Lectures on the Life, Writings, and Times of Edmund Burke', *Athenaeum* (29 Aug. 1868), 265–6; W. T. Marriott, 'Lectures on the Life, Writings, and Times of Edmund Burke', *FR* (Dec. 1868), 699–701.

[143] Goldwin Smith, *Three English Statesmen: A Course of Lectures on the Political History of England* (1868), 193.

1870, Smith's close friend J. A. Froude, historian and author of *The Nemesis of Faith* (1849), published his highly controversial *The English in Ireland in the Eighteenth Century* (1872–4). Froude was similarly inclined to stress the Catholicity of Burke: though 'not himself a Catholic', he was just as little a Protestant in Froude's view. He might have been swept into the world of English politics, but his true sympathies lay with the old faith and his old friends. Hence Burke's 'advice to the world' was to 'save his countrymen from the revolutionary temper by restoring to them the privileges of citizenship'.[144] Evidently, anti-Catholicism did not simply disappear at the close of the nineteenth century; and the equation of Catholicism with Irish identity—which developed throughout the century—became much more pronounced after 1885. But neither Smith's nor Froude's analyses were based on the old belief that Burke was a practising Roman Catholic. Moreover, an increasing number of popular texts regretted that Burke had suffered 'a double disadvantage' from both his Irish parentage and the Roman Catholicism of his mother. That had been a time, the Liberal T. Dundas Pillans claimed, when 'racial and religious prejudice existed to a degree hardly conceivable by the present generation'.[145] Though anti-Catholicism—at either an elite, intellectual, or popular level—did not simply vanish after this time, even Edwardian Protestant Associations exhibited a markedly more tolerant stance towards Catholics than their predecessors.[146] The example of Burke therefore conforms to the accounts of D. G. Paz and John Wolffe on the decline of anti-Catholic sentiment and organization as a 'major public issue' from the 1870s.[147]

By the 1870s, therefore, it was widely acknowledged that Burke's connection to Catholicism and his support for Catholic relief did not stem from a secret Roman Catholic faith. Instead his tolerant Anglicanism attracted admiration from pro-Catholic Tories as well as many Liberals, and disdain from more staunchly Anglican Tories and anti-Catholic Liberals. The parliamentary debates over the disestablishment of the Irish Church in 1869 demonstrate the ambivalence surrounding Burke's religious identity. As in the reform debates of the 1830s, he was invoked as an authority by both parties and on both sides of the debate. Previously, Gladstone had defended his decision to pursue disestablishment by reference to Burke's criticism of the penal laws ('hideous scandals'), and was in

---

[144] J. A. Froude, *The English in Ireland in the Eighteenth Century* (1872–4), iii. 23–4.
[145] T. Dundas Pillans, *Edmund Burke: Apostle of Justice and Liberty* (1905), 11–12.
[146] John Wolffe, *The Protestant Crusade in Great Britain, 1829–1860* (1991), 306–8.
[147] Ibid., 305–7; D. G. Paz, *Popular Anti-Catholicism in Mid-Victorian England* (1992), 18.

return attacked by an anonymous pamphleteer for 'trott[ing] out Burke's horses'.[148] This author maintained that Burke had nonetheless spoken highly of the Irish Church, and argued for its preservation: 'Wishing to make a clatter with them [Burke's "horses"], and to raise a little dust in our eyes, let him [Gladstone] look to it that he does not get knocked down and trampled upon himself.'[149] Similarly, the Irish Conservative member for Trinity College, Dublin (TCD), John Ball (1815–98) cited Burke in parliament as in favour of the maintenance of the established church (as Peel had done earlier in the century[150]), but in response the Liberal Chancellor Robert Lowe countered that Burke had also detailed the evil effects the Church of Ireland had had on the populace—an evil which could now be remedied as it could not have been in Burke's day.[151] Even Leigh Hunt's radical *Examiner* ran a favourable front-page leader with the headline 'How Burke Would Have Governed Ireland' which lamented how the English had ignored his earlier warnings that laws 'should suit the people and the circumstances of the country'.[152] These somewhat muddled readings of Burke portrayed him once more as a sympathetic friend of Catholic relief and a critic of the Church of Ireland, but they did not attempt to explain this compassion via speculations about Burke's own religious faith, nor did Liberals promote Burke as an opponent of established churches per se. Though they fall short of the positions adopted by Gladstonian Liberals examined in Chapter 5, still they lay a foundation.

The issue of church establishment was especially significant to so-called 'Liberal Anglican' thinkers, from Coleridge, F. D. Maurice and Thomas Arnold, to Matthew Arnold and later Liberal Idealists, all of whom upheld the concept of a moralized state.[153] To these writers and educators, Burke was seen to have supported the view that the church and the state were not merely allied, but one and the same thing. Thomas Arnold (1795–1842)

---

[148] W. E. Gladstone, *A Chapter of Autobiography* (1868), 33; Gladstone, *The Vatican Decrees in their Bearing on Civil Allegiance: A Political Expostulation* (1874), 23; 'Philip Plainspoken', 'Short Notes on a Long Chapter of Mr. Gladstone's Autobiography, reprinted from John Bull' (1868), 17.

[149] Plainspoken, 'Short Notes', 17–18.

[150] See p. 38 in this volume.

[151] *Hansard*, 19 Mar. 1869, vol. 195, cc.1802–14 (Ball); 22 Mar. 1869, vol. 194, cc.1993–4 (Lowe). See also [Anon.], 'Church and State', *WR* (July 1868), 151–83; W. Maziere Brady, 'The Irish Establishment under Papal and Protestant Princes', *CR* (Sept. 1868), 9; [Anon.], 'The Irish Church Measure', *North British Review* (July 1869), 568–601.

[152] 'How Burke Would Have Governed Ireland', *Examiner* (2 Jan. 1869), 1.

[153] Jones, *Victorian Political Thought* (2000), 44–52. See also Parry, *Democracy and Religion*, 72–3; Peter Mandler, '"Race" and "Nation" in Mid-Victorian Thought', in Stefan Collini, Richard Whatmore, and Brian Young, eds., *History, Religion, Culture: British Intellectual History, 1750–1950* (2000), 227–8.

drew on Burke's 'Speech on the Petition of the Unitarians' (1792) in an 1826 article for the *Edinburgh Review* as well as in the Appendix for his subsequent lectures as Regius Professor of Modern History at Oxford published in the 1840s. In the former, Arnold used Burke's 1792 speech to argue for the importance of the laity in the governance of the Church of England, while in his lectures of 1841–2 he cited it in order to reinforce his claim that 'in a Christian commonwealth the church and the state are one and the same thing, being different integral parts of the same whole'.[154] In his widely read biography of Arnold, fellow Broad Churchman A. P. Stanley (1815–81) also made this link when he stated that Arnold's 'theory' of the 'absolute identity of the Church with the State', and with it the aim of the 'highest welfare of man', had been previously sanctioned 'by Burke, and in part by Coleridge'.[155] Like Burke, and unlike Coleridge, Arnold had been an Anglican supporter of Catholic emancipation, based on his belief in the existence of a distinct Irish nationality.[156] In a similar vein, Arnold's son Matthew (1822–88) would later produce his own essay entitled 'The Church of England' in which he took inspiration from Burke while defending the established church as peculiarly suited to the English national character: 'all the constituents assigned to the English people's nature by Burke,— our people's piety, their integrity, their good nature, their good humour, but above all, their *integrity*— contribute to incline them [to the Church of England]. That the Church should show a like inclination, is in its favour as a National Church.'[157] All this was derived from an older Anglican tradition which stressed the role of national churches within a universal Christian community, and indeed Maurice (1805–72) had also recommended Burke (a passage from *Reflections*), discussing the distinct religious quality of the English state in *Kingdom of Christ* (1838 and later editions).[158] He regretted later, however, that Burke was not only *too* 'National' (i.e. he was the 'masterly protester' against every attempt to merge national constitutions and obligations into 'some general theory which concerned all men equally'),

---

[154] [Thomas Arnold], 'The Church of England', *ER* (Sept. 1826), 501, 510–11; *Introductory Lectures on Modern History*, 4th edn (1849), 53.
[155] A. P. Stanley, *The Life and Correspondence of Thomas Arnold* (1844), i. 206.
[156] Ibid., i. 379, 402; S. T. Coleridge, *On the Constitution of Church and State, according to the idea of each; with aids towards a right judgement on the late Catholic Bill* [1830], *The Collected Works of Samuel Taylor Coleridge*, eds. Kathleen Coburn et al. (1969–2002), x. 7.
[157] Matthew Arnold, 'The Church of England', *Last Essays on Church and Religion* [1877] (1903), 126–30. See also Arnold, *A French Eton, or Middle Class Education and the State* (1864), 75.
[158] F. D. Maurice, *Kingdom of Christ: or, Hints to a Quaker respecting the Principles, Constitution and Ordinances of the Catholic Church*, 2nd edn (1842), ii. 487.

he had also failed to see, during the French Revolution, that 'the more awful they [the revolutionaries] were, the more they bore witness of the guidance of Him in whom all awe dwells'—that is, Maurice criticized Burke for failing to take a more progressive view of providential development.[159] This was a theme which would be taken up again by Burke's Idealist admirers, raised in the Broad Church environment of T. H. Green's Balliol (Chapter 6).

The growing sense of Burke's Anglicanism—and its potential rigidity— also lies at the root of Acton's move away from Burke in the 1880s. He retracted his earlier statements, and now concluded that Burke's French writings were inconsistent with his earlier views. In the 1790s Burke had become less Roman Catholic, and, as a defender of the Glorious Revolution, more Anglican: 'A liberal wishes that which ought to be—above what is—Burke too historic—The most historically-minded of English statesmen. To the detriment of his reasoning power—and of his moral sense. He looked for what ought to be in what is. Is that not essentially Anglican?'[160] He voiced this private musing publicly in an 1889 review of James Bryce's *American Commonwealth*: 'I descry a bewildered Whig emerging from the third volume with a reverent appreciation of ancestral wisdom, Burke's *Reflections*, and the eighteen Canons of Dort, and a growing belief in the function of ghosts to make laws for the quick.'[161] Here, in his description of Bryce (an Ulsterman), Burke's *Reflections*—in part a defence of French Catholicism—is associated with excessive historicism and even Calvinism. Deane convincingly illustrates, therefore, that from the 1880s—a pivotal period in Burke reception more generally— Burke ceased to offer significant intellectual inspiration for Acton.[162]

Overall, Burke was rarely presented as having a definitive denominational identity before 1880. Instead, he was used in a variety of ways by both Tories and Liberals in debates on the extension of Catholic relief as well as on the value and maintenance of established churches in Britain and Ireland. It should also be clear, in this context, that by this date British

---

[159] F. D. Maurice, *Moral and Metaphysical Philosophy*, new edn (1872), ii. 586–95; 'Edmund Burke' [1857], *The Friendship of Books and Other Lectures*, ed. Thomas Hughes (1874), 254–7.

[160] Acton MSS, cited in Deane, 'Lord Acton and Edmund Burke', 329; 'Freedom Betrayed: Acton, Burke and Ireland', *Irish Review*, 30 (2003), 13–35, 20. See also Derek Beales, 'Edmund Burke and the Monasteries of France', *HJ*, 48 (2005), 434–5; Gertrude Himmelfarb, 'The American Revolution in the Political Theory of Lord Acton', *Journal of Modern History*, 21 (1949), 293–312.

[161] Lord Acton, *The History of Freedom and Other Essays*, eds. J. N. Figgis and J. V. Laurence (1907), 580.

[162] Deane, 'Lord Acton and Edmund Burke', 332. For Acton on Burke in the 1890s, see Chapter 7 in this volume, pp. 211–12.

public life was much more religiously pluralistic thanks to successive legislation from Catholic emancipation to university reform. Acton's later appointment as Regius Professor of History at Cambridge in 1895 is in itself an excellent example of this transformation. At a popular level, anti-Catholic and anti-Irish tensions were largely confined to areas of high Irish immigration, such as Merseyside and Lancashire.[163] And though intellectual anti-Catholicism still lingered, staunchly Protestant stances increasingly appeared old-fashioned to contemporaries: by 1907, for instance, Edmund Gosse noted how ' "Down-with-the-Pope" men' were increasingly viewed as 'illiberal'.[164] This was a subtle but significant shift: Burke's personal links with Catholicism became less politically and socially potent at a time when his thought was increasingly portrayed as 'Anglican'. One important result was that, by the early 1900s, Burke's religion was portrayed in a rather baggy sense by his critics: as Chapter 6 will detail, he could now be easily presented as a supporter of a tolerant broad-based Christianity; as a believer in the religious nature of the state and thus more inclined towards national churches/Anglicanism; and/or as a bulwark against secularizing, disestablishmentarian, 'Jacobinical' atheism.[165] So although the Protestant Liberal (later Unionist) historian, W. E. H. Lecky, in a 1903 edition of his popular *Leaders of Public Opinion in Ireland*, saw in *Reflections* 'the most profound and eloquent of all defences of the Conservative view of the Constitution', he was also quick to highlight the fact that 'at a time when he was preaching with unrivalled power the danger of tampering with the framework of the existing British Constitution, he urged that the Constitution of Ireland could not be better strengthened than by introducing gradually and carefully a Catholic element of property and education into political life'.[166]

CONCLUSION

In spite of his supposed 'madness', Catholicism, inconsistency, and obstructionism, Burke retained a substantial reputation as a man of letters and one of the greatest writers of English prose. It was this which ensured Burke continued to be drawn upon by Radicals, Whigs and Tories, and

---

[163] Although Daniel Jackson argues that the Third Home Rule Bill crisis (1912–14) reignited Protestant prejudices *across* Britain, he himself notes how 'popular attitudes to Ireland may have softened in some places' except in the 'strongholds of resistance', which included Liverpool and Lancashire: *Popular Opposition to Irish Home Rule in Edwardian Britain* (2009), 2–3.
[164] Wolffe, *Protestant Crusade*, 306–7.   [165] See Chapter 6 in this volume.
[166] W. E. H. Lecky, *The Leaders of Public Opinion in Ireland*, new edn (1861; 1903), i. 140–1.

Liberals and Conservatives, despite the ambivalence in his religious and political views when applied to nineteenth-century constitutional debates and party politics before 1880. Indeed, almost all commentators found it convenient to shelter in literary appreciation when struggling to swallow their partisan bile: Burke had, at least, brought poetical imagination to dry abstract ideas. This sentiment lay behind the well-known quip from Macaulay, recorded in his diary, that Burke was 'the greatest man since Milton'.[167] In Macaulay's eyes Milton was above all a poet, and the author of *Areopagitica*, rather than a political actor and Cromwell's Secretary. In a literary perspective even the Radical Hazlitt could describe Burke's passage on the constitution as the 'proud keep of Windsor' as 'the most splendid passage in his works'.[168] As a result of bipartisan literary praise he came to be increasingly referred to as a writer who was beyond party political categorization.

Bipartisanship was positively promoted in some quarters: it was to the class of bipartisan politicians to which Burke belonged, according to the *Westminster Review* in 1852, that England owed its 'peculiar character of... progress, to which must be attributed both its durability and its safety'. At the same time, however, it was to these men 'to whom she is in general most scandalously ungrateful'.[169] Here again we see the tug-of-war between the virtues of political independence and party spirit. Burke could be presented as offering guidance to both political parties as a uniquely 'philosophical statesman', or a 'philosopher in action', in possession of wide, penetrating views.[170] This was particularly so in the decade 1846–55 when the disintegration of the party structure brought about by Peel was at its height. An early statement of Thomas Macknight's reverence for Burke appears in his hostile biography of Disraeli (1854), where Burke appears as a precursor of Peel: a statesman who took 'a more

---

[167] Thomas Macaulay, *Journals of Thomas Babington Macaulay*, ed. William Thomas (2008), iv. 17. Cf. Macaulay, 'Burke on France', in ibid.: v. 201. On Macaulay's primarily imaginative, literary, and aesthetic appreciation of Burke, see Peter Ghosh, 'Macaulay and the Heritage of the Enlightenment', *EHR*, 112 (1997), 386; Fuchs, *Edmund Burke, Ireland, and the Fashioning of the Self*, 2–3.

[168] William Hazlitt, 'Character of Burke' [1807], *Political Essays*, 376. Intellectual problems arose when Hazlitt attempted to associate this kind of admiration for Burke with his known political opinions and, after much agonizing, decided that it was impossible: if, on the great question of constitutional change in favour of a more democratic electorate, Hazlitt and Burke could not be reconciled, then on no topic could this occur. For an example of Hazlitt's approach in more popular literature, see 'Local Recollections of Great Men: Burke', *The Penny Magazine of the Society for the Diffusion of Useful Knowledge*, 10 (1841), 129–31.

[169] [Anon.], 'Sir Robert Peel and His Policy', *WR* (July 1852), 216–17. See also, for example, [Anon.], 'Earl Grey on Reform', *NR* (Apr. 1858), 431.

[170] See, for example, Montgomery, *Edmund Burke*, viii–xxviii.

comprehensive view of mankind' standing above the pettiness of parliamentary and party business.[171] Both Peel and Disraeli revealed a degree of interest in Burke and smatter their writings and speeches with occasional references and quotes from his works. But rather than acting as mediums divining the future construction of Burke's 'conservatism', it is clear that these Conservative leaders cannot be cast as significant actors in the story of how C/conservatives came to adopt the dissident Whig Burke as one of their own. It is similarly impossible to suppose that these Conservative leaders shared any significant affinity with the modern conception of Burke's 'conservative' thought.

This bipartisan treatment, however, did not resolve the significant problems which still surrounded Burke's legacy: problems of consistency, personal identity, and character. In his study of *Blackwood's*, Anthony Jarrells concludes that the frequent and often favourable references to Burke generally referred to his notorious eloquence or his ability to transcend party politics. But even Croly, Jarrells notes, made no attempt to link Burke's statements on the empire to *Blackwood's* own politics.[172] Literary appreciation was of course important in its own right. Burke's parliamentary oratory positioned him as the modern Cicero or Demosthenes; and commentators were still preoccupied with the question of whether Burke had authored the mysterious 'Letters of Junius', whose anonymous author was noted for his eloquent satires of Georgian political figures.[173] The utilitarian philosopher Henry Sidgwick encapsulated this non-doctrinal sentiment perfectly when he noted, in a *Fortnightly Review* article of 1877, that 'Burke lives' not merely by eloquence, but through 'a kind of wisdom, fused of intellect and emotion, which is as essentially independent of the theorizing in which it is embedded as metal is of its mine'. But literary appreciation came at a cost, and many-sidedness could be a problem. Hence the dictum: 'though Burke lives, we meet with no Burkites'.[174] Thus, the Tory historian Montagu Burrows could equally claim in the *Quarterly* the following year that 'Burke is not for either party—now he is for both. He is "English, or Imperial" in spirit.'[175]

Burke held a peculiar place in English, and British, constitutional politics and thought: until the late nineteenth century he was reviled

---

[171] [Macknight], *Disraeli: A Literary and Political Biography*, 325–6.
[172] Antony Jarrells, 'Tales of the Colonies: Blackwood's, Provincialism, and British Interests Abroad', in Robert Morrison and Daniel S. Roberts, *Romanticism and Blackwood's Magazine: 'An Unprecedented Phenomenon'* (2013), 272.
[173] O. D. Edwards, 'Macaulay's Warren Hastings', in Geoffrey Carnall and Colin Nicholson, eds., *The Impeachment of Warren Hastings* (1989), 585–8.
[174] Sidgwick, 'Bentham and Benthamism', in *Miscellaneous Essays*, 95.
[175] [Montagu Burrows], 'Burke; Select Works', *QR* (Oct. 1878), 332.

and claimed by members of both political parties, and was generally acknowledged to be a great prose writer. Whatever his particular views, there was little doubt that he had argued his cases eloquently, and his love for the constitution could not be doubted. Burke as a wise and great statesman was also a kind of model for aspiring MPs. He had given impressive justification for some issues that would shape much nineteenth-century political discourse: from political parties to free trade. Burke's Irish background also led writers from across the British Isles to reflect upon his connections with Catholicism. Though this distanced him from Tory-Conservatives in the early nineteenth century, it was a cause for celebration and elaboration by Catholics, and his ejection at Bristol in support of religious liberty and free trade for Ireland was portrayed as martyrdom by Liberals and pro-Catholic Irish Tories.

Yet what Burke provided was an inspiring example of a life in literature and politics, not a usable political creed. Burke's zeal for a constitution long since reformed created an apparently impossible problem for any attempt at party political appropriation. He had been a Whig of sorts: but he had left his sting in the constitution and died. This made him important in a literary and historical sense, but also in a way irrelevant; he was an antiquity that could be drawn upon by both sides, but only within strict limits. Even in the 1860s and 1870s, most Tories could not yet forgive Burke for his anti-monarchical and pro-Catholic tendencies, and Whigs were no more willing to absolve Burke from blame with regard to his behaviour during the Revolutionary period. His political reputation and contemporary relevance were also complicated by his reverence for a stationary version of the constitution, which appeared to be a contradiction in terms—especially to reform-minded writers and politicians. After *c.*1880 the construction of a 'conservative' tradition based on more flexible ideas about tradition and the preservation of institutions would transform this position almost completely. Before moving on to a more chronologically focused analysis, however, it is necessary to consider a theme that spans our entire period: the issue of Burke's Irishness and the extent to which national identity played a role in his reception history.

3

Irishness, National Character, and the Interpretation of Political Thought, c.1830–1914

Though he is today cited as a key figure in the history and development of ideas about the *English* national character,[1] Burke was, of course, an Irishman: from his rural childhood experiences of Ballitore to university life at Trinity College, Dublin. In 1886, Augustine Birrell (1850–1933), Liberal author and later Chief Secretary for Ireland (1907–16), remarked in the *Contemporary Review*: 'The first great fact to remember is, that the Edmund Burke we are all agreed in regarding as one of the proudest memories of the House of Commons, was an Irishman.' Burke was not, to Birrell, only an Irishman, but 'a typical one—of the very kind many Englishmen, and even possibly some Scotchmen, make a point of disliking'. That was to say, Burke's Irish pedigree could be dated back for at least six centuries and was thus far superior to that of Charles Stewart Parnell. From Burke's first appointment as Rockingham's private secretary, he was, 'so ran the report, supposed to be a wild Irishman, whose real name was O'Bourke, and whose brogue seemed to require the allegation that its owner was a Popish emissary'.[2] Clearly it is necessary to examine the role Burke's Irish identity played in his reception history. This chapter therefore examines the extent to which Burke was in fact seen as 'a typical Irishman', and to what extent he was portrayed as a quasi-Englishman. It also addresses the question of how Burke's Irishness impacted upon interpretations of his work and thought.

---

[1] Mandler, *English National Character*, 3. For Burke as the originator of the 'British Political Tradition', see Hall, *Political Traditions*, 18–19.
[2] Birrell, 'Edmund Burke', 28, 36. This was later re-printed in Augustine Birrell, *Obiter Dicta: Second Series* (1887). Compare T. B. Macaulay, 'Chatham' [1844], *Critical and Historical Essays*, i. 454.

Ideas about national character are common in discussions of nineteenth-century social and political thought.[3] Likewise, there are ample elaborations of conceptions of Englishness and Irishness at a more abstract level within nineteenth-century literature. According to these, the English were deemed to have been blessed with virtues of reason, self-control, love for order and freedom, sobriety, respect for law, and a firm dislike of abstraction, enthusiasm, and emotionalism. The Irish, by contrast, were seen to exhibit energy, wit, and sociability, but remained enslaved (from the English point of view) by their inclinations to be superstitious, feckless, improvident, violent, and excitable; they were subservient to priests and demagogues, and given to drink.[4] Irish history was often used to explain these differences. Leading *Edinburgh Review*(ers) such as Francis Jeffrey, Sydney Smith, McVey Napier, James Mackintosh, Henry Hallam, and James Mill all agreed that English policy in Ireland was the ultimate cause of any defects in their national character.[5] The alternative, more deterministic approach, saw the crucial division as resulting from the balance of the respective Celtic and Teutonic elements in each nation: the Irish were predominantly Celtic, the English were predominantly Teutonic. That said, it could not be denied that Britain and Ireland's heritage was somewhat mixed: Anglo-Saxons, Celts, Britons, and Normans had played a part in the history of both islands. The English were also seen as combining Celtic and Teutonic elements to produce energy and versatility alongside steadiness and love of order.[6]

Historians interested in the development of Irishness and the stereotypical Irish national character have often focused on the issue of racial superiority.[7] Much of this literature tends to emphasize the predominantly pejorative and patronizing treatment of the Irish by inhabitants of

---

[3] Roberto Romani, *National Character and Public Spirit in Britain and France, 1750–1914* (2004); Varouxakis, *Victorian Political Thought on France*; Georgios Varouxakis, 'National Character in John Stuart Mill's Thought', *HEI*, 24 (1998), 375–91; D. M. Craig, 'Democracy and "National Character"', *HEI*, 29 (2003), 493–501; Joanne Parker, 'The Dragon and The Raven: Saxons, Danes and the Problem of Defining National Character in Victorian England', *European Journal of English Studies*, 13 (2009), 257–73.

[4] Michael de Nie, 'Britannia's Sick Sister: Irish Identity and the British Press, 1798–1882', in Neil McCaw, ed., *Writing Irishness in Nineteenth-Century British Culture* (2004), 174.

[5] Roberto Romani, 'British Views on Irish National Character, 1800–1846: An Intellectual History', *HEI*, 23 (1998), 193–219. Romani, however, deals exclusively with 'Irish character' as synonymous with the Irish peasantry.

[6] Creasy, *Progress of the English Constitution*, 4th edn (1858), 32.

[7] Beginning with the seminal L. P. Curtis, *Anglo-Saxon and Celts: A Study of Anti-Irish Prejudice in Victorian England* (1968). 'Race' is understood here in the sense that it was used in the period: namely, a more inclusive term which invoked ideas of climate, religion, language, and primitive mode of government as well as physical characteristics.

Great Britain, and often focuses, in class terms, primarily on the Irish peasantry. Both Roy Foster and Terry Eagleton have, however, recognized that Irish stereotypes were not entirely negative. To Foster, the Irish were no worse off than other groups, including the Scots and the French. For Eagleton, it was also clear that when the Victorian English desired a mode of sensibility less 'frigid' than their own, they often turned to the 'Celtic fringes' for inspiration.[8] As we shall see, these insights are particularly helpful when considering Burke's perceived contribution to nineteenth-century British intellectual culture. His was a different brand of Irishness: not the extreme social outcast, the 'Other' creature, but the Irishman who *almost* integrated into the English/British political world; a liminal figure. What matters here, therefore, are the particular characteristics—whether viewed positively or negatively—applied to Irishmen[9] and how they contributed to the legacy of Burke in the century following his death. Not only is Burke's Irish identity integral to the history of his reputation as a political thinker, it also presents an alternative representation of Irish national character to that conveyed in the historiographical literature of the 'whisky and potatoes'-fuelled Irish peasant.

'In a word,' stated the critic Bliss Perry (1860–1954) in a 1908 edition of 'selections' from Burke's works, 'Burke was an Irishman; he had the hot head, the queer logic, the warm heart, and the ill luck of his race.'[10] My aim in this chapter is to show that the characteristics which were most frequently criticized in Britain (especially England) are those which were also connected to general conceptions of Irish national character, though this was mitigated by the fact that Burke was not Catholic, but a member of the (Anglican) Church of Ireland—and thus of the island's social elite, with privileged access to TCD. The allegations made against him are not of drunkenness and physical violence, but of a passionate zeal that could tip over into hysteria. The further charges levied against Burke were extensive: he was an Irish adventurer, a deathbed Catholic convert, and heavily in debt.[11] Others sought to explain why Burke had never held a senior position in government—usually by reference to his irritable

---

[8] R. F. Foster, *Paddy and Mr Punch: Connections in English and Irish History* (1993), 173; Terry Eagleton, *Figures of Dissent* (2003), 2–3. See also S. Gilley, 'English Attitudes to the Irish in England, 1780–1900', in C. Holmes, ed., *Immigrants and Minorities in British Society* (1978); D. G. Paz, 'Anti-Catholicism, Anti-Irish Stereotyping, and Anti-Celtic Racism in Mid-Victorian Working-Class Periodicals', *Albion*, 18 (1986), 601–16.

[9] It could be assumed that these also applied indirectly, additionally modified by gendered considerations, to Irish women. Women were rarely mentioned directly in these discussions.

[10] Edmund Burke, *Selections from Edmund Burke*, ed. Bliss Perry (1908), ix. Perry was an American, but this was a British publication.

[11] For a succinct catalogue, see Morley, *Edmund Burke: A Historical Study* (1867), 75–6.

temper, or his non-aristocratic social standing.[12] As such, the chapter is structured around concepts which illustrate the positive, negative, and more ambivalent aspects of Burke's Irish identity: wisdom, passion, and madness. These were not clearly defined concepts which were applied uniformly, but they do offer continuous threads which are apparent in the interpretation of Burke's thought throughout the century.

WISDOM

The most laudatory commentary on Burke's Irish roots appears in the proclamations of his peculiar 'wisdom' or 'genius'. Like the praise of Burke's literary style, the ascription of wisdom or genius (the terms were used interchangeably) was almost universal—bar the most unflattering of Radical commentators from Mary Wollstonecraft to Marx and Engels.[13] Yet, the concepts wisdom and genius are elusive and subject to multiple interpretations. The lengthiest exposition of Burke's genius in the early nineteenth century can be found in James Prior's 1826 *Life of Burke*. The 'first characteristic of genius' which Burke possessed was 'originality', but Burke was also unparalleled as an orator in 'his force of language, his striking phraseology, or that inexhaustible fertility upon every topic which constitutes the soul of eloquence'.[14] Prior, rejecting and anticipating Radical criticism, was quick to stress the manly basis of Burke's extravagant rhetoric: he stated clearly that there was nothing 'flowery' in Burke's work, as his greatness came from his strength.[15] This was a way of distancing Burke from effeminate sentimentalism and pointing towards a literary style that connoted restraint, firmness, candour, and independence, which were seen as the fundamental conditions for political health.[16] Moreover, Burke's genius was connected by Prior, an Irishman himself, to his status as an Irishman in an English parliament. 'Certain peculiarities in his eloquence,' Prior explained, 'such as the strength of his imagination, the vehemence, the force of invective, the almost morbid acuteness of feeling...belong as much perhaps to his country as to the individual.' In coupling reason with imagination, Prior argued, Burke had given to English parliamentary oratory a flavour of which it had previously tasted

---

[12] William Massey, *A History of England during the Reign of George III* (1865), ii. 421–3.
[13] For example, the description of Burke's 'Speculative cobwebs, embroidered with flowers of rhetoric, steeped in the dew of sickly sentiment', in Karl Marx and Friedrich Engels, 'The Communist Manifesto' [1848], *Collected Works* (1996), xxxiv. 269.
[14] Prior, *Life and Character of the Rt. Hon. Edmund Burke*, ii. 455–7.
[15] Ibid., 460.   [16] Burrow, *Whigs and Liberals*, 88.

little.[17] In doing so, Prior (a pro-Catholic unionist) suggested that it was his combination of different—but complementary—national traits which gave the most potent effects.

Burke's wisdom was often linked to a capacity for foresight, or 'prophecy'. This had been a classic trope in Burke commentary following his apparently inspired early predictions, in *Reflections* (1790), that the French Revolution would lead to death, destruction, and military despotism. In reality this was an accident which tells us a good deal about the peculiarities of Burke's mind and political situation, but, as events unfolded, their apparent correlation with what was predicted in the *Reflections* gave Burke great authority. This unique insight marked him out as a wise statesman and thinker. Burke was, to Coleridge in 1817, 'a *scientific* statesman; and therefore a *seer*. For every *principle* contains in itself the germs of a prophecy.'[18] Prior's conception of Burke's wisdom went beyond this by linking capacity for foresight with the general ability to look above ephemeral party interests and point out consequences.[19] Burke's 'foresight' was as notable on issues such as American Independence as on the French Revolution: he had seen the danger of enforcing an abstract right to taxation on a colony, and had prophesied both the bloodshed of the Reign of Terror and the military despotism of Napoleon as early as 1790. Burke's belief in the need for the regulation of the slave trade, the relief of Irish Roman Catholics, and reform of the Penal Code were also significant as evidence for his foresight and, for Prior, this was another Irish trait. Burke was able to render 'even the common and temporary affair of an election, a medium for promulgating great and permanent political truths'. If Burke was presented as un-English, still the result of this had been to illuminate political truths which were for the benefit of Britain and Ireland as a whole. He transcended mere political history: an example of the rare union of politician and philosopher. It gave a 'value to his writings so as to cause them to be quoted every night in both houses of parliament, as the greatest authority of our time'.[20] Burke's was an enlightened patriotism, rooted in party (as elaborated in *Present Discontents*), but superior to all party considerations. The call for more politicians to revere Burke's thinking, and to appreciate the Irish element in British politics, is implicit in this political eulogy.

---

[17] Prior, *Life and Character of the Rt. Hon. Edmund Burke*, ii. 465–6.
[18] S. T. Coleridge, *Biographia Literaria* [1817], *Collected Works of Coleridge*, vii.i 191–2. See also William Wordsworth's exclamation 'Genius of Burke!' in bk. 7 of the 1850 version of *The Prelude: The Four Texts (1798, 1799, 1805, 1850)*, ed. Jonathan Wordsworth (2004).
[19] Prior, *Life and Character of the Rt. Hon. Edmund Burke*, ii. 502.
[20] Ibid., i. 307, 370, ii. 482. For another, later, Irish example of this argument, see D. O. Madden, *The Age of Pitt and Fox* (1846), 2, 310.

Wisdom and genius are not, however, rigorous concepts. For George Cornewall Lewis, who was well-known for his attempts to define elusive or difficult political concepts,[21] there were pre-requisites before either 'wisdom' or 'genius' could be reached by any 'man'. Aside from gender, these included: superior mental powers; a wide-ranging and far-seeing mind; comprehensive and synoptic viewpoints on extensive subjects; and the ability to trace the consequences of abstract principles. In order to earn the title of genius, one must possess 'That high degree of intellectual power, which we call *genius*... [It] is in itself inexplicable, and can only be judged by its effects. But some ray of that light is requisite in order to enable a person to be classed among the original teachers and guides of mankind.'[22] Genius was therefore something indefinable, precisely because of its peculiarity: but, to Cornewall Lewis, writing in the late 1840s, this made its presence no less apparent. Again, it is worth noting that this is not a theoretically rigorous definition; rather it was the intellectual equivalent of beauty is in the eye of the beholder.

Cornewall Lewis, whose work was reissued in 1875, did however add one further layer to his understanding of wisdom: the necessity of a moral compass in addition to insight. Immoral men 'may be *great*, but cannot be *wise*; for by *wisdom* we mean the power of judging, when the intellectual and moral faculties are *both* in a sound state.'[23] In order to be wise, therefore, a thinker must be morally sound. It was this power of judgement in Burke which Cornewall Lewis found particularly striking. In an 1862 letter to the historian Lord Stanhope, a staunch Pittite, Cornewall Lewis disagreed with Pitt's interpretation of Burke's writings on France and on Warren Hastings. Pitt might see there 'rhapsodies in which there is much to admire and nothing to assent to', but Cornewall Lewis' opinion was that though 'there is much in them [that is] wild and rhapsodical', Burke's 'view of both subjects is substantially right'.[24] Lewis' view here was followed by later writers. For example, the Brighton-based naturalist E. A. Pankhurst claimed in 1886: 'The difference between talent and genius is difficult to express in words, but the reader is conscious of it as he passes from... the speeches of Pitt to those of Burke.'[25] In reference to

---

[21] Though this in itself was seen by two of his reviewers (Mill and Bagehot) to be somewhat unusual: George Watson, *The English Ideology: Studies in the Language of Victorian Politics* (1973), 91.
[22] George Cornewall Lewis, *An Essay on the Influence of Authority in Matters of Opinion*, 2nd edn (1875), 21–2. The first edition appeared in 1849.
[23] Ibid., 27.
[24] Cornewall Lewis to Earl Stanhope, 5 May 1862, *Letters of George Cornewall Lewis*, ed. Gilbert Frankland (1870), 415.
[25] Pankhurst, *Burke: A Study of his Life*, 46. See also Macknight, *Life of Disraeli*, 82–4.

Burke's wisdom, Pankhurst explained: 'Nature and truth have given him a large wisdom, and his thought has that moral force which is in its essence religious.'[26]

In his 1867 study *Edmund Burke*, John Morley had also made the connection between Burke and wisdom. 'It is difficult to name another publicist whose writings are so thickly studded with those unsystematic products of an acute, enlarged and reflective mind, which are vaguely labelled as wisdom.'[27] Morley would later explain, at an address in Edinburgh in 1877, that wisdom could stand for knowledge, learning, science, and systematic reasoning, but that it could also represent 'the unsystematic truths that come to shrewd, penetrating and observant minds, from their own experience of life and their daily commerce with the world, and are called the wisdom of life'.[28] Following this, Morley proclaimed that 'When the splendid genius of Burke rose like a new sun into the sky, the times were happier, and nowhere in our literature does a noble prudence wear statelier robes than in the majestic compositions of Burke.'[29] Here, Morley, like Prior, suggests that Burke was not merely a wise 'sun', but a *new* sun: he was original. Indeed, to many nineteenth-century onlookers Burke was a peculiarly individual thinker, writer, and orator (a verdict with which the twenty-first century will hardly disagree). Birrell applied this dual conception of wisdom more explicitly in 1886 when he remarked that Burke's writings were 'a storehouse of wisdom, not the cheap shrewdness of the mere man of the world, but the noble, animating wisdom of one who has the poet's heart as well as the statesman's brain'. It was an alchemical combination that could bring practical results and, as such, 'Nobody is fit to govern this country who has not drunk deep at the springs of Burke.'[30] Burke had succeeded in combining Mr Gradgrind's 'wisdom of the Head' with the 'wisdom of the Heart'.[31]

Burke's promoters, therefore, had identified Burke's writings and speeches with a uniquely useful conception of wisdom, or genius. But what did this wisdom or genius owe to his Irish background? It is notable that the ascription of wisdom, particularly 'political wisdom'—the area which Burke chose for the application of his gifts—was sometimes seen to be peculiar to him despite his Irish origin. This was still considered remarkable at the very end of the century, as the Idealist Scot Hugh

---

[26] Ibid., 45.   [27] Morley, *Edmund Burke: A Historical Study* (1867), 30.
[28] John Morley, 'Aphorisms' [1887], *Oracles on Man and Government* (1923), 154.
[29] Ibid., 170.
[30] Birrell, 'Edmund Burke', 43. See Chapter 7 in this volume for Burke in university syllabuses at this time.
[31] Charles Dickens, *Hard Times* (1854), 264.

Walker, Professor of English Literature at St David's College, Lampeter, explained in the popular magazine *Good Words*:

> If the average Briton were asked to say what was the special gift of the Irish people, he would probably answer, their bright, good-natured wit; if he were further asked what was their peculiar defect, he would be not unlikely to say, the lack of political wisdom. In view of this very general opinion, supported as it is by a great deal of evidence, it is not a little strange that several of the greatest Irish writers have shown little or none of the kind of wit in question, while they have given evidence of quite an extraordinary endowment of political wisdom... [Burke was] the chief of Irish literary men; and Burke's style is characterized by his majestic and sonorous eloquence, not by wit, while his great bequest to posterity is a political philosophy certainly unsurpassed and probably unequalled in the English language for its scope and profundity.[32]

So Burke's political wisdom in fact made him *un*-Irish. But Burke was not of course the sole representative of political wisdom, and his wisdom had taken an unusual form. A standard division was drawn throughout the period which contrasted Burke with the Benthamite utilitarians and Philosophic Radicals. Disraeli, for instance, had claimed that the 'fallacy of the great Utilitarian schoolmen consists in confounding wisdom with knowledge'. Instead, in his *Vindication of the English Constitution* (1835), he defined the notion of wisdom as encompassing the 'wisdom of our ancestors': 'those rare great men, who in seasons of singular emergency, difficulty, and peril, have maintained the State, and framed, fostered, developed and established our political institutions'. In his list of 'wise ancestors' since the period of the Reformation, Disraeli offered a routine listing of Burke alongside figures ranging from Henry VIII to Robert Walpole.[33] This division was also highlighted by Burke's major Liberal biographers (and Disraeli haters), Macknight and Morley,[34] and by his later Irish academic critics. Edward Dowden (1843–1913), Professor of English Literature at TCD, remarked in the *Fortnightly Review* in 1889 that 'the chief rival political teachers of England [at the time of the French Revolution] were the doctrinaire Godwin with his haughty abstractions of

---

[32] Hugh Walker, 'The Right Hon. W. E. Hartpole Lecky', *Good Words* (Dec. 1899), 114. Walker (1855–1939) was educated at Glasgow and the University of Wales, later becoming Professor of English Literature at St David's College, Lampeter. He produced numerous books on English literature and contributed towards several periodicals and the Cambridge Modern History and History of English Literature. *Good Words* was targeted at a lower-middle-class Evangelical and nonconformist readership.

[33] Disraeli, *Vindication of the English Constitution*, 141–2.

[34] Macknight, *Life and Times of Edmund Burke*, iii. 357; Morley, *Burke* (1879), 214. The 'utilitarianism' of Burke is explored in Chapter 4 in this volume.

reason, and Edmund Burke who inspired the historical British habit of thinking with the perfervid passion of the Celt'.[35] A less sympathetic Irish critic of Burke's, William Graham (1839–1911), Professor of Jurisprudence and Political Philosophy at Queen's, Belfast, stated that Bentham 'was a typical Englishman of the best kind; a representative of the peculiar genius of the English race, which Burke was not; practical, clear-sighted, of much common sense, filled with popular sympathies and public spirit'.[36] For Morley in 1905 this alternative, English form of political wisdom was found in John Stuart Mill and exemplified in his style: 'Even when anger moves him, the ground does not tremble, as when Bossuet or Burke exhorts, denounces, wrestles, menaces, and thunders.'[37] In each of the three cases—Godwin, Bentham, Mill—Burke was seen to provide a balance or contrast to Englishness, though despite this he remained an oddity because this meant he was essentially un-English. There was a passion and a fire in his political wisdom that had no precedent in English political thought. Simultaneously, however, although men like Bentham, Mill, and other Philosophic Radicals were much easier to slot into a traditional canon of political theory writing, they too were deemed by many commentators to have been un-English: unhistorical, doctrinaire, and unconvincing because remote from the historical English Constitution.[38] Dowden, at least, appeared to recognize that Godwin was just as strange a political teacher as Burke. Yet, they were still British (and, indeed, English) and were thus exempt from the national characteristics attributed to Burke. Burke, the Irishman, was an outsider, but no less important for that.

Burke's peculiar brand of political wisdom was also elaborated by Matthew Arnold—a significant and original commentator on Burke. In his 1864 'Essay on the Function of Criticism', Arnold proposed:

> Burke is so great because, almost alone in England, he brings thought to bear upon politics, he saturates politics with thought... It does not hurt him that [after *Reflections*] Dr Price and the Liberals were enraged with him; it does not even hurt that George the Third and the Tories were enchanted with him. His greatness is that he lived in a world which neither English Liberalism nor English Toryism is apt to enter; the world of ideas, not the world of catchwords and party habits... That return of Burke upon himself has always seemed to me one of the finest things in English literature, or

---

[35] Edward Dowden, *New Studies in Literature* (1895), 315. This was originally published as 'Coleridge as a Poet', *FR* (Sept. 1889), 342–66.
[36] William Graham, *English Political Philosophy, from Hobbes to Maine* (1899), 178.
[37] Morley, 'A Great Teacher' [1905], *Oracles*, 17.
[38] See, for example, [M. M. M.], 'Letter', *Gentleman's Magazine* (May 1830), 412: 'Un-English in their hearts, Un-English in their thoughts, and consequently Un-English in their designs.'

indeed in any literature. That is what I call living by ideas; when one side of a question has long had your earnest support, when all your feelings are engaged, when you hear all around you no language but one, when your party talks this language like a steam-engine and can imagine no other,—still to be able to think, still to be irresistibly carried, if so be it, by the current of thought to the opposite side of the question, and ... to be unable to speak anything *but what the Lord has put in your mouth*. I know nothing more striking, and I must add that I know nothing more un-English.[39]

Arnold is here attacking the perceived English antipathy to thought and abstract thinking. Though Arnold did not laud abstractions as such, his aim was to stress the importance of broad, elevated thinking. Arnold also attempted to de-politicize Burke in a similar way to previous writers such as Prior and Macknight. Through an emphasis on Burke's centrality to the production of political wisdom, he was portrayed as providing an essential service to intellectual life as a whole, and was therefore above the petty ephemeral squabbles of partisan party politics. This made Burke an easier sell to the English, even if, by doing so, Arnold stripped Burke of the party political identification which Prior claimed was the stamp of all Englishmen. There was some sense in the manoeuvre, however. It meant that Burke could be appreciated across educated society as a thinker as well as a stylist. In a letter of 1865, Arnold explained again: 'What makes Burke stand out so splendidly among politicians is that he treats politics with his thought and imagination; therefore, whether one agrees with him or not, he always interests you, stimulates you, and does you good.'[40] But in living by *one* idea during the period of the French Revolution, Burke's actions became even more un-English: they evaded all considerations of political compromise and pragmatism found in English parliamentary government.

This notion of 'living by ideas' identified Burke as exemplifying national character traits which Arnold recognized as imported; but still they provided a much needed service. This theme had been highlighted earlier in the century by the Christian Socialist F. D. Maurice, who claimed in *The Kingdom of Christ* (1838 and frequently reprinted) that Burke, though 'an adventurer, an Irishman, a philosopher', had yet been 'the instrument of restoring the tone of English feeling, both amongst the men of action and of meditation, both in the upper and middling class'.[41]

---

[39] Matthew Arnold, 'Essay on the Function of Criticism' [1864], *Essays in Criticism* (1965), 13–14.
[40] Matthew Arnold to Jane Martha Arnold Foster, 23 Jan. 1864, *Letters of Matthew Arnold*, ed. Cecil Lang (1996–2001), ii. 268.
[41] Maurice, *Kingdom of Christ*, 2nd edn (1842), i. 268. Maurice also made an early link between Burke and the historical jurisprudence of Savigny on p. 269. On Savigny and Burke see also pp. 164–5, 207 in this volume.

Maurice believed that distinct and heterogeneous national characteristics strengthened universal human bonds—whether one was English, Irish, French, or otherwise, each 'brings in his quota to the common treasure of humanity'.[42] It was an important point for Matthew Arnold, too, in *On the Study of Celtic Literature* (1877).[43] For Arnold, the English 'genius' was found in the mixture of 'energy with honesty', while the Celtic genius was located in its energy and sentimental element. What constituted special power and genius in an individual seemed to Arnold to result from a person 'blending with the basis of his national temperament, some additional gift or grace not proper to that temperament'. Arnold now linked Burke's greatness explicitly with his Irish identity: it was located 'in his *blending* a largeness of view and richness of thought, not English, with the English basis'.[44] For Arnold, Burke's Celtic heritage was an interesting question: in his English integration Burke was, to some degree, able to transcend the confines of his native 'genius', and by doing so became a singular and remarkable historical figure.

The idea of Burke 'blending' national characteristics had deep roots. From the Irish perspective, however, there was a sense in which the English were operating a double standard in which talented Irishmen and women were granted honorary English status. Though Prior had insisted on the importance of Burke's eloquence in constituting part of his genius, he was evidently not entirely successful in persuading all of his readers. Charles Lever, the Irish novelist, used Burke as the classic example of this 'English' double standard in *Cornelius O'Dowd* (1865):

> Burke, the great orator, the master of every form of eloquence, we might be permitted to claim [as Irish], because, by calling it Irish eloquence, its condemnation was fixed for ever. But Burke the logician—Burke the statesman—Burke the philosopher—the man who foresaw more in the working out of events than any man of his age, who could trace the effects to their causes, and predicate from the actual to what must be the future—him they deny us, and declare that all these gifts were English.[45]

Here political wisdom is again associated with the English. Yet despite the claim that Burke's eloquence was of secondary importance, it was (as

---

[42] Quoted in Jones, 'The Idea of the National in Victorian Political Thought', 16.
[43] Between 1910 and 1946 the Everyman edition sold an estimated 15,521 copies. The *Essays Literary and Critical* containing 'The Function of Criticism' sold an even more impressive 47,793 copies between 1908 and 1958: Bill Bell, 'Beyond the Death of the Author: Matthew Arnold's Two Audiences, 1888–1930', *Book History*, 3 (2000), 159.
[44] Matthew Arnold, *On the Study of Celtic Literature* (1877), 78, 100–1. My emphasis.
[45] Charles Lever, *Cornelius O'Dowd upon Men, Women, and Things in General* (1865), bk. 2, ch. 28; Andrew Blake, 'Writing from the Outside In: Charles Lever', in Neil McCaw, *Writing Irishness in Nineteenth-Century British Culture* (2004), 122–3.

we have already seen) a major factor in securing his reputation as a master of the English language and should not be underestimated as another form of appropriation. Anthony Trollope's *The Eustace Diamonds* (1872), for example, features a chapter entitled 'Mr. Burke's Speeches' in which a governess and an Under-Secretary of State discuss the high literary status accorded to Burke's writings, but his name is invoked merely as a synonym for exceptional parliamentary oratory.[46] Similarly, in George Eliot's *Middlemarch* (1874), (the English) Mr Brooke compliments (the foreign) Will Ladislaw by declaring: 'when I think of Burke, I can't help wishing somebody had a pocket borough to give you, Ladislaw'. Brooke believed that, like Burke, and despite Ladislaw's obvious talent, he would never win the popular vote. This similarity extends to style and delivery: 'That avalanche and the thunder, now, was really a little like Burke. I want that sort of thing—not ideas, you know, but a way of putting things.'[47] Here was another route by which Burke was made amenable to men and women who did not share his politics, ensuring his dissemination as an English prose writer across a broad political spectrum—regardless of whether men such as Mr Brooke were desirous of Burke's specific ideas, or, indeed, 'ideas' at all. The importance both of Burke's eloquence and his blending of national character traits to his distinctive constitutionalism was summarized succinctly by Goldwin Smith (to whom we will return), then Regius Professor of Modern History at Oxford, in his widely read work *Irish History and Irish Character* (1861):

> We see the different political tendencies of the Irish and English races combined, yet distinguishable from each other, in the political character of Burke, to whose writing we owe, more than we are aware, the almost religious reverence with which we regard the Constitution. Trained among English statesmen, Burke had learnt to love English institutions, but he loved them not like an Englishman, from a practical sense of their usefulness, but like an Irishman, with the passionate fervour of personal attachment, and rendered to their imagined founders, collectively, the homage of a heart which devoted loyalty pays to a king. His feelings, diffused by his eloquence, have become those of our whole nation.[48]

---

[46] Anthony Trollope, *The Eustace Diamonds* (1872), bk. 1, ch. 7. For the case for reconsideration of Trollope's Palliser novels by historians, see Roy Foster '"Fatal Drollery": Parliamentary Novels, Outsiders, and Victorian Political History', in *Paddy and Mr Punch*, 139–70.
[47] George Eliot, *Middlemarch* (1874), bk. 1, ch. 46.
[48] Goldwin Smith, *Irish History and Irish Character* (1861), 19. For Smith see E. Wallace, *Goldwin Smith: Victorian Liberal* (1957).

PASSION

A second key feature of nineteenth-century commentary was Burke's Celtic 'passion'. But on this subject critics were often divided. Most fundamentally, Burke's passionate style was seen to have brought imagination and life to dry political affairs. Imagination was of course a key Romantic concept—seen by some literary scholars as *the* defining Romantic attribute—and Burke was, of course, admired in different ways by figures now central to canons of British Romanticism such as Coleridge, Wordsworth, and Southey.[49] But imagination was also linked by contemporary literary authors to Irish national traits. Byron's sentiments on this subject were distinctly anti-Romantic: 'It is the fashion of the day to lay great stress upon what they call "imagination" and "invention", the two commonest of qualities: an Irish peasant with a little whisky in his head will imagine and invent more than would furnish forth a modern poem.'[50] On the one hand, Burke's unusual passion and imagination had provided him with a foresight that allowed him to see more than bare 'facts' or reality. On the other hand, this passion had a dark side. This was another legacy from Burke's behaviour during the Regency debates of the 1780s, and subsequently his response to French affairs in the 1790s. Writing in 1796, for example, the Radical John Thelwall described Burke as 'a very desultory and excentric [*sic*] writer. His combustible imagination fumes, and boils, and bursts away, like the lava from a volcano (as bright and destructive) in a thousand different directions; apparently without art or design.'[51] Both positive and negative interpretations of Burke's passion became stock features of nineteenth-century commentary.

---

[49] For Coleridge's further comments, see pp. 50, 71–2 in this volume. Intellectual histories of the lake poets have outlined their admiration for Burke, but suggest limits to this connection. John Morrow, for example, contrasts Coleridge's fundamentally philosophical style with that of Burke in *Coleridge's Political Thought* (1990), 69–72, 161–4; Richard Bourke's 'Burke, Enlightenment and Romanticism' in David Dwan and Christopher Insole, *The Cambridge Companion to Edmund Burke* (2012), criticizes the anti-Enlightenment, reactionary Burke portrayed in Alfred Cobban's well-known study of Burke and the lake poets, *Edmund Burke and the Revolt Against the Eighteenth Century: A Study of the Political Thinking of Burke, Wordsworth, Coleridge and Southey* (1929); and David Craig's *Robert Southey and Romantic Apostasy: Political Argument in Britain, 1780–1840* (2007) demonstrates the problems with referring to a canon of British Romanticism identifiable before the late nineteenth century (pp. 4–8). It is certainly suggestive that it is the later studies by figures such as Morley and Acton (pp. 98–100, 105–6, 211–12 in this volume) and English literature professors (Chapter 7 in this volume), which increasingly draw a line of influence between Burke and Romanticism as an identifiable body of thought.

[50] Quoted in Maurice Bowra, *The Romantic Imagination* (1961), 153; Tim Blanning, *The Romantic Revolution* (2011), 167.

[51] John Thelwall, *The Rights of Nature against the Usurpations of Establishments* (1796), 11–12.

For Thomas Macknight, the Englishman who adopted Ireland as his home country, Burke 'unite[d] political eloquence and philosophy as they had never been before united in ancient or modern times', bringing together 'philosophical reflection', 'power of insight', and 'richness of imagination'.[52] Though Macknight was an unusually effusive eulogist, the distinctive novelty of Burke in this respect was noted by other Victorian commentators, including J. R. Green in his *Short History of the English People*. To Green, Burke's eloquence was 'of a wholly new order in English experience' and therefore produced 'an impassioned expression of a distinct philosophy of politics':

> His ideas, if conceived by the reason, took shape and colour from the splendour and fire of his imagination. A nation was to him a great living society, so complex in its relations, and whose institutions were so interwoven with glorious events in the past, that to touch it rudely was a sacrilege. Its constitution was no artificial scheme of government, but an exquisite balance of social forces which were in itself a natural outcome of its history and development.[53]

In John Morley's opinion also, it was Burke's passion that provided the crucial element in understanding the underlying consistency of Burke's thought and character: 'Few men's opinions hang together so closely and compactly as his did. The fiery glow of his nature fused all his ideas into a tenacious and homogeneous mass.'[54] Both Morley and Green intertwine what they perceive to be Burke's passion and his elevated political thought; he is separated from rivals such as Bentham not simply by content, but also in style and imagination. This was no less important a consideration because of the fact that he was also a political actor; a cool, rational Englishman he was not and, as we will see, this was an important tool for interpreting Burke's personal history in addition to his political thought. Passion became a marker and an explanation for Burke's individuality, both good and bad.

Burke's passion was seen to have given him a zeal for the welfare of others and a hatred of oppression: the Celtic 'warm heart' cited by Perry.[55] This national characteristic was, perhaps unsurprisingly, most forcefully promoted by Burke's Irish biographer Prior. Here Burke's support for toleration and liberty, against tyranny, is not 'just' a 'moral principle', but an 'engrafted feeling'—whether for Americans, kings, nobility, or clergy—deriving from

---

[52] Macknight, *Life and Times of Edmund Burke*, i. 201.
[53] Green, *Short History of the English People*, 776.
[54] Morley, *Edmund Burke: A Historical Study* (1867), 46.
[55] Burke, *Selections from Edmund Burke* (1908), ix. See also [Anon.], 'Burke', *Academy* (16 July 1898), 64–5.

his earliest days in Ballitore.[56] On slavery, Burke's 1780 'Sketch of a Negro Code' had planned for a minute regulation of the trade though 'very little hope' could be entertained of its total abolition. Likewise, his India Bill would have guarded 'against future robberies and oppression', and its highest honour and title would have been that 'of securing the rice in his pot of every man in India'.[57] Across all topics, Burke's sentiments came from one 'whose public exertion has been a struggle for the liberty of others'.[58] It was a portrait of Burke that was transmitted throughout the century, painting an image of a generous character with a genuine concern for the welfare of his fellow men and women, regardless of creed, social class, or ethnicity. Though a Protestant, he was a fiery advocate of toleration for all creeds. He would not support a system which inflicted humiliation on one group, while elevating another, and was seen to have held a deep antipathy for violent social inequalities.[59] A similar picture is painted in Macknight's fulsome biography. Burke's hospitality for labourers near his home at Beaconsfield apparently knew no bounds; nor did his patronage of struggling young poets and artists. He had a happy marriage and was a doting father. His sympathies stretched back home to native Ireland and across the globe towards India.[60]

Burke's 'Irish' sense of empathy and generosity could be applied in a more negative sense, however—particularly with regard to his personal finances. The stereotype of an 'Irish adventurer' seeking his fortune was a common one and, as Augustine Birrell noted in 1886, Burke's finances had always been 'marvels and mysteries', particularly concerning the question of how he could have afforded to purchase his large estate at Beaconsfield, when he was only a self-made Irishman and an unpaid MP. As discussed in Chapter 2, rumours spread that Burke was a corrupt hireling available to whoever paid the most. Birrell does note, however, that both Burke's 'Tory enemies and Radical enemies' had 'never succeeded in formulating any charge of dishonesty against him that has not been at once completely pulverized, and shown on the facts to be impossible'. Birrell explains that he got the capital for Beaconsfield, 'After an Irish fashion—by not getting it at all', which is to say that he left a large, unpaid mortgage. Birrell was not without sympathy, however, and he further notes that this was no worse than Burke's corrupt wealthy peers,

---

[56] Prior, *Life of Burke*, 2nd edn, i. 473.
[57] Ibid., i. 368, 439.   [58] Ibid., ii. 102.
[59] [Anon.], 'Burke and Goldsmith', *London Journal* (1 May 1868), 392.
[60] Macknight, *Life and Times of Edmund Burke*, ii. 190. Disraeli did not come close to measuring up: Macknight, *Life of Disraeli*, 8–9, *passim*. See also H. M. Butler, *The Character of Edmund Burke: An Oration* (privately printed, 1854), 10–12, J. R. M. Butler Papers, Trinity College, Cambridge, JRMB/M3/8/1.

who would have simply retained 'the interest on all balances of the public money from time to time in his hands as Paymaster of the Forces' for their own use. Unlike these men, and in particular Henry Fox (1704–75), father of Charles James, Burke 'carried his passion for good government into actual practice' by cutting down the emoluments of his office to a salary.[61] The positive comparison with Henry Fox was an important development because the Holland House line of praising the Foxite Whigs while slandering Burke had done much damage to Burke's reputation in the first half of the century.[62]

It was acknowledged, however, that Burke's passionate zeal could be misplaced. Prior, for example, had argued that Burke 'hated the old despotism of France, and still more he hated the new': a 'plundering, ferocious, bloody, tyrannical democracy'.[63] But where was his passion for the oppression of the Third Estate? This was another old trope from the 1790s, when caricaturists increasingly depicted Burke's spectacles as providing him with a faulty or foggy view.[64] Tom Paine's famous verdict continued to be echoed through the period: Burke had pitied the plumage, but forgot the dying bird.[65] A more sympathetic, though still critical, example can be found in an 1868 issue of the *London Journal* which stated that 'The cruelties of the Reign of Terror no doubt shocked his delicate susceptibilities, and, being incapable himself of nursing feelings of revenge, he could see no righteous judgement in the long pent-up indignation of a whole people breaking out in its worst and lowest form.' It was therefore the execution of Marie Antoinette, rather than the sufferings of the people, that 'drew from his indignant soul the loftiest flights of his rich eloquence'.[66]

Burke's passion was seen to transform his literary style—so praised for its special characteristics—into a double-edged sword when invoked on questions of political reform. As noted, Burke was opposed to the issue of parliamentary reform in Britain from at least the 1780s, and when the Conservative and Pittite historian Stanhope described Burke's behaviour in 1782 upon the issue of parliamentary reform, he was portrayed in almost hysterical terms:

> The member for Malton could no longer be restrained. There, as Sheridan relates it in a secret letter to Fitzpatrick, 'Burke acquitted himself with the

---

[61] Birrell, 'Edmund Burke', 36–40.
[62] Macknight, *Life and Times of Edmund Burke*, i. xiv.
[63] Prior, *Life of Burke*, ii. 72. [64] Robinson, *A Life in Caricature*, 152–3.
[65] Thomas Paine, *Rights of Man*, 2nd edn (1791), 26. See, for example, J. F. Stephen, 'Burke and de Tocqueville on the French Revolution' [1863], *Horae Sabbaticae* (1892), iii. 160–7; The *Daily Telegraph* (5 July 1867), 4; H. A. L. Fisher, *The Republican Tradition in Europe* (1911), 142.
[66] 'Burke and Goldsmith', 392.

most magnanimous indiscretion, attacked William Pitt in a scream of passion, and swore Parliament was and always had been precisely what it ought to be, and that all people who thought of reforming it wanted to overturn the Constitution.'[67]

Macaulay had previously deplored the fact that Burke's gift, which could have been used for the seeking of political truth, was so disfigured by his passionate nature in an 1830 issue of the *Edinburgh Review*: Burke 'generally chose his side like a fanatic, and defended it like a philosopher'. His reason was mighty, yet 'It did whatever work his passions and imagination might impose.'[68] It was this sudden passionate anger that was deemed 'Burkean' by later Victorian writers. Morley explained how Burke's discussions of proposals to increase the frequency of parliamentary elections were filled with sensible (or 'wise') arguments, such as that they would 'tear to pieces the fortunes of independent men' as well as making the people 'more lawless, more idle, and more debauched'. But Burke would then launch into sudden exaggeration: '"I do not seriously think that this constitution, even to the wrecks of it, could survive five triennial elections."' It was an 'intensely Burkean end to solid, reasoned argument'.[69] In 1886, discussing Burke's fiery letters to his friends regarding his ill-treatment by William Hamilton, Birrell exclaimed that in this there was 'nothing more delightfully Burkean'. All the same Birrell continued: 'I not only excuse Burke for his heat, but love him for letting me warm my hands at it after a lapse of 120 years.'[70] But still this posed a problem for those who wished to interpret him as a political thinker.

To be 'Burkean' was to connote images of passionate, wild exaggeration. Burke was no simple empiricist, yet he did not write in the fashion of political thinkers before, or indeed after, him. Even Coleridge who had described Burke as a '*seer*' and a great man in 1817, lamented in 1833 that Burke was 'a mere dinner-bell' whose speeches emptied the House of Commons except when he combined 'his general principles with some sordid interest, panic of property, jacobinism, &c'. Burke's writings, therefore, contained only 'germs' of political truth, or 'half-truths' which could not be sufficient in themselves.[71] So to Coleridge Burke was no straightforward political or philosophical idol—not to mention Burke's

---

[67] Mahon, *History of England from the Peace of Utrecht*, vii. 167. The letter of 20 May 1782 was also cited in Russell, *Life and Times of Charles James Fox*, i. 322.
[68] T. B. Macaulay, 'On Southey's Colloquies on Society' [1830], *Critical and Historical Essays*, ii. 187–8.
[69] Morley, *Edmund Burke: A Historical Study* (1867), 106.
[70] Birrell, 'Edmund Burke', 38–9.
[71] S. T. Coleridge, '5 Apr. 1833', *Table Talk*, in *Collected Works of Coleridge*, xiv.i 358-9. See also '[7 January–13 February 1823]' in ibid., pp. 36–7.

support for Catholic emancipation; a position Coleridge opposed.[72] A more positive spin could be provided by the close of the century by a fellow Irishman, the Irish Liberal (and then Unionist) historian, W. E. H. Lecky, in a speech at TCD on the centenary of Burke's death in 1897:

> Burke is not one of those great men of calm and lucid judgement who stand out in history like some Greek temple, faultless in its symmetry and its proportion. He was a man of strongly contrasted lights and shades, of transcendent gifts united with very manifest defects. His intellect was in the highest degree both penetrating and comprehensive. He saw further and he saw deeper than any of his contemporaries, and none of them could illuminate a subject with such a splendour of eloquence and such a wealth of knowledge and thought. But this judgement was often obscured by violent gusts of passion, by the force of an overmastering and almost ungovernable imagination—which sometimes seemed not merely to adorn but to transfigure what it touched—by violent personal likings and dislikings.[73]

It was not until the end of the century that Burke came to be seen as the author of a political philosophy in the academic sense of the term, but—excepting his fiercest Radical critics—he had always been held to possess political principles and morality. The physical form of his writings might have taken shape as pamphlets, speeches, and letters applied to issues as they arose, but they nonetheless contained wide, general principles in application to specific political events: thus, Burke's writings, as their 'mass of detail' became less relevant, had to be plucked to reveal the timeless truths underneath that mass of overlying detail. This was done particularly savagely at the end of the nineteenth century, when books of Burke's popular one- or two-sentence aphorisms began to appear for sale.[74] Yet—as we will see—even writers such as Green, Morley, and the Stephens did not attempt to shape Burke's 'distinct philosophy of politics' in a systematic sense. This was left to later writers and is a subject for a later chapter.

MADNESS

It was when Burke was seen to depart completely from reason in the 1790s—his descent into 'madness'—that he appeared to be most starkly

---

[72] See 'Church and State' in Chapter 2 of this volume. These comments may also explain, in part, Mill's position on Burke as outlined in Chapter 4.
[73] Reprinted in Lecky, *Memoir of the Rt. Hon. W. E. H. Lecky* (1909), 305.
[74] See 'Autodidacticism' in Chapter 7 of this volume.

separated from the manners of the English. Yet it was also, inconsistently, the period in which his command of the English language was seen to reach its peak. To Macaulay, Burke had written on emotions, beauty, and nature 'in the style of a parliamentary report'. By contrast, in his old age, he discussed treatises and tariffs 'in the most fervid and brilliant language of romance'. For Macaulay, it was 'strange that the Essay on the Sublime and Beautiful, and the Letter to a Noble Lord, should be the productions of one man. But it is far more strange that the Essay should have been a production of his youth, and the Letter of his old age.'[75] It was indeed widely accepted that Burke's greatest literary triumphs were to be found in his later writings, including the four *Letters on a Regicide Peace* (1795–6), but it was also assumed that this had come at the price of his sanity. How, then, did Burke's nineteenth-century critics explain this development?

France was widely held to be the interpretative key. From the first publication of the *Reflections*, it was suggested by his opponents that the French Revolution had sent Burke into a frenzy—a classic example being Mary Wollstonecraft's depiction of Burke as feminine, hysterical, and irrational.[76] (The notion that Celtic attributes were almost feminine was also common in the period.[77]) During the early nineteenth century, it was laid down by Whigs and Radicals that France had indeed sent Burke mad. This thus legitimized any division in his oeuvre that would be necessary for party political purposes. Earlier Radicals such as T. B. H. Oldfield, writing in 1816, described Burke's French writings as 'a melancholy contrast to the speeches of his better days'. But, more importantly, 'The public mind was so distempered at this period, that the violent ebullitions of this eloquent madman were received with admiration and applause. While the house thought itself enlightened by his arguments, it was only inflamed by his invectives.'[78] This was still a major theme mid-century. Lord John Russell was a major protagonist here in accusing Burke of 'his usual vehemence, passion, and inconsistency' in his *Memorials of Charles James Fox*. He quoted a letter from Fox to Lord Holland from 26 May 1791: '"I have not read Burke's new pamphlets, but hear a very different account of it from yours. It is in general thought to be mere madness, and

---

[75] Macaulay, 'Bacon' [1837], *Critical and Historical Essays*, ii. 394.
[76] Mary Wollstonecraft, *A Vindication of the Rights of Men*, 2nd edn (1790), 6, 9, 28.
[77] For example: 'Not only do . . . Celtic words all apply to inferior employments, but that by far the larger number of them apply to articles of feminine use or to domestic feminine occupations [e.g. dainty, darn, mop].' Saxon masters had married Celtic wives and allowed them to keep old terms to do with 'household drudgery'. Creasy, *Progress of the English Constitution*, 31.
[78] Oldfield, *The Representative History of Great Britain and Ireland*, ii. 2.

especially in those parts where he is for a general war, for the purpose of destroying the present government of France."'[79]

The most infamous assessment of Burke's madness, however, was H. T. Buckle's *History of Civilization in England* (1857–61). Buckle's positivistic approach to history bears some resemblance to the kind of sociological and ethological history J. S. Mill calls for in Book VI of his *System of Logic* (1843),[80] though Buckle himself (b. 1821) died in 1862 without a significant following, and leaving his *History* incomplete. Yet the *History* created something of a *succès de scandale* through its attempt to apply scientific laws to historical processes, and as such was read with great interest by the authors to be discussed in Chapter 4.[81] In his discussion of Burke, more specifically, Buckle asserted that during the French Revolution he 'fell into a state of complete hallucination'. It was only then that 'the feelings of Burke finally mastered his reason; the balance tottered; the proportions of that gigantic intellect were disturbed.'[82] It displayed 'an increasing, and at length uncontrollable, violence'.[83] This could be seen most clearly in his writings on declaring war on France: 'Such cruel, such reckless, and yet such deliberate opinions, if they issued from a sane mind, would immortalize even the most obscure statesman, because they would load his name with imperishable infamy.' Yet, to Buckle's surprise:

> they proceed from one who, a very few years before, was the most eminent political philosopher England has ever possessed. To us it is only given to mourn over so noble a wreck. More than this no one should do. We may contemplate with reverence the mighty ruin; but the mysteries of its decay let no man presume to invade.[84]

To E. J. Payne, an editor of Burke's *Works* in the 1870s, the story of Burke's madness was stated in its most absurd form here. In Payne's view, Buckle had mischievously clothed his 'silly notion' with the 'dignity of history'.[85] Buckle's analysis of 'the mighty ruin' and blatant statement of 'madness' at a time when Burke's command of the English language was

---

[79] Lord John Russell, *Memorials and Correspondence of Charles James Fox* (1853–7), ii. 21, 363. See also J. Mackintosh, *Memoirs of the Life of the Rt. Hon. Sir James Mackintosh*, ed. R. J. Mackintosh (1835), i. 72–3; Richard Cobden, '1793 and 1853, in Three Letters' (1853), 21–2; Walter Bagehot, 'William Pitt', *NR* (July 1861), 223.
[80] J. S. Mill, *A System of Logic* (1843), bk. vi; Bernard Semmel, 'H. T. Buckle: The Liberal Faith and the Science of History', *British Journal of Sociology*, 27 (1976), 379. On Mill see H. S. Jones, 'John Stuart Mill as Moralist', *JHI*, 53 (1992), 287–308. 'Ethology' was Mill's term for the scientific study of 'character'.
[81] Semmel, 'Buckle', 373, 379–83; Thomas William Heyck, 'Buckle, Henry Thomas', *ODNB* (2004).
[82] Buckle, *History of Civilization in England*, i. 334.   [83] Ibid., i. 336.
[84] Ibid., i. 340.   [85] Burke, *Select Works*, ed. E. J. Payne, i. x.

simultaneously seen to reach its peak clearly invited rebuttal and, in doing so, served to inspire a new generation of Burke scholarship.

Even Burke's most sympathetic mid-century biographer, Macknight in his *History of the Life and Times of Edmund Burke* (1858–60), admitted that there was a perception of Burke's madness after 1790, and that Burke's fiery vehemence could be injurious to his object. This could be seen in his French writings and his opposition to parliamentary reform in Britain, but also in the impeachment trial of the first Governor-General of India, Warren Hastings (1787–95). Although to Macknight his speeches at this time abounded in 'imagery, philanthropy, wisdom', the manner of their delivery was so 'impetuous and fervent' that 'plain men, who knew nothing and cared less about the crimes which he declared to have been perpetrated in India, thought his zeal... to be almost incompatible with soundness of mind. His madness, which had hitherto been only hypothetical, was considered at last to be most probable.'[86] Constitutional philosophy, Macknight noted, was 'likely to make less impression when the speaker's manner appears wild and eccentric'.[87] But he criticized those who had 'delighted to impute Burke's conduct during the stormy events of the latter period of his life to sudden passion and unreasonable anger'.[88] Despite the fact that Burke's temper in debate had become 'almost uncontrollable', Macknight insisted that 'no allowance was made for age, sensibility, virtue and genius, goaded by cruel wrongs, and not less cruel neglect; misunderstood, depreciated, impoverished, contemned', or for the loss of his beloved son Richard in 1794.[89] Burke's wisdom had provided him with a prescient foresight, and 'Foreseeing as he did, it was impossible for him not to be excited and violent, and to ordinary mortals to appear on the verge of madness... If he was mad, it was that madness which was in old times characterized by the prophet, as mad for the sight of his eyes which he saw.'[90]

Of course, Tories and Conservatives were no keener to adopt a madman than Liberals. In 1824 the Tory *British Critic*, for example, denied Prior's claim that Burke was a great statesmen on the basis of his 'bitter', 'ungovernable temper', while his praise of France was an 'outrage on common sense'.[91] T. E. Kebbel, in his review of Macknight's biography of Burke, criticized Buckle's conclusion of attributing Burke's change of party in the last ten years of his life to mental derangement, although 'there is a mixture of ingenuity and simplicity of this solution of an

---

[86] Macknight, *Life and Times of Edmund Burke*, iii. 93.
[87] Ibid., iii. 224.   [88] Ibid., iii. 231.
[89] Ibid., iii. 236.   [90] Ibid., iii. 344.
[91] [Anon.], 'Prior's Life of Burke', *British Critic* (Nov. 1824), 525–33.

embarrassing phenomenon that really commands our admiration'. Because of this, Kebbel regretted that Macknight did not consciously attack these charges more vigorously, and expose 'the flimsy attempts at proof' upon which they depend. Yet to Kebbel, as with Macaulay and Macknight, there was some merit within Burke's violence: during the 1790s, Burke's powers were at their zenith. Therefore, Kebbel cited the *Appeal from the New to the Old Whigs* (1791) and the *Letter to a Noble Lord* (1796) as 'undoubtedly among the finest of all Burke's productions'.[92]

'Madness' was also enlisted as explanation for Burke's exclusion from high office. While a popular jibe against the Whigs, and particularly Whig aristocratic exclusiveness, claimed that Burke had been kept from the Cabinet due to his lack of noble birth, this was countered by reference to Burke's irascibility.[93] Joseph Napier (1804–82), an Irish Tory, went further in 1862 in suggesting that Burke's exclusion was simply part of the habitual exclusion of Irishmen, no matter how talented, from ministerial posts.[94] But while the notion that Burke was an important man of letters remained, the idea that Burke was not a practical politician, or, more specifically, a man of government, gathered strength. Though the accusations of madness were largely an early to mid-nineteenth century phenomenon, the issues surrounding Burke's temper remained. Birrell would claim, for instance, that the reasons for Burke's exclusion from high office were threefold: one being Burke's temper, the second his debts, and finally his opposition to parliamentary reform, which also indicates the importance attributed to the latter concern in defining the nineteenth-century Whig–Liberal party.[95] For Goldwin Smith, in 1905, it was clear that aristocratic exclusiveness had been exaggerated. To Smith, whose tone towards Burke had changed significantly since 1861, political merit could always triumph and he listed Addington, Jenkinson, and Canning as 'distinctly plebeian'. Burke's failure to progress was deemed to be not only personal, but Irish:

> The vehemence of Burke's temper... was the Celtic part of his character, and the violence of his impulses, caused him, even when he was battling for the right, to commit errors of judgement and taste which cost him the confidence of the House of Commons and made those who witnessed them speak of him as insane. Insanity itself, indeed, could hardly have

---

[92] Kebbel, 'Edmund Burke', *Essays upon History and Politics*, 180–1.
[93] This had been the conclusion of the third Lord Holland's posthumously published *Further Memoirs of the Whig Party, 1807–1821*, ed. Lord Stavordale (1905), 238. For a supportive review, see [Anon.], 'The Maecenas of the Whigs', *SR* (18 Nov. 1905), 658.
[94] Napier, *Edmund Burke: A Lecture Delivered*, 70.
[95] Birrell, 'Edmund Burke', 40–1.

been less of a qualification for dealing with high matters of state than the fury which broke all bounds not only of good sense and moderation, but of the commonest decency, in Burke's conduct in the impeachment of Warren Hastings. The *Reflections*... recklessly inflaming public feeling at the most dangerous of all possible junctures, when it was the manifest object of statesmanship to keep it cool, is another proof of the unfitness of the author for the highest trust.[96]

Although Burke's specifically Irish identity became less important as time went on, Smith shows that the Irish element of his character as an explanatory factor for his political thought did not completely disappear at the end of our period. 'Burke was', he claimed, 'half Irish in mind as well as face.'[97] While he does not suggest that it was because Burke was Irish that he was excluded from office, as Napier argued in 1862, Smith indicated that it was nonetheless Burke's Irish 'traits' that were a primary cause of his unsuitability for political promotion. For Smith, as Chapter 2 illustrated, this Irish element in Burke's thought was undoubtedly connected to his 'Catholicity'—though it should be remembered that this association and its connotations had become less problematic in wider political and social discourse and, by the turn of the twentieth century, Burke's religious beliefs were more commonly associated with a tolerant form of Anglicanism rather than Roman Catholicism.

Meanwhile Burke was becoming distanced from a more consciously modern Ireland, in the shape of the burgeoning Gaelic Revival movement in Ireland, and W. B. Yeats in particular. Yeats rejected Burke, Swift, and Goldsmith, from inclusion in his 'Celtic Revival' canon of writers as overly anglicized Irishmen.[98] When Burke became overwhelmingly identified in contemporary terms with the Unionist cause (see Chapter 5), he ceased to be exclusively Irish and was as a result open to ever greater appropriation by the British. This was the source of Yeats' rejection of Burke and other Anglo-Irish Georgians as true Irishmen at the turn of the twentieth century:

> Goldsmith and Sheridan and Burke had become so much a part of English life, were so greatly moulded by the movements that were moulding England, that, despite certain Irish elements that clung about them, we could not think of them as more important to us that any English writer of equal rank. Men told us that we should keep our hold of them, as it were, for they were a part of our glory; but we did not consider our glory very important.[99]

---

[96] Goldwin Smith, *Burke on Party* (1905), 6.
[97] Goldwin Smith, 'Burke', *Cornhill* (July 1896), 26.
[98] Yeats to the Editor of the *Daily News*, 11 May 1904, *The Collected Letters of W. B. Yeats*, eds. John Kelly and Ronald Schuchnard (1986–), iii. 592–3.
[99] W. B. Yeats, 'Samhaim' [1904], *Explorations*, ed. Georgie Yeats (1962), 159.

This English context should be set alongside that identified by Yeats scholars, who identify his early interests as replicating the ideology of Gaelic nationalism which denied the Anglo-Irish a legitimate place in the nation in terms of identity. As a result, Burke, alongside Goldsmith and Swift, became 'part of the English system'.[100] It was not until the interwar period that Yeats revised this view and reintegrated the eighteenth-century Anglo-Irish into his Irish literary canon, as in his poem 'The Seven Sages'.[101]

CONCLUSION

Ireland and ideas of Celtic and Irish character were crucial in the development of the interpretations of Burke as a political thinker. On the one hand, what were perceived to be the Celtic parts of his character were seen to have furnished Burke with his unique powers and status in history, but they were also used against him. Burke's passion and madness were deemed to have been derived from his Celtic roots, and therefore prevented his progression and final assimilation in an English parliament. This was only heightened by readings of the years preceding his death under the impact of events in France: there was no progressive narrative in his own lifetime of slow transformation or anglicization.

The three central psychological threads of Burkean portraiture, wisdom, passion, and madness, are, however, odd categories. They provide a specific kind of analysis, showing that the English/British reader had little interest in deducing generalized political lessons from Irishness; but a great deal of interest in establishing a peculiarly Irish psychological make-up, which was so helpful in Burke's case in explaining his individuality. They are not rational analytical categories which form part of an 'Irish political method' or an Irish 'science of politics'. Instead, the idea that Burke *blended* national character traits was established early and grew in popularity throughout the century. This helped to fashion him as something of a quasi-Englishman, though 'blending' came in various forms, whether within his own person (as in Matthew Arnold), or by bringing Irish qualities to England (as in Prior and Maurice). Significantly, in both cases Burke's 'blending' of national characteristics intrinsically linked him to English history, politics, and literature. It provided a way

---

[100] Quoted in Clare Nally, *Envisioning Ireland: W. B. Yeats' Occult Nationalism* (2010), 41–2; D. T. Torchiana, *W. B. Yeats and Georgian Ireland* (1992), 4.
[101] Roy Foster, *W. B. Yeats: A Life* (1997), ii. 411; W. B. Yeats, *The Collected Works of W. B. Yeats*, eds. W. H. O'Donnell and D. N. Archibald (2002), iii. 532–3.

of celebrating his unusual, unorthodox social and intellectual position in the history of British politics and thought.

Over time, Burke continued to be admired in his native Ireland by Catholics and Protestants alike, but there was an important turn away from the eighteenth-century Anglo-Irish writers by the key 'Celtic Revival' figure of Yeats at the *fin de siècle*. In Britain, meanwhile, memories of Burke's distinctive 'Irish brogue' delivering lengthy 'dinner-bell' speeches had faded, and caricatures of him depicted as a bespectacled Jesuit were no longer regular features of popular political culture. Despite the complaints of anti-Catholic men of letters such as Froude and Goldwin Smith, Burke was increasingly praised as a master of English prose, who blended Irish traits with English constitutionalism. It was not, however, until the debates over Unionism and Irish Home Rule from the 1880s that Burke moved towards a more clear-cut 'English' position. Burke was in no way fully anglicized by the turn of the twentieth century, but, as we will see, he certainly did become an established member of an English/British political, literary, and intellectual canon. First, however, it is essential to explore the work that in retrospect laid the foundations for this re-interpretation in the years 1860–80.

4
Critical Recovery, *c*.1860–1880

As the preceding chapters have demonstrated, Burke's political reputation and personal character during the first half of the nineteenth century were complex and ambiguous. His eulogies of the English, or British, Constitution and his eloquent prose earned him widespread admiration. Politically, however, he was condemned by Whigs for splitting the party and consigning them to forty years of opposition. At the same time, Burke was held up by Tories and Conservatives as an anti-French totem, although still problematically Irish—and we have also seen how Burke's Irish identity continued to play a critical role in evaluating his life and work, with both positive and negative results. The further charges levied against Burke were extensive: he was an adventurer, a suspected Catholic, and heavily in debt. Others sought to explain why Burke had never held a senior position in government—usually explained by his irritable temper, or his non-aristocratic social standing. But perhaps the most famous conundrum—one which still resonates in modern academic discussions of Burke's thought—was the question of his consistency. Belief in the division between Burke's writings on Revolutionary France and his earlier work, such as the *Thoughts on the Cause of the Present Discontents* and his American speeches, all from the 1770s, was a widespread phenomenon. Burke's political legacy was divided between Whig praise of earlier texts and Tory adulation of *Reflections on the Revolution in France*.

In the 1860s one particular verdict of this kind stood out. H. T. Buckle divided up Burke's oeuvre into pre- and post-French Revolutionary categories in his well-known *History of Civilization in England* (1857–61), and went so far as to claim that, despite his great genius, Burke's Revolutionary writings were the work of a man in a state of 'complete hallucination'.[1] Though Buckle represented no party or group of opinion, there was no denying the intellectual ambition of his project.[2]

---

[1] Buckle, *History of Civilization in England*, i. 424–32. Cf. G. Cornwall Lewis, *Essays on the Administrations of Great Britain*, 124.
[2] Semmel, 'Buckle', 370–86.

So in the years that followed this categorization became infamous, and the works of men such John Morley (1838–1923), in *Edmund Burke: A Historical Study* (1867) and *Burke* (1879), and Leslie Stephen (1832–1904), in his *History of English Thought in the Eighteenth Century* (1876), marked a turning of the tide in Burke criticism. They substantially revised the idea that Burke was an inconsistent political thinker and a man of dubious moral character, and provided a rebuttal.[3] This was a seminal moment in his reception history, and these re-evaluations therefore deserve more extensive scrutiny. Notable contributions were also made by James Fitzjames Stephen (1829–94), E. J. Payne (1844–1904), Matthew Arnold (1822–88), Edward Dowden (1843–1913), and W. E. H. Lecky (1838–1903). Through their books and periodical articles, these authors asserted Burke's political consistency, his intellectual power, and his possession of a generous moral character, and thus laid the foundations for the much more far-reaching revaluation that took place after 1880. It was now clear that Burke's contribution to the history of political thought was of far greater importance to mankind than any irregularities in the way he paid for his house. In a society increasingly preoccupied with the need to control historical change, the period between the Second Reform Act and with it the incipient arrival of 'democracy', and the conversion of Gladstone to the cause of Irish Home Rule, was one in which Burke first became associated with the organic, developmental thought which would later make him so appealing to Idealist philosophers and Conservative politicians.

All the major Burke revisionists in this period were Liberals, though of very different kinds. This has led commentators to argue that they presented a view of Burke as a 'liberal utilitarian', and 'utilitarian-positivist-liberal'.[4] Pithy quotes can certainly be found in support of this. Fitzjames Stephen found Burke to be from 'first to last a utilitarian of the strongest kind', and, to Morley in 1867, Burke was 'the greatest statesman' who adhered to the 'doctrine' of 'general utility'.[5] One problem with this argument, however, is that scholars of Burke are at odds with more general conceptions of nineteenth-century intellectual history. Over several decades, the 'conveniently pre-fabricated label' of 'Utilitarian Liberal' and its exaggerated impact on political discourse and action has come under challenge. Stefan Collini observes correctly that Victorian political discourse was largely drawn from other sources—constitutional, historical,

---

[3] Morley, *Edmund Burke: A Historical Study* (1867); *Burke* (1879); Leslie Stephen, *History of English Thought in the Eighteenth Century* (1876).
[4] See pp. 3–4 in this volume.
[5] J. F. Stephen, 'Burke on the English Constitution' [28 Dec. 1867], *Horae Sabbaticae* (1892), 115–16 (hereafter *HS*); Morley, *Edmund Burke: A Historical Study* (1867), 309.

religious, and moral. It is crucial to note that notions now associated with utilitarian philosophy such as 'general happiness' and 'expediency' outside a systematically deployed framework have a limited connection to utilitarianism proper.[6] So linking Burke with either of these two concepts did not automatically conscript Burke into a utilitarian canon. It is possible, for instance, to find examples of the 'happiness of the people' in Whig rhetoric from the eighteenth century.[7] The same can be said for references to 'expediency' and pragmatism. In a stereotypical formulation, it was the 'distinctive peculiarity of the English mind', according to the Lord Chancellor, Lord Westbury, in 1863, to love precedent and 'appealing to the authority of past examples rather than indulging in abstract reasoning'.[8] Victorian intellectual historians have shown the insufficiency of categorizing any part of the historically minded nineteenth century as being dominated by ahistorical utilitarian political or moral philosophy, and, moreover, of categorizing utilitarianism itself as static and unchanging.[9]

The same can be said for the description of these interpretations as utilitarian-positivist-liberal. If 'positivist' means merely a more scientific or materialistic reading of Burke's thought, then the definition is so broad that it may be found almost anywhere. If, on the other hand, it refers specifically to English Positivism, a set of doctrines deriving from Comtean Positivism, then it is too narrow to take in Burke's revivers. The Liberals in this chapter were not fully fledged English Positivists on the model of Frederic Harrison or E. S. Beesly. The secularized Catholicism of Comte's 'Religion of Humanity' was particularly problematic for one-time Evangelicals such as Morley,[10] while Fitzjames Stephen profoundly disliked Positivism as a whole.[11] Comte, and elements of his stadial theory

---

[6] Stefan Collini, 'Manly Fellows: Fawcett, Stephen, and the Liberal Temper', in Laurence Goldman, ed., *The Blind Victorian: Henry Fawcett and British Liberalism* (1989), 44–5.

[7] Cf. Joseph Addison, 'Monday, June 25',*The Freeholder* (25 June 1716): 'They [the Tories] tacitly do honour to the Whig scheme, and own it more accommodated to the happiness of the people, than that which they espouse'; Henry Brougham, *Government without Whigs* (1830), 3: '[Tories] would make that constitution, with the wealth and happiness of the people who live under it, subservient to the views of discontented faction'; and Lord John Russell, *Correspondence of Charles James Fox*, iii. 24: '[Fox] was purely and simply a Whig: devoted to the popular principle of that party'.

[8] T. A. Nash, *Life of Lord Westbury* (1888), ii. 58. For a pithy overview of the English, Scottish, and French 'minds', see Lord Macmillian, *Two Ways of Thinking* (1934). See also Mandler, *English National Character*, 175.

[9] Burrow, *Whigs and Liberals*, 9–10, 193.

[10] Parry, *Democracy and Religion*, 239–44.

[11] Christopher Harvie, *The Lights of Liberalism: University Liberals and the Challenge of Democracy, 1860–1886* (1976), 42.

of history undoubtedly influenced the thought of Morley and Leslie Stephen, but neither was a doctrinaire English Positivist.

What Comte (and indeed J. S. Mill, whose project was in some respects akin to Comte's) did give these Liberal interpreters was a stadial and progressive notion of history. They also shared a view of the French Revolution as a fundamental turning point in modern history, especially in the history of ideas. Yet despite this interest in the French Revolution and the history of ideas, Burke did not come directly recommended by either Mill or Comte or the English Positivists, for none of them had any great interest in him.[12] Mill had very little to say about Burke—a clear sign of want of interest in such a prolific writer—and the gulf between them both in politics and intellectual method is clear enough: Mill's stringently social-scientific historicism was a world away from Burke's rhetorical presentation of the past. So what Mill did say was negative: Burke's sentimental eloquence was deplorable, while his aphorisms were 'the only valuable portion of his writings'.[13] Mill stated quite clearly, in 1865, that Burke was 'too often a polemic [sic] rather than a connected thinker'. Hence while his aphorisms were valuable, they were simply 'weapons snatched up for the service of a particular quarrel' and thus less admirable than 'the matured convictions of a scientific mind'.[14] It is also true that Comte recommended the reading of Burke alongside William Godwin in a letter of 1857 to the English Positivist Richard Congreve so that he might fully appreciate Comte's positive philosophy, but the subsequent references to Burke by these writers demonstrate that their reception of his thought was overwhelmingly negative.[15] Congreve, for instance, claimed that Burke lost his mental powers defending the *ancien régime* in France as well as Britain.[16] Frederic Harrison and E. S. Beesly similarly depicted Burke as a raving madman in the style of Buckle in 1866.[17] If anything, therefore, Burke's new generation of Liberal admirers were far removed from Mill and the Positivists in their interest in Burke as an admirable political thinker.

---

[12] Christopher Kent, *Brains and Numbers: Elitism, Comtism, and Democracy in Mid-Victorian England*, (1978), 118; John Morley, 'A New Calendar of Great Men', *NC* (Feb. 1892), 312–28.
[13] J. S. Mill, 'Periodical Literature: Edinburgh Review' [1824], *Collected Works of John Stuart Mill*, ed. J. M. Robson (1979), i. 311; 'Aphorisms: Thoughts in the Cloister and the Cloud' [1837], i. 424.
[14] Ibid., 'An Examination of William Hamilton's Philosophy' [1865], ix. 160.
[15] Mary Pickering, *Auguste Comte: An Intellectual Biography* (2009), ii. 525 n.67.
[16] Richard Congreve, 'Modern and Revolutionary Europe', *Essays Political, Social, and Religious Lectures* (1874–1900), iii. 659.
[17] Frederic Harrison, 'England and France', in Richard Congreve, ed., *International Policy* (1866), 84, 110; E. S. Beesly, 'England at Sea', in ibid., 178, 219.

Why, then, did a new cohort of men of letters became interested in Burke in the 1860s? Several historians have tried to explain this change. For John Burrow, the men of the 1850s and 1860s represented a significant generational intellectual shift: to Morley and Leslie Stephen, the eighteenth century now receded into a detached historical past. Unlike earlier writers they lacked a direct connection to eighteenth-century traditions, such as Holland House Whiggism.[18] It was at this point, Burrow argues, that Burke became a particularly useful intellectual figure as proto-Darwinian and utilitarian.[19] A new perception of Burke's 'organicism' also underlines Jeffrey von Arx's explanation of the Burkean revival.[20] To Christopher Kent, the central force behind Morley's 1867 text was Comte's progressive philosophy of history with its emphasis on the French Revolution as a transformative moment; one which brought mankind towards the final 'positivist' stage of human history. Kent expounds Morley's belief that Burke had played a vital intellectual role—providing one side, or a 'half-truth'—which Comte and the Positivists had overlooked.[21] Georgios Varouxakis then sees this need to combine 'half-truths' as a widespread phenomenon in nineteenth-century thought, tracing it as a mental habit through Goethe, Coleridge, J. S. Mill, and the Arnolds.[22] Each of these accounts makes a valuable contribution, but these suggestive fragments must now be brought together and combined with a much deeper exploration of the texts and their authors taken together.

At the most basic level, it is clear that writers were rediscovering the eighteenth century as a period of considerable historical interest. Yet Brian Young is correct when he claims that the eighteenth century did not become of historical interest in a purely antiquarian sense, but instead became more clearly defined as the intellectual basis for subsequent religious, political, and philosophical developments.[23] Morley, Leslie Stephen, and Lecky were historians of opinion, and even Fitzjames Stephen—known for his rugged commonsense—adored reading political thought (his favourite philosopher was Hobbes), and wrote hundreds of articles on political thinkers for the *Saturday Review*. It was the eighteenth

---

[18] Burrow, *Whigs and Liberals*, 10–11.   [19] Ibid., 14.
[20] J. P. von Arx, *Progress and Pessimism: Religion, Politics, and History in Late Nineteenth-Century Britain*, (1985), 47–8.
[21] Kent, *Brains and Numbers*, 118–21. Cf. Morley, *Edmund Burke: A Historical Study* (1867), 225.
[22] Varouxakis, *Victorian Political Thought on France*, 14. Hence Fitzjames Stephen, who disliked Comte, can still be found rejecting the negative view of the Revolution as a revolt against God as 'imperfect, one-sided, and radically sophistical': 'De Maistre's Minor Works', *HS*, iii. 279–80, quoted in Young, *Victorian Eighteenth Century*, 123–4.
[23] Ibid., 1–2.

century, in Leslie Stephen's words, that formed the 'borderland' between past and present.[24] This was a new attitude: as Edward Dowden remarked in 1878, the declining aversion to the eighteenth century as a whole could be seen in the work of Morley and Leslie Stephen, and in Mark Pattison's 'Tendencies of Religious Thought in England, 1688–1750'.[25] But rescuing the 'Bankrupt Century' meant that its historical actors were in need of reinvention, including Burke.[26] Given their philosophical bias these writers were less interested in the party squabbles and personal greed that had previously dominated conceptions of this period, and instead focused on identifying systems of thought and guiding principles; they wished to investigate the 'truthfulness' of past thought, and so re-evaluate the contribution of the eighteenth century to the nineteenth. Yet, although many of Burke's new critics were admirers of Bentham, Mill, and Comte who shared their interest in intellectual systems and principles, they were also products of English public schools and Oxbridge—the educational establishment. An interest in philosophy was combined variously with the pursuit of 'manly' outdoor activities; praise of straightforward commonsense; and involvement in practical party politics. The result was a much higher admiration for the English, or British, eighteenth century—whether in thought or in literature—than Radical Mill or French Comte.

The purpose of this chapter, therefore, is to demonstrate the distinctive contribution that was made by a younger generation of Liberal men of letters in the recovery of Burke's political reputation. The mid-Victorian reinvention of Burke was a holistic one: his moral, as well as his political, consistency was asserted. In doing so, this heterogeneous group of writers established Burke as an important political thinker and reaffirmed his position as an author worthy of study on all accounts, ranging from his prose style to his statesmanship. The mid-1860s was also a period of significant political reform and it is here that Burke's constitutional conservatism was first revealed as a major obstacle, which prevented him from being a source of inspiration for modern Liberals. Hence, this chapter argues, rather than moulding Burke into a 'liberal-utilitarian', Burke's Liberal interpreters actually played a fundamental role in establishing Burke as a C/conservative political thinker, although they could

---

[24] Leslie Stephen, 'Defoe's Novels', *Hours in a Library* (1874), i. 26.
[25] Edward Dowden, *Studies in Literature, 1789–1877* (1878), 3; For Pattison, see Mark Pattison, 'Tendencies of Religious Thought in England, 1688–1750', in *Essays and Reviews* (1860); H. S. Jones, *Intellect and Character in Victorian Britain: Mark Pattison and the Invention of the Don* (2007).
[26] John W. Bicknell, 'Leslie Stephen's *English Thought in the Eighteenth Century*: A Tract for the Times', *VS*, 6 (1962), 106.

not have anticipated the later consequences of their actions after 1880. This was a crucial first stage in a much longer process.

This chapter is structured around four main parts. Section one provides an introductory survey of our three main writers—Leslie and Fitzjames Stephen, and John Morley—including their shared backgrounds and intellectual interests, as well as their points of divergence. Next, section two examines earlier Burke biographies, their reception, and the questions they raised which remained unanswered to reviewers. This sets the scene for section three, which discusses the ways in which Burke's life and thought were reinterpreted, including Burke's claim to the label of 'thinker' and his consistency of thought. This section concentrates primarily on the political–philosophical side of Burke's recovery, whereas section four addresses a somewhat broader area: the assertions that Burke was also a great moral character and a guide for future statesman, and hence the positioning of Burke within a British or English political and intellectual tradition.

INTELLECTUAL CONTEXT

In order to explain the ways in which Burke's thought was reconstructed, it is necessary first to consider the intellectual worlds of our key commentators: James Fitzjames Stephen, his younger brother Leslie, and Leslie Stephen's close friend in adulthood John Morley. All three grew up in Evangelical Anglican households; all underwent varying degrees of mental and personal trauma during their 'crises', and eventual loss of faith; and both Morley's Oxford and the Stephens' Cambridge held J. S. Mill's *System of Logic* (1843) as the supreme authority on moral and political questions.[27] When he refused to take clerical orders in 1859, Morley's father severed all contact and income, forcing Morley to leave Oxford with only a pass degree, and leaving him to make his way as an isolated journalist in London. After resigning his Cambridge tutorship in 1862, Leslie Stephen too chose journalism, and the two soon became intimately acquainted.[28]

Indeed, all three men are notable for their contributions to the newly founded periodicals, such as the *Fortnightly Review* (founded in 1865, edited by Morley from 1867) and the *Cornhill Magazine* (founded in 1859, edited by Leslie Stephen from 1871), that were becoming a defining feature of Victorian intellectual and cultural life. Presenting their work in

---

[27] Harvie, *Lights of Liberalism*, 38.
[28] F. W. Maitland, *Life and Letters of Leslie Stephen* (1906), 255–6.

periodical form—this was how Morley's *Edmund Burke* (1867) first appeared—increased their readership far beyond those who would specifically purchase a new book on Burke. Sales of the explicitly 'advanced' views of the *Fortnightly* were at 1,400 copies in 1867, and between 2,500 and 3,000 by 1872, while those of the weekly *Saturday Review* stood at approximately 10,000 around the year 1860, and had doubled to 20,000 by 1870. Morley estimated, however, that once one allowed for the multiple readership of an issue, the pages of the *Fortnightly* reached a readership of 30,000 of the 'influential classes'—the controversial nature of featured articles ensured that they were talked about, and brought the library down to the parlour.[29]

The oldest of our three men, Fitzjames Stephen has a reputation of being, at one and the same time, a Benthamite jurist, a religious sceptic who defended the value of unifying religious belief, and a 'conservative' political thinker who unsuccessfully stood as a Liberal parliamentary candidate.[30] Like Morley and his brother Leslie, he made his reputation through contributions to the fledgling *Saturday Review* (founded in 1855), including a number of articles on Burke, republished later in *Horae Sabbaticae* and described by the author as 'the best things I ever wrote'.[31] His capacity for scholarly application was apparently less evident in his Cambridge years, although unlike Leslie he had been a member of the Apostles, following a nomination from his friend Henry Maine (1822–88), the jurist whose celebrated work *Ancient Law* was published in 1861. Fitzjames Stephen's powerful, if not academic, intellect was combined with a profound dislike of humbug and 'wind-baggery'.[32] He is now known predominantly for his critical response to Mill's *On Liberty* (1859), *Liberty, Equality, Fraternity* (1873), in which he doubted the overall benefit of free discussion for ordinary men and women, and defended moral coercion and the 'self-evident' divisions of social strata. Yet whatever this may connote in modern terms, Stephen thought of himself as a Liberal and this is vital: even when he is more

---

[29] Patrick Jackson, *Morley of Blackburn: A Literary and Political Biography of John Morley* (2012), 34–5; Alvar Ellegård, *The Readership of the Periodical Press in Mid-Victorian Britain* (1957), 22, 27, 32.

[30] B. E. Lippincott, 'James Fitzjames Stephen: Critic of Democracy', *Economica*, 33 (Aug. 1931), 296–307; Russell Kirk, 'The Foreboding Conservatism of Stephen', *Western Political Quarterly*, 5 (Dec. 1952), 563–77. Lippincott, who read for his PhD at the London School of Economics under Harold Laski (another great admirer of Burke), places Stephen in 'the tradition of Burke'.

[31] J. F. Stephen to Lord Lytton, 21 Sept. 1890, quoted in J. A. Colaiaco, *James Fitzjames Stephen and the Crisis of Victorian Thought* (1983), 26.

[32] R. C. J. Cocks, 'Maine, Sir Henry James Sumner', *ODNB* (2004); K. J. M. Smith, 'Stephen, Sir James Fitzjames', ibid.

inclined to favour existing institutions and social structures, he always believes that Burke goes too far in this direction. He was, his brother stated, a Puritan and a utilitarian, even after he had embraced agnosticism. In 1885 Fitzjames Stephen described his mental state in 1865 (during the publication of his Burke articles) as 'too hot in his Benthamism', but at that date he had not yet lost his faith.[33] Mill's *Logic* may have been formative, but Stephen was no uncritical follower of his political and moral views.[34] He found Comte repulsive, describing Positivism as a 'Ritualistic Social Science Association'.[35] Instead, Fitzjames Stephen was a great admirer of Macaulay: both derived from and rejected Clapham Sect Evangelicalism. In particular he admired Macaulay's essays and the *History of England* but not the essay on Warren Hastings, whom Stephen, a one-time member of the Indian Colonial Council, saw as a great man.[36] He held strong sympathies with political arrangements which had developed over time and hence did not identify Liberalism with constitutional destruction or an inevitable teleology of progress, like Buckle.[37] It was still possible to be a utilitarian (though perhaps a poor Philosophic Radical) if one identified maximum expediency with the continuation of established institutions. Hence, on the polarizing question of Irish Home Rule, Fitzjames Stephen (along with such fellow utilitarians as his brother Leslie, Henry Sidgwick, and A. V. Dicey) opposed Gladstone's constitutional overhaul.

The major intellectual difference between Fitzjames and Leslie Stephen lay in the questions they asked of their historical subjects, Burke included. To the elder brother, the important issue was 'is it true?' Leslie, in contrast, sought to situate past thought contextually, within a larger framework of intellectual development.[38] It was this historicism which prevented Benthamite or even Millite utilitarianism from being a completely comfortable fit with Leslie Stephen.[39] Despite his love of empiricism, he believed that Bentham was especially deficient in historic sense, for which Burke provided the antidote. Leslie Stephen held Comte in much higher regard

---

[33] Leslie Stephen, *Life of James Fitzjames Stephen* (1895), 117, 217; Julia Stapleton, 'James Fitzjames Stephen: Liberalism, Patriotism, and English Liberty', *VS*, 41 (1998), 257–8.
[34] Ibid., 299, 308–9.
[35] J. F. Stephen, *Liberty, Equality, Fraternity* (1873), 110, 122.
[36] J. F. Stephen, *The Story of Nuncomar and the Impeachment of Sir Elijah Impey* (1885), ii. 8; Stephen, *Life of James Fitzjames Stephen*, 226, 233.
[37] Stapleton, 'James Fitzjames Stephen', 247; [J. F. Stephen], 'Liberalism', *Cornhill* (Jan. 1862), 70–83; [J. F. Stephen], 'Buckle's Theory of Civilization in England', *ER* (July 1861), 183–211.
[38] Stephen, *Life of James Fitzjames Stephen*, 226; D. D. Zink, *Leslie Stephen* (1972), 77.
[39] Stephen, *History of English Thought*, ii. 126.

than his brother, and once claimed he would have been a Positivist if he had gone to Oxford.[40] Even so, Leslie Stephen believed that Comte's stadial theory of history had been superseded by Darwin and the evolutionists, who had placed historic development upon a more solidly scientific base.[41] Leslie Stephen, as we will see, did much to construe Burke in exactly the kind of historical and organicist light which would be utilized by students of T. H. Green around the turn of the century. Historical organicism thus provided a common (and one might add, conveniently elastic) language for empiricists and Idealists alike, as an authoritative discourse which aligned political thought with natural science and dominant conceptions of British history. It is interesting to note here, then, that Stephen read and approved of much of Green's *Prologomena to Ethics* in 1883, excepting Green's difficult prose style.[42] His philosophy of history was also somewhat different from that of Mill, Comte, and Buckle. Rejecting Buckle's 'rationalistic' view of history, Stephen turned Mill and Comte on their heads when he argued that ideas resulted from social conditions, rather than the other way round.[43] Leslie Stephen's specific interest in the eighteenth century went back to his youthful love of the literature of the period, which had developed during his time at Cambridge reading for the mathematical tripos. Besides his recreational mountaineering book, *The Playground of Europe* (1871), by 1876 Stephen had published fourteen essays on eighteenth-century figures, and his later biographies for Morley's English 'Men of Letters' series were dominated by them too—where his subjects included Johnson, Pope, and Swift.[44]

As time went on, Leslie Stephen increasingly sunk his energies into literary and ethical studies.[45] In contrast, while Morley became well-known for his editorship of the *Fortnightly Review* and the English Men of Letters series, his treatise *On Compromise*, and volumes on Voltaire, Rousseau, and Diderot (1872–8), he gradually turned away from his research on the French Revolution and began to look towards a career in active politics.[46] Morley, who finally became a Liberal MP in 1883 and a cabinet minister shortly afterwards, was constantly drawn to a life of

---

[40] Maitland, *Life of Stephen*, 172. On the contrast between Leslie and Fizjames' views on Comte, see T. R. Wright, *The Religion of Humanity: the Impact of Comtean Positivism on Victorian Britain* (1986), 143–6.
[41] Maitland, *Life and Letters of Leslie Stephen*, 350–1, 489; Noel Annan, *Leslie Stephen: The Godless Victorian* (1984), 140, 162.
[42] Maitland, *Life and Letters of Leslie Stephen*, 374–5.
[43] Zink, *Leslie Stephen*, 20; Collini, 'Manly Fellows', 43; Leslie Stephen, 'An Attempted Philosophy of History', *FR* (May 1880), 672–95.
[44] Leslie Stephen, *The Playground of Europe* (1871); Zink, *Leslie Stephen*, 80; Annan, *Leslie Stephen*, 241.
[45] Collini, 'Manly Fellows', 43.   [46] Jackson, *Morley of Blackburn*, 74.

political action. Collini labels him as 'Mill's representative on earth', and David Hamer has described Morley's thought as an unoriginal hybrid of key intellectual movements: utilitarianism, Positivism, and organicism.[47] Despite Morley's association with Mill and utilitarianism, however, his interest in Burke was not simply as an advocate of expediency in politics. Practically, Burke was held up as an example of an intellectual in politics and, ideologically, Morley disliked impatient 'sudden reformation' and believed in the uselessness of 'reformatory rebellion'—his view of expediency was bound up with 'natural' morality, which he saw as identical to the order inherent in nature.[48] It is thus paradoxical, to say the least, that Morley was one of Gladstone's strongest supporters over Home Rule from December 1885. He was certainly perceived by contemporaries as an 'advanced' Liberal, though Morley would write of himself in 1909 that, 'the man whose first literary task and first success was a glorification of Burke can never have been at heart a revolutionary champion'.[49]

From these potted biographies, it should be clear that each of these writers was eclectic. They derived ideas from a broad and diverse range of sources, including divergent aspects of utilitarianism, Positivism, and evolutionary organicism, as well as less exclusively philosophical interests: law, party politics, the empire, and literature. Another factor which linked Burke's new admirers was a profound interest in developing new ideas and principles to meet present and future needs. For this reason, it was not necessary that Burke's Liberal admirers should share the same religious views. Although somewhat older, Matthew Arnold (b. 1822) also published his most important work concerning Burke between the mid-1860s and the mid-1880s.[50] In Ireland, Lecky, an Anglo-Irish Protestant rationalist, was a life-long admirer of Burke, although the volumes of his *History of England in the Eighteenth Century* which included considerable commentary on Burke were not published until 1882.[51] As outlined in Chapter 2, a continental, philosophical, and Catholic interpretation of Burke can be found in J. B. Robertson's lectures on Burke, published in 1868, but they were met with hostility in the mainstream British press.[52] The common link was a tendency to look to Burke, as Robertson did, for

---

[47] Collini, *Public Moralists*, 103; David Hamer, *John Morley: Liberal Intellectual in Politics* (1968), 38, 384; Varouxakis, *Victorian Political Thought on France*, 123.

[48] Morley to Lord Minto, 26 Mar. 1908, quoted in Hamer, *John Morley*, 69. This is also the theme which runs throughout Stephen E. Koss, *John Morley and the India Office, 1905–1910* (1969).

[49] Hamer, *John Morley*, 384. Conveniently, however, the Irish Question was not a vital issue for Liberal politics in 1909.

[50] See also pp. 64–5, 118–19 in this volume.   [51] Ibid., 119–20.

[52] See pp. 46–7 in this volume.

hints on constructing a moral and social brand of 'inductive philosophy' to replace 'dreamy discussion of theories'. In the same way Leslie Stephen lamented that no 'political science as a coherent body of doctrines, deduced from certain axioms of universal validity, but leading to different conclusions according to the varying conditions of human society' yet existed.[53] Likewise, Morley regretted that the Revolutionary experiments of 1848 did more than any other event to harden the English against political theory, and Matthew Arnold (as we have seen) promoted the reading of Burke to set the English 'on thinking'.[54] There was a general interest in well-formed principles and the power of ideas to regulate the progress of human society, and not only 'when the vision of God becomes faint'.[55]

To sum up: those who wrote on Burke were not intellectual doctrinaires who interpreted his thought in one or two specific ways. What was produced instead was much more fluid and there are disagreements between authors, as well as apparent contradictions and inconsistencies within the texts themselves. Before discussing these texts in more detail, however, it is necessary to establish the problems which then existed within Burke literature in order to establish the evident shift in tone and substance of later work.

CRITICAL PROBLEMS

Before the new erudition of the 1860s, earlier biographical studies had done little to convince Burke's critics of his merits as a man or as a political figure. James Prior's standard *Life of Burke* was still going strong in the 1850s, as is evidenced by its inclusion in Bohn's edition of Burke's works in 1854.[56] It had, however, received a lukewarm Tory reception upon its initial publication,[57] and was still deemed unconvincing in the 1850s. Its weakness was made all the worse, the *Athenaeum* remarked, by its pretensions to sufficiency. For the *Athenaeum* as well as the Radical *Leader*, Prior had failed to account for the fundamentally problematic issues of Burke's finances, his possible conversion to Catholicism, and the extent to which his political views were simply reflections of his monetary interests such as

---

[53] Stephen, *History of English Thought*, ii. 130.
[54] Varouxakis, *Victorian Political Thought on France*, 79; Morley, *On Compromise*, 18. See also Parry, 'The Impact of Napoleon III', 175.
[55] Stephen, *History of English Thought*, ii. 2. See also Hamer, *John Morley*, 7; Harvie, *Lights of Liberalism*, 20.
[56] Prior, *Life and Character of the Rt. Hon. Edmund Burke*, 5th edn (1854).
[57] Sack, 'The Memory of Pitt and the Memory of Burke', 623–40.

his position as Agent for New York in the 1760s and 1770s and his royal pension during the war with France.[58]

It was this deficiency that Thomas Macknight's *History of the Life and Times of Edmund Burke* (1858–60) intended to remedy. His main purpose at the time of writing was to rescue Burke from the hands of his Whig declaimers.[59] In contrast to the party political chaos of the mid-1850s and early 1860s, Burke was presented as a wise, philosophical, consistent political actor. He had been chosen by no less than 'the dispensation of Providence' to be 'the greatest, and the wisest of the emancipators of Ireland', 'the most brilliant and far-sighted of British statesman', 'the most enlightened and eloquent defender of established governments', and 'the most profound and comprehensive of political philosophers that had yet existed in the world'.[60] Macknight's enormous text—three large volumes—was praised for its detailed research and his inclusion of new material from (for example) Fox's correspondence and Grenville's memoirs.[61] The main problem with Macknight's work lay in his 'biographical passion' for his subject: his effusive style and adulation was seen as excessive by reviewers.[62] Hence, rather than convincing them of Burke's greatness, the work invited criticism. The *Athenaeum*, again, admitted that Burke was a 'great public man' but twice lamented that Macknight had simply provided an 'unbroken eulogy' rather than expounding Burke's finances in a convincing manner.[63] This was also the conclusion of the *Daily Telegraph*: 'The character of Edmund Burke has been, at all times, a problem.'[64] Likewise, the *Critic* retorted that Macknight's 'hero-worship would even sicken Mr. Carlyle' and described Burke as merely a 'trading politician' who was concerned only in advancing his own interests: how else did the 'poor young Irishman, the son of a struggling attorney in Dublin ... become the landed gentleman?'[65]

The High Church *Christian Remembrancer* was somewhat more sympathetic to Burke, painting him as a 'lover of liberty' who nonetheless rekindled Toryism in the years following the French Revolution. However, his political identity was that of a Whig and he had been wrong to 'squeez[e] himself in between Pitt and Dundas, at the head of the English

---

[58] 'Life of the Right Honourable Edmund Burke', *Athenaeum* (17 Feb. 1855), 195–7; 'Edmund Burke', *Leader* (13 Feb. 1858), 160.
[59] Macknight, *Life and Times of Edmund Burke*, i. xiv.
[60] Ibid., i. 9.
[61] 'History of the Life and Times of Edmund Burke', *Examiner* (2 Mar. 1861), 133.
[62] [J. F. Stephen], 'Edmund Burke', *SR* (10 Apr. 1858), 372–3.
[63] 'Life and Times of Edmund Burke', *Athenaeum* (20 Feb. 1858), 236–8; 'History of the Life and Times of Edmund Burke', *Athenaeum* (22 Dec. 1860), 866–7.
[64] 'History of the Life and Times of Edmund Burke', *Daily Telegraph* (4 Mar. 1858), 2.
[65] 'History of the Life and Times of Edmund Burke', *The Critic* (31 July 1858), 428–9.

Conservatives'.⁶⁶ Scottish periodicals were also more positive. The *Scottish Review* argued in favour of Burke's pension, for which he received so much criticism: 'Men who... devote themselves, without any patrimony, to the promotion of political principles, deserve every encouragement from the state.'⁶⁷ Despite this, a substantial part of the article is still taken up with a defence of Burke's financial situation, a denial of his Catholicism, and an explanation of how Burke could have contributed to the 'Letters of Junius' without actually writing them himself.⁶⁸ The *North British Review* also defended Burke's pension and cited his early advocacy of free trade, Catholic emancipation, the petition of the Dissenters, and law and financial reform as examples of his wide views. Most unusually, however, this review goes on to expound Burke's 'political philosophy', even if its treatment was somewhat simplistic. His political thought was likened to moral philosophy because it landed every question 'in the arms of virtue or vice'. It was also a way of demonstrating Burke's consistency: he is stated as having a love of 'the old principle of "political expediency"'—a dislike of metaphysics in politics'.⁶⁹

Overall, the reviews of Macknight's biography illustrate the confused reputation Burke held in the mid-nineteenth century. He was described as an important historical and political figure, and a great writer of English prose, but the questions which preoccupied his English reviewers especially were personal rather than theoretical. His literary reputation was employed to sugar-coat rather barbed speculation on how Burke funded himself, and this tainted his entire reputation, political and moral. The *North British Review* was unique in its more expansive views, but this should be less surprising given that political philosophy had been an important component of Scottish higher education since the turn of the century.⁷⁰ Given that this focus on Burke's financial history is almost wholly absent from later commentary, it is therefore significant that in 1862 a series of lectures by the Irish Tory MP Joseph Napier were published which directly addressed the topic of Burke's credit, including

---

⁶⁶ 'History of the Life and Times of Edmund Burke', *Christian Remembrancer* (Oct. 1861), 297–318. For earlier Tractarian praise of Burke as a 'Saxon', see [E. A. Freeman], 'The Conquest and the Conqueror', *The Theologian and Ecclesiastic* (Oct. 1848), 197–211 and 261–77, especially pp. 265–6.

⁶⁷ 'Macknight's Life of Burke', *Scottish Review* (July 1861), 215. Burke's pension was also defended in 'History of the Life and Times of Edmund Burke', *New Quarterly Review* (Jan. 1861), 47.

⁶⁸ Ibid., 216–17.

⁶⁹ 'History of the Life and Times of Edmund Burke', *North British Review* (Nov. 1861), 445–79.

⁷⁰ Collini, Winch, and Burrow, *Noble Science of Politics*, ch. 1.

an explanation of his purchase of the Beaconsfield estate.[71] Napier's lectures appear finally to have settled this question in Burke's favour and became a significant reference for those, such as Morley, who wanted to overthrow charges against Burke convincingly, 'in a clear and legal manner, with references to conclusive documents'.[72]

What was still missing, the Liberal *British Quarterly Review* claimed, was a study of Burke by a man of genius who held large, mature, and discriminating views.[73] For this reason, it is of the utmost importance to note that Burke's subsequent critics balanced their interest and admiration with clear and precise analyses of his respective merits and demerits. The works produced were still essentially histories and biographies, rather than systematic theories, but they displayed a markedly different approach: not unbroken eulogy, but a critical analysis of Burke's adherence to his proclaimed beliefs, situated contextually as well as within a longer trajectory of the development of political thought. Geniuses or not, the 'lights of Liberalism' displayed a new learning, and a fresh desire for principles and systems that would bring the minds of men together. It is to the work of these Burke scholars that we now turn.

CRITICAL RECOVERY: THOUGHT

From the mid-1860s a series of articles and monographs began to cast Burke's thought and historical legacy in a different light. The most important of these were Fitzjames Stephen's articles in the *Saturday Review* (1863–8), (mostly republished in *Horae Sabbaticae*), Leslie Stephen's *History of English Thought in the Eighteenth Century* (1876), which contained a substantial chapter on Burke, and Morley's two books: *Edmund Burke: A Historical Study* (1867) and *Burke* (1879). Oxford's Clarendon Press also released a three-volume *Select Works* between 1874 and 1878, with a learned introduction from a lesser-known figure, E. J. Payne, Fellow of University College, Oxford, who wrote primarily on what was then called colonial history. In limiting Burke's works to three volumes (the *Present Discontents* and American speeches, *Reflections*, and the *Letters on a Regicide Peace*), Payne's edition aimed at providing schools with accessible editions of English Classics. In size and critical commentary, however, Payne's introductions are of a very different breed

---

[71] Napier, *Edmund Burke: A Lecture Delivered*, 59–64.
[72] Morley, *Edmund Burke: A Historical Study* (1867), 76.
[73] 'History of the Life and Times of Edmund Burke', *British Quarterly Review* (July 1858), 232–3.

from the brief, straightforward, abridged schoolbooks produced from the 1890s (detailed in Chapter 7, 'At School'), and his scholarly ability was recognized by reviewers too.[74] Payne is therefore treated alongside better-known figures such as Morley and the Stephens, as being primarily concerned with the task of recovering Burke as a significant, consistent political thinker. Finally, Burke was also publicized within much more broadly based texts, such as J. R. Green's *Short History of the English People* (1874).[75]

In contrast to the queries raised about Burke's debts to Lord Rockingham, Fitzjames Stephen's response to Macknight's biography described Burke as a founder of 'modern Liberal Conservatism'.[76] At first sight this appellation is reminiscent of Russell's 1852 quip that 'Conservative-Liberal' expressed in seven syllables what 'Whig' said in one—as was also the case for Lord Aberdeen's 'Conservative Progress'.[77] Nonetheless, Fitzjames Stephen's review represents a first step in the long process which established Burke as a canonical 'conservative' political thinker. It was not until the 1860s, however, that Stephen began his scheme of articles on political thinkers for the *Saturday Review*, including a series on Burke which appeared intermittently between 1863 and 1868.[78] Stephen was in no doubt, in 1865, that Burke could be comfortably labelled a 'political thinker'. Burke had an 'eminently un-English temper of holding political principles absolutely, applying them without modification or compromise, and enforcing them with acrimonious and unsparing vehemence'. Clearly, this was not a characteristic Stephen held in high regard—Burke was *too* principled a thinker. Burke's 'chief merit as a political thinker', however, was that the principles themselves, practical utility and expediency, were 'totally removed from French models'.[79]

It was this which led Fitzjames Stephen to believe that it was possible to demonstrate Burke's overall consistency of thought. He argued, in 1867, that there were not one but two ways to do this: the first was to take the 'broad expositions' of the ideas contained in Burke's *Reflections* and the *Appeal from the New to the Old Whigs*, and demonstrate their existence in

---

[74] 'School-Books', *Academy* (23 Oct. 1875), 426.
[75] Green, *Short History of the English People*, 775–80.
[76] [Stephen], 'Edmund Burke', 372.
[77] Spencer Walpole, *Life of Lord John Russell* (1889), ii. 156. See also David Craig, 'Advanced Conservative Liberalism: Party and Principle in Trollope's Parliamentary Novels', *Victorian Literature and Culture*, 38 (2010), 355–71.
[78] Stephen, *Life of James Fitzjames Stephen*, 178; Colaiaco, *James Fitzjames Stephen*, 26.
[79] [J. F. Stephen], 'Burke on Popular Representation', *SR* (18 Sept. 1865), 394. Cf. Arnold on living by ideas as 'un-English'—although for Arnold, unlike Stephen, this was a good thing: 'The Function of Criticism at the Present Time' [1864], *Essays in Criticism*, 17–18.

his earlier 'political speculations'; the second option, which was less systematic but 'more instructive', was to follow a 'natural and chronological order, collecting principal doctrines on political and moral subjects'.[80] It was from this latter method that it could be shown that 'expediency is... the basis of all his speculation, and the first rule of expediency is to set out from existing facts'. This made Burke 'from first to last a utilitarian of the strongest kind' but—crucially—this was 'like almost all the principal writers, on what may broadly be called the orthodox side in the eighteenth century'.[81] Burke was in fact accused of being *too* consistent because he refused to apply new principles between the American and French Revolutions.[82] The result was to place Burke within a broad empirical tradition, but this was not Stephen's final judgement on the nature of Burke's thought.

Fitzjames Stephen admired Burke as 'the one Englishman [*sic*] who has succeeded in attaining first-rate eminence both in politics and literature by one and the same set of writings'.[83] Yet he fluctuated in his assessment of Burke's thought itself. By 1868, in his articles on Burke's French writings, he had decided that Burke's interest in practical utility, including his belief in working within existing institutional arrangements, was an important component of his 'system' but this was subservient to a higher 'duty to God'. Burke was therefore 'an a priori reasoner on politics' because, Stephen wrote, Burke believed that God appointed an order for the whole human race; that this order must be reverenced as the work of God; but that it must also be improved because it was designed by God for the benefit of man.[84] It was therefore the French Revolutionary writings which best displayed 'the nature of his political philosophy'.[85] So Burke was presented as an empirically minded thinker, but *not* as a pure empiricist: 'an immutable divine decree lies at the root of every part of Burke's political theories', although this gives rise to the occasional incredulous query: 'did Burke mean to say that God gave two members to Old Sarum?'[86] Admiration for Burke is however ultimately outweighed by Stephen's profound dislike of inductive reasoning. Burke was an important and consistent political thinker, but not a suitable guide to a truly

---

[80] Stephen, 'Burke on the English Constitution' (28 Dec. 1867), *HS*, iii. 113–14.

[81] Ibid. That English ethical thought in the eighteenth century was utilitarian—in contrast to the Scots—was a commonplace that long predated Stephen: see James Mackintosh's *Dissertation on the Progress of Ethical Philosophy* (1830).

[82] Stephen, 'Burke on the English Constitution', iii. 121.

[83] Stephen, 'The Works of Burke' (19 Oct. 1867), *HS*, iii. 93.

[84] Stephen, 'Burke on the French Revolution' (29 Feb. 1868), *HS*, iii. 140, 142.

[85] Ibid., iii. 131. [86] Ibid., iii. 144.

deductive political theory, even for a 'conservative' utilitarian who placed great emphasis on the utility of existing institutions.

John Morley's analogous demonstrations of Burke's political thought were published in book form in 1867 as *Edmund Burke: A Historical Study*. 'It is surely impossible,' he pleaded, 'to deny the title of thinker to one who perceived, as Burke did, the profound speculative truth that politics is not a science of abstract ideas, but an empirical art, with morality for its standard.' Burke had mastered the 'great doctrine' that 'nothing universal can be rationally affirmed on any moral or political subject'.[87] Again, then, Burke's empiricism and pragmatism were again praised. But this was not Morley's final judgement either. Like Fitzjames Stephen, he believed in Burke's internal consistency—an intellectual attribute which Morley held extremely high. He later stated in *Rousseau* (1873) that 'a man's life ought to be steadily composed to oneness with itself in all its parts'.[88] Thus, in 1867, Morley explains how Burke's later history (his 'contempt of the philosophic cabal') was the development of earlier principles and not separated, 'as Buckle, Brougham, and others maintained, by a deep chasm—impressed by age, toil, and the anguish of his son's death'.[89] Burke's consistency could also be found in his championship of minorities—French aristocrats as well as the 'friends of the people'.[90] Another principal element of consistency was that he had always revered, and refused to reform, the existing constitution— even though to Morley this was merely a 'machine'.[91]

That Morley was still a relatively little-known figure can be seen in the length and quantity of his reviews. While in 1867 he received only one paragraph in the *Athenaeum*, by 1879 *Burke* commanded two pages.[92] The general state of opinion regarding Burke in 1867 was, however, best exemplified by the article in the *Saturday Review*. It was extremely positive in its assessment of Morley's work, and conceded that Morley gave to the view of Burke's consistency, 'a force... it never had before, and with a slight hesitation we are inclined to admit that he has proven his point'. The spine of this consistency was as follows: 'Anything thoroughgoing, radical, or revolutionary, whether in politics, theology or ethics, was

---

[87] Morley, *Edmund Burke: A Historical Study* (1867), 20–3.
[88] John Morley, *Rousseau* (1873), i. 207–8.
[89] Morley, *Edmund Burke: A Historical Study* (1867), 35. For similar sentiments, see J. E. Thorold Rogers, *Historical Gleanings: A Series of Sketches* (1869), 150–2.
[90] Ibid., 54–5.
[91] Ibid., 133–4. Gladstone agreed: *Gleanings of Past Years, 1843–1878* (1879), i. 137.
[92] 'Edmund Burke: a Historical Sketch', *Athenaeum* (30 Nov. 1867), 723; 'English Men of Letters—Burke', *Athenaeum* (13 Sept. 1879), 334–6.

hateful to him in the last degree.'[93] But still, the *Saturday* continued, this did not amount to granting Burke the status of political thinker. His hatred of speculation, while 'useful and becoming in a statesman', sat 'strangely on a philosopher': there was 'little of the matter, and still less of the manner, of a thinker' in his contempt for paper constitutions and the rights of man.[94] In short, Morley could not reverse existing preconceptions overnight, and there was still work to be done that could convincingly establish antipathy to theory as part of a system of political thought, but the argument for Burke's consistency was beginning to take hold.

Morley continued to insist that Burke was due the title of political thinker in 1879. By this time, Morley's personal reputation had increased dramatically, and his second text on *Burke* garnered much more attention, and was by far the more popular of his two Burke studies.[95] Here Morley can be seen exploring the implications of any movement from literary work into politics, and the possible parallel that this had with his own life, as an intellectual in politics.[96] Having decided to leave his projected history of the French Revolution and turn to more practical work, Morley writes that Burke's union of practical politics with thought was not only consistent in principle, but that he saw public life as the 'field in which to test, and work out, and use with good effect' the moral ideas which were his 'genuine interest'.[97] The reason why people saw *Reflections* as a 'living' text could not simply be for its literary and rhetorical qualities. *Reflections* 'lives' because it 'contains a method, a set of informal principles, which, awakened into new life after the Revolution, rapidly transformed the current ways of thinking and feeling about all the most serious objects of our attention and have powerfully helped to give a richer substance to all modern literature'. *Reflections* was 'the first great sign that ideas on government and philosophy [set out by Locke] ... did not comprehend the whole truth nor the deepest truth about human character'.[98] It further signalled the beginning of a reaction covering 'the whole field of thought' of the next generation, by demonstrating the negative consequences of 'pure individualistic rationalism'.[99] This is, unmistakably, a second

---

[93] 'Mr. Morley on Burke', *SR* (9 Nov. 1867), 605. See also 'Edmund Burke: A Historical Sketch', *Examiner* (30 Nov. 1867), 757.
[94] Ibid., 606.
[95] 'Morley's Life of Burke', *SR* (16 Aug. 1879), 208–9; 'English Men of Letters—Burke', *Athenaeum*, 334–6; 'English Men of Letters – Burke', *QR* (Oct. 1879), 488–90. Leslie Stephen wrote to an American correspondent, Charles Norton, after reading *Burke*: 'Morley has just done "Burke" for his own series, and done it, I think, exceedingly well. To read Morley always makes me envious.' Quoted in Maitland, *Life and Letters of Leslie Stephen*, 338.
[96] Hamer, *John Morley*, 126.   [97] Morley, *Burke* (1879), 207.
[98] Ibid., 171.   [99] Ibid., 172.

attempt to assert Burke's status as a political thinker within the wider transformative moment of the French Revolution. On Burke's consistency he preached that

> It is unreasonable to tell us that he turned back on his course; that he was a revolutionist in 1770 and a reactionist in 1790; that he was in his sane mind when he opposed the supremacy of the Court, but that his reason was tottering when he opposed the supremacy of the Faubourg Saint Antoine.[100]

Morley refused, however, to go so far as to endorse Burke's writings after the *Appeal* (1791) as 'political philosophy': 'Our appreciation of Burke as a political thinker and contributor to political wisdom is at an end. He is now only... Cicero shrieking against Mark Antony.'[101] Morley's criticism here displayed lingering remnants of previous—unreconstructed—views. This placed a limit on how far he was prepared to admit Burke to the status of political thinker, and so supports the argument that this was only an early stage of a much wider process. In spite of this, as an earlier review of *Edmund Burke* in the *Examiner* suggested, it was because Morley dissented so much from Burke's politics, that his 'apology', or in Morley's later words 'glorification', became 'all the more noteworthy'.[102] He appeared as a fair judge in a way that Burke's earlier, more enthusiastic, biographers had not.

Contrastingly, and very reasonably, Edward John Payne was outraged by Morley's claim in *Burke* that the later Revolutionary writings were not the work of a serious thinker.[103] Previously, Payne had gone further than Morley and the Stephens in his critical sympathy and in his belief in the sanity and consistency of Burke's thought. After graduating from Oxford with first-class honours in the classical schools, Payne was elected Fellow of University College and his first scholarly enterprise had been the *History of the European Colonies* (1872). He then turned his attentions to an edition of Burke's works, the bar, and went on to contribute further historical scholarship on the colonies (notably for the Cambridge Modern History), and on the history of musical instruments.[104] In the first two volumes of Burke's works, published in 1874 and 1875, Payne criticized earlier French and German appropriators of Burke who 'forced him into

---

[100] Ibid., 169. This is lifted from *Edmund Burke: A Historical Study* (1867), 53–4.
[101] Morley, *Burke* (1879), 184.
[102] 'Edmund Burke: A Historical Sketch', *Examiner*, 757.
[103] E. J. Payne, 'Mr. Morley on Burke', *Academy* (18 Oct. 1879), 287. For Morley's response, see 'A Word with Some Critics', *FR* (Oct. 1879), 581.
[104] 'Obituary: Edward John Payne', *Geographical Journal* (Feb. 1905), 224–5; John R. Catch, 'Edward John Payne: Victorian Gambist', *Galpin Society Journal*, 50 (Mar. 1997), 127–35.

their systems' by turning him into a Catholic. Instead, Payne positioned Burke within a 'legal' (i.e. English constitutionalist) tradition, which viewed British liberty as something which advanced precedent by precedent, directly opposed to the 'rights of man method'—describing the former as the 'half-conscious tradition of this English philosophy of the State'.[105] However Payne was also deeply interested in speculative thought, 'the philosophy of history', and the evolution of groups and nations—all of which were noted by reviewers of his later works, such as his *History of the New World Called America* (1893-9) in which he traced the development of American civilization.[106]

These interests can also be seen in his editorial introduction to Burke's works. Here Payne described the 'political philosophy of Burke' as 'systematic and complete', although it did not pretend to be what was commonly understood as 'scientific theory'. Burke's main thesis, Payne explained, centred on a belief that society's motive force was incomprehensible to men and, as a consequence, it was futile to try to reconstruct it on allegedly analytical, but in reality mechanical, lines.[107] Payne's belief in Burke's consistency was paramount. He even argued, in his third and final volume of Burke's works, an edition of the *Letters on a Regicide Peace* published in 1878, that the *Letters* were in point of fact superior to *Reflections* for their knowledge, eloquence, and logical ability—they were 'the author's masterpiece'.[108] The French Revolution had not made him mad: 'He maintained to the last the perfect consistency of his political opinions...Burke was always what would now be called a *Conservative*.' This was not, however, directly connected to the political party, but represented instead a more general preference for existing establishments and 'distrust of what exists only in speculation'.[109] Thus, the *Examiner*, who commended Payne's scholarship, dismissed such a general label, since by the same logic 'the [Socialist] Internationalists would call [the atheist anti-socialist Radical] Mr. Bradlaugh a Conservative'.[110]

---

[105] *Burke: Select Works*, ed. E. J. Payne, i. viii; ii. xix, xxxvi.
[106] Franklin H. Giddings, 'History of the New World Called America', *Political Science Quarterly* (Dec. 1893), 733–6. For further reviews, see also Justin Winsor in *EHR* (Apr. 1893), 346–51; O. T. Mason in *American Anthropologist* (Jan. 1900), 170–2; and Frank Russell in the *American Historical Review* (July 1901), 796–9. Giddings accused Payne of reviving Buckle's 'theory of history, of social evolution'. To Payne this theory of historical progress was based upon physical conditions, such as whether animals were fit for domestication and plants for cultivation, as it was food supply that transformed social organization, religion, thought, and morals.
[107] *Burke: Select Works*, ed. E. J. Payne, ii. xxxvi.   [108] Ibid., iii. l.
[109] Ibid., i. xi.   [110] 'Notes on Books', *Examiner* (24 Oct. 1874), 1166.

In the midst of Morley and Payne's publications appeared Leslie Stephen's *History of English Thought in the Eighteenth Century* (1876).[111] Here was another example of a clear statement of Burke's status and consistency as a significant political thinker. To Leslie Stephen, all English theorists—Bentham as well as Burke, along with Delolme and the 'constitution-mongers'—agreed substantially that political truth must be based upon experience. This was due to the 'social condition of England' as well as the 'English dislike' of 'sweeping abstract theories' which 'prevented us from adopting the metaphysical or quasi-mathematical mode of political reasoning'.[112] So Burke is placed firmly within a broad-based *English* tradition, centred not on the constitution but on a more general 'English' dislike of theory. Unlike Bentham or the constitutionalists, however, Burke's 'magnificent imagination and true philosophical insight' led him to 'a genuine historical theory'.[113] Burke had seen that the majority of 'men's' thoughts and interests were developments and inheritances from their ancestors, and therefore held 'the corresponding doctrine, that reform is impractical in the sense of an abrupt reconstruction'.[114] It was Burke's evolutionary historicism which the Darwinian Stephen most approved of, but which—as he later remarked in *The English Utilitarians* (1900)—was as uncongenial to utilitarians as to revolutionists.[115] Hence, Stephen saw Burke's 'greatest title to speculative eminence' as lying in his early realization that

> a nation was a living organism, of infinitely complex structure, of intimate dependence upon the parts, and to be treated by politicians in obedience to a careful observation of the laws of its healthy development. To them [the French Revolutionaries], a nation was an aggregate of independent units, to be regulated by a set of a priori maxims.[116]

Burke also had a 'triumphant and conclusive' answer to any charge of inconsistency: throughout his political life, his efforts had always sought to maintain the equipoise of the constitution. Stephen noted: 'It is only on the theory that a man who approves of one is bound to approve of all revolts, or that a man who is opposed to corrupt influence of any power, must be opposed to its existence, that the charge [of inconsistency] could be made plausible.'[117] Stephen, who like Payne was much less interested in practical politics than Morley, explicitly looks beyond the 'narrow

---

[111] Maitland includes a letter noting that a preliminary 250 copies were ordered by one American publisher: *Life and Letters of Leslie Stephen*, 293.
[112] Stephen, *History of English Thought*, ii. 280.   [113] Ibid., ii. 266.
[114] Ibid., ii. 230.
[115] Leslie Stephen, *The English Utilitarians* (1900), ii. 367.
[116] Stephen, *History of English Thought*, ii. 248–9.   [117] Ibid., ii. 249.

limits' of party to stress that Burke, 'as a thinker', always expounded 'the same principles, applies the same tests, and holds to the same essential truths'.[118] The Revolutionary context simply strengthened 'Burke's conservatism': 'his whole conception of political science is radically unaltered, and his method shows the same characteristic peculiarities'.[119]

Still, as with the other authors, Leslie Stephen is critical of Burke. According to Stephen, Burke had failed to see the link between the American and French revolutions, and hence the significance of the role he himself had played challenging established rights (of taxation) in the American case. In contrast to his brother's judgement that Burke's thought was primarily inductive, Stephen placed Burke with 'the cruder empiricists' because he believed that Burke denied the possibility of basing general principles upon experience. Burke was therefore presented by Stephen as of limited use, either to himself or to other writers such as Morley who wanted to reconcile 'expediency with morality': what they were looking for was a much broader ethical framework that went beyond Benthamite utilitarianism. Burke, as the greatest exponent of the historical method, had provided a 'road' to constructing such a system, but he and 'the Conservatives' had not solved the problem itself.[120] So Burke was useful as a guide, but stopped short of developing a positive system acceptable to Stephen. 'The problem of constituting a science of politics,' Stephen regretted, 'has not yet been solved.'[121] Hence Stephen's inference, present both here and in his later work, that Burke's thought was still essentially philosophical. Stephen would later remark, in *Hours in a Library*, that although it was tempting to compare Burke with Macaulay, there was a fundamental difference which made this impossible: 'Burke's superiority is marked by this, that he is primarily a philosopher... Macaulay, on the contrary, gets away from theory as fast as possible.'[122]

The reader is therefore left with an unclear diagnosis of Burke's relative empiricism, or utilitarianism. Morley, Fitzjames, and Leslie Stephen all describe Burke in places as a 'utilitarian' but they also contrast his thought directly with Bentham. Clearly this 'utilitarianism' was not classical, Benthamite utilitarianism, whatever else it might have been. Nor is any systematic exploration of Burke's utilitarianism offered; these authors simply apply the general label. If we then ask what kind of utilitarianism was portrayed by these writers, the answer is a very vague utilitarianism that might be better described as a broad empiricism, which was linked to a much longer-standing English tradition of empiricism, of which

---

[118] Ibid., ii. 249–50. [119] Ibid., ii. 249. [120] Ibid., ii. 280, 266.
[121] Ibid., ii. 281.
[122] Stephen, 'Macaulay', *Hours in a Library*, new edn (1892), iii. 360–1.

utilitarianism was just one part. It is equally evident that the assumed link between utility, expediency, and 'liberal' or 'radical' beliefs must be queried: utility and expediency, even within a systematically deployed theoretical framework, are not intrinsically 'liberal' or 'radical' and can be used equally to support the maintenance or reform of existing institutions, beliefs, or habits. In this sense it is perfectly plausible to be both 'utilitarian' and 'conservative'.

Yet even this broadly empirical reading was not clear-cut. Fitzjames Stephen judged Burke to have been an inductive thinker, who nonetheless believed in divine providence, and this 'mysticism' also formed an important part of Payne's analysis. In fact, it was the perception of Burke's overarching religious beliefs that posed the greatest problem for his new interpreters—all of whom were interested in the place of religion and belief in systems of thought and this in turn affected the usefulness of Burke for mid-Victorian agnostics. Morley, Leslie, and Fitzjames Stephen were all admirers of Lecky's *History of Rationalism in Europe* which, inspired by Buckle, charted the decline of belief in magic and miracles, and the rise of rationalism.[123] Burke's belief in a divinely ordered world (whether Catholic or Anglican[124]) therefore limited his usefulness to these advanced Liberals because it came to be seen as a hindrance to free thought, the questioning of established norms, and the subsequent exposition of 'truth', which would ensure the future progress of mankind.[125] Thus, to Morley in 1867, Burke's defence of mandatory subscription to the Thirty-Nine Articles in 1772 was 'an attitude identical with that of the least liberal and enlightened people amongst ourselves'.[126] A few pages later Morley proclaimed:

> He [Burke] never swerved in his antipathy to free thought, whether in politics, in theology, or in ethics. To examine with a curious or unfavourable eye the bases of established opinions was to show a leaning to anarchy in one order, to atheism in another, to unbridled libertinism in the third.[127]

A year later, in 1868, Fitzjames Stephen stated that it was the 'possibility and morality' of a non-religious association in France that Burke 'denied and branded atheism and anarchy'. But as this possibility, Stephen asserted, was now beyond doubt, Burke's 'most cherished doctrines' had

---

[123] W. E. H. Lecky, *History of the Rise and Influence of the Spirit of Rationalism in Europe* (1865); Stephen, *Life and Letters of Leslie Stephen*, 200. For Lecky and Buckle, see Semmel, 'Buckle', 381–3.
[124] See 'Church and State' in Chapter 2 in this volume.
[125] Stephen, *Life and Letters of Leslie Stephen*, 230; Morley, *On Compromise*, 10, 112, passim. For Stephen, see Young, *Victorian Eighteenth Century*, ch. 4.
[126] Morley, *Edmund Burke: A Historical Study* (1867), 37.   [127] Ibid., 46.

been 'emphatically and directly contradicted by experience'. The French Revolution had unearthed a live question: is any system of religion and morals true? It was this question which demanded immediate attention, and was one to which Burke's response was not deemed adequate.[128] In the same way, Leslie Stephen's *History of English Thought* criticized Burke's defence of the established church. Stephen's text, which also served as a rationalist attack on the church, unsurprisingly belittled Burke on this matter: 'he seems almost to think that the truth of the doctrines preached by so useful a body should never be questioned'.[129] This was the 'weaker side of Burke's teaching', because he wished to strengthen faith by stifling free discussion, and forgot 'that a religion supported by a dread of awkward discussions must crumble when assailed by active opponents'.[130] Burke had appreciated the fundamental continuity of the social organism, but—drawing on a different organic metaphor—had failed to see the rot and decay in systems of religious belief, as well as in politics and society more generally, and the correlative germination of new ideas and beliefs.

As a result, these writers frequently, though not always, label Burke's thought as 'C/conservative'. In 1867, Morley described Burke's theory as the 'Whig and oligarchic theory at its best'.[131] This was government for the people, but not by the people.[132] Burke had recognized quite correctly that there was a 'collective reason of ages' which even in a time of revolution it was 'monstrous to overlook'. This was more than 'mere conservative passion', and Morley evidently approved. 'This may be Toryism,' he concluded, 'but it is Toryism on its noble and exalted side.'[133] J. R. Green came to the same conclusion a few years later: 'his temper was... conservative, but his conservatism sprang not from a love of inaction but from a sense of the value of the social order, and from an imaginative reverence for all that existed'.[134] It was this reverence for order and existing institutions that, in 1879, Morley identified as the basis of his rage against Hastings as well as the French revolutionaries: 'a noble and philosophic conservatism rather than philanthropy... raised that storm in Burke's breast against the rapacity of English adventures in India'.[135] By 1879 Morley was also able to set Burke's 'conservative' Whiggism in an international context, which blurred the 'minute' differences of opinion between English Whigs (such as Burke) and English Tories (such as

---

[128] Stephen, 'Burke on the French Revolution', *HS*, iii. 150–2.
[129] Stephen, *History of English Thought*, ii. 229; Zink, *Leslie Stephen*, 100.
[130] Ibid., ii. 230.
[131] Morley, *Edmund Burke: A Historical Study* (1867), 115.
[132] Ibid., 14.   [133] Ibid., 281–2.
[134] Green, *Short History*, 776.   [135] Morley, *Burke* (1879), 130–1.

Samuel Johnson) in comparison to the 'French philosophic party', and led him to conclude that *Reflections* placed Burke 'among the great Conservatives of history'.[136] This was also the conclusion of J. R. Seeley (1834–95), a Broad Church historian influenced by Maurice and Arnold who also nurtured an interest in Positivism. Writing in *Macmillan's* later that year, he claimed that Burke believed in the 'divine right of the constitution, though not of the king. He denies the right of human reason to discuss fundamental political institutions...And therefore without consciously abandoning his old Whiggism he founded modern Conservatism.'[137]

It is crucial to note, however, that Morley in particular was fully aware that Burke lacked clear political descendants, and that his 1879 audience still needed to be persuaded. It is worth quoting the final passage of *Burke* at length in order to obtain the full sense of this:

> The Coleridgean school are Burke's direct descendants, whenever they deal with the significance of Church and State. But they connected these views so closely with their views on metaphysics and theology that the association with Burke was effectively disguised...The conservative movement in England ran on for many years in the ecclesiastical channel, rather than among questions where Burke's writings might have been brought to bear. On the political side the most active minds, both in practice and theory, worked out the principles of liberalism, and they did so on a plan and by methods from which Burke's utilitarian liberalism and his historic conservatism were equally remote. There are many signs around us that this epoch is for the moment at an end. The historic method, fitting in with certain dominant conceptions in the region of natural science, is bringing men round to a way of looking at society for which Burke's maxims are exactly suited; and it seems probable that he will be more frequently and more seriously referred to within the next twenty years than he has been for the whole of the last eighty.[138]

The *Saturday Review* agreed, and explained to readers that Morley was referring to 'hereditary tendencies' and 'historical evolution' in the wake of Darwinism and the related impact of 'science' on Victorian thought.[139]

---

[136] Ibid., 110, 174. See also Morley's *Life of Richard Cobden*, new edn (1895), 167: Here Morley uses Burke, 'the most magnificent genius that the Conservative spirit has ever attracted' and 'one of the earliest assailants of legislative interference in the corn trade', to argue against the idea that there was an 'essential bond' between agricultural protection and 'Conservative policy'.

[137] J. R. Seeley, 'History and Politics', *Macmillan's* (Oct. 1879), 449–58.

[138] Morley, *Burke* (1879), 215–16.

[139] 'Morley's Life of Burke', *SR*, 206. See also Mark Francis and John Morrow, *History of English Political Thought in the Nineteenth Century* (1994), 205; J. W. Burrow, *Evolution and Society: A Study in Victorian Social Thought* (1966).

Payne had also claimed that in Britain the 'school of Burke' was best represented by Coleridgeans (the 'Liberal Anglicans' discussed in Chapters 1 and 2), but still that no useful line of descent could be drawn. For Payne too, Burke held 'a peculiar place in general literature' because he had no clear successors in British political life, even though *Reflections* was the 'best text-book of Conservatism which has ever appeared'.[140] This was in complete contrast to his afterlife in France and Germany, and Payne discussed England's aloofness from Europe further in the following volume, quipping that England was closer to New York and Bombay than Paris and Vienna.[141] It was also at this time that the philosopher Henry Sidgwick made the comment, noted in Chapter 2, that 'though Burke lives, we meet with no Burkites'.[142] Burke's legacy was given new life by these admiring critics, but it had yet to be sufficiently connected to a particular political party or group.

CRITICAL RECOVERY: CHARACTER

Besides their interest in Burke as a consistent political thinker, his new interpreters were also keen to raise the status of Burke's character after years of gossip and speculation on his personal affairs. This was part and parcel of a holistic recuperative effort: Burke's greatness in part stemmed from his wider personal character. As avid readers of Mill's *System of Logic*, Morley and the Stephens were well acquainted with Mill's argument, from Book VI, on the difference between higher and lower 'types' of characters; the need to foster the creation of the higher 'type'; and the desirability of founding a 'science of character', which Mill called 'ethology', in order to achieve this end.[143] In addition to the ethical concerns contained within his writings, Mill himself was revered for his personal radicalism and political courage,[144] and it has been widely established that ideas of 'character' permeated Victorian thinking more generally.[145] These have then been linked to changing conceptions of 'manliness' which increasingly favoured stout, rugged independence, and denigrated puny,

---

[140] *Burke: Select Works*, ed. E. J. Payne, ii. xxv. [141] Ibid., iii. xliv–xlv.
[142] Henry Sidgwick, 'Bentham and Benthamism in Politics and Ethics' [1877], *Miscellaneous Essays*, 136.
[143] Mill, *System of Logic*, bk. vi; Jones, 'John Stuart Mill as Moralist', 287–308.
[144] Harvie, *Lights of Liberalism*, 151.
[145] Stefan Collini, 'The Idea of "Character" in Victorian Political Thought', *TRHS*, 5th ser., 35 (1985), 29–50; Craig, 'Statesmanship', in Craig and Thompson, *Languages of Politics*, 56–60.

effeminate 'sentimentalism'.[146] This forms an important context for considering the ways in which Burke was made appetizing through new interpretations, as his whole personality was made more appealing—but this was done in a very different manner from previous, overenthusiastic biographers such as Macknight. 'Burke was a real man,' Abbey and Overton proclaimed in their *History of the English Church in the Eighteenth Century* (1878), 'if there ever was one.'[147] This re-working of Burke's public and personal character was explicitly ethical. The highest object of Morley's 1867 book, he stated, was to estimate Burke's contribution to the progress of mankind—the study of history itself being 'moral training'.[148] Likewise, for Leslie Stephen, an acceptable view of morality had to take into account whether a person had made the world better or worse, and take into consideration the impact of an individual's actions on society and their relationship to the moral code of the time.[149] These writers were not 'public moralists' in a Christian sense, but they did possess a kind of ethical system.[150]

An extraneous source of inspiration here was Giuseppe Mazzini (1805–72), who was an important intellectual influence on Morley in particular, as well as a number of other Victorian Liberals.[151] Mazzini has been described as 'the greatest ideologue of nineteenth-century European nationalism', and his work—especially *The Duties of Man* (1858, English trans. 1862) was celebrated by progressive Liberals in England.[152] Mazzini, along with a number of European thinkers such as Johann Gottlieb Fichte and Ernest Renan, as well as—crucially—the 'Liberal Anglican' Coleridgeans Thomas Arnold and Maurice, was preoccupied with ideas of nationality, culture, and the organic state.[153] Mazzini would also be a formative influence on the Idealist Burke scholars who are discussed in later chapters, such as John MacCunn and C. E. Vaughan. Morley, who knew and corresponded with Mazzini, was of course far from being a

---

[146] John Tosh, 'Gentlemanly Politeness and Manly Simplicity in Victorian England', *TRHS*, 6th ser., 12 (2002), 455–72.
[147] C. J. Abbey and J. H. Overton, *The English Church in the Eighteenth Century* (1878), ii. 407–8.
[148] Morley, *Edmund Burke: A Historical Study* (1867), 55.
[149] Annan, *Leslie Stephen*, 245.   [150] Morley, *On Compromise*, 137–8.
[151] Morley, *Recollections*, i. 72–3.
[152] G. Mazzini, *The Duties of Man* (1862); Jones, *Victorian Political Thought*, xii. See also Christopher Bayly and Eugenio Biagini, *Giuseppe Mazzini and the Globalization of Democratic Nationalism, 1830–1920* (2008); Marcella Pellegrino Sutcliffe, *Victorian Radicals and Italian Democrats* (2014); Harvie, *Lights of Liberalism*, 101–2; Alon Kadish, *Apostle Arnold: The Life and Death of Arnold Toynbee* (1986), 2; Arnold Toynbee, *Lectures on the Industrial Revolution in England* (1884), 200: 'Not Adam Smith, not Carlyle...but Mazzini is the true teacher of our age.'
[153] Jones, *Victorian Political Thought*, 44.

'Liberal Anglican', but it is nonetheless possible to identify in his thought a sincere belief that the nation acted as a 'moral arena' in which we learn our duties to others.[154] Mazzini was, to Morley, 'the moral genius who spiritualized politics, and gave a new soul to public duty in citizens and nations'.[155] Politics could therefore be seen as a branch of ethics, and this necessitated a combined re-evaluation of Burke's moral nature as well as his political thought.

In what ways was Burke's character presented positively? In a similar vein to the writers discussed in Chapter 3, Burke was rendered as having a noble and generous spirit. He had a deep concern for the welfare of others, whether they were farmers on his estate or mistreated Indian and Irish subjects. It was stated once more that there was nobility in Burke's zeal for the well-being of mankind, and in his drive to use his position as an MP as a means to this end. Leslie Stephen announced that 'Burke alone felt that even the machinery of party might be used in the interest of mankind.' In doing so, Burke was judged to have elevated the status of parliament itself. 'The greatness of Burke as a political thinker,' Stephen continued, 'cannot be adequately appreciated without noticing the nobility of his moral nature.' He stood above all of his contemporaries in his 'combination of width of view with keenness of sympathy', and this was displayed in his arguments regarding the wrongs of Massachusetts, the Middlesex electors, and Ireland.[156] On this occasion Stephen even defended Burke's irritable temper, by asserting that he was always 'the most powerful and least selfish [voice] on the side of honour, justice, and mercy'. This was, to the rational empiricist Stephen, of even greater importance than the fact that his views on political economy were far in advance of his time.[157]

Similarly, Morley, in 1867, followed Burke 'from the heat and violence' of the House of Commons where drunken squires 'derided the greatest man of their time', to his home in Beaconsfield. Here Burke would give food to the starving beggar, medicine to the sick peasant, and talk farming with the labourers.[158] Meanwhile Fox, the hero of Burke's Whig detractors, was squandering thousands of pounds through gambling.[159] Fox, portrayed as a licentious Georgian, was used as a contrast to further emphasize Morley's presentation of Burke as a selfless public figure, suited to Victorian ideals of public duty. His public and private moralities were one:

---

[154] Ibid., 50. [155] Morley, *Recollections*, i. 75.
[156] Stephen, *History of English Thought*, ii. 222. [157] Ibid., ii. 223.
[158] Morley, *Edmund Burke: A Historical Study* (1867), 56. [159] Ibid., 57.

He really did what so large a majority of public men feign to do. He forgot that he had any interests of his own to be promoted, apart from the interests of the party with which he acted and from those of the whole nation, for which he held himself a trustee... Above all things, he achieved honourable and independent political distinction, at a time which it was much harder for a plebeian to achieve distinction on such terms as it is now.[160]

To Morley, Burke's attack on the mistreatment of the Indian people affected a 'revolution' in the spirit of English government: he single-handedly produced a substantial shift in public opinion on imperial abuses, and therefore the ethics of empire.[161] Burke is made to seem morally powerful—regardless of his actual political influence at the time, or the fact that the impeachment of Warren Hastings was unsuccessful—and this Anglocentric view seems to have governed Morley's later attitude to India as Secretary of State from 1906.[162] This sense of Burke's authoritative moral character can also be seen in Morley's 1879 text, which is peppered with adjectives describing Burke as 'stout' and 'manly'. Similarly, Burke's pragmatic engagement with political issues contributed to the development of his sincerely moral political thought: Burke lived 'in the real world' rather than a 'false dream of the past' and this was what produced his 'moral, historic, conservative imagination'. For Morley this was really quite different from the 'literary or romantic conservatism' of a thinker such as Chateaubriand. He was very clear that Burke's 'conservative doctrine' was a profound instinct, political and moral, but mostly moral.[163] And by stressing the nobility of Burke's whole character, in tandem with the account of his thought discussed above, Morley could convincingly argue that any monetary debts left outstanding were of minor significance compared to Burke's magnificent 'greatness'.[164]

A second important component of Burke's character lay in his perceived 'independence'. Mill had claimed in 1824 that a true representative of the people would speak up for the public good on each occasion, regardless of party.[165] As noted in Chapter 2, praise of Burke's independence more often than not focused on his relationship with party politics, and the actions which he took that were consistent with his professed principles (for example, on Catholic relief or the French Revolution), but were nonetheless in defiance of either popular opinion (in the former

---

[160] Ibid., 57–8.   [161] Ibid., 208.
[162] Jon Wilson, 'The Silence of Empire: Imperialism and Empire', in Craig and Thompson, *Languages of Politics*, 233–4; Koss, *Morley and the India Office*, 127–30, 136–7, 162; Hamer, *John Morley*, 346–7, 385.
[163] Morley, *Burke* (1879), 66.   [164] Ibid., 36–7.
[165] J. S. Mill, 'Periodical Literature', *WR* (Apr. 1824), 527–30; Collini, Winch, and Burrow, *Noble Science of Politics*, 109.

instance) and/or members of his political party (as in the latter). In each case, Burke was seen to have upheld his principles and refused to conform to the expectations of either popular public opinion or high political party loyalty. This quality was celebrated by Fitzjames Stephen who stood as a parliamentary candidate, and by Morley who became an MP and cabinet minister.[166] As an outspoken advocate, Burke was again positioned as an early sponsor of the liberties enjoyed, or beginning to be enjoyed, in the nineteenth century—free trade and the emancipation of slaves as well as Catholics—though this was of course offset by Burke's noted aversion to free thought in other areas, such as parliamentary reform. Leslie Stephen, who in our trio of writers was the least interested in party politics, saw Burke as 'incomparably the greatest intellectual power of all English politicians' who threw his labours into fighting against the tyranny of kings, penal laws, and English brutality in India.[167] Here was a way of promoting Burke as a national, non-partisan political figure, and an example for modern statesmanship.

But again, this praise was not without limitations—the critical approach of these authors was, after all, precisely what made their studies reputable. Burke was criticized when he was seen to act against his 'long-held' principles in the name of party loyalty. For Morley he damaged his integrity on the few occasions in which he followed the party leadership, rather than acting out his own previously stated principles.[168] Fitzjames and Leslie Stephen also disliked Burke's lapses into 'sentimentalism' or 'sentimental rhetoric' in the cases of Marie Antoinette (for Leslie[169]) and Warren Hastings (for Fitzjames). In his *Life* of his brother, Leslie Stephen remarked how 'hard' Fitzjames had been on Burke in *Nuncomar and Impey* (a study of one the supposed judicial wrongs of Hastings and his Chief Justice Elijah Impey). Burke had been 'misled', Leslie explained, by generous feelings into 'the sentimental rhetoric by which he [Fitzjames] was always irritated'. As a result, Burke was then treated by Fitzjames like 'a barrister trying to introduce totally irrelevant eloquence'.[170]

---

[166] [Stephen], 'Burke on Popular Representation', 395; Morley, *Edmund Burke: A Historical Study* (1867), 27; W. C. Lubenow, *The Cambridge Apostles, 1820–1914: Liberalism, Imagination, and Friendship in British Intellectual and Professional Life* (1998), 13.
[167] Stephen, *History of English Thought*, ii. 223.
[168] Morley, *Burke* (1879), 125.
[169] Stephen, *History of English Thought*, ii. 247.
[170] Stephen, *Life and Letters of Leslie Stephen*, 433; Stephen, *Nuncomar and Impey*, ii. 87. It has been suggested that pure sensationalist sentimentalism is the reason why Fitzjames turned away from a clerical career towards Benthamite 'facts' and evidence: James C. Livingston, 'The Religious Creed and Criticism of Sir James Fitzjames Stephen', *VS*, 17 (1974), 279–300.

Clearly, Burke was not perfect, nor without weakness. Criticism aside, the overall effect of the reconsideration of Burke's character was to provide a non-partisan assessment of Burke as a man. Mainstream opinion began to follow where the critical recoverers had led the way. For example, in his review of Payne's *Select Works* for the Tory *Quarterly Review* in 1878, Montagu Burrows (1819–1905), a Tory constitutionalist and the first Chichele Professor of Modern History at All Souls College, Oxford, did not attempt to claim Burke for the Conservatives, but instead described Burke, out of all political writers, as 'the most resolute in striking into the middle path between party-views'.[171] Burke was 'a patriot before all things', but never a selfish or isolated patriot. It was this which made Burke such an important source for all future politicians and public servants, Liberal or Conservative.[172] Shortly afterwards, in *Imperial England* (1880), Burrows hailed Burke as 'the High Priest of the British Constitution'.[173] Thanks to these re-readings of Burke's life and work, it was becoming far easier to celebrate Burke as a national hero.

CONCLUSION

There can be no doubt that, by 1880, a substantial body of revisionist historiography on Burke's thought and character had been produced. Its authors, and their more sympathetic reviewers, promoted Burke as a significant historical, literary, and political-philosophical figure. They saw his direct relevance to a mid-Victorian audience increasingly preoccupied with organic and evolutionary thinking. Burke was greatly admired by his new, Liberal, commentators, but this did not equate to a simple appropriation of Burke as a Liberal—utilitarian, Positivist, or otherwise. Unsurprisingly, however, they preferred Burke attacking George III and his friends to the sentimental eulogies of Marie Antoinette and a 'rotten' *ancien régime*. Hence they were all willing to admit the limitations Burke had for advanced thinkers: his religious beliefs and love of things established made Burke 'conservative'. In a fight between truth and order, Burke would have sided with order. What Morley, the Stephens, Payne, and others actually presented was a morally admirable, intellectually consistent political thinker who had pioneered the historic and organic conception of society and was more or less rooted to a long-standing English empirical tradition.

---

[171] [Burrows], 'Burke, Select Works', 332. For similar sentiments, see [Anon.], 'The Expansion of England', *QR* (July 1884), 161. This had also been Macknight's view.
[172] Ibid.   [173] Montagu Burrows, *Imperial England* (1880), 85–7.

The books of Morley, Leslie Stephen, and Payne were well-received when they were published and became even more notable as the influence and status of their authors increased. Morley went on to serve as an MP, a cabinet minister, and eventually accepted a peerage and the Chancellorship of the University of Manchester. Fitzjames Stephen became a judge and a baronet, and his essays on Burke obtained second hearing as they were re-published in his own name in 1892. Leslie Stephen, meanwhile, was awarded a number of professorships and honorary degrees, and after the death of Matthew Arnold came to be seen as the country's most preeminent man of letters. Morley and Leslie Stephen also forged links with America: not only were American editions of their work commissioned, but connections were developed by regular correspondence, lecture tours, and through the liberal periodical *The Nation*, which published Stephen's letters and reviewed Morley's books. Even E. J. Payne, though not a major figure in Victorian intellectual history, had an important afterlife as his edition of Burke's works went through a number of twentieth-century reprints.

But while the overall effect of these texts was to present Burke as a consistent political thinker there was still variation and vagueness in the analysis: he is presented within the same text or group of texts (such as Payne's editions or Fitzjames Stephen's articles) as a C/conservative, a constitutional Liberal, and as a patriot who was between parties. Vital as these presentations were, they were still an early stage of a longer process, which was some way away from what would in fact prove to be the end result: self-conscious *Conservative* integration of Burke within a deliberately remodelled 'Tory' or 'Conservative' tradition. The starting point for this remarkable transformation lay in the Irish Home Rule Bill of 1886.

5
Irish Home Rule, *c.*1886–1893

> It is the fashion now to quote Burke.
> *Fortnightly Review*, 1887[1]

The status of Edmund Burke as a political thinker was transformed by the debates over Ireland and Home Rule in the 1880s. By this point his Irish identity was already strongly entrenched, but his authority on Irish and British politics was now raised to an entirely new level. One of the first expressions of this development was Matthew Arnold's publication of Burke's writings on *Irish Affairs* (1881), accompanied by the explicit wish that they would influence present-day thinking on Ireland.[2] In subsequent discussions, Burke was invoked by Home Rulers, such as Gladstone, by political opportunists such as William Harcourt, and by Unionists, including W. E. H. Lecky and A. V. Dicey. Already considered a master of political wisdom on topics such as political parties and the duties of an MP to his constituents, this sphere was expanded by Home Rule. Burke was quoted in speeches, letters, pamphlets, articles, and books on the topic, and his works were recited with enthusiasm in parliament. Of course, this also precipitated a critical backlash against Burke's new celebrity. Nonetheless, the Home Rule debates were a crucial moment in the formation of Burke's reputation and his integration within the mainstream of English thought. Without Home Rule, it would have been impossible to make statements such as the epigraph above or the remark of the Tory bishop of Ripon, William Boyd Carpenter (1841–1918), in 1897 that 'every politician of the nineteenth century was happy if he could only shelter himself under the authority of Edmund Burke'.[3]

---

[1] [Anon.], 'Home Affairs: A National Party', *FR* (July 1887), 151.
[2] Burke, *Irish Affairs*. For a light polemical introduction to this topic, see Conor Cruise O'Brien, 'Setting People on Thinking: Burke's Legacy in the Debate on Irish Affairs', in Ian Crowe, ed., *Edmund Burke: His Life and Legacy* (1997).
[3] 'Extension Students at Oxford', *The Times* (2 Aug. 1897), 8.

Ireland was a pre-eminent theme of British politics throughout Gladstone's second ministry from 1880 to 1885, and this was the context for Arnold's edition of Burke. Nonetheless, Home Rule—the proposal for a devolved Irish parliament in Dublin—remained a marginal issue and it received little notice from the British parties in the general election of autumn 1885, the result of which left Gladstone as the prime minister designate. The political universe was then transformed by the 'Hawarden Kite' of December 1885, when news first broke of Gladstone's conversion to the cause. The Home Rule Bill he introduced to parliament on 8 April 1886 proposed a single chamber assembly in Dublin, which would legislate for Ireland within well-defined limits. This not only meant the retention of specific powers at Westminster (such as some powers of taxation, defence, and foreign policy) but, so far as the provisions of the bill were concerned, the maintenance of the Act of Union. Yet this was the principal bone of contention.[4] Apart from distant colonies such as Canada, the idea of a devolution of power from the Westminster parliament was unheard of—the modern term 'devolution' was unknown—and its operation within the United Kingdom was regarded by critics as a derogation of the sacrosanct principle of the 'sovereignty of parliament' which must inevitably lead to the dissolution of the Union and perhaps even the entire empire. Home Rule was therefore not just an Irish issue but a constitutional argument about parliamentary sovereignty within the UK. To Gladstone, however, sovereignty was historically defined, and to this extent malleable, whereas to a leading intellectual opponent such as Dicey, its definition was rigid and theoretical.[5] On 7 June 1886 the first Home Rule Bill was defeated in the Commons, but the issue was established as the most bitterly contested feature of British politics in the years down to Gladstone's retirement in 1894. Thereafter it remained an ever-present possibility, before returning to the forefront of the high political agenda in the frenetic debates of 1909–14.

In this context various themes from Burke's oeuvre took on an obvious relevance. Particularly crucial were his views on the American colonies from the 1770s when, for the first time, the question of a devolution of parliamentary authority lay close to the surface. Another relevant subject was 'Grattan's Parliament' of 1782, named after the leading Irish politician Henry Grattan, which might be portrayed as a precursor to the Home Rule proposal. The historical circumstances were indeed different: there was then no Act of Union and this was an exclusively Protestant

---

[4] Alvin Jackson, *Ireland, 1798–2008* (2010), 130.
[5] John-Paul McCarthy, 'Gladstone's Irish Questions: An Historical Approach, 1830–1886', DPhil thesis, University of Oxford, 2010, 208.

body but it was regarded by many in Ireland as a golden age of autonomy, between the oppression of the earlier eighteenth century and the creation of the Union in 1801. Burke was of course a leading contemporary of Grattan and his parliament, and most of his contributions on this subject, first made available by the four volumes of correspondence published in 1844, had been republished in more accessible and topical form by Arnold in 1881. In addition to his Irish identity outlined earlier, this combination of abstract maxims of political thought combined with eloquent historical commentary gave Burke a uniquely authoritative voice. Moreover, the centrality of these themes to Gladstone's reasoning on the necessity for Home Rule suggests an underdeveloped aspect of the Gladstonian argument: Burke was, in Paul Bew's words, 'the icon of icons'.[6] Burke was not, of course, the only historical point of reference, but his relevance has generally been discussed only briefly, as for example by Bew and James Loughlin,[7] and when he is invoked, his meaning is often distorted by anachronism, as can be seen in Colin Matthew's assumption that reference to Burke indicates a distinctive 'conservative' flavour.[8]

This chapter begins, therefore, with an overview of Burke's position within the existing literature on Irish history and Irish issues before 1885. It works on the assumption that many of the figures involved in the Home Rule debates, both on the Unionist and Gladstonian sides, had genuine intellectual and/or ideological convictions which shaped their conclusions.[9] It seeks to examine these conclusions when they are supported by reference to Burke and, therefore, is divided into (firstly) Home Rule and (secondly) Unionist arguments. This is not to say that Gladstone's scheme was received uncritically by Irish Nationalists, but that the Gladstonian and Unionist sides were the most crucial with regard to their use of Burke and this is primarily the story of how Burke was canonized by the British as one of their own. Intellectually, Liberal Unionists are not considered here simply as Whigs seeking a reason to join ranks with the Conservative party. In actual fact, they were an independent and (as regards Burke) the principal scholarly source of opposition to Gladstone. Our interest lies in their rival interpretation of Liberal principles—most

---

[6] Paul Bew, *Ireland: The Politics of Enmity* (2009), 349.
[7] Bew, *Ireland*, 349; J. Loughlin, *Gladstone and the Ulster Question, 1882–1893* (1986), 59, 195; Patrick Maume 'Burke in Belfast: Thomas Macknight, Gladstone and Liberal Unionism', in D. G. Boyce and Alan O'Day, eds., *Gladstone and Ireland: Politics, Religion and Nationality in the Victorian Age* (2010).
[8] H. C. G. Matthew, *Gladstone, 1809–1898* (1997), 469.
[9] Ian Cawood, *The Liberal Unionist Party* (2012), 13. See also Christopher Harvie, 'Ideology and Home Rule: James Bryce, A. V. Dicey, and Ireland, 1880–1887', *EHR*, 359 (1976), 298–314; John Roach, 'Liberalism and the Victorian Intelligentsia', *HJ*, 8 (1957), 71–88; Collini, *Public Moralists* (1991), 230–4.

centrally, 'civil and religious liberty'—and the idea that it was in Ireland's union with Great Britain that these 'historic' Liberal values could be best secured.[10] Both sides drew considerably on the writings of Burke, but it was the Liberal Unionists who, in the end, made the stronger claim as they were able to deploy Burke's work as a whole, in contrast to the more selective Gladstonians. Equally interesting are the learned politicians who had made a study of Burke, such as John Morley and Lord Salisbury, but declined to reinforce their arguments with his oeuvre. Finally, the chapter brings to light the historical parallel between the Liberal party split over Home Rule and Burke's schism from the Whigs a century earlier and what this meant for party identity. The Liberal Unionist identification with Burke, and their subsequent integration within the Conservative party, was a significant moment in the assimilation of Burke into (what would become) the Conservative tradition. The impact of the Home Rule debates produced not only the reimagining of Burke's political identity, but the creation of new party identities in order to combat intense instability.

BURKE BEFORE THE KITE

There was, of course, a pre-history of invoking the authority of Burke in Irish matters. Paul Bew notes how Wolfe Tone mythologized Burke as the greatest Irishman of his era and a supporter of Irish reform; his was a name to be employed to encourage those who were fearful of a reformist strategy.[11] Likewise, in the 1830s and 1840s, the Irish Tory (and future Home Ruler) Isaac Butt and the *Dublin University Magazine* lauded Burke as someone who, though less distinctively Irish than men such as Tone, could still be cited as an intellectual genius of Protestant Ireland.[12] Again, as the literature produced over the disestablishment of the Irish Church in the late 1860s demonstrated, Burke was upheld and quoted as in favour of established churches, though his reported remark that the

---

[10] For examples from pamphlet literature: Earl of Derby, 'The Irish Question' (1886), 2–3; [Anon.], 'Lord Hartington's Address' (1886), 6–7; Gilbert Mahaffy, 'The Attitude of Irish Churchmen in the Present Political Crisis' (1886), 10; [Anon.], 'From Liberal Ulster to England' (1886).
[11] See Wolfe Tone, 'An Argument on Behalf of the Catholics of Ireland' (1791), *Writings of Theobald Wolfe Tone*, eds. T. W. Moody, and R. B. McDowell (1998–2007), i. 119. Tone cites Burke in a later fifth edition: Bew, *Ireland*, 4.
[12] Joseph Spence, 'Isaac Butt, Irish Nationality and the Conditional Defence of the Union, 1833–70', in D. G. Boyce and Alan O'Day, eds., *Defenders of the Union* (2001), 72.

established Church of Ireland was 'wholesale robbery' stung many anti-disestablishment Victorians.[13]

It was not until the publication of Arnold's volume of 1881, however, that Burke's thoughts on Ireland were presented to the British public in a popular and easily accessible form. Moreover, this was a distinctly 'Irish' Burke who was being introduced by a prominent English cultural critic: it held the weight of an authoritative recommendation.[14] The volume was well received. Although a review by Burke's editor E. J. Payne claimed its interest (to him at least) would be 'mainly historical',[15] this betrayed his own academicism, and was contradicted by Arnold's preface which regretted the English habit of forgetting their great writers, in contrast to the French, who excelled at such commemorative practices. He wished that a consideration of Burke on Ireland would 'set people on thinking'. This was an activity which, according to Arnold, who later became a Liberal Unionist, needed much encouragement in England. Unfortunately, 'setting people on thinking' without clear direction tended to produce diverging results. Thus, material was taken from Burke to support both Gladstonian and Unionist arguments. Arnold's interest in Burke did not, however, spring from party politics or the Land War troubles of the late-1870s and early 1880s: it can be traced throughout his writings, beginning in 1864, when he cited Burke as someone who lived by ideas. Similarly, Arnold's wider interest in the Celtic element in Britain and Ireland became apparent after the publication of his 1867 work, *On the Study of Celtic Literature*; a work which demonstrated that those who blend national characteristics—such as Burke—were representative of true genius and creativity.[16]

At the same time as *Irish Affairs*, Arnold published an article entitled 'The Incompatibles' in the April and June 1881 issues of the *Nineteenth Century*. Both were therefore produced between the 1881 Land Bill and the discussion of the suspension of *habeas corpus*. 'The Incompatibles' provided his readership with more direction as to his thoughts on Irish issues, and would be republished in a collection of Arnold's *Irish Essays* in 1882, with a popular edition appearing in 1891 (Arnold died in 1888). In the book's preface he demanded measures and policies which would be

---

[13] See 'Church and State' in Chapter 2 in this volume. See also, for example, Brady, 'Irish Establishment', *CR* (Sept. 1868), 9.
[14] Compare, for instance, the extracts in the second volume of Charles Read, *The Cabinet of Irish Literature* (1879): Burke on the sublime; on American taxation; on the French Revolution, including the digression on Marie Antoinette; on the trial of Warren Hastings.
[15] E. J. Payne, 'Letters, Speeches, and Tracts on Irish Affairs', *Academy* (9 July 1881), 22.
[16] See 'Wisdom' in Chapter 3 in this volume.

'healing'—an idea also taken from Burke.[17] The article features a comparison between Burke's constituents at Bristol who refused to support free trade with Catholic Ireland, and the 'Philistines' of Arnold's day who refused to make amendments to land ownership.[18] Arnold argued that Britain held the Irish through conquest and confiscation, and had never converted those initial angry memories into a peaceful attachment.[19] This evidently shaped Arnold's opinions regarding Home Rule, as we will see below.

Another set of texts that would prove seminal in 1886 was published by the Irish Protestant historian W. E. H. Lecky, a product of Trinity College, Dublin, who had written his own interpretation of Burke and of Irish history. Several of his works came to be seen as a vindication of Home Rule, though Lecky's aim was a patriotic one, to produce a more broadly bipartisan defence of Irish history. His *Leaders of Public Opinion in Ireland* was originally published in 1861, with a new edition in 1871. It traced ideas of 'nationalism with loyalty' through the careers of Swift, Flood, Grattan, and O'Connell. The first edition also contained a chapter on the problem of clerical influence in Irish politics and argued that progress could only follow a reduction of the power of the priest—what would later be termed 'Rome Rule'—but this was removed from subsequent editions. Here, Burke was held up as without equal in his production of condensed, valuable political maxims, and these aphorisms would become increasingly popular after 1886.[20] Lecky sent *Leaders* to Arnold when he was compiling his Burke source book and 'The Incompatibles', and Arnold subsequently 'pillaged [it] for a few notes... to explain Burke's Irish papers... conformably to the recommendation give of them in the "Incompatibles".'[21] These works existed in a network of sorts; with notable writers who wrote publicly on Burke also sharing their interests in private.

Lecky also published a popular *History of England in the Eighteenth Century* in eight volumes between 1878 and 1890. It became notable for incorporating Irish history into the more familiar English story as a way of introducing Irish history to a previously uninterested English audience. In his review for the New York *Nation*, Dicey claimed Lecky was an essayist rather than an historian. Despite this unlikely judgement, given Lecky's researches in Dublin archives, Dicey nonetheless admits that his *History*

---

[17] Matthew Arnold, 'The Incompatibles' [1881], *Irish Essays* (1882), 3–4.
[18] Ibid., 5.   [19] Ibid., 9–10.
[20] W. E. H. Lecky, *The Leaders of Public Opinion in Ireland*, new edn (1871), i. 99.
[21] Arnold to Lecky, 13 Apr. 1881, *Letters of Matthew Arnold*, v. 144.

was in fact full of information neglected by ordinary historians.[22] The third and fourth volumes of Lecky's work, which brought the reader to 1782, Grattan's Parliament, and an admirable profile of Burke, were published in 1882, although volumes five and six, which stretched to 1793, did not appear until 1887. Gladstone himself issued a favourable review in 1887, a clear illustration of Lecky's historical influence.[23] As with Arnold, this *History* was written with contemporary Irish issues in mind. Hence a letter to Lecky from J. P. Prendergast, an Irish Liberal Unionist historian and barrister, noted a modern parallel with Burke in his fight against Revolutionary France: 'Your study of Edmund Burke shows how you are overflowing with his wisdom—never more wanted than at the present... We are on the road to a more Jacobinical revolution than the Jacobins!'[24] Following the success of the *History of England*, Lecky extracted from it a *History of Ireland in the Eighteenth Century* in five volumes (which referenced Burke copiously), published in 1892. It was this exposition of Irish history and Irish character which led Home Rulers to adopt his texts as evidence, though Lecky himself was a Liberal Unionist and sat for TCD as a Unionist MP in the period from 1895 to 1902.

Finally, Goldwin Smith's works on Irish history, also referenced in Chapters 2 and 3, provided an alternative historical proof of English misrule in Ireland. The most popular of his works was *Irish History and Irish Character*, published in 1861 during his tenure of the Regius Professorship of Modern History at Oxford. Both this, and his 1868 lectures, *Three English Statesmen*, gave vivid accounts of Burke. Yet, whereas *Irish History* stressed Burke's unique blending of Irish and English qualities, *Three English Statesman* gave more room to Smith's anti-Catholic tendencies by likening Burke to Bossuet and 'Roman friars' in his defence of 'superstitions'.[25] *Irish History* was, however, the more popular choice for Gladstonian readers. James Bryce later described it, in 1914, as one of Smith's best works, and the most powerful indictment of English rule in

---

[22] Cited in Norman Pilling, 'Lecky and Dicey: English and Irish Histories', *Éire-Ireland*, 16 (1981), 47. See also his 'The Reception of the Major Works of W. E. H. Lecky, 1865–1896', MPhil thesis, University College, London, 1978.

[23] W. E. Gladstone, 'Lessons of Irish History in the Eighteenth Century', *Special Aspects of the Irish Question: A Series of Reflections in and since 1886* (1892). The 1882 volumes were well-received by the Tory reviewer and friend of Disraeli, T. E. Kebbel: 'Mr Lecky and George III', *FR* (July 1882), 41. Lord Acton was also taken with Lecky's 'masterly' account of Burke: Lecky, *Memoir of the Rt. Hon. W. E. H. Lecky*, 161.

[24] Prendergast to Lecky, 2 June 1882, quoted in Donal McCartney, *W. E. H. Lecky: Historian and Politician, 1838–1903* (1994), 112. See also W. E. H. Lecky, *History of England in the Eighteenth Century* (1878–90), iii. 181–211.

[25] See pp. 47–8, 67, 77–8 in this volume.

Ireland from an English historian by offering a survey of the causes of Irish misfortunes and discontent. It therefore came as a surprise to him, and others, when Smith opposed Gladstone's Home Rule Bill in 1886.[26] A closer reading of Smith's portrait of Burke in 1868, however, would have suggested otherwise. When discussing his *Irish History* in 1894 Smith denied any 'apostasy', stating his support, with John Bright, for the disestablishment of the Irish Church, but (again like Bright) he was 'always for the union'.[27] Smith's persistent distrust of the Celtic character was still evident in an 1887 address on Home Rule, during which he asserted: 'It is impossible that British statesmen can allow a separate realm of Celtic lawlessness to be set up in the midst of the Anglo-Saxon realm of law.'[28]

Taken together, these works make up a solid body of literature for consideration of the Irish Question and they of course gained greater importance when the Home Rule issue exploded in 1886. Since they provided accessible material which could be used in support of a variety of arguments, they were considered essential reading in the period following the Hawarden Kite.[29] Most simply, these texts provided a much needed grounding in Irish history when there had previously been little public interest in the subject. Produced by Arnold, Lecky, and Smith, they originated from a broadly 'liberal' base; yet all these men would prove to be future Liberal Unionists. They condemned historical Irish misrule and promoted the moral statesmanship of Burke, but they did not see the solution to Ireland's problems in constitutional change and devolution. The Gladstonians, including Gladstone himself, drew opposing conclusions. There were, therefore, instances where authors felt it necessary to reassert their control of their work: one example is Lecky, who refused to publish a popular, cheap edition of *Leaders* in 1886 to avoid its continued appropriation by Home Rulers.[30] The point to note here is that in the early 1880s, Burke's identity was still fairly flexible as a thinker and he had not been incorporated into any narrow or specific Conservative or Liberal tradition. However, there are boundaries to malleability and there were limits to his usefulness in generating diverging arguments. By analysing the texts which were identified, quoted, and avoided by opposing sides, it is possible to consider how much of Burke's oeuvre was considered helpful or discarded by each party.

---

[26] James Bryce, 'Goldwin Smith', *North American Review* (Apr. 1914), 521.
[27] Goldwin Smith, *Essays on Questions of the Day, Political and Social* (1894), xiv. Compare his 'The Fallacy of Irish History', *FR* (Jan. 1884), 41.
[28] Goldwin Smith, *The Schism in the Anglo-Saxon Race* (1887), 30.
[29] R. B. O'Brien, 'The "Unionist" Case for Home Rule', in J. Bryce, ed., *Handbook of Home Rule*, 2nd edn (1887), 154.
[30] J. J. Auchmuty, *Lecky: A Biographical and Critical Essay* (1945), 40.

THE GLADSTONIAN ARGUMENT

Gladstone was central in the positioning of Burke within the argument for Home Rule on his side. Burke, in his letters and speeches, was both a critical source in providing him with detail of Irish issues, such as the history of the Penal Code, the position of Catholics, and Grattan's Parliament of 1782, and a more general fountain of political wisdom, particularly regarding ideas of conciliation and the need for voluntary political ties in a 'union of hearts'. He had a life-long intellectual relationship with Burke (as evidenced by his leaving gift to Arthur Hallam in 1827[31]) and he venerated his work.[32] It would be a mistake, however, to think that this was necessarily representative of mainstream Liberal opinion. Gladstone had no ordinary or orthodox Liberal pedigree, and he was similarly eccentric in his intellectual preferences. Hence he found his sustenance in his four 'doctors' (Aristotle, Augustine, Dante, and Bishop Butler) rather than in any identifiably Liberal authors.[33] By the end of 1886, however, he had orchestrated a Burkean reading revolution.

Gladstone's intense reading of Burke begins in December 1885, a fortnight before his son Herbert flew the Hawarden Kite in *The Times*. During this period, his interest in Burke is well documented. John Morley's 1903 *Life of Gladstone* was seminal in stressing the connection, stating that Gladstone was reading Burke almost daily and quoting from his *Diary*: 'What a magazine of wisdom on Ireland and America... *sometimes almost divine.*'[34] *The Gladstone Diaries* confirm that, during the month of December 1885, Gladstone was reading Burke constantly, particularly his speeches on American taxation and conciliation from the 1770s.[35] Colin Matthew interprets this as indicating that Burke was something of an add-on, after the strategic decision had been made.[36] However, it would be a mistake to dismiss his reading merely as padding for his argument. Contrary to Matthew's suggestion that Burke was

---

[31] See p. 29 in this volume.
[32] Gladstone, *Correspondence on Church and Religion*, ii. 326. See also H. C. G. Matthew, *Gladstone, 1809–1898*, 547; McCarthy, 'Gladstone's Irish Questions', 36, 64, 85.
[33] Morley, *Life of Gladstone*, i. 207 and n.2. See also Matthew, *Gladstone*, 635; J. P. Parry, *The Rise and Fall of Liberal Government in Victorian Britain* (1993), 250–60.
[34] Morley, *Life of Gladstone*, iii. 280 [original emphasis].
[35] W. E. Gladstone, *The Gladstone Diaries*, eds. M. R. D. Foot and H. C. G. Matthew (1968–1996), xi. 443–54. 'Burke on America' was generally considered to consist of two speeches: on taxation [1774], and on conciliation [1775]. 'Burke on Ireland' was made up of a collection of letters and speeches, as published by Matthew Arnold in 1881.
[36] Matthew, *Gladstone*, 469, 547.

marginal, the rich heritage of Gladstone's prior reading of Burke (which Matthew himself brought into the public domain),[37] and the profusion of his use of Burke from 1886 onwards, are extremely powerful arguments for both the continuity of Gladstone's policy-making and the force of ideas in politics.[38] His opponents may not have agreed with him, but for Gladstone Home Rule was part of a process of continuous constitutional evolution, and Burke was both a guide to the possibilities of change and a guarantor of fundamental continuity.

The material that Gladstone read was almost exclusively Burke on America and Ireland. It is not until after the 'American' reading that he explored Burke's correspondence, including the Irish writings recently published by Arnold. Here lay the Gladstonian Achilles heel: the Gladstonian argument used only a specific section of Burke's oeuvre, not the whole. In contrast, as we will see, the opposition enlisted a much broader Burkean source base. Still, Gladstone's selections from Burke provided him with a more stimulating influence than Matthew allows. He interprets Gladstone's reading of Burke as 'old historicism', and it was Burke's 'conservative whiggery' that provided balance to the 'new deductivism' of another writer on his reading list—A. V. Dicey. In this way, Matthew makes a connection between 'history' and 'conservatism' which has much more to do with modern received wisdom on Burke and conservatism than with Gladstone's reading in this instance.[39] In fact, Gladstone used Burke to define and support his central moral argument and Burke was clearly considered to be a force for change. Throughout his life, from 1845 when he quoted Burke's critique of the penal laws to support his conversion over Maynooth, through to Home Rule, Gladstone used Burke in quite radical ways.[40] At the heart of Gladstone's understanding of Burke is the idea that the argument for granting Home Rule rested on the importance of history in Irish politics.[41] Therefore, his prescription for his Unionist opponents was, as he wrote to R. H. Hutton, editor of the *Spectator*, on 2 July 1886: 'Soak and drench yourselves with the writings of Mr. Burke on Ireland, especially on the Grattan Parliament: most of all, his writings on the American war.'[42] While Matthew correctly identified

---

[37] Gladstone, *Gladstone Diaries*, xiv. 321.
[38] Morley, *Life of Gladstone*, i. 42; Matthew, *Gladstone*, 547; McCarthy, 'Gladstone's Irish Questions', 276; D. Bebbington, *The Mind of Gladstone: Religion, Homer and Politics* (2004).
[39] Matthew, *Gladstone*, 469.
[40] McCarthy, 'Gladstone's Irish Questions', 61.
[41] J. L. Hammond, *Gladstone and the Irish Nation* (1938; 1964), 651; Bew, *Ireland*, 350.
[42] Gladstone, *Gladstone Diaries*, xi. 580.

Gladstone's historicism, this was Burke the Irish Whig and not the founder of conservatism.

Nonetheless, without Gladstone's actions the debate on Burke would never have existed in the form it took. His engagement with Burke was not simply a personal matter: on 13 April he called upon Members of Parliament to utilize Burke as he had:

> I should like to quote Mr. Burke—and I hope we shall hear much of Mr. Burke in the course of this discussion—for the writings of Mr. Burke upon Ireland, and still more upon America, are a mine of gold for the political wisdom with which they are charged, applicable to the circumstances of to-day, and full of the deepest and most valuable lessons to guide the policy of a country.[43]

The Gladstonian argument with reference to Burke covered four main points: the importance of voluntary political ties in maintaining the Union; the choice between Home Rule and coercion; the idea that Home Rule was a final measure that would not lead to separation; and the use of Grattan's Parliament of 1782 as an historical and constitutional precedent. The problem with the Gladstonian argument lay in its softness: could an appeal to organic, historical, and moral arguments derived from Burke outweigh hard-edged appeals to constitutional law and power politics? Effectively, it presented voluntary political ties as the essence of Burke's political thought, which was simply not consistent with previous or subsequent analysis—particularly regarding Burke's constitutional thought. A closer examination of each of the four Gladstonian 'Burkean' arguments is therefore revealing.

A key justification for Gladstonian Home Rule lay in the perceived necessity for voluntary political ties, which became known by the slogan 'the union of hearts'. This was derived largely from Burke's American speeches, according to which enforcing abstract rights of taxation through coercive measures unnecessarily risked the unity of the empire. In contrast, Burke argued for conciliation, by allowing American assemblies to be recognized but remain united under the crown. He also argued in favour of governing with knowledge of the nature and feelings of the governed, which in America was shown to be an extreme love of liberty. It was in this way that political ties with the colonies could be secured; and, moreover, they were the strongest ties. Burke's American speeches were combined with a selection of Irish writings, including his writings to the electors of Bristol, who (as we have already noted) would eventually eject him from his seat for his support of Irish free trade. These arguments were taken up

---

[43] *Hansard*, 13 Apr. 1886, vol. 304, cc.1544–5.

by the Home Rulers, who based their case on a perceived need to rectify past Irish misgovernment to secure such connections and maintain the Union. It was thus an historical argument, which offered a political solution to the conundrum of how to provide 'justice to Ireland'.

Gladstone's earliest allies also upheld the importance of voluntary political ties. John Redmond, the Home Rule MP, asserted that the Union must be supported by the will of the people: 'Edmund Burke said—"A voluntary tie is a more secure link of connection than subordination borne with grudging and discontent."' Unfortunately, Redmond continued, English political leaders had refused to trust the people of Ireland.[44] Gladstone also quickly converted many Liberal backbenchers, such as Alfred Pease, who recorded in his diary in 1887 that 'There are no grander passages in Burke's speeches than those on Conciliation with America.' He claimed, in his memoir of 1932, that hearing a speech on the history of Irish landlords by Thomas Sexton in 1886 had driven him to consult Burke, his 'Whig mentor', and quotes Burke's 1777 'Letter to the Sheriffs of Bristol': 'I was persuaded that Government was a practical thing made for the happiness of mankind and not to furnish a spectacle of uniformity to gratify the schemes of visionary politicians.'[45] Gladstone had provoked a course of reading for many politicians and public men, as they either read or re-read the works of Burke to fashion their arguments.

Cabinet support was also forthcoming. The Home Secretary, Hugh Childers (1827–96), drew on Burke to explain the union of hearts. Childers, with an Irish peerage in his ancestry and colonial experience in Australia, had been in favour of Home Rule since 1880 and informed Gladstone of his intention to raise the issue on the platform in 1885. By 1886, he was also winding up his speeches with words from Burke, such as his 'Letter to Lord Charlemont'; a text which, Childers claimed, was already famous among Irish Members of Parliament, though he regretted it was unknown to English and Scottish members. Like Gladstone, Childers stressed the need for voluntary political ties and drew on Burke when asserting:

> Mutual affection will do more for mutual help and mutual advantage between the two Kingdoms than any ties of artificial connection whatever.

---

[44] *Hansard*, 13 May 1886, vol. 305, c.968.
[45] Alfred Pease, *Elections and Recollections* (1932), 100, 156. Pease's memoir covers the period 1885–92, and he also wrote to *The Times* in support of his Burkean argument for Home Rule: 'The Constitutional Course', *The Times* (14 June 1886), 4. For later arguments on the necessity for voluntary political ties between countries in the periodical press, cf. Frederic Harrison, 'A Rejoinder to the Duke of Argyll', *CR* (Feb. 1889), 306–7; J. A. Partridge, 'Ireland and the Empire', *WR* (July 1889), 466.

> No reluctant tie can be a strong one. At the present time the tie which exists between Great Britain and Ireland is not only a reluctant tie, but one which I believe is deeply disliked.

For Childers, the Home Rule Bill would create a 'new bond of amity' and would 'result in a permanent attachment to, and affection for, this country'.[46]

In closing the debates on the second reading of the bill, Gladstone drew on Burke as an example of an Irishman with Catholic ties loyal to Britain, and as a means to understand the ways to secure similar loyalty from the Irish a hundred years later. He quoted a 1796 'Letter to Windham' in stating his belief that disaffection had cast deep roots in the principles and habits of the majority among the lower and middle classes of Ireland: '"Catholics, who are in a manner the whole people, are as yet sound; but they may be provoked, as all men easily may be, out of their principles."' Gladstone then went on to explain Burke's meaning to the House: 'the Protestants, not having grievances to complain of, have become loyal'. In contrast, the Roman Catholics, since 1796, 'as Mr. Burke says, have been provoked, as all men easily may be, out of their principles of loyalty. And these are words, and these are ideas, which show us what is the way in which to promote loyalty, and what is the way in which we can destroy it.'[47] This was, no doubt, a genuine attempt to secure a positive relationship between the kingdoms under devolution. Yet still here we get a sense of what many Liberal Unionists would later complain of: in their view, the Catholics were not 'the whole people', but a majority only. The Gladstonians also failed to demonstrate why only constitutional change could secure this loyalty.

Shortly afterwards, Gladstone again used Burke to stress the importance of offering Home Rule in good will, and not under coercion. He continued:

> We wish it [Home Rule] to be granted in the mode prescribed by Mr. Burke. Mr. Burke said, in his first speech at Bristol—'I was true to my old-standing invariable principle, that all things which came from Great Britain should issue as a gift of her bounty and beneficence rather than as claims recovered against struggling litigants, or at least, if your beneficence obtained no credit in your concessions, yet that they should appear the salutary provisions of your wisdom and foresight—not as things wrung from you with your blood by the cruel gripe of a rigid necessity.' The difference between giving with freedom and dignity on the one side, with acknowledgment and gratitude on

---

[46] *Hansard*, 21 May 1886, vol. 305, c.1742.
[47] *Hansard*, 7 June 1886, vol. 306, c.1221.

the other, and giving under compulsion—giving with disgrace, giving with resentment dogging you at every step of your path—this difference is, in our eyes, fundamental, and this is the main reason not only why we have acted, but why we have acted now.[48]

This brings us to the second component of the Gladstonian argument: the choice was between Home Rule and coercion. For Liberals, the problem with coercion—the suspension of civil and religious liberty in Ireland—is easy to understand if one considers 'liberty' to be the central Liberal principle. This was the historic Whig and Liberal motto, and of far greater importance to party identity than the alternative 'Peace, Retrenchment, and Reform' with its ephemeral fiscal and foreign policy emphasis.[49] The appeal to liberty was nothing less than a summons to constitutional reform. This is really the foundation of the Gladstonian argument: Home Rule was necessary to prevent further coercion and restore civil and religious liberty to Ireland. Moreover, coercion was seen to be an unstable basis for both immediate political action and for a long-lasting union between countries. Thus, Home Rule must be granted quickly, and granted in good spirit. This idea too could be derived from Burke. In short, there is both a positive and a negative argument: Home Rule must be granted willingly, in order to inspire and promote the union of hearts, but it must also be done to prevent coercion and the suspension of liberty.

The positive argument for supporting Home Rule over coercion was also made by Lyon Playfair, the Liberal MP and chemist (1818–98), who proceeded from the assumption that Ireland had become a 'nation' with a 'people'—a conception of nationality by historical association, as opposed to language or religion. In contrast, Unionists both Liberal and Conservative generally denied this.[50] Playfair concurred with his leader that 'Burke has the kernel of truth in many of his speeches and writings' and concluded his speech with a quotation from Burke's 1778 'Letter to Edmund Pery': '"You [Ireland] are now beginning to have a Country"'. Moreover, Burke argued that '"when that thing called a Country is once formed in Ireland, quite other things will be done than were done"': in other words, the energies fuelling zeal and anger would be put to better use, and there would be peace.[51] Playfair's quotation suggested that Home Rulers believed that Ireland had become a nation in her own right and,

---

[48] Ibid., c.1237.
[49] For example, F. A. Hayek, 'Liberalism', in *New Studies in Philosophy, Politics, Economics and the History of Ideas* (1978), 129; Eugenio Biagini, *Liberty, Retrenchment and Reform: Popular Liberalism in the Age of Gladstone, 1860–1880* (2004), 424.
[50] Such a denial continued into the twentieth century: Robert Anderson, *Sidelights on the Home Rule Movement* (1906), 189–90.
[51] *Hansard*, 18 May 1886, vol. 305, c.1380.

this being the case, Burke would have been a force for change—perhaps the change willed by the Home Rulers—rather than a supporter of maintaining the existing Union.[52] Moreover, the English had nothing to fear with regard to violence: Irish energy would be redirected into nation-building, and there would be no need for further coercion. This was an interesting conception of nationhood: one that recognized an alternative heritage, but stopped short of full independence.

Another example is found in R. Barry O'Brien's contribution to the *Handbook of Home Rule*—a key compilation of essays which includes contributions by Gladstone and Morley. He illustrated how Burke would support an anti-coercion argument using examples from Irish history, in order to establish a union of hearts. His argument was in fact taken from Lecky's *Leaders of Public Opinion in Ireland*:

> Such were the principal articles of this famous [penal] code—a code which Burke truly described as 'well digested and well disposed in all its parts; a machine of wise and elaborate contrivance, and as well fitted for the oppression, impoverishment, and degradation of a people, and the debasement in them of human nature itself, as ever proceeded from the perverted ingenuity of man.'[53]

The insinuation here is that Burke, who understood the problems that English coercion in Ireland had caused via the Penal Code, would seek 'justice for Ireland' (in the form of an Irish parliament) over constitutional continuity and the maintenance of the Union. Elsewhere outside Westminster, the National Liberal Association published and distributed pamphlets quoting Burke in support of Home Rule, thus popularizing this gospel.[54]

---

[52] Some commentators were not so sure: H. O. Arnold-Forster, 'An English View of Irish Secession', *Political Science Quarterly*, 4 (1889), 79–82. Cf. Matthew Arnold: 'Ireland has been a nation—a most unhappy one...Wales too, and Scotland, have been nations. But politically they are now nations no longer, any one of them...This country could not have risen to its present greatness if they had been.' *On Home Rule for Ireland: Two Letters to The Times* [22 May and 6 Aug. 1886] (1891), 4–5.

[53] O'Brien, 'The "Unionist" Case for Home Rule', in Bryce, *Handbook of Home Rule*, 166; Lecky, *Leaders of Public Opinion*, 120–3. According to a modern commentator, Lecky treated 'the whole penal code in the spirit of Edmund Burke and Henry Grattan': McCartney, *Lecky*, 78.

[54] [Anon.], 'A Few Extracts from the Works and Speeches of Edmund Burke, in support of the case of present policy of the Liberal Party towards Ireland' (1887). There were numerous Liberal pamphlets which were published and distributed (many of them through official Liberal channels) which evoke Burke in relation to the 'union of hearts' and Irish history, including Grattan's Parliament: Malcolm MacColl, 'Reasons for Home Rule' (1886), 38–42; Edmund Harvey, 'A Summary of Irish Grievances, still existing in 1886; with some Remarks on Home Rule' (1886); H. J. Leech, 'Henry Grattan: A Lecture, delivered at the Manchester Liberal Club, Oct. 8 1886' (1886); John W. Willans, 'Grattan's Parliament: What Led up to it; What it was; What it did; and How it Fell' (1887); J. Hirst Hollowell, 'Ireland: The Story of Her Wrongs, and a Plea for her Rights' (1886).

The Gladstonian argument also insisted that Home Rule was a final measure and not a stepping stone towards Irish independence. In fact, Gladstonians argued, the reality would be quite the opposite. Home Rule was necessary for the continued unity of the three kingdoms and the avoidance of total separation. One example of such argument is found in a speech by the Liberal MP George Shaw Lefevre, later Lord Eversley. He quoted Burke to support the declaration that 'Ireland could not be separated from England', as it would lead to ruin. Furthermore, he insisted that this was even truer in the late nineteenth century because 'the resources of Great Britain are so infinitely greater in proportion to those of Ireland than they ever were before'. Where Unionists saw Home Rule as a first step towards disintegration of the empire and Irish independence, Home Rulers argued for finality:

> It is my confident belief [that] it is possible to concede to Ireland all she really requires in the direction of local government [meaning Home Rule] without imperilling any of the great interests of this country; and in so doing we shall add much to the real union of the two countries, and we shall secure and increase, rather than diminish, the real strength and force of the Empire.[55]

Constitutionally, it was an argument intended to maintain the existing Union, though no doubt many Nationalists would have hoped for more.

Support for this view outside Westminster can be found in Lord Thring's essay on 'Home Rule and Imperial Unity' in the *Handbook of Home Rule*. Like O'Brien, Thring quoted Burke profusely and, like Gladstone, he focused on Burke's American speeches to support his position on Ireland. In discussing the 'futile' attempts by the British parliament to diminish by concession or repress by coercion Irish aspirations or discontent, Thring, a chief parliamentary draftsman in 1886 for both Home Rule and Land Bills, quoted Burke.[56] He continued: 'How strange to Burke would have seemed the doctrine that the restoration of a limited power of self-government to Ireland, excluding commerce, and excluding all matters not only Imperial, but those in which uniformity is required, should be denounced as a disruption of the Empire!'[57] Furthermore, Thring used Burke to counter Unionist arguments against the

---

[55] *Hansard*, 18 May 1886, vol. 305, cc.1314–15. The idea of a higher, sentimental connection between Britain and Ireland with reference to Burke did appear in pamphlet literature: in addition to those listed above, see Thomas J. Ewing, 'Mr. Gladstone and Ireland; or, Lord Salisbury and the Orange Faction' (1886), 16; J. A. Fox, 'From Galilee to Gweedore, a Drama with a Purpose' (1889), 13.

[56] Lord Thring, 'Home Rule and Imperial Unity', in Bryce, *Handbook of Home Rule*, 67–8.

[57] Ibid., 76.

finality of the measure: 'To those who urge such arguments I would recommend the perusal of the speech of Burke on Conciliation with America.' He then cites: '"When will this speculating against fact and reason end? What will quiet these panic fears which we entertain of the hostile effect of a conciliatory conduct? Is it true that no case can exist in which it is proper for the Sovereign to accede to the desires of his discontented subjects?"'[58] This was, evidently, a widespread form of argument.

The final component of the Gladstonian argument for Home Rule attempted to show historical support for the scheme: the pre-existence of Grattan's Parliament from 1782 until the Act of Union came into force in 1801. This was important not because the Irish parliament established in 1782 would resemble that proposed by Gladstone—it was a relic of the Protestant Ascendancy—but because it illustrated, as a piece of historical evidence, that the Irish were capable of self-government and that Home Rule had a kind of constitutional precedent: an Irish parliament would therefore be a restoration, or reform in the true sense, rather than a revolution. These arguments for historical constitutional precedent— always a favourite with reformers attempting to 'reclaim' lost liberties— were given added authority by the apparent support of Burke.

Again, it was Gladstone who directed his party towards this evidence. He drew on Grattan's Parliament, and Burke's support of it, from the earliest stages of the debate.[59] In insisting upon the influence of Burke, he raised the question, 'what were the old Whig traditions' to be respected and upheld?[60] The great organ of Whig tradition, he claimed, was Burke—even above Fox. Despite the claims of Burke's apostasy over the French Revolution, on the subject of the relations with Ireland Burke never modified 'by one hair's breadth' the generous and wise declaration of his younger years. To Gladstone, although Burke did not live down to 1800, he placed on record both 'his political adhesion to the opinions of Mr. Grattan', and 'his full satisfaction with the state of things that prevailed in Ireland—the political state of things, especially the Acts of 1782 and 1783, and in a letter written not long before his lamented death he said that he trusted that Ireland had seen the last of her revolutions'. By that, Gladstone asserted, Burke meant to imply that the Act of 1782 did amount to a revolution, 'a blessed and peaceful revolution, but still a

---

[58] Ibid., 77–8.
[59] Aside from his parliamentary speeches, see Gladstone, 'Lessons of Irish History in the Eighteenth Century', in Bryce, *Handbook of Home Rule*, 85–6.
[60] *Hansard*, 10 May 1886, vol. 305, c.583; 'The Government of Ireland Bill', *The Times* (11 May 1886), 8.

revolution—a revolution effected by those peaceful means, by . . . bold and wise British statesmanship'.[61] And, furthermore, that there should be no more subsequent 'revolution' such as the Act of Union. He even attempted to convince a sceptical J. G. Swift MacNeill (1849–1926), an Irish Home Rule MP, and the Belfast *Northern Whig* editor and biographer of Burke, Thomas Macknight, on the evidence of the speech by Burke's friend and executor, French Lawrence in January 1799, that Burke would have opposed the Union.[62]

Home Rulers then began to gather any evidence of support given by Burke to the idea of an independent Irish parliament. It was at this point that William Vernon Harcourt (1827–1904), then Chancellor of the Exchequer, entered the debate. Harcourt was by no means an instinctive friend to the Irish cause, but his interest in eighteenth-century precedent (not least because of his family background—the first Earl (Simon) Harcourt (1714–77) succeeded Lord Townshend as Lord Lieutenant of Ireland in 1772) was considerable:

> Burke, who knew something of the question, and who had always been, and was in 1782, an enthusiastic supporter of the independence of the Irish Parliament, towards the close of his days, when he had become a Whig seceder, bore his testimony to the success of the Irish Parliament. In one of his letters, when he was invoking and stimulating Pitt to continue the Great War, and pointing out the great resources that England possessed at that time for carrying on the war, he contrasted the condition of Ireland then with the condition of Ireland as it had been at former periods during the great wars of Marlborough. And this is what Burke says in his letter on 'A Regicide Peace' in the year 1796, when Grattan's Parliament had been in operation for 14 years—'Ireland, now so large a source of the common opulence and power, and which wisely managed might be made much more beneficial and much more effective, was then the heaviest of burdens. An army not much less than 40,000 men was drawn from the general effort to keep that Kingdom in a poor, unfruitful, and resourceless subjection.'[63]

Harcourt's argument was that Grattan's Parliament had had a vital impact on the welfare and status of Ireland. The wider argument was the idea that Ireland should be governed by Irish ideas: it was this that would lead to

---

[61] *Hansard*, 10 May 1886, vol. 305, cc.583–4.
[62] J. G. Swift MacNeill, *What I Have Seen and Heard* (1925), 248; Bew, *Ireland*, 349; Maume, 'Burke in Belfast', 179; Matthew, *Gladstone*, 469. Gladstone even spoke of 'the ideas about the distressful nature of the country' which he had been discussing with Morley, including Burke, Parnell, and Ireland, when he met the young *Comédie Française* actress, Mme Reichenberg, at this time: 'French Recollections of Mr. Gladstone', *Daily Telegraph* (26 May 1898), 10.
[63] *Hansard*, 1 June 1886, vol. 306, c.762.

measures and policies that would have the greatest impact and the best results there. Local knowledge of the governed—which Burke had also argued for in his American speeches, seen above—by governors, was essential.

Home Rulers repeated these parliamentary assertions through various media out of doors. For instance, in December 1886, A. J. Mundella (1825–97), the Liberal politician and manufacturer, wrote in a letter to *The Times*: 'There is contemporary confirmation, if confirmation were needed, that Burke was in favour of the maintenance of an Irish Parliament.' The source called upon here is again second-hand: French Lawrence, who claimed in 1799 that Burke used to say to him: 'England and Ireland have grown up under circumstances which do not admit of incorporation with each other.' Mundella then asks, rhetorically: 'Was Burke a "Separatist" or an advocate "of the disruption of the Empire"?'[64] The implication was that an appeal to Burke was a defence of Home Rule; that is, that there could be a separate Irish identity, without separation from Britain.[65] Going further, however, Burke himself could be held up as the embodiment and personification of such an idea.

The use of Grattan's Parliament as a precedent continued into the twentieth century. In 1911, the historian Alice Stopford Green produced *Irish Nationality*. Stopford Green was a leading Irish nationalist historian and the widow of the staunchly Liberal J. R. Green (who, as detailed in previous chapters, had read and written about Burke in the 1870s); she herself had been raised in the Church of Ireland and now sought to assert Ireland's claims as a nation. She referenced Burke firstly as an historical source to describe the Protestant Ascendancy.[66] But then she offered a reading of Burke which positioned him as recognizing 'Irish nationality' in accordance with Grattan's views: '"The Irish Protestant," cried Grattan, "could never be free till the Irish Catholic had ceased to be a slave." "You are now," said Burke, "beginning to have a country." Finally a great cry for the independence of their parliament rose in every county and from every class.'[67] Stopford Green was, perhaps, one of the few intellectual Liberals who used Burke in this way besides Gladstone, but her actions

---

[64] A. J. Mundella, 'Mr. Gladstone and Burke', *The Times* (14 Dec. 1886), 10. For similar sentiments, see O'Brien, 'The "Unionist" Case for Home Rule', in Bryce, *Handbook of Home Rule*, 174.
[65] ['Radical'], 'How Ireland Flourished under Home Rule 100 Years Ago' (1884).
[66] Alice Stopford Green, *Irish Nationality* (1908), 170. Although she was criticized for doing so: T. M. Kettle, 'Home Rule and Antiquarianism', *Academy* (14 Oct. 1911), 466–7. For a later popular rendering of Grattan's Parliament, see M. McDonnell Bodkin, *Grattan's Parliament: Before and After* (1912).
[67] Ibid., 205.

(i.e. enlisting Burke) at this time should be contrasted with those of the Gaelic Revivalists who excluded the Anglo-Irish from their canons.[68]

Read in ways such as these, it seems unsurprising that Burke, an Irishman and an English MP, would be a source for the Gladstonians. Yet there was one notable silence which demonstrated the relative weakness of the Gladstonian argument: John Morley. Morley supported Home Rule as an issue which had the potential to unite the Liberal party, but also because he had a long-standing hatred of English misgovernment in Ireland—especially coercion.[69] But despite being the most knowledgeable Burke scholar on the Home Rule side and an ardently Gladstonian Liberal MP, Morley did not produce Burke propaganda for his Irish cause: his speeches and writings on the subject are clear of any reference to Burke. It is always interesting to see where men of letters, upon entering the political, 'practical' realm, apply their knowledge. Morley, given the time he spent reading and studying Burke, would beyond doubt have had an opinion. The fact that he does not share this learning, or invoke Burke to support his arguments (as he does elsewhere, for instance in his work of 1874, *On Compromise*[70]) is suggestive to say the least.[71] One could infer from Morley's silence that he deemed Burke too irrelevant to use due to the altered context. Hence his assertion regarding the 1886 bill, when writing in 1903: 'Historical parallels in the politics of the day are usually rather decorative than substantial.'[72] Perhaps too he came to the conclusion that Burke would not have supported Home Rule, since Morley, like Dicey, accepted that it was indeed a constitutional revolution.[73] And whereas Morley had previously argued (and asserted again in an 1886 review of Henry Maine's *Popular Government*[74]) that a constitution was merely a machine, he recognized that for Burke it was something much more sacred, and thus untouchable.[75] This fundamental difference in outlook was noted by Chamberlain—who, as we will shortly see, now claimed an affinity with Burke—in a letter to Morley, in which he likened

---

[68] See pp. 78–9 in this volume.   [69] Hamer, *John Morley*, 198–9, 232–5.
[70] Morley, *On Compromise*, 177–8: Burke's definition of 'compromise' is stated as the 'true' definition.
[71] See, for example, Morley's review of Dicey: 'The Government of Ireland', *NC* (Jan. 1887), 19–39.
[72] Morley, *Life of Gladstone*, iii. 313.
[73] A. V. Dicey, *England's Case against Home Rule* (1886); *Why England Maintains the Union* (1887); *A Leap in the Dark, or, our New Constitution* (1893; 2nd edn 1911); *A Fool's Paradise: being a Constitutionalist's Criticism of the Home Rule Bill of 1912* (1913).
[74] John Morley, 'Maine on Popular Government' [1886], in Morley, *Oracles on Man*, 81.
[75] Morley, *Burke* (1879), 58–9. Not forgetting his *Edmund Burke: A Historical Study* (1867).

their political and personal separation over Home Rule to that of 'Fox and Burke'.[76]

It was therefore possible to extract from Burke a defence for the union of hearts, but what about the Union itself as a part of the British Constitution which Burke held as sacred? Of course, the Union of 1801 did not exist in Burke's lifetime and had, therefore, already altered Burke's revered constitution well before 1886 (something the focus on Grattan's Parliament tended to overlook). Even so, for a knowledgeable Burke scholar such as Morley, it would be an extremely tenuous argument that attempted to claim Burke as a supporter of constitutional change per se, and Home Rule was, after all, a constitutional argument. His aphorisms were certainly malleable—but only up to a point. Silence would also have avoided contradicting Gladstone at a time of party disunity. This is of course speculation, but it is necessary to address Morley's absence from this discussion. Whatever the reason, the silence on the matter from the most famous living British scholar of Burke at the time, as a Home Ruler, was a deafening one.

Similarly, Lord Rosebery, although no Burke scholar, also refused to join his leader's appropriation of Burke's work: though he was politically crucial for Gladstone in 1886, Rosebery was not ultimately loyal to his Irish policy of devolution. This could perhaps be traced to his reverence for Pitt (the instigator of the Act of Union)—he published a *Life of Pitt* in 1891—and also his Scottish frame of reference: his historical addresses often focused exclusively on Scotland.[77] His later appreciations of Burke in the 1890s, after he had succeeded Gladstone as prime minister, usually when unveiling a statue or plaque, seem moderate and critical in comparison to the tone of the Home Rule debates. When he unveiled the new Burke memorial at St Mary's and All Saints Church, Beaconsfield, for instance, he stated that 'if you are one of those who are disgusted by his [Burke's] violence and bad taste' it would be better to reflect on his peaceful home life instead.[78] The Gladstonian argument for Home Rule, therefore, was largely made by politicians and the Liberal party *en masse*, through pamphlets and speeches. However, it was not usually made at a higher intellectual level, other than that produced by the Liberal party's highly cerebral leader.

---

[76] Morley, *Recollections* (1917), i. 204.
[77] Lord Rosebery, *Life of Pitt* (1891); Rosebery, *Miscellanies, Literary and Historical* (1921), especially vol. ii.
[78] 'Edmund Burke at Beaconsfield', *Speaker* (16 July 1898), 3. See also Lord Rosebery, 'Burke', *Appreciations and Addresses*, ed. Charles Geake (1899).

OPPOSITION: LIBERAL UNIONISTS AND CONSERVATIVES

The opposition to Home Rule, consisting of Liberal Unionists and Conservatives, attacked the Gladstonian argument both in content and in its interpretation of Burke. However, in 1886 it was mostly Liberal Unionists who attempted to reclaim Burke, rather than the Tories. Indeed, though the Liberal Unionists have rarely received analysis in these terms, it is evident that much of the intellectual work against Gladstone's 'Burkean' argument was theirs. The Liberal Unionists contained a number of esteemed men of letters, science, and the universities, such as Arnold, Dicey, Lecky, and Goldwin Smith, as well as T. H. Huxley, John Tyndall, Leslie and Fitzjames Stephen, and Edward Dowden. Tyndall, in a letter to *The Times* in June 1887, stated: 'A former worshipper of the ex-Prime Minister said to me some time ago: "Never in the history of England was there such a consensus of intellect arrayed against statesmen as is now arrayed against Mr. Gladstone."'[79] This was certainly true of the Liberal Unionists in particular, though not every scholarly Liberal Unionist felt qualified to contribute to the debate. So, for instance, Leslie Stephen, who wrote extensively on Burke, could claim in 1896: 'I feel that if I were to suggest any arguments bearing directly upon home rule or disestablishment, I should at once come under that damnatory epithet "academical," which so neatly cuts the ground from under the feet of the political amateur.'[80] The Liberal Unionist party, however, would not have survived as long as it did (it was a separate body until 1895) without grassroots support. Nor was the party driven solely by intellectuals: politicians in Westminster also played a part in responding to the Gladstonian trigger. What is notable for our purposes is that all types (intellectual, parliamentary, grassroots) had some sort of engagement with Burke: whether they quoted him, studied him, or published his works.

While the Gladstonian argument was selective, the responses of the opposition were diverse. For most Liberal Unionists, the reason for their opposition to Home Rule was based on a belief that it would be disastrous in terms of social cohesion, individual liberties, and the unity of the empire. It went against their deepest principles: they felt they must protect the liberty of the Protestant minority in Ireland. A classless, national Liberalism which strove for civil and religious liberty was as deeply

---

[79] Quoted in Hammond, *Gladstone*, 532. For Hammond (pp. 543, 546), the main difference was that, to Gladstone, Home Rule was not just a political issue—it also possessed a mystical, religious aspect.
[80] Leslie Stephen, 'Science and Politics' [1892], *Social Rights and Duties* (1896; 2011), i. 46.

entrenched in these writers as in the Gladstonian Liberals. This is why they felt able to call upon their Whig traditions and upon Burke. Yet, to them, Home Rule was also a constitutional revolution. Thus they found support—along with some Conservatives—across Burke's wider oeuvre, most notably his writings on France. For example, Lecky asserted the Unionist case against 'Rome Rule' in favour of civil and religious liberty and refuted the Gladstonian reading of Grattan's Parliament, while Dicey defended the established constitution. Arnold insisted that Home Rule was an unnecessary 'mechanical' political solution to a much wider problem, and therefore suggested a scheme of local self-government to gain Irish loyalty. He offered a different version of the union of hearts; one which maintained the existing Act of Union. The Duke of Argyll (1823–1900)—who broke with Gladstone over Home Rule, but whose personal eccentricity and ferocious independence were such that he remained outside the Liberal Unionist party proper—spoke against the dissolution of the Union and the related worry about the disintegration of the empire. On the other hand, the Conservative use of Burke was less prominent, and the silence of a genuinely intellectual commentator such as Lord Salisbury is particularly notable.

The Liberal Unionist response centred round the idea of civil and religious liberty.[81] As with the Gladstonians, this was the historic party motto in which they rooted their identity. However, in 1886 their aim was to protect the liberty of the Protestant minority against a Catholic majority. This was often connected to a fear of clerical influence on political affairs and a more general anti-Catholic feeling. Burke's *Reflections on the Revolution in France*, in which he defended the liberty of aristocrats and clergymen against atheists and the multitude, became a key source. For instance, Lecky—the Protestant believer in rational religion—acknowledged that the vast majority of Irish political thinkers, including Burke, Sheridan, Flood, and Grattan, had preferred a dual monarchy with Ireland a distinct and independent nation connected with England by the crown: 'Burke aided it when he wrote in approval of the movement of '82 and denounced the Penal Laws and the travel restrictions which shackled the energies of Ireland.' For Lecky, this was historical: 'The enthusiasm which springs from the memory of the past will ever sustain... the patriotic passion, which makes the independence of the land its primary

---

[81] W. S. Lilly, 'Illiberal Liberalism', *FR* (Nov. 1895), 651–2, 655. It was later claimed that one of the most definite differences between Gladstone and Hartington was their conception of liberty: [Anon.], 'The Duke of Devonshire and the Liberal Unionist Party', *QR* (Jan. 1912), 275.

object, will foster and inspire it.'[82] Many Home Rulers felt that, given this historical tradition, Lecky would become a Home Ruler. He did not. Lecky, though he condemned English misrule, still had more confidence in the improvement that could be wrought by the British government and the elimination of Catholic influences, such as the perceived influence of priests over voters.[83] His concern for the civil and religious liberty of the Protestant minority included himself. Again, awareness of English misrule did not necessarily require constitutional change. Previously, in 1882, Lecky had discussed the representative system of the early 1880s in order to make Burke's views clearer in his *History of England*. Here, the first objective was to bring together men of ability, knowledge, and integrity in Parliament: men who were best suited to maintain the health of the empire. Moreover, Lecky argued, using Burke, that political power should be concentrated in the hands of those classes whose material interests would be most affected by upheaval and war.[84] The underlying message was, of course, an anti-Catholic view of Irish intelligence and wealth: despite measures of Catholic emancipation dating back to 1793, the land imbalance remained prominent.

Fear of the oppression of minorities was often linked to the Terror of Revolutionary France. Thomas Macknight, as we have seen, was an English Liberal with a deep knowledge of Burke and of Ireland. Yet though a firm follower of Gladstone before 1886, he was unconvinced by Gladstone's interpretation of Burke drawn from his speeches on conciliation with America. Macknight believed that a change in the constitution to reduce executive power at Westminster was as mistaken as Fox's benign reaction to the French Revolution which (he argued) resulted in anarchy, revolution, and absolutism.[85] Macknight, now a Liberal Unionist, did not believe that the Catholic Irish majority housed the talent required to govern competently and, consequently, Home Rule would bring about economic disaster and civil war. He also rejected the idea that the newly empowered Irish would govern fairly: again we see the Liberal Unionist preoccupation with the civil and religious liberty of the Protestant minority.[86] Macknight therefore turned away from Gladstone, once a friend and model statesman, towards Hartington, who became his new ideal of Burkean statesmanship and consistency.[87] Similarly, Huxley

---

[82] Quoted in Auchmuty, *Lecky*, 72.   [83] Ibid., 73.
[84] Lecky, *History of England*, iii. 212–13. He was still asserting this in 1897: see Lecky, *Memoir of the Rt. Hon. W. E. H. Lecky*, 309.
[85] Maume, 'Burke in Belfast', 163–4.   [86] Ibid., 177.
[87] Ibid., 178; Thomas Macknight, *Ulster as it is: or, Twenty-Eight Years' Experience as an Irish Editor* (1896), ii. 221.

demanded to know: 'Is there among us a man of the calibre of Burke' who would 'stand up and tell his countrymen that the disruption of the union is nothing but a cowardly wickedness, an act base in itself, and fraught with immeasurable harm, especially to the people of Ireland?'[88] Of course, the anti-Catholic views of Lecky and Macknight are hardly examples of magnanimous behaviour, yet they were both supporters of Irish Church disestablishment who argued for 'civil and religious liberty'—a concept which could include a minimum of Catholic toleration and a Gladstonian moral ideal of respect and redress of past misrule, without necessitating Irish self-government.

A second fundamental theme for the Unionists, therefore, was to refute the Gladstonian interpretation of Grattan's Parliament. While Gladstonians had suggested its importance as a constitutional precedent, Unionists—mostly Liberal Unionists—argued that it was no such thing. Lecky, for example, in an 1886 letter to *The Times*, used Burke to argue against the Gladstonian view of Grattan's Parliament. He insisted that the Parliament of 1782, as supported by Burke, was a product of the Protestant Ascendancy 'of property' which left that Ascendancy entirely unshaken and was exclusively loyal. It was thus completely different from a Home Rule parliament, which would empower those who would wish to sever the British connection for good. Lecky not only wrote to the press but further disseminated this argument via a pamphlet produced by the Liberal Unionist Association.[89]

In addition, Unionists often argued that Burke had changed his mind and his tone about the Irish parliament of 1782 in his later writings. They also insisted, like Lecky, that the modern context was completely altered. This refutation was used by the Duke of Argyll, Lecky, and backbench MPs, such as the Whig scion, Edmond Wodehouse (1835–1914). Morley would later describe Argyll as 'a more definite representative of old-fashioned and current Liberal doctrine than Gladstone ever was'[90] and he was vocal in the debates. Furthermore, despite Argyll's mocking tone when discussing perpetual references to Burke,[91] he produced one of the

---

[88] *Evening Standard* (13 Apr. 1886), quoted in Bew, *Ireland*, 349. This was also quoted in a pamphlet for general distribution: William Wileman, 'Rome Rule in Ireland, the Facts of the Case Plainly Stated: Opinions of Eminent Men' (1886), 23–4.
[89] [W. E. H. Lecky], 'Grattan's Parliament: a Letter by Mr. W. E. H. Lecky, addressed to the Editor of the Times, June 7 1886' (1887), 1. For similar sentiments, see Hugh de Fellenberg Montgomery, 'Burke and Gladstone', *The Times* (16 June 1886), 7. This was extended into a pamphlet: 'Gladstone and Burke' (1886).
[90] Morley, 'Liberalism and Reaction' [1904], *Oracles on Man*, 141.
[91] For instance, 'Gladstone is very fond of referring to Edmund Burke. Here is a passage from Edmund Burke, in which he uses this expression in a letter—"I must speak the truth; I must say that all the evils of Ireland originated within itself." I venture to propound in this

longest orations on Burke in *Hansard*. After declaring that the use of Burke and the comparisons with Grattan's Parliament were irrelevant, Argyll exclaimed:

> But there is one passage, written by him towards the close of his life, which I can confidently recommend to your Lordships' reading as having some reference to the present condition of affairs. Burke was at the time one of those who were in favour of the Parliament of 1782. As an Irishman, he rejoiced at the election of that independent Parliament; but in the year before his death, in a letter to the Rev. Dr Hussey, he recognized the danger of that which you are now wishing to do—washing your hands of the responsibility of Irish affairs, by handing them over to an exclusively Irish Parliament.

He then quoted a 1796 letter from Burke which had been used earlier in the debate by Wodehouse. Both quoted the same passage: '"Ireland has derived some advantage from its independence of the Parliament... [But] I cannot but think that even these great blessings were bought clearly enough when... they have totally lost all benefit from the superintendence of the British Parliament."' Wodehouse described this as 'faint praise' for Grattan's Parliament; while Argyll asked, 'Is that the condition of things to which you wish to reduce Ireland by handing over all its affairs to the local Parliament and washing your hands of all responsibility?'[92] Argyll and others sought to disprove the relevance of Burke's support for Grattan's Parliament by stressing the entirely changed context. The very idea that Burke was continuously supportive of the parliament was questioned by Unionists who placed his doubts over its cumulative benefits, when compared with political coexistence with the British in Westminster. By pointing to these changed circumstances and Burke's later concerns, Argyll was able to claim Burke as a source of political wisdom and authority, while disproving the Liberals' particular use of his works as legitimating their proposals. Despite Argyll's lack of enthusiasm on quoting Burke, both in parliament and when writing to *The Times*,[93] and his belief in Burke's irrelevance to late nineteenth-century debates on Ireland, it is telling that he could not resist mentioning him anyway.[94] This sense

---

House now that the miseries of Ireland are not mainly due to misrule, but to the mischievous customs of the people themselves.' *Hansard*, 19 Aug. 1886, vol. 308, c.49.

[92] *Hansard*, 3 June 1886, vol. 306, cc.912–13; 10 June 1886, vol. 306, cc.1266–7. The latter prompted an immediate response—Burke included—from Lord Herschell (1837–1889), then Liberal Lord Chancellor: *Hansard*, 10 June 1886, vol. 306, c.1283.

[93] Duke of Argyll, 'Mr. Canning on the Irish Question', *The Times* (23 June 1886), 10.

[94] He quoted Burke again in 1889: 'The Duke of Argyll's Speech', *Spectator* (20 July 1889), 8–9.

of Burke's irrelevance as an authority on contemporary Irish issues was shared with Hartington and, most probably, Morley.[95] Yet he chose to end his 1893 book, *Irish Nationalism: An Appeal to History*, with a quotation from Burke.[96]

A third argument was to insist that Home Rule was unnecessary: it was a narrowly political solution to a multi-faceted problem and measures could be taken to rectify this problem without resorting to constitutional change. It became known by the slogan, 'killing Home Rule with kindness', and in tone it resembled the union of hearts argument. This was true of Matthew Arnold, who viewed the situation as requiring exceptional statesmen: 'It needs an Irishman of Burke's calibre', he wrote to *The Times* on 6 August 1886, 'to be a reasonable politician under such circumstances.' Those circumstances were, he explained, the treatment of Irish issues as desired by the Irish Protestant minority and the British 'Philistine': he saw no generosity of spirit in either group and it was only to be expected that the Catholic section of Ireland reacted badly, when English politicians and writers told them they were treated as their equals in the same manner as the Scots.[97] But, even so, Arnold believed that the Union should be maintained. Here, Nathan Wallace argues, he took two guidelines from Burke when considering what political concessions one might make: firstly, to remain constant to an agreed position, and, secondly, never to make decisions under the threat of violence.[98] To Arnold, Home Rule was an untried 'plunge into the unknown'. Local self-government was needed, and in earnest, but that was all. Arnold's is an argument imbued with the necessity for a union of hearts, but also of the Union. He therefore urged Liberal Unionists to act uniformly with Lord Salisbury and the Conservative party to create a system of local self-government for Ireland, an idea associated primarily with Joseph Chamberlain: Hartington had the good temper to counter Salisbury's bad, and Goschen (1831–1907), who went on to serve as Chancellor of the Exchequer from 1887 until 1892, had a particular knowledge of local government.[99]

---

[95] Hartington, at a speech at a loyalist meeting, dryly commented: 'I have no doubt that before the end of this debate we will hear much more of Mr. Burke, and Mr. Burke's sayings.' 'The Government of Ireland', *The Times* (15 Apr. 1886), 6.
[96] Duke of Argyll, *Irish Nationalism: An Appeal to History* (1893), 264.
[97] Arnold, *On Home Rule for Ireland*, 11.
[98] Nathan Wallace, 'Matthew Arnold, Edmund Burke, and Irish Reconciliation', *Prose Studies: History, Theory, Criticism*, 34 (2012), 210.
[99] Arnold, *On Home Rule for Ireland*, 4, 12. See also Lilly, 'Illiberal Liberalism', 651–2. A pamphlet published and distributed by the Liberal Unionist Association also positions Burke as in favour of local self-government under the control of a unitary parliament: John Guthrie Smith, 'Home Rule in Ireland, the Colonies, and the United States. An Address Delivered in the College Division, Glasgow, 17 Dec. 1886' (1889), 4.

Arnold's view was not simply a rejection of Irish self-government, but a reworking of the solution to Irish grievances that would not shake the equipoise of the British Constitution. The chief aim was to reconcile the Irish to Britain on more than a merely 'mechanical' level. As Lord Monteagle explained, in 1897, Arnold 'used never to be tired in reminding us in connection with Irish affairs of Burke's guiding principle, "Sir, your measures must be healing"'.[100] These arguments were later popularized by others in lesser-known speeches and lectures, such as that by William Willis (1835–1911), a largely self-educated barrister and judge, who argued that the root of Irish discontent had been attributed 'to matters wholly foreign to their real origin'; that is, to political and constitutional matters rather than to low wages and land and rent disputes.[101]

Unionists also insisted on the danger to the empire that granting Home Rule posed. It raised the fear of the separation of Britain from Ireland by stimulating Irish nationalist feeling, and also of provoking a chain reaction across the entirety of the British Empire, in which colony after colony would demand independence from the sovereign parliament at Westminster.[102] Burke was used in this context by R. W. Dale (1829–95), an influential Nonconformist minister and former 'Gladstonian'. Dale's ministry was in Birmingham, and he had a longstanding link to the leading radical politician among the Liberal Unionists, Joseph Chamberlain (who served as mayor of the city from 1873, and as an MP from 1876). Like Arnold and Huxley, Dale depicted Burke as an exemplary statesman of political combat:

> It may seem presumption on a person like myself to express a strong adverse judgement on proposals submitted to us by a statesman like Mr. Gladstone, but there is a sentence of Edmund Burke's which ought to be remembered by the chiefs of the political parties, by their colleagues, and their followers . . . 'In my course,' says Mr. Burke, 'I have known and, according to my measure, have co-operated with great men, and I have never yet seen any plan which has not been mended by the observations of those who were much inferior in understanding to the person who took the lead in the business.' [Cheers.] I am encouraged by that sentence to criticize one of the main provisions of the Bill now before us. My principal objection to the Bill

---

[100] Lord Monteagle, 'The New Irish Policy', *NC* (June 1897), 1018. The preface to Arnold's Irish essays certainly laid great stress on the idea of 'healing': *Irish Essays*, vi, xv.
[101] William Willis, 'Edmund Burke: the Story of His Life, a lecture delivered at Beaconsfield 5th December 1888' (1889), 24; J. B. Atlay, 'Willis, William', rev. Eric Metcalfe, *ODNB* (2004). Gladstone read this in 1889: Gladstone, *Gladstone Diaries*, xii. 245.
[102] [L. J. Jennings], 'Mr. Gladstone and Ireland', *QR* (July 1886), 282.

is the provision which imposes taxes on the Irish people for Imperial purposes and excludes them from the Imperial Parliament. [Cheers.][103]

Dale saw the exclusion of the Irish from Westminster as undesirable, and still more so given the continuation of taxation. No doubt this would have had resonance with his Nonconformist audience, who had only relatively recently seen compulsory church rates abolished in 1868, and hints at the trouble such payments could cause. This was an appeal to the principled, voluntaryist strand of Nonconformity who identified themselves with the Roman Catholics as the fellow oppressed; it illustrates, therefore, the diverse ways in which the reading and use of Burke passed through all the component groups of Liberal Unionism, including the more radical section. We can even find examples of Joseph Chamberlain himself finishing speeches with flourishes from Burke.[104] Chamberlain and Dale combined were two of the few Liberal Unionists who had the power to steer Nonconformists—and not only more traditionally anti-Catholic Evangelicals—away from Gladstone's alliance with the Catholic Irish, and towards Unionism.[105] Their combined use of Burke is therefore significant.

The final, and most fundamental, argument was the insistence that Home Rule was a constitutional revolution. As we have seen in Morley's case, it was easy to come to the conclusion that Burke would have rejected any such measure outright. Likewise, although the Act of Union had already altered Burke's ideal of the British Constitution, there was equally little ground for using him in support of changes in political structures, particularly those man-made 'paper constitutions' which he had denounced so loudly during the French Revolution. Using *Reflections* and other French writings allowed Liberal Unionists to position Burke as a proto-Unionist, since any reading of Burke on the topic of the British Constitution, particularly during the Revolutionary period, would undeniably strengthen the Unionist cause. By contrast, there was very little ground for promoting an image of Burke as a constitutional modernizer, as he had opposed parliamentary reform in Britain long before events in France were underway.[106]

---

[103] 'Mr. Chamberlain and the Birmingham Association', *The Times* (22 Apr. 1886), 10.
[104] [Anon.], 'Speech Delivered by the Rt. Hon. Joseph Chamberlain, M.P. to the Members of the Liberal Union Club, at Willis' Rooms, June 14 1887' (1887). Published and distributed by the Liberal Unionist Association.
[105] Peter Marsh, *Joseph Chamberlain: Entrepreneur in Politics* (1994), 304; Loughlin, *Gladstone and the Ulster Question*, 199; John Wolffe, *God and Greater Britain: Religion and National Life in Britain and Ireland, 1843–1945* (1994), 147–8.
[106] See pp. 26–7 in this volume.

For this argument, the most commanding figure was the constitutional lawyer, A. V. Dicey. His widely-read tract, *England's Case against Home Rule*, referenced Burke largely as a broad-minded supporter of Irish Catholics against the Penal Code, against the wishes of his 'selfish' Bristol constituents.[107] This was followed by a section on the 'democratic sentiment' influencing Home Rule and used Burke as a way to highlight its dangerous and cruel elements, as he had been ejected from his seat at Bristol for following an enlightened principle. *Why England Maintains the Union* was a popular rendering of *England's Case against Home Rule*, published in 1887, and it consoled readers by reminding them that Burke's prediction of England's ruin as a result of separation from the American colonies did not come true.[108] It looks here as if he is following the textual agenda set by the Gladstonians. However, *A Leap in the Dark*—composed as resistance to the Second Home Rule Bill in 1893—quoted *Reflections*. For Dicey, the 'essential difference' in constitution-making was between guessing and foresight.[109] To him, Burke's diatribe against the French constitution was an example of the latter: his French writings worked out previously held principles and this was what made Burke a philosophic statesman. Perhaps, *contra* Matthew, Burke and Dicey were not such polar opposite reading choices for Gladstone after all.[110] That Dicey made use of the *Reflections* is predictable given its status as an enthusiastic panegyric on the constitution as it then stood, but his emphasis on Burke's fundamental consistency is also indicative of the wider success of the critical reappraisals discussed earlier. Unionists were able to exploit all of this to great effect, given the importance Gladstone had ascribed to Burke's opinion in the debate.

In light of this Liberal Unionist counterargument, the relative Conservative silence on Burke is noteworthy. The omission of Lord Salisbury, a highly intellectual and well-read politician, from the Conservative deployment of Burke is a particularly revealing. In fact, Salisbury appears to have kept Burke at a distance in his political thinking—or at least publicly. Andrew Roberts notes Salisbury's preference for Castlereagh, while Michael Pinto-Duschinsky's *The Political Thought of Lord Salisbury* concludes by explicitly contrasting the 'Conservatism' of Salisbury and Burke.[111] Salisbury's son, Lord Hugh Cecil, would rectify his father's

---

[107] Dicey, *England's Case against Home Rule*, 22.
[108] Dicey, *Why England Maintains the Union*, 50.
[109] Dicey, *A Leap in the Dark*, 134.   [110] Matthew, *Gladstone*, 547.
[111] J. J. Sack, 'Edmund Burke and the Conservative party', in Ian Crowe, ed., *Edmund Burke: His Life and Legacy*, 81; Andrew Roberts, *Salisbury: Victorian Titan* (1999), 50, *passim*; Michael Pinto-Duschinsky, *The Political Thought of Lord Salisbury, 1858–1868* (1967), 153. Burke is not discussed in Michael Bentley, *Lord Salisbury's World: Conservative Environments in Late-Victorian Britain* (2001).

lack of interest in his volume on *Conservatism* in 1912.[112] Two very modest exceptions to this rule are Colonel Edwin Hughes (1832–1904), member for Woolwich, who felt 'called upon to abandon my common sense, and believe in truth and justice as expounded by the present Prime Minister'. Yet he did not see the route to 'justice' through Home Rule, and supported his arguments with quotes from Burke's Irish writings from the 1790s which stated that '"Great Britain would be ruined by the separation of Ireland"'.[113] Later that month, Disraeli's old companion from Young England, Lord John Manners, began his speech on the 1886 bill by stating: 'The Prime Minister wanted to hear as much as possible of Mr. Burke's views.' Accordingly, Manners took issue with Gladstone's incorporation of features of both single- and dual-chamber models in his bill. He employed the element of Burke which was safest for his Tory position, that is, Burke on France, to establish his counterargument. He enlisted Burke to assert that any meeting of multiple 'Orders' in one chamber in an Assembly—as happened during the French Revolution, and as was proposed for the Irish parliament—would end in failure as it had in France, 'the melancholy result of that frightful disaster'.[114] As with Liberal Unionists such as Dicey, Manners saw revolution—constitutional revolution—in the proposed changes and Burke was invoked as a defensive weapon. Largely, however, Tories were not enthusiastic to make use of Burke for support, and this is evident in comparison to Liberals both Gladstonian and Unionist. That Salisbury declined to fight for the Burkean mantle at this time is even more arresting.

HISTORY AND PARTY IDENTITY

The debate over Home Rule and the use of Burke was in the first instance an argument about Liberal political traditions: only subsequently did it impact on their previous opponents, the Conservatives. But when it became apparent that the Liberal split was going to be permanent, the debate over Burke's legacy began to move into a new gear and a new phase. In this context, a critical aspect of Burke's appearance in the Home Rule debates are the historical parallels which were drawn between the Liberal split of 1886 and Burke's secession from the Whigs over the French Revolution at the close of the eighteenth century.[115] This was

---

[112] See Chapter 6 in this volume. [113] *Hansard*, 17 May 1886, vol. 305, c.1214.
[114] *Hansard*, 31 May 1886, vol. 306, c.527.
[115] See, for example, [Anon.], 'The Party Future', *BM* (Nov. 1896), 721; [Anon.], 'Lord Hartington', *WR* (Apr. 1887), 929: 'It is not unlike the difference between Burke and Fox.'

the popular analogy, not with Peel and the Conservatives in 1846.[116] While Gladstonian Liberals invoked the pre-revolutionary part of Burke's corpus in reference to the evils of British rule in Ireland, the Liberal Unionists were able to claim all of him. Indeed, they *were* Burke (and the rest of the Portland Whigs, who crossed the floor of the House of Commons to support Pitt's administration); and the Gladstonians, in their own minds, *were* the Foxite Whigs (who supported the revolutionaries). Their union with the Conservatives, who had previously been fond of using Burke to proclaim the dangers of constitutional revolution—but not much else—was a principal step in divorcing him from Liberal politics and constitutional reform.

The debate between Fox and Burke over the French Revolution incorporated many of the same themes which arose in 1886. The eighteenth-century debate had been, firstly, an argument about liberty and despotism: what was liberty? Who had liberty? Who was being tyrannized?[117] This then led on to the question of the protection of individuals and institutions versus the rights of majorities and (in Burke's notorious phrase) the 'swinish multitude'. Yet both Fox and Burke and their followers had admired the constitution while differing in their interpretation. The similarities between the two situations, the late eighteenth and the late nineteenth centuries, were the invocation of the idea of 'betrayal' by those who deserted their leader; the counter-statement of consistency; and, finally, a fear of violence. The differences that were claimed related, first, to the number of party members taking part in the 'betrayal', and, secondly, the existence of a 'catastrophe' in the Revolutionary period which was not apparent in 1886. Indeed, the Revolutionary comparison was so popular that Morley was led to write a debunking article in 1888, stating that the analogy was 'moonshine'.[118]

The idea of the betrayal and inconsistency of the seceders in relation to their previously held principles was well-documented on both sides of the debate. On the Gladstonian side, one example is found in Harcourt, in April 1886, as he addressed the House as follows:

---

[116] Ghosh, 'Gladstone and Peel', 68–9.
[117] For example, Lilly, 'Illiberal Liberalism', 642, 655–6: 'The Liberal party has always been understood to be the party upholding "the good old cause" as earlier generations delighted to call it; the cause of civil and religious liberty. But what does liberty mean? ["Genuine freedom" cannot be voted for.] This truth has been forgotten or disbelieved of late years by the Liberal Party, and most of all by the Radical section which has tyrannised over it. They have imagined the vain thing that liberty consists in a spurious and mechanical individualism.'
[118] John Morley, 'A Few Words on French Revolutionary Models', *NC* (Mar. 1888), 468–80.

I may be reminded that Burke in his later years proved unfaithful to the principles he then taught. He became the leader of a great secession, most disastrously in my opinion to the history of this country. You may think differently, but permit us who cherish the traditions of the Whig Party to think so. Yes, the secession of the Portland Whigs was the potent cause of most of the disasters which attended the close of the last and commencement of the present century. It was a bad thing for the Liberal Party—it was a bad thing for the Tory cause—and led them into excesses into which they never would have been betrayed but for that secession of the Whigs. There remained, however, still faithful to their principles and their Party a small but illustrious band of statesmen who in those dark and stormy times kept alive the sacred fire and preserved the ark of the Liberal Party, men who were faithful and not afraid, and among that band there were no names more famous than those of Cavendish and of Grey.[119]

The Liberal Unionist retaliation to this, like Burke's before them, was to insist on the consistency and strength of their previously held principles and their relation to their current political actions. Yet they too accused their opponents of betrayal. Lecky wrote an anonymous letter to *The Times* (4 February 1886) entitled '1793–1886', where he described his new position as analogous with that of Burke and the Portland Whigs. But, whereas the Whigs had blamed Burke for causing their forty-year political relegation at the beginning of the nineteenth century, Lecky, as a Liberal Unionist, placed the blame on the Foxite (and hence Gladstonian) leaders, who acted like unpatriotic radicals. In doing so, *they* had betrayed their political principles. This, to Lecky, was the true cause of the Whig exclusion from office until the ministries of the 1830s. He signed the letter, 'An Old Whig', thereby aligning himself with Burke the Whig seceder in his 1791 *Appeal from the New to the Old Whigs*.[120] Burke's *Appeal* had been designed to show his continued adherence to Whig traditions and so too his own long-standing beliefs. Lecky similarly, like Burke before him, saw *his* own constancy to long-held Liberal principles as in no way contradictory of his opposition to a scheme of Home Rule.

The reclamation of Burke by Liberal Unionists through the history of party identity continued in letters to *The Times*. In December 1887, 'Anti-Jacobin' wrote to *The Times* to insist on the importance of doing so. They contested Rosebery's conviction that 'the Separatists [i.e. Gladstonians] are heirs of the Whig tradition' and, in doing so, appealed to the authority of Burke: 'Other Separatists have patronized the great Whig, since

---

[119] Although Hartington was, of course, a Cavendish and a Liberal Unionist. *Hansard*, 13 Apr. 1886, vol. 304, cc.1454–5.
[120] *The Times* (4 Feb. 1886), quoted in McCartney, *Lecky*, 126.

Mr. Gladstone praised him in a recent letter.' 'Anti-Jacobin' accused the Liberal (and Macaulay's biographer) George Trevelyan (1838–1928), who had first opposed Home Rule and then returned to the Gladstonian side, of wrongly invoking Burke's authority in the name of radical causes, such as assailing the established church and the House of Lords. Since the Gladstonians had invoked Burke's authority, it was not necessary to argue for his 'infallibility'. What was required instead was 'merely to show that that authority, whatever its intrinsic value, is not upon the side of "those who have coined themselves Whig principles from an Irish die, unknown to the impress of our fathers in the Constitution"'.[121] The choice of the term 'Anti-Jacobin' as a pseudonym, and the reference to Burke's French writings once more, was therefore a highly considered move. Likewise, in his memoirs of 1898, the Liberal Unionist Lord Selborne recalled a letter to Sir Arthur Gordon from 6 June 1887, in which Selborne stressed the similarities with the eighteenth century and described Burke as an 'anti-Jacobin Liberal', presumably, like himself.[122]

Dicey also drew on the history of party identities to reclaim Burke and focused on the violence apparent in both the French Revolution and the Irish Question. In an 1888 article for the *Contemporary Review* entitled 'New Jacobinism and Old Morality', he began by restating the tale of Burke during the Revolutionary period. For Dicey, the Jacobins and the Gladstonian Liberals represented not just new, democratic politics, but a new morality; a new set of ethics. He linked the violence of the Irish to the violence of the French Revolution and quoted another of Burke's writings from the 1790s, his *Letters on a Regicide Peace*. He then turned his attention to the Gladstonian Liberals and stated: 'Burke's anti-revolutionary writings teem with sentences which might appear to be prophetically aimed at the favourite dogmas of Gladstonian Liberals.' He continued: 'the whole spirit of his teaching is as hostile to the new Jacobinism patronized by Mr. Gladstone as to the old Jacobinism patronized or tolerated by Fox'. Home Rulers were, however, becoming

> dimly conscious that the spirit of Burke is opposed to the spirit which inspires the Home Rule Movement. They never cite Burke's later writings; and eulogies of Fox are a sort of admission, that Home Rulers find the sentimentalism of the Whig rhetorician far more congenial to their taste than the political philosophy of the statesman whose hatred of the revolution spirit broke the Whig party to pieces.[123]

---

[121] ['Anti-Jacobin'], 'Mr. Burke and the Separatists', *The Times* (17 Dec. 1887), 9.
[122] Lord Selborne, *Memorials, part II: Personal and Political, 1865–1895* (1898), ii. 272.
[123] A. V. Dicey, 'New Jacobinism and Old Morality', *CR* (Apr. 1888), 476, 485–6. See also his 'The Protest of Irish Protestantism', *CR* (July 1892), 8, 13.

It is hardly surprising that Dicey again plumped for Burke's anti-revolutionary writings. They were an obvious source for the defence of the constitution and Dicey was a constitutional lawyer. He highlighted the selectiveness of the Gladstonian appropriation of Burke: in avoiding sections of his work, they misrepresented Burke's 'spirit' which, Dicey suggested, was more truly aligned with the Unionist side. But, more significantly for Burke's theoretical and political reputation, Burke's 'political philosophy'—i.e. his defining principles—was aligned with the Liberal Unionists, while the Gladstonians could only lay claim to a much weaker (and less fundamental) sentimental rhetoric. Establishing the respectability of Burke's French writings was also important as, if the Liberal Unionists were to be aligned with Burke and his conduct over the French Revolution, it was important that they be considered wise and sound, like his earlier speeches.

One can find examples of the 'dim consciousness' of Gladstonian uncertainty claimed by Dicey in the speeches of George Trevelyan and Rosebery. Trevelyan, speaking at the Durham and Northumberland Liberal conference in December 1887, used only Burke's 'kind' attitude to the Irish to query the Liberal Unionists' commitment to satisfying Irish grievances: in other words they had failed to mimic his benevolent spirit.[124] Trevelyan, who had only recently returned to the Gladstonian fold, was very much a moderate in this context. Similarly, in a speech to the United Leeds Liberal Association in 1888, Rosebery took inspiration from Burke's *Appeal from the New to the Old Whigs*. 'I confess,' Rosebery claimed, 'that I should be greatly inclined to write an appeal from the new to the old Liberals, because the new Liberalism that is now developed is one of such very exceptional character.'[125] Here Rosebery, who declined the Burkean mantle in 1886, aligned himself and the Liberal party in opposition to Burke's position—which helps to explain his reluctance to praise Burke in the 1890s mentioned earlier. Both underline the point that prominent Gladstonian Liberals were beginning to alter their tone when speaking about Burke.

The Liberal split then led on to the idea of possible convergence with the Conservative party, in the manner of Burke and the Portland Whigs when they crossed the floor of the Commons in the 1790s. This was being argued by the prominent Liberal Unionists Dicey and Henry James as early as 1887.[126] At the National Radical Union in Birmingham, presided

---

[124] 'Sir G. Trevelyan at Sunderland', *The Times* (13 Dec. 1887), 10.
[125] 'Lord Rosebery at Leeds', *The Times* (10 Oct. 1888), 10.
[126] A. V. Dicey, 'On the Fear of Alliance with Conservatives', *Unionist Delusions* (1887), 77. Burke features on p. 78.

over by Chamberlain, James drew on Burke's maxim, as he put it, that 'when bad men combined it was time for good men to associate'. James asserted that an alliance (between Gladstonians and Irish Nationalists) had been created to destroy a valued institution, and so its opponents were bound to seek partners in order to effectively defend the Union.[127] A. H. A. Hamilton, a Conservative Old Etonian and public official, saw this too: in a pamphlet of 1888 entitled 'The Past and Present Schisms of the Liberal Party', he predicted that the closer the connection between the Gladstonian and the Parnellite Home Rulers, the more intimate would be the alliance between the Liberal and Conservative Unionists. For him, the Liberal Unionists were deeply patriotic. Taking up Burke's maxim on party as stated by James, Hamilton continued:

> The Liberal Unionists, I think, must gravitate to the party of Lord Salisbury—as Burke, and Portland, and Fitzwilliam, and Windham, and the rest, gravitated to the party of William Pitt. Whether, as some of us may hope, they will merely bring strength and permanence to the Conservative party; or whether, as others may prefer, the two sides will combine to form a new party, to be called the Constitutional, or National, or Patriotic, or Country party, still remains to be seen. Parties grow up, and acquire new names, as it were naturally, and not in obedience to any previously arranged system.[128]

Allusions to Burke's *Appeal* became increasingly popular. Even Chamberlain, a man very short on interest in English history, claimed inspiration in a speech of 1889: 'I am inclined to imitate Mr. Burke, *longo intervallo* of course, and to make an appeal from the new Radicals to the old.' Chamberlain aligned himself with the 'old' Radicals—Bright and Cobden—whose chief aim was to improve the condition of the people, and condemned the 'new', who sought only to 'attack the Constitution'.[129] Liberals and Liberal Unionists of all stripes were beginning to conceptualize and position Burke within political traditions more explicitly and publicly than in previous decades, in accordance to their contemporary political understanding of party difference.

The inevitability of this convergence was upheld by other Conservatives. T. E. Kebbel, the Tory journalist, wrote in an article of 1890 that just as Burke was an old Whig, Lord Hartington was an old Liberal. As

---

[127] 'The National Radical Union', *The Times* (2 June 1887), 6.
[128] A. H. A. Hamilton, 'The Past and Present Schisms of the Liberal Party: A Historical Parallel' (1888), 21.
[129] 'Mr. Chamberlain at Greenwich', *The Times* (1 Aug. 1889), 6. This analogy continued to be used into the 1900s: [Lord Crewe], 'The Disintegration of the Opposition', *The Times* (1 Nov. 1900), 10. Crewe was a Liberal.

such, Kebbel argued, they represented the principles of their party far better than their rivals. Yet because, like Burke before him, Hartington was deemed to have renounced Liberal principles and traditions, he would only ever be able to become leader of the Conservative party.[130] There was at this time, not coincidentally, a vast outpouring of discussion literature on the future of party politics and whether it was in the national interest to continue the form of party government that Burke had so eloquently defended in 1770.[131] In a similar vein, though drawing on a later (1774) speech of Burke's, Chamberlain used Burke in an 1892 speech to question the theory of party that insisted on constant adherence to the whip, and for members to relinquish the idea of exercising private judgement.[132]

The drawing of an historical parallel about changing party alignments was not simply an ephemeral product: it had staying power precisely because the fortunes of the Liberal Unionists had to be resolved. Thus, an 1893 article in the *Contemporary Review* entitled 'The Evolution of Liberal Unionism' began: 'The period which has passed since Mr. Gladstone's accession to office in 1886 has witnessed the most memorable secession from a great political party since Edmund Burke issued his famous "Appeal to the Old Whigs",' leaving Fox and Sheridan 'almost alone to do battle with a Parliament driven to the verge of frenzy by the horrors of the French Revolution'. However, its author, Sir George Osborne Morgan (1826–97), a Welsh lawyer and Gladstonian Liberal, saw an essential difference between the two defections:

> The great Whig disruption on 1792 was the work of timid men unnerved by an appalling catastrophe. The Liberal revolt of 1886 carried away with it not only the cautious and 'moderate' Liberals, but the most robust and advanced Radicals who once professed allegiance to Mr. Gladstone—not only the Argylls, the Selbornes, and the Goschens, but the veteran 'Tribune of the People', the hero of the 'unauthorised programme', and the author of the once popular social nostrum, summed up in the magic words, 'Three acres and a cow' [Chamberlain].[133]

The Liberal split of 1886 was different because it carried a more diverse body of men across the floor of the Commons than its eighteenth-century predecessor. It had had an effect on 'robust' Radicals, as well as the weak and 'cautious' moderates. Burke, as one of the 'timid men' in the 1790s,

---

[130] T. E. Kebbel, 'Party Prospects', *NC* (Feb. 1890), 324.
[131] Examples of such discussions which explicitly reference Burke include: J. R. Seeley, 'The Impartial Study of Politics', *CR* (July 1888), 53–65; Smith, *Burke on Party*, 1–6.
[132] 'Mr. Chamberlain and Mr. Matthews at Birmingham', *The Times* (18 Aug. 1892), 4.
[133] George Osborne Morgan, 'The Evolution of Liberal Unionism', *CR* (Aug. 1893), 299.

was evidently no hero in this version of the story, yet the basic interpretation had taken root. The effect of these historical associations was to attach the 'spirit', as Dicey had described it, of Burke to the Liberal Unionists—and not the Gladstonians, who were seen to have been radically misguided in their interpretation of Burke as a constitutional modernizer. In doing so, Burke became indirectly attached to the Conservative party, as the Liberal Unionists gradually merged into close political cohabitation.

This can be clearly seen in the debates around the Second Home Rule Bill, which was introduced to Parliament by Gladstone in 1893. Not only did many Gladstonians loosen their ties with Burke, there was also a considerable Conservative uptake of his work. Harcourt, in 1892, acknowledged that it was the Liberal Unionists who now claimed to represent the principles of Burke, though he insisted that, in failing to replicate his spirit towards the Catholics, they no longer represented the Whig–Liberal tradition of 'civil and religious liberty':

> The Party which sits on this side of the House is the Party that for generation after generation, and at the cost of political power for year after year, has maintained the doctrine not only of civil freedom, but of religious equality... The Liberal Party first demanded and obtained religious equality for the Non-conformists, afterwards for the Catholics, then for the Jews, and lastly in the struggle in which you engaged against the late Mr. Bradlaugh... I speak of the principles to which we have always adhered, and which we have perpetually maintained[.] I should like to ask, where are the Whigs on this subject? If there ever was a subject to which the Whigs by tradition and principle were bound, it is this question of religious equality. Where are the men who profess—shall I say who pretend—to be the representatives of the principles of Burke? What was it that Burke taught with reference to the Catholics of Ireland? The principles of Fox, Grey, Grenville, and Russell. Where are the Fitzwilliams, the Carlisles, and the Cavendishes? Are the Whigs prepared to sacrifice these principles, as they have thrown overboard all the rest? I hope not. But if they are, we need not wonder why they are perishing out of the land, why they have ceased to influence the people amongst whom they were once a power, and why, like the Greeks of the Lower Empire, they will carry a memorable name to an unhonoured grave.[134]

Redmond was now a lone voice on the Home Rule side in drawing on Burke when calling for conciliation.[135] For Gladstonians in both the Commons and the Lords, Burke became an off-hand reference as one of a number of distinguished Irishmen, including Grattan, Swift, and

---

[134] *Hansard*, 9 Feb. 1892, vol. 1, cc.69–70.
[135] *Hansard*, 9 Feb. 1893, vol. 8, c.936.

Flood.¹³⁶ In addition there was increasing reference to Gladstone as an idealistic moral crusader in politics. His original invocation of Burke in 1886 could hardly be forgotten, and in this way Burke was introduced once removed: 'when Mr. Gladstone has most alienated and angered those Conservatives who would boast themselves to be the political descendants of Burke, he has himself, to his own satisfaction, justified his statesmanship by the precepts of the political philosophy of Burke.'¹³⁷ Hereafter, Gladstonian Liberal references to Burke remained similar to Redmond's and focused on the need for benevolence and conciliatory action. Asquith, for instance, in a speech of 1894, spoke of the importance of capturing Burke's generous and benevolent attitude, yet insisted that he and the Liberal party were maintaining the 'old Liberal' traditions.¹³⁸ It appears to be another separation of philosophical principles and rhetorical or moral sentiment. But taken overall the centrality of Burke to the Gladstonian argument was fading away.

By contrast, Burke continued to be used by Liberal Unionists in parliament, including Gladstone's former Attorney General Henry James (1828–1911), who fought against a Unionist coalition with the Conservatives, and James Parker-Smith (1854–1929), Cambridge Apostle and Chamberlain's future Private Secretary (1900–3).¹³⁹ James used Burke's aphorism from the 1777 'Letter to the Sheriffs of Bristol'—that 'general', or national, rebellions are always provoked—to argue that Home Rule would provoke rebellion in the form of separation (and not, as the Gladstonians would argue, that English misrule provoked Irish insurgence).¹⁴⁰ Elsewhere, Lecky also continued to denounce the relevance of Grattan's Parliament and the dangers of separation with the help of Burke, 'the greatest and truest of all our political thinkers'.¹⁴¹

Simultaneously, the rise of Conservative appropriation of Burke by 1893 is notable. Burke increasingly appeared in Conservative arguments against the bill in Parliament, including those of Balfour, who cited Burke as an example of Irish genius which belonged to the 'race', 'religion', and

---

¹³⁶ *Hansard*, 12 Apr. 1893, vol. 11, c.163 (E. J. C. Moreton); 7 Sept. 1893, vol. 17, c.413 (Lord Thring).
¹³⁷ T. H. S. Escott, 'Mr. Gladstone and Mr. Chamberlain', *WR* (July 1894), 16. See also 'The Second Reading', *Speaker* (8 Apr. 1893), 387.
¹³⁸ 'Mr. Asquith in Berwerkshire', *The Times* (28 Mar. 1894), 4.
¹³⁹ Lubenow, *The Cambridge Apostles, 1820–1914*, 152.
¹⁴⁰ *Hansard*, 21 Apr. 1893, vol. 11, c.938 (Henry James); 7 Aug. 1893, vol. 15, c.1504 (James Parker-Smith).
¹⁴¹ W. E. H. Lecky, 'Address Delivered Before the Birmingham and Midland Institute' [10 Oct. 1892], *The Political Value of History* (1892), 25; *Historical and Political Essays*, new edn (1910), particularly, 'Ireland in the Light of History' [1891] and 'Empire: Its Value and Growth' [1893].

'class' of those who, in the late nineteenth century, repudiated Home Rule (i.e. the Anglo-Irish).[142] Balfour was joined by backbench Tory MPs, such as Percy Thornton and Thomas Gibson Bowles,[143] and, in the Lords, by Cranbrook and William Boyd Carpenter, bishop of Ripon, who all invoked the authority of Burke. Cranbrook, very much the elder statesman who had served in Conservative ministries under Derby, Disraeli, and Salisbury, made use of Burke's Irish letters to insist on the disaster that separation would bring upon Ireland and Britain, before asserting that Home Rule would inevitably lead to this. He was, as ever, a good index of conformity. Shortly afterwards, Boyd Carpenter drew upon Burke's idea of the British parliament as a national institution, devoid of local attachments ('Speech to the Electors of Bristol', 1774), as a refutation of the interpretation of Burke as supportive of an Irish parliament governing on Irish issues by 'Irish ideas'.[144]

Outside Westminster, Lord Randolph Churchill, once the leader of the Fourth Party and a spokesman for 'Tory Democracy', made a speech which asserted that Home Rule was the greatest incident in parliament since the days of Burke, Fox, and Pitt. He then called on Gladstonians to revert to their 'old Liberal' faith and realize their true traditions.[145] The arguments for and against Home Rule were, evidently, not radically altered. The sea change is instead found in the increasing number of prominent Conservatives who felt comfortable quoting and referencing Burke, especially the Gladstonian favourites on Ireland and America. This is crucial. It was not enough for Radicals and Liberals to 'reject' Burke; Conservatives had to embrace him too.

CONCLUSION

In 1886 Gladstonian Liberals had viewed Burke on Ireland and America as a source of authority for their 'union of hearts'. Voluntary political ties were, they argued, the very essence of Burke. He was also quoted as a historical authority on Irish matters, such as the Penal Code. His early support of Grattan's Parliament—positioned as a constitutional precedent for Home Rule—was considered conclusive. For most Liberal Unionists, by contrast, the reason they opposed Home Rule was that its result could only be disastrous in terms of social cohesion, individual liberties, and the

---

[142] *Hansard*, 21 Apr. 1893, vol. 11, cc.990–1 (Balfour).
[143] *Hansard*, 14 Feb. 1893, vol. 8, c.1448 (P. M. Thornton); 14 Aug. 1893, vol. 16, c.193 (T. Gibson Bowles).
[144] *Hansard*, 8 Sept. 1893, vol. 17, c.574 (Cranbrook), c.611 (Ripon).
[145] 'Lord Randolph Churchill in Rossendale', *The Times* (13 July 1893), 12.

unity of the empire. It went against their deepest principles: they had to protect the liberty of the Protestant minority in Ireland, just as Burke had argued for the protection of nobility and clergy in France. A classless, national Liberalism which strove for 'civil and religious liberty' was as deeply entrenched in these writers as in the Gladstonian Liberals. However, Home Rule was also a constitutional revolution. Thus they found support—eventually, with Conservatives too—in Burke's wider oeuvre.

The extent to which Burke's works were drawn upon by both Home Rulers and Unionists was paramount in raising his status as a canonical political thinker. But Liberal Unionists became Conservatives, in practice if not always in their hearts, and certainly in the eyes of the opposition, for the Gladstonian party was bent on crowning itself the true inheritor of Liberal principles and denigrating its rivals as simply traitors and turncoats. Moreover, the Liberal Unionists acted as consistent political allies of the Conservatives. There was, from 1895, a Unionist alliance between Liberal Unionists and Conservatives, formalized in 1912 by the creation of the Conservative and Unionist Party. For this reason, the historical similarities between the Liberal Unionists and Burke's secession over the French Revolution were called into play. This is a key moment of the assimilation of Burke into the Conservative tradition: Home Rulers used aspects of Burke—on Ireland, on America—to give authority and eloquence to their arguments from an Irish 'master of civic wisdom', but they avoided Burke's writings on France. Liberal Unionists were able to take all of Burke: they often used the same quotes as Liberals but offered an alternative interpretation and did not confine themselves to a particular body of texts.

The Liberal Unionists, in joining with the Conservative party, took their version of Burke with them. This convergence of party identity is illustrated clearly in the increasing Conservative appropriation of Burke's works for political ends: some Tories had always been happy to cite Burke—especially favourite passages which denounced French Revolutionaries and delivered a splendid panegyric on the constitution—but only after their convergence with the Liberal Unionists did Conservatives come to love Burke in his entirety. Whereas Burke had been a bipartisan figure before 1886, admired by constitutionalists of both parties, after 1886 he increasingly came to be seen as Conservative and Unionist, and not Liberal, property. By 1911, Hartington's biographer could write that, following the Whig schism over the French Revolution, 'the Cavendishes went with Burke'.[146] If, at the close of the nineteenth century, old Liberals could be palatable and dependable political allies to Conservatives, so

---

[146] Bernard Holland, *Life of the Duke of Devonshire, 1833–1908* (1911), i. 7.

could an eighteenth-century old Whig. Home Rule was not the sole explanation for this—the increasing importance of extra-constitutional social and economic issues in shaping party identity was another factor—but it is a significant one. Burke, hitherto the Whig-turned-Tory, slowly became the Liberal (Unionist)-turned-Conservative. What remains to be seen are the ways in which Burke's C/conservative thought was fashioned in the aftermath of 1886–93.

6
The New Conservatism, c.1885–1914

> It is only within the last thirty or forty years that Edmund Burke has been conceded universally his true place 'as the greatest of political philosophers'.
>
> *Speaker*, 1899[1]

In order for Burke to become the 'founder of modern conservatism', it was essential that Conservatives identified him as such. It is therefore significant that the late Victorian and Edwardian period saw the construction of political traditions of an entirely novel kind. It was from this process that Burke could be claimed as a political thinker whose conservatism was both the basis of a specific British party political tradition and an abstract cosmopolitan political philosophy. By this point in time, Burke was increasingly referred to as a 'philosophic statesman' who was guided by (mostly) consistent political 'principles'. Critical work on Burke, such as John Morley's, was primarily biographical, historical, and with thematic chapters divided by location: Britain, France, India, and America.[2] Even Leslie Stephen did not attempt to construct a system of 'Burke's political philosophy': he remarked in an 1891 letter to Henry Sidgwick that 'there does not appear to be any English book worth much as a systematic statement of any political theory', noting that he was especially interested in a work covering Locke, Hume, Burke, Godwin, and Bentham.[3] It was in fact from the 1890s that commentary on Burke's thought developed in two distinct but related ways. First, Burke's work began to be systematized into a 'political theory'—defined here as a coherent body of abstract concepts which were separate from, yet clearly affiliated to, party political divisions—which emphasized his historic, conservative organicism.

---

[1] [Anon.], 'Burke's Reverence for Order', *Speaker* (5 Aug. 1899), 126.
[2] Prior, *Life and Character of Edmund Burke*, 2nd edn; Macknight, *Life and Times of Edmund Burke*; Morley, *Edmund Burke: A Historical Study* (1867); Morley, *Burke* (1879).
[3] Leslie Stephen to Henry Sidgwick, 19 May 1891, Trinity College, Cambridge, Add. MS.c/95/96.

Secondly, this political philosophy was increasingly recognized by Conservative Unionists as part of their own political and intellectual heritage.

This chapter outlines, first of all, the development of Burke's thought, seen as the work of an individual canonical thinker, into a 'political philosophy'. The literature responsible for this not only provided justification for discussing Burke's work in abstract terms, but also defined his thought as a political philosophy of conservatism. This was bolstered in the periodical press and in various histories, anthologies, and reviews. The subsequent section will discuss how, in a party political context, partisan commentators variously rejected and claimed Burke and his revitalized intellectual legacy. Its specific focus is on Conservative Unionists—whether styled as Tories, Conservatives, or Unionists—and the ways in which Burke's legacy and thought became intellectually foundational and polemically valuable in a contemporary political setting. A primary consideration here is the relative place of Burke, and political thought more generally, within a C/conservative political and intellectual tradition.

THE POLITICAL CONTEXT

Before this, however, it is worth pausing to consider the political climate in the wake of the Home Rule crisis. Although historians have said much less about it, the search for a 'New Conservatism' after 1885 is as recognizable as that of New Liberalism. Liberals and Unionists (whether previously Tory, Conservative, Whig, or Birmingham Radical) were both in search of new identities in the wake of the Reform Acts of 1884–5, which, by creating a franchise that was widely regarded as democratic,[4] implied a degree of closure to the constitutional agenda which had dominated party politics since 1832. The vacuum and uncertainty this implied was compounded by the new political alignment created by Home Rule and, after 1900, by the growing prominence of the Labour movement and the associated threat of 'Socialism'.[5] With the exception of Ireland, the traditional party divisions generated by constitutional disputes over 'Church and State' began to look outdated. So far as the church was concerned, the 1880 Burials Act, which legalized non-Anglican burial

---

[4] H. Matthew, R. McKibbin, and J. Kay, 'The Franchise Factor and the Rise of Labour', *EHR*, 91 (1976), 723–52.

[5] E. H. H. Green, 'Radical Conservatism: The Electoral Genesis of Tariff Reform', *HJ*, 28 (1985), 682, 684. On anti-Socialism specifically, see James Nicholas Peters, 'Anti-Socialism in British Politics c.1900–22', DPhil thesis, University of Oxford, 1992. Peters' otherwise illuminating thesis identifies an underlying 'Burkeanism' in much anti-Socialist writing which would be more accurately described as an underlying organicism.

services in Anglican churchyards, marked the accomplishment of the Dissenters' 'six grievances' (presented in the wake of the 1832 Reform Act).[6] The 1902 Education Act established a system of denominational education that was maintained without any resignations or defections, though it remained controversial among Nonconformists, serving as a driver of the 1906 Liberal landslide.[7] So not all constitutional issues were settled overnight, and further examples include the cases of the House of Lords and the Welsh Church. This was a transitional period; and so the traditional centrality of constitutional politics and the centuries-old reverence from which it ultimately derived did not simply vanish. It continued to play a role, albeit altered, in national issues, and hence in party political and ideological alignments. The status (and possible reformation) of the House of Lords, for instance, had been raised by Liberal Unionist and Tory commentators such as Goldwin Smith and T. E. Kebbel, long before—and after—the 1911 Parliament Act. This was also true with regard to the party system itself: contemporaries who noted the decline of nineteenth-century constitutional politics worried that they were witnessing the disintegration of the British two-party system.[8] And while both parties would increasingly migrate towards a socio-economic and extra-constitutional programme (though with different policies and at different speeds), the continued presence of the constitution was particularly strong within the Unionist party, both for those who called themselves Tories and Conservatives, and for those who embraced the writings of Burke. The specific foundation of the Unionist party, which became formalized as an alliance in 1895, and as a united political party in 1912, was after all a constitutional one—the maintenance of the Act of Union with Ireland. As the 1910s progressed, impending legislation on the Lords, the disestablishment of the Anglican Church in Wales, and Irish Home Rule drove many Unionists into an even more desperate search for ideological invigoration. Burke's spotlight shone ever brighter: his fears of Jacobinical destruction of the British Constitution began to ring true.

Still, the belief that a constitutional standpoint was an increasingly insufficient basis for party identity was also evident, as individuals and organizations simultaneously turned towards constructive policies on non-constitutional issues. This can be seen at a high-political level and in a

---

[6] G. I. T. Machin, *Politics and the Churches in Great Britain, 1832–68* (1977), 42–3.

[7] E. H. H. Green, *The Crisis of Conservatism: The Politics, Economics and Ideology of the British Conservative Party, 1880–1914* (1995), 8.

[8] ['An Old Liberal'], 'A National Party', *Daily Telegraph* (5 Jan. 1891), 5; Goldwin Smith, 'Reform the House of Lords!', *CR* (Apr. 1897), 511–16; T. E. Kebbel, 'Is the Party System Breaking Up?', *NC* (Mar. 1899), 502–11. See also William Thomas Charley, *The Crusade against the Constitution: An Historical Vindication of the House of Lords* (1895), 453.

broader intellectual context. Thus, much of the principal, English-centred party agenda also focused a great deal of attention on empire, financial issues (such as tariff reform versus progressive taxation), and social reform.[9] On the Liberal side this led to the penning of a number of celebrated expositions of 'New Liberalism', as seen in the work of J. A. Hobson, L. T. Hobhouse, Herbert Samuel, and Charles Masterman, to name only a few.[10] But less attention has been paid to the Unionists who, in the same context, underwent an analogous process of change.[11] Yet they also needed to survive electorally and ideologically on the new terrain, and many Conservative Unionists became disillusioned with what they perceived to be an 'unconstructive' approach to party policy.[12] Further impetus came from the influx of Liberal Unionists and their subsequent impact on how Tories and Conservatives conceptualized their political thinking. Robert Taylor and Peter Marsh both suggest that Liberal Unionists would not have joined the Unionist ranks in such numbers if Conservatives had been 'incorrigible reactionaries'.[13] A new kind of question began to be posed: how does one reform in a Conservative or Unionist way? Self-proclaimed Tories and Conservatives began to construct their own traditions and values of cautious reform and organic national harmony in an attempt to transcend unequal material divisions and so appeal to a cross-class base. As with the Liberals this can be seen in high-political terms through the appeals to empire and Tariff Reform protecting native, working-class jobs. But it can also be traced at an intellectual level as numerous authors began to theorize and historicize C/conservatism. Major examples include F. E. Smith's *Toryism* (1903), Lord Hugh Cecil's *Conservatism* (1912), and Geoffrey Butler's *The Tory*

---

[9] Martin Pugh, *Lloyd George* (1988), 43.
[10] For a sample of the extensive historiographical work on New Liberalism, see Michael Freeden, *The New Liberalism: An Ideology of Social Reform* (1978); Peter Clarke, *Liberals and Social Democrats* (1981); Michael Bentley, *The Climax of Liberal Politics: British Liberalism in Theory and Practice, 1868–1918* (1987); Sandra den Otter, '"Thinking in Communities": Late Nineteenth-Century Liberals, Idealists and the Retrieval of Community', *Parliamentary History*, 16 (1997), 67–84.
[11] E. H. H. Green, *Ideologies of Conservatism: Conservative Political Ideas in the Twentieth Century* (2002), 2; Philip Williamson, 'Review: Ideologies of Conservatism', *EHR*, 475 (2003), 270–1; Martin Francis and Ina Zweininger-Bargielowska, eds., *The Conservatives and British Society* (1996).
[12] Martin Pugh, *The Tories and the People, 1880–1935* (1985).
[13] Robert Taylor, *Lord Salisbury* (1975), 187; Peter Marsh, *The Discipline of Popular Government: Lord Salisbury's Domestic Statecraft, 1881–1902* (1978), 131. For an example from the periodical press (including Burke), see William John Courthope, 'A Conservative View: Prophecy and Politics', *NR* (June 1886), 475–86. Courthope was responding to Matthew Arnold's plea for constructive Conservatism (which also cited Burke) that is outlined best in Arnold's 'The Zenith of Conservatism', *NC* (Jan. 1887), 148–64. Arnold argued that stability did not exclude the possibility for development.

Tradition (1914).[14] The intellectual and moral cornerstone of such texts was, more often than not, Burke.

THE INTELLECTUAL CONTEXT

This development indicates, therefore, that besides the political context there are also independent intellectual contexts for his reception in this period. In particular, the historically-minded intellectual atmosphere of the late Victorian period was explicitly cited as favouring a 'return to Burke', and John Morley's prediction in 1879 that there would be a Burkean renaissance before the end of the century was frequently repeated in commentary.[15] The sources of this renaissance lay variously in historicist, organic, Idealist, and utilitarian thought.

It is now well-established that the nineteenth century placed extraordinary emphasis on the importance of history.[16] The historical method stressed the complexity and interdependence of institutions, beliefs, and habits. One of the most important devices for evoking historical change lay in the 'organic' metaphor—the idea that societies are not made, but grow—and this became increasingly significant to understanding the historic and future development of nations across the political spectrum. But, of course, 'organicism' was part of a general vocabulary that could be invoked by different people with quite different aims. Most generally, it can stand for the method of interpreting the past stated as a continuous evolutionary process. Applied to future action it could, however, suggest very different approaches. Organic metaphors could, on the one hand, imply inevitable growth and development and thus support arguments for reform. On the other hand, they could be used to defend the status quo, cautioning against the kind of rapid change that could cause irreversible damage to slow-growing institutions. Organic metaphors were also deployed in likening institutions and the body politic to biological processes—nutrition, decay, rebirth, and so on—providing an accessible metaphor for interpreting the past, diagnosing contemporary problems, and suggesting options for the future. For some the idea that society was

---

[14] F. E. Smith, *Toryism* (1903); Lord Hugh Cecil, *Conservatism* (1912); Geoffrey Butler, *The Tory Tradition: Bolingbroke, Burke, Disraeli, Salisbury* (1914).

[15] Morley, *Burke* (1879), 215–16.

[16] See, for example, Valerie Chancellor, *History for their Masters. Opinion in the English History Textbook: 1800–1914* (1970); Rosemary Mitchell, *Picturing the Past: English History in Text and Image 1830–1870* (2000); R. D. Anderson, 'University History Teaching, National Identity and Unionism in Scotland, 1862–1914', *Scottish Historical Review*, 91 (2012).

an organism led to interest in ideas regarding the 'general will': the idea that a nation holds a collective consciousness above the aggregate desires of individuals. Today it is conventional for scholars to couple historicism and organicism with Burke's name,[17] but this is not a self-evident or context-free reading of his texts. In fact, it was not until this time that Burke's name became synonymous with a political philosophy of organic historic conservatism, and this was undoubtedly a fundamental moment of change in Burke's reception history.

Organicism was a very general trend, but it drew on more specific intellectual contexts. Some of the most prominent exponents of Burke had been strongly influenced by Idealist philosophy. Although Idealism was primarily associated with Balliol College, Oxford under Benjamin Jowett and T. H. Green, Jose Harris, Stefan Collini, and Clive Dewey have all sought to show the pervasiveness of Idealist thought throughout British intellectual life and culture in the late nineteenth and twentieth centuries—highlighting the role played by Idealists in introducing new concepts and vocabulary to British thought.[18] British Idealism, a part-Germanic import from Kant, Hegel, and Fichte, stressed the unity and developmental nature of organic society. Many of the Idealists who feature in this thesis first studied at Scottish universities, for example, during the Idealist Edward Caird's tenure of the Chair of Moral Philosophy at Glasgow (1866–93), and then went down to Balliol as Snell exhibitioners.[19] Although Idealism was not usually allied with Darwinian or Spencerian evolutionary thinking, it did still reflect the later nineteenth-century preoccupation with organic developmental intellectual processes. As philosophers cum social reformers, Idealists sought to mediate between an a priori conceptual framework and concrete facts, all of which formed an organic whole: hence the seemingly paradoxical Hegelian concept of the 'concrete universal'. Burke's specific appeal lay in the perception that he offered an organic and historicist *theory* of the state which simultaneously emphasized the importance of the locality, the 'little platoon', as a stepping-stone towards wider integration within the nation. Indeed, John MacCunn, Professor of Philosophy at Liverpool, stated in *Six*

---

[17] For a scholarly example, see Burrow, *Whigs and Liberals* (1988), 9–10, *passim*. Equally important are the more popular political accounts offered by, for instance, the Edmund Burke Institute: <http://www.edmundburkeinstitute.org/edmundburke.htm>.

[18] C. J. Dewey, '"Cambridge Idealism"': Utilitarian Revisionists in Late Nineteenth-Century Cambridge', *HJ*, 17 (1974), 63–78; Stefan Collini, 'Idealism and "Cambridge Idealism"', *HJ*, 18 (1975), 171–7; Jose Harris, 'Political Thought and the Welfare State, 1870–1940: An Intellectual Framework for British Social Policy', *Past and Present*, 135 (1994), 116–41.

[19] The Snell Exhibition sponsored Glaswegian graduates wishing to study at Balliol: Bentley, *Climax of Liberal Politics*, 76.

Radical Thinkers (1907) that Green instructed his students to read Burke.[20] Another of MacCunn's Glasgow and Balliol contemporaries, J. H. Muirhead (1855–1940), likened Green's belief in the providential basis of society to that of Burke, and the following year cited him as an influence alongside (though subordinate to) Hegel.[21]

Utilitarianism forms another context. Utilitarian thought was undergoing significant changes as Henry Sidgwick, Professor of Philosophy at Trinity College, Cambridge, replaced J. S. Mill as its chief representative. Sidgwick's modern commentators have described his approach as using 'the method of Bentham' to arrive at 'the conclusion of Burke'. This is a modification of the Idealist philosopher D. G. Ritchie's comment that Sidgwick used the method of Bentham to arrive at the conclusion of 'an end-of-the-nineteenth-century Blackstone,' or 'an English Hegel'.[22] Sidgwick had been no 'Burkite' in 1877, but his constitutional conservatism became abundantly clear following the Home Rule debates.[23] Like all Liberal Unionists, Sidgwick upheld his 'old Liberal' legacy, while his thought, notably *Elements of Politics* (1891), moved closer to the existing constitution than Bentham or Mill ever did.[24] This was also true of A. V. Dicey. In his seventy-seventh year Dicey (1835–1922) was still describing himself as an 'old, an unconverted, and an impenitent Benthamite', yet his writings explicitly cultivated Burke from 1886 on.[25]

Dicey himself is thought to have made his creed seem out of touch through his 1895 lectures which divided the Benthamism of 1830 to 1870 from modern 'Collectivism'.[26] The waning of ahistoric 'old Liberalism' is also suggested by Collini's study of the posthumous reputation of Mill.[27] But any condemnation of utilitarianism as static or outdated is too simple. Instead, Sidgwick's utilitarianism drew on evolutionary and organic theories of progress to argue for a non-interventionist limited state. Utilitarianism was not Philosophic Radicalism any more. Instead,

---

[20] John MacCunn, *Six Radical Thinkers* (1907), 229, 241.
[21] J. H. Muirhead, *The Service of the State: Four Lectures on the Political Teaching of T. H. Green* (1908), 68–9.
[22] Stefan Collini, 'The Ordinary Experience of Civilized Life', in Bart Schultz, ed., *Essays on Henry Sidgwick* (2002), 351; David Boucher and Andrew Vincent, *British Idealism and Political Theory* (2000), 61. Ritchie's review in *International Journal of Ethics*, 2 (1891–2), 254–5, is cited in B. Schultz, *Henry Sidgwick—Eye of the Universe: An Intellectual Biography* (2004), 561.
[23] Henry Sidgwick, 'Bentham and Benthamism in Politics and Ethics' [1877], *Miscellaneous Essays*, 136. See also Francis and Morrow, *History of English Political Thought*, 285.
[24] M. W. Taylor, *Men versus the State: Herbert Spencer and Late Victorian Individualism* (1992), 67.
[25] A. V. Dicey, *A Fool's Paradise* (1912), ix.
[26] A. V. Dicey, *Lectures on the Relation between Law and Public Opinion in England during the Nineteenth Century* (1905), 125–209.
[27] Collini, *Public Moralists*, ch. 8.

Sidgwick the Unionist emphasized organic, cautious, developmental change which, as this chapter will show, was unquestionably pinned to Burke in this period.[28] Burke was not, of course, an Idealist or a utilitarian. His appeal was much broader: Burke became extraordinarily attractive to thinkers, writers, and educators as the intellectual father of organicism and the historical method (even if Rousseau remained the sire of collectivist notions of the 'general will').[29]

THE POLITICAL PHILOSOPHY OF EDMUND BURKE

The condensation of Burke's thought into a 'political philosophy of (small-c) conservatism'—that is, an intellectual system standing once removed from (capital-C) political Conservatism—was most visibly carried out by Liberal intellectuals, Unionists or otherwise. Throughout the nineteenth century, there had been excellent critical interpretations of Burke's life and thought which presented certain characteristics, such as passion and wisdom, and principles, such as devotion to the mixed constitution of 1688, as cornerstones in understanding his ideas, consistency, and character. After 1885, however, this historical and biographical scholarship was superseded by more abstract expositions of Burke's political thought. Unlike other political philosophers, Burke never produced a theory of government and so the quest to systematize his speeches and letters was fraught with problems, but it also allowed a good deal of room for interpretative construction. Burke's 'conservatism' thus came to symbolize relatively vague concepts such as hostility to constitutional change (including the related issues of the place of abstract ahistorical thought in politics, and the balance of the constitution); support for private property and religion; and a belief in the historic, organic nature of society. Ironically, therefore, Burke's heyday as an organic historicist thinker was the product of his abstraction from his original historical context.

Needless to say, this 'political theory' lay well outside of pure philosophy and systematic doctrine. Nonetheless, the language used to describe Burke's thought becomes increasingly couched in more abstract terminology from

---

[28] As a young man Sidgwick read *Reflections* aloud to overcome his stammer, as it was better than 'even Macaulay': Henry Sidgwick to Mary Sidgwick (undated—between 1 Feb. and 21 Feb. 1865 letters), Trinity College, Cambridge, Add. MS.c/99/43.

[29] G. Lowes Dickinson wrote on the intellectual shift towards 'relativist' political theory, including both Idealists and Utilitarians while a Political Science lecturer at Cambridge. The cause, he claimed, was the influence of the 'historic method': 'Recent Political Theory and Practice', *QR* (Oct. 1900), 359–80.

the 1880s, and description of Burke as a 'political philosopher' with a distinct 'political philosophy' became widespread.[30] This trend can be seen earlier, as documented in Chapter 4, but it snowballs from the 1880s. A key explanatory factor here is that those who were interested in Burke came from moral sciences and philosophy backgrounds, including Oxford 'Greats' (a degree which included not only the classics but philosophy, ancient and modern). The diversification of university degrees, discussed in more detail in Chapter 7, meant that scholars who had been formally trained in classics or mathematics could expand and explore new (but related) disciplines. This was, after all, the period in which the study of historically situated 'political thought' was established as a subject across the United Kingdom. That this was distinct from what we regard as the 'History of Political Thought' today will be clear from the fact that, in conjunction with the academic creation of Burke as a conservative political philosopher, his thought was recruited for party political purposes. This interconnectedness is crucial: Burke's legacy as a conservative thinker would not have the weight it had—and continued to have long afterwards—without Conservative Unionists adopting Burke, or at least a specific interpretation of his work.

But before Burke's thought was fully worked into a 'political theory', he was first christened as the British pioneer of the historical method. In 1879 Morley described the twin pillars of Burke's thought as 'utilitarian liberalism' and 'historic conservatism'.[31] The former, conceived in the loosest sense as a preference for outcomes over abstractions, would remain an important facet in interpretations of Burke's thought; but it was the latter notion of 'historic conservatism' which took on greater prominence in subsequent years. This in itself is symptomatic of the status of historicist and organicist thought in the late Victorian period. The Liberal Unionist jurist Frederick Pollock's *Introduction to the Science of Politics* (1890) was instrumental in identifying Burke as the generator of an international tradition of historical thought, which included the jurisprudence of Friedrich Savigny (1779–1861) and the recently deceased Henry Maine (d. 1888).[32] Pollock, a firm believer in Burke's consistency of principles, confessed that Burke would never have constructed a formal theory of politics—though the *Appeal from the New to the Old Whigs* (1791)

---

[30] I use terms like 'doctrine', 'theory', and 'philosophy' in this chapter synonymously, as did his commentators.
[31] Morley, *Burke* (1879), 215–16.
[32] See also Chapter 3 in this volume, n.41. For a modern discussion of this, see Seán Patrick Donlan, 'Burke on Law and Legal Theory', in Dwan and Insole, *Companion to Edmund Burke* (2012), 71. Pollock would, however, break with the LUs over the 'fair' vs. free trade controversy: Lubenow, *The Cambridge Apostles, 1820–1914*, 193.

brought him closest to an explicit statement. To Pollock, Burke 'restored history to its place in politics', but, echoing Sidgwick, he claimed that 'like some of the greatest thinkers in pure philosophy, he left no disciples'.[33] One American reviewer, the publisher J. L. Stewart, noted that both Pollock and Morley had succeeded in placing Burke 'in a new light', confirming that his 'contribution to solid political thought is an important one'.[34]

In placing Burke in a specifically English canon of historical method, however, the crucial figure is Leslie Stephen. As previously discussed, his *History of English Thought in the Eighteenth Century* (1876) made Burke the foundational 'English' exemplar of the organic and historical method.[35] This was a point Stephen went on to repeat regularly throughout his life and its force grew as his reputation grew in scope and influence. Thus, in 1892, Stephen lamented that abstract reasoning, condemned by Burke, 'the greatest of our philosophical politicians', still held its place, and countered with the assertion that the value of a political theory could only be determined by national circumstances.[36] In an article on Thomas Paine, Stephen remarked: '[the] whole pith of Burke's teaching' lay in the historical method, and the truth recognized 'by every philosophical writer' that the state was an organism which derived its vitality from its evolution.[37] In *The English Utilitarians* (1900), Burke's opposition to the French Revolution was seen to arise as a response to its attack on organic principles of society, its breach of historical continuity, and 'war' on the prescription and tradition essential for 'healthy development'. Again, the historical method is mixed with organic metaphor. On Burke's consistency, Stephen quoted Mackintosh, from 1806, pointing to the fact that this lay in his abhorrence of 'abstract politics'.[38] Finally, Stephen's 1903 Ford Lectures, published in 1904, the year of his death, again reaffirmed Burke's historicism:

> Burke represents above all things the political application of the historical spirit of the period. His hatred for metaphysics, for discussions of abstract rights instead of practical expediency; his exaltation of 'prescription' and 'tradition'; his admiration for Montesquieu and his abhorrence of Rousseau; his idolatry of the British constitution, and in short his whole political doctrine from first to last, implies the profound conviction of the truth of

---

[33] Frederick Pollock, *Introduction to the Science of Politics* (1890), 85–92, 118–19, 125.
[34] John L. Stewart, 'Introduction to the History of the Science of Politics', *Annals of the American Academy of Political and Social Science*, 1 (Jan. 1891), 505–7.
[35] Stephen, *History of English Thought*, ii. 280; see also 'Critical Recovery: Thought' in Chapter 4 of this volume.
[36] Leslie Stephen, 'Science and Politics' [1892], *Social Rights and Duties*, i. 56–7.
[37] Leslie Stephen, 'Thomas Paine', *FR* (Aug. 1893), 273.
[38] Stephen, *English Utilitarians*, ii. 100–2.

the principles embodied in a thorough historical method. Nobody, I think, was ever more consistent in his first principles.[39]

Burke's historic organicism was also admired and promoted by Idealist philosophers. Henry Jones (1852–1922), Professor of Philosophy and Political Economy at Bangor and a Welshman himself, can be found arguing for a version of Home Rule for Wales in 1890 using ideas of 'Burkean' organic development: 'the idea of a continuity that is self-enriching has been held for nearly a hundred years by the leaders of thought with considerable unanimity'; and the idea that 'Society is an Organism', 'which touched the reflections of Burke as with the light of a new day, has now become a truism of popular science'.[40] Likewise, D. G. Ritchie, a contemporary of MacCunn and Arnold Toynbee at Balliol who ended his career as Professor of Logic and Metaphysics at St Andrews, envisioned a harmonious and interdependent society along Burkean lines. When attacking Herbert Spencer in 1891, Ritchie argued in association with Burke 'that the State is not simply a joint-stock company or a private club. Some of us really do believe that, in some respects, society is an organism.'[41] Yet Ritchie's politics were not what he took Burke's to be and he also regretted that a consequence of the evolutionary and historical method had been 'to support a political and social conservatism of the type so brilliantly illustrated in this country by Burke'.[42] Burke's strict adherence to the constitution of 1688 was still a problem for Liberal admirers of Burke, both politically and intellectually, and this will be seen again shortly in the work of MacCunn and Jones. Ritchie himself went on to write a radical communitarian critique of natural rights which began with Burke, but once more criticized his refusal to evolve from 1688.[43] This appreciation of Burke as an organic historic thinker of course went beyond Idealism—the historian and Anglican clergyman J. N. Figgis stated in 1896 that it was because Burke understood the organic nature of society that he was seen to be a leading political thinker[44]—but Idealism had a profound impact on the construction of

---

[39] Leslie Stephen, *English Literature and Society in the Eighteenth Century* (1904), 198.
[40] Henry Jones, 'Wales and its Prospects' (1890), 3–4, 52. See also his *Idealism as a Practical Creed* (1909), 61, 216–17.
[41] D. G. Ritchie, *Principles of State Interference: Four Essays on the Political Philosophy of Mr. Herbert Spencer, J. S. Mill, and T. H. Green* (1891), 72–3.
[42] D. G. Ritchie, *Darwin and Hegel* (1893), 65. See Edmund Neill, 'Evolutionary Theory and British Idealism: The Case of D. G. Ritchie', *History of European Ideas*, 29 (2003), 313–38.
[43] D. G. Ritchie, *Natural Rights*, 2nd edn (1903), 5–6, 10, 12, 17.
[44] J. N. Figgis, *The Value of Historical Study* (1896), 20. See also his anonymous review of F. W. Maitland's *Gierke's Political Theories of the Middle Ages*: *Athenaeum* (2 Feb. 1901), 133–4.

Burke's reputation, not just as an organic thinker, but as a principally *conservative* organic thinker. Since Idealist academics dispersed into teaching positions around the country, this theme also runs into Chapter 7 on education.

Although Burke came to be comfortably placed in a canon of organic historical thought, he was nonetheless seen to have lacked 'disciples' in the late Victorian period—which was in fact very convenient if he was to be reinvented or reshaped. His 'influence' began to be traced through more abstract terms such as 'spirit' or approach. The historical method was a central part of this, although this was a many-sided school and appreciations varied between critics. Thus, on the one hand, Pollock placed Burke alongside Maine's historical jurisprudence—attractive as an antidote to analytical writers like John Austin—within a broad tradition of historicism, while, on the other hand, Ritchie praised Burke's historic organicism for progressing *beyond* Maine's celebrated individualistic 'contract theory' towards a conception of society as an organism.[45] The staying power of the association of Burke with this broadly defined historical organicism can be seen, twenty-five years later, when Morley described Maine as 'the most eminent English member of the Burkian school'—a remarkable act of intellectual appropriation by any standards.[46] Ernest Barker did something similar but with more skill (or evasion) when he traced Maine's historical method back to the French Revolution and Burke: 'Rather as a spirit than a method, this tendency already appears in the splendid romanticism of Burke.'[47] It was this flexibility which extended Burke's staying power and continuing relevance to changing contexts, once his canonical position had been established. As Barker's comment suggests, this had much broader implications as Burke's historicism became the basis of a concept variously traced not only from the reaction to the French Revolution but also the Romantic Movement in literature. More generally, the literary quality of Burke's prose outlined earlier continued to be a significant factor in the continued interest and inclusion of Burke within the authorial canons of English literature, political thought, and history in this period.

One example of literary interest is Edward Dowden (1843–1913), Professor of English Literature at Trinity College, Dublin, who used his 1896 lectures on 'The French Revolution and English Literature' at Princeton to assert Burke's speculative credentials. This was a distinctive

---

[45] Pollock, *Science of Politics*, 119; Richard A. Cosgrove, 'Pollock, Sir Frederick', *ODNB* (2004); Ritchie, *Darwin and Hegel*, 225.
[46] John Morley, *Notes on Politics and History* (1914), 27.
[47] Ernest Barker, *Political Thought from 1848–1914* (1915), 162.

approach: as a student Dowden had devoted himself to philosophy and much of his later work, including his internationally acclaimed work on Shakespeare, was viewed by contemporaries and predecessors as bearing this psychological and philosophical stamp.[48] Dowden's interest in the French Revolutionary era was similarly long-standing: Wordsworth was a literary hero and Dowden had been lecturing on the Revolution's impact on English literature from the mid-1860s at the Alexandra College for women in Dublin.[49] Dowden was an Irish Protestant who doubted; a philosophically-minded professor of English literature interested in Germany, the French Revolution, Wordsworth, Romanticism, and Burke. In many ways Dowden resembled the (mostly Liberal) Idealists, but he also differed from them in fundamental ways: he was a staunch Liberal Unionist and, though he was obliged to teach increasing numbers of women (especially following their admittance to TCD in 1904), he had opposed women's inclusion in a co-educational TCD. The 1896 lectures were published in Britain in 1897, the year of Burke's centenary and the occasion for a celebratory event at TCD which featured speeches from Dowden and W. E. H. Lecky. Dowden, in his speech and his lectures, celebrated Burke as an Irish–British statesman and devoted considerable space in his lectures to an exposition of the 'root' of Burke as a political theorist.

In Dowden's eyes, Burke's thinking was essentially abstract. Dowden, who went on to write *Puritan and Anglican* in 1900, presented Burke's thought as metaphysical on the basis that it was, above all, supremely religious. Elaborating on James Fitzjames Stephen's recently republished articles from 1863–8, he argued that Burke, 'our highest teacher of political wisdom, was himself a speculator, a reasoner in politics; but he tried to reason and to speculate with the facts of the case before him'.[50] Thus, Burke's anger, found in *Reflections*, at the 'metaphysical theorists' of pre-Revolutionary France, did not originate in the fact that they were theorists, but that they were devious 'sophisters': 'he could have no claim to the title of political thinker if he had despised ideas.'[51] Yet Dowden defended Burke's religiosity against the assertions made by the recently deceased Stephen, a fellow Liberal Unionist, as well as the Gladstonian

---

[48] H. O. White, *Edward Dowden, 1843–1913: An Address Delivered in the Chapel of Trinity College, Dublin* (1943).
[49] Edward Dowden to John Dowden, '(Saturday) 1867', *Letters of Edward Dowden and his Correspondents*, eds. Elizabeth and Hilda Dowden (1914), 37; Christina Hunt Mahoney, 'Women's Education, Edward Dowden, and the University Curriculum in English Literature: An Unlikely Progression', in Margaret Kelleher and James H. Murphy, eds., *Gender Perspectives in Nineteenth-Century Ireland* (1997).
[50] Edward Dowden, *The French Revolution and English Literature* (1897), 104.
[51] Ibid., 101.

Morley, that Burke's works contained an element of 'mysticism': 'If to believe that the order of the world is a providential order be mysticism, then the teaching of Burke may be described as political mysticism.' He further retorted that Morley and Mill propounded their own mysticism of atomistic individualism.[52] It was a political appropriation of Burke and, to a degree, religion, for the Unionists—or at least a particular version of Unionism—as well as being a significant argument about the philosophical nature of Burke's thought in an international, educational context. Dowden's sympathetic view of the broadly 'religious' nature of Burke's thought was also to be repeated later by Liberal Idealists, as well as Edwardian Conservatives. By 1915 Ernest Barker felt comfortable in pronouncing that 'the religious basis of human society...has been the strength of conservatism from Burke to to-day'.[53]

Soon after Dowden's lectures, another Irishman produced one of the first attempts at a systematic work of political philosophy featuring Burke. This was William Graham's *English Political Philosophy* (1899). An Ulsterman and Professor of Jurisprudence and Political Economy at Queen's, Belfast, Graham was a product of TCD and also well-integrated in London society. He was steeped in Idealist philosophy and explicitly desired 'a connected political thought'.[54] Through considerations of Hobbes, Burke, Bentham, Mill, and Maine, Graham illustrated 'the different schools of political thought—Conservative, Liberal, Radical, and even Socialist'.[55] Graham sought to illustrate the 'truth' of political science that natural law, in the form of an instinctive moral sense of justice, could be 'proved' by the historical method: his favourite example being the demonstrable rights of property.[56] Nevertheless, he gave Burke a chilly reception. Given his opposition to parliamentary reform, the extension of the suffrage, and the relief of the Dissenters, Burke was by implication a Liberal Unionist: 'nothing of a Democrat, but merely a Whig with Conservative instincts, whom Dr Johnson believed to be a Tory at heart'.[57]

---

[52] Ibid., 107–9. [53] Barker, *Political Thought from 1848–1914*, 172.
[54] Graham, *English Political Philosophy*, xix. See his *Idealism: An Essay Metaphysical and Critical* (1892), in which his 'chief object' was to defend the Idealism of Berkeley (p. xii), and its extension by Hegel (p. xvi). This was reasserted again in his widely-read *The Creed of Science* (1881). Here, Graham sympathized with scientific thinkers, but argued for an alternative creed applicable to the non-scientific realms of religion, morals, and metaphysics: the existence of a divinely guided evolutionary process. His argument in favour of 'natural laws' provoked a response from Darwin: see Bernard Lightman, 'The Creed of Science and its Critics', in Martin Hewitt, ed., *The Victorian World* (2012), 457–9.
[55] Graham, *English Political Philosophy*, xxi.
[56] Ibid., 377–88. [57] Ibid., 90.

On the other hand, his political philosophy as expounded in *Reflections* and twinned with the *Appeal* constituted 'something like a complete and coherent political system with a political doctrine'. This system covered the origin of society and government; the advantages and disadvantages of different forms of government; the justification of property; the essential relationship between church and state in Britain (Graham was evidently in favour of disestablishment[58]); and the 'real' rights of man. Burke's appeal lay in the fact that, unlike the abstractions of Hobbes and Rousseau, he wrote in an original and attractive style.[59] Burke's view of inequality and natural aristocracy was also presented as an essential part of a 'conservative' 'theory'[60] and was inherently linked with his perpetual distrust of 'the mass of men'.[61] Graham summarized Burke's political philosophy thus:

> What do we find in sum? A system of opinions that rejects the possibility of discovery in moral or political philosophy; that forbids honest inquiry on religious questions[;] ... a mental temperament that would make a difference of speculative dogma in religion or politics a ground of a prolonged war with a neighbouring nation... We find a system of politics that rests property mainly on prescription, whatever injustices and abuses may be connected with it[;] ... that rests government as well as property on prescription, and that accordingly approves of an irresponsible and corrupt oligarchy governing England[;] ... we find a view of morals that rests right conduct on opinions, manners, habits, as external objective guides, or else on prejudice and mere strong feeling as internal instructors, instead of on conscience, reason, or utility.[62]

'In every direction', therefore, Burke was a 'conservative, in full and entire sympathy with things as they are, with no belief in and no sympathy with progress': his ideal was in the past, rather than the future. And while Graham believed that both conservative and progressive castes of mind were necessary, it was to the progressive aspect that he looked towards as a way of ensuring progress and development: Burke would make only minor adjustments in practical politics, while 'in religion and morals and political science he does not even believe that any further truth is to be found'.[63] His conservative political philosophy was then linked by Graham to party political divisions. It furnished 'a new creed or body of principles for the Tory party, as well as a definite practical policy'. It was superior to Bolingbroke's 'unenlightened' Patriot King as it gave Tories 'new and more reasonable principles' and 'transformed the party in some considerable degree in respect to its main function and aims' (that is, it suggested a

---

[58] Ibid., 139.   [59] Ibid., 94.   [60] Ibid., 147.
[61] Ibid., 149.   [62] Ibid., 166.   [63] Ibid., 167.

more positive, active approach to constitutional maintenance, rather than negative, passive, reactionary resistance).[64] This did not mean, however, that as a Liberal Idealist Graham was correspondingly celebratory of Bentham and Mill. On the contrary, he attacked their utilitarian attempts to base considerations of 'justice' on utility rather than natural law or Kantian natural rights.[65] By contrast, although Burke aimed (in Graham's eyes) at constructing a set of abstract principles, he must be placed, as a thinker, into the 'historical' (rather than metaphysical) school.[66]

English Political Philosophy was well received in reviews as a contribution to the 'history of political ideas'.[67] The section on Burke was singled out as the most excellent by both the *Speaker* and Carveth Read (1848–1931), Grote Professor of Philosophy at University College, London and 'Sunday Tramp', in the *Economic Journal*.[68] Likewise, the Fabian and ethical Socialist Sidney Ball described the book as 'the most convenient introduction to English political philosophy that exists'. Yet Ball criticized Graham's obviously polemical argument that the 'justice' of private property could be 'proved' by the historical method and that (despite his own criticism of Burke on this point) the climax of human progress was nigh.[69] Read noted these same points and recognized Graham's approach as being influenced by Herbert Spencer, whom he frequently cited.[70] The *Saturday* and *Quarterly* reviews were also positive, though they questioned whether such a thing as political philosophy actually existed.[71] Indeed, to some the very idea of political philosophy was un-English—whether Scottish or continental. That said, editors of the schoolbooks and cheap editions discussed later relied on Graham as an authority, and it was built upon in later critical examinations of Burke.[72]

Another notable systematization is John Maynard Keynes' 1904 Cambridge University prize-winning essay, *The Political Doctrines of Edmund Burke*. Keynes had first read Burke at Eton—he used some of his substantial (Etonian) prize money to purchase twelve volumes of Burke's

---

[64] Ibid., 174. [65] Ibid., xxv. [66] Ibid., xxvi.

[67] 'English Political Philosophy from Hobbes to Maine', *Athenaeum* (2 Dec. 1899), 754. See also 'English Political Philosophy', *Academy* (16 Dec. 1899), 720–1.

[68] ['H. B.'], 'English Political Philosophy', *Speaker* (16 Dec. 1899), 289–90; Carveth Read, 'English Political Philosophy', *Economic Journal* (Mar. 1900), 83–5; William Whyte, 'Sunday Tramps (act. 1879–1895)', *ODNB* (2013).

[69] Sidney Ball, 'English Political Philosophy', *International Journal of Ethics* (July 1900), 520–5.

[70] Read, 'English Political Philosophy', 84.

[71] [Dickinson], 'Recent Political Theory', *QR*, 359; 'English Political Philosophy', *SR* (20 Jan. 1900), 83–4.

[72] MacCunn, *Political Philosophy of Burke*, 85; Ivor Brown, *English Political Theory* (1920), 73.

works in 1901—and, in his final year, delivered Burke's panegyric of Fox in dress clothes for a 'Speeches' event.[73] Keynes' Cambridge essay (the University Members' Prize for English), meanwhile, is generally used in Keynes scholarship as a means of uncovering his political thought, often with the explicit aim of reconciling Keynes with 'the prophet of twentieth-century conservatism'.[74] Burke was, as Keynes' biographer notes, the only political hero that he ever acknowledged.[75] For our purposes, however, this is not a question of Keynes' politics, but of uncovering typically Edwardian ideas about Burke. From the standpoint of the intellectual historian, Keynes' unpublished essay—which had no wider discursive consequence—was nonetheless a response and contribution to the then existing literature on Burke: Keynes' motivation lay in what he perceived to be deficiencies in this criticism. Most centrally, *Political Doctrines of Burke* is of interest as an interpretation and synthesis of Burke that was considered award-winning in Edwardian Cambridge. Keynes' essay was further commended by his examiners in *The Times*: the essay—which bore the celebratory motto '"Burke at his best is English at its best"'—was considered 'most worthy' of honourable mention in a national newspaper.[76]

Keynes' aim was to establish Burke's consistent and underlying political philosophy, and he did so by rejecting the historical method in favour of the abstract.[77] His notes begin conventionally enough on 'the constitution' but were followed with subtitles such as 'property', 'church establishment', 'consistency', and 'the popular element'.[78] The essay itself admitted the modern importance of Burke: 'Burke is perhaps the only political writer, the direct bearing of whose works is wholly topical and contemporary, who could be approached as the source of a consistent and coherent body of political theory.'[79] What Keynes refused to do, however, was assign Burke's 'political theory' to any particular school of political thought. Despite criticizing Morley for overemphasizing Burke's 'moderate' utilitarianism, Keynes explained Burke's relevance accordingly:

> Perhaps it was as an exponent of... the glorious Constitution that he liked himself best; but it is as one of the earliest exponents of Laisser Faire, of a

---

[73] Robert Skidelsky, *John Maynard Keynes* (1983–2001), i. 98, 101.
[74] Suzanne Helburn, 'Burke and Keynes', in B. W. Bateman and J. B. Davis, eds., *Keynes and Philosophy: Essays on the Origin of Keynes' Thought* (1991), 30. See also G. R. Steele, *Keynes and Hayek* (2002), 55; Zohrah Emami and Paulette Olsen, *Engendering Economics* (2004), 97.
[75] Skidelsky, *Keynes*, i. 154.
[76] 'Election Intelligence', *The Times* (5 Dec. 1904), 6.
[77] J. M. Keynes, *The Political Doctrines of Edmund Burke* (1904), John Maynard Keynes Papers, King's College, Cambridge, JMK/UA/20/2/94.
[78] Ibid., JMK/UA/20/1.   [79] Ibid., JMK/UA/20/3/4.

modified political utilitarianism, and of expediency against abstract right, that he is most important in the history of opinion.[80] In light of this claim, the dissertation that Keynes actually produced was a forceful argument for Burke's belief in intrinsic and universal goods: the organic constitution;[81] religion and the necessity of church establishment;[82] and the 'sanctity of property'.[83] Burke had held these beliefs, however, while destroying what remained of divine right, and it was this aristocratic sensibility which made Burke the Whig, rather than a monarchical Tory such as Bolingbroke, a modern conservative.[84] Keynes therefore constructed an a priori philosophy of Burke's political thought which emphasized key concepts identical to Graham's explicitly 'conservative' theory of Burke's political thought, although the essay was in fact produced in response to non-metaphysical categorizations of Burke's thought like Graham's.[85] At the same time, the Liberal Keynes stressed that the 'utilitarian' strand of Burke's writings remained his most important contribution to political thought. Like the Liberals of Chapter 4, however, his essay told a much broader story.

Burke's 'political philosophy' was further developed in John MacCunn's *The Political Philosophy of Burke* (1913). MacCunn, a Snell exhibitioner tutored by Caird at Glasgow and Green at Balliol, later became Professor of Philosophy at the University of Liverpool and consistently demonstrated a practical concern for social work and education.[86] MacCunn's Liberal Idealism (he had been an honorary member of the Oxford University Palmerston Club[87]) was fused with an interest in Burke and Mazzini and, as noted earlier, MacCunn claimed that Green recommended Burke to his students.[88] Central to MacCunn's conceptual framework was a typically Idealist concern for the organic growth of the nation, particularly with regard to active, ethical citizenship and the related issue of how individuals connected to communities and the state.[89] MacCunn's evident respect for

---

[80] Ibid., JMK/UA/20/3/21.   [81] Ibid., JMK/UA/20/3/45.
[82] Ibid., JMK/UA/20/3/69–76.   [83] Ibid., JMK/UA/20/3/24.
[84] Ibid., JMK/UA/20/3/84.   [85] Ibid., JMK/UA/3/10.
[86] John MacCunn, *Liverpool Addresses on the Ethics of Social Work* (1911).
[87] University of Oxford Palmerston Club, *Rules and List of Members* (1891). The label suggests that the Palmerston Club was the less radical of the two Oxford Liberal Associations, the other being the Russell Club. Yet Sidney Ball, a thorough-going radical, was a founder member.
[88] MacCunn, *Six Radical Thinkers*, 229. Julia Stapleton explains this as a gloss rooted in MacCunn's passionate devotion to Burke in *Englishness and the Study of Politics*, 37–8. I would suggest, however, that a number of second-generation Idealists demonstrate a clear—though less extensive—interest in Burke.
[89] MacCunn, *The Ethics of Citizenship* [1894], 6th edn (1922). For MacCunn and citizenship see H. S. Jones, 'Education for Citizenship in Great Britain, c.1880–1944: The Renewal of a Civic Tradition', in Inge Botteri, Elena Riva, and Adolfo Scotto di Luzio, eds., *Fare il cittadino. La formazione di un nuovo soggetto sociale nell'Europa tra XIX et XXI secolo*

Burke, particularly in relation to his organicism, sets the tone of the whole book: 'Nothing... is more constantly reiterated in Burke's pages than this idea of balance, equipoise, harmony, organic unity. Nor is it only to the political constitution in the narrower sense that he applies these and suchlike categories; it is to the constitution of civil society as a whole.'[90] His study nonetheless painted Burke as a conservative, devoting an entire chapter to Burke's 'conservatism'. This had also been the conclusion of Henry Jones in 1910, who noted (briefly) that Burke urged organic reform over revolution due to his 'social and political conservatism', whereas Jones' own aim was genuinely progressive reform.[91] The distinctive aspect of MacCunn's political philosophy of Burke, however, is not only its length, but that it arrived at 'conservatism' systematically through Whig political theory: there was no tension between Burke's historical Whig position and the 'small-c' conservatism of 1913.

MacCunn still felt it necessary to show that Burke had a political philosophy. Like Fitzjames Stephen, Dowden, Graham, and Keynes, MacCunn asserted that, regardless of his protests, Burke was a theorist. He justified himself by saying that the modern idea of political philosophy was much wider than Burke's narrow conception. Thus Burke was the owner of a distinctive political philosophy.[92] MacCunn reiterated: 'when one has well-defined and coherent principles, as Burke will be shown to have, it is difficult to explain the difference' between 'principles' and 'political philosophy'.[93] He demonstrated that Burke's 'conservatism' could be traced to philosophical principles rather than sentiment or prejudices,[94] and further that any overemphasis on the pragmatic 'utilitarian' interpretation of Burke's thought was narrow and simplistic.[95]

For MacCunn, Burke's metaphysical thinking was rooted in his religious temperament. Though Burke lived according to a belief in the impracticality and implausibility of radical reform, this was subordinate to the broader religious framework of Burke's thought.[96] MacCunn criticized Graham for enrolling Burke in the ranks of inductive historical thinkers and canonizing *Reflections* as the first deployment of the historical method in Britain. Instead, MacCunn insisted on the deductive nature of Burke's political thought and asked: 'What else can be said of a thinker

(2012); Edmund Neill, 'Conceptions of Citizenship in Twentieth-Century Britain', *Twentieth Century British History*, 17 (2006), 427–8. For the longer intellectual context, see Jones, 'The Idea of the National in Victorian Political Thought', 12–21; Harris, 'Political Thought and the Welfare State', 121, 126.

[90] MacCunn, *Political Philosophy of Burke*, 25.
[91] Henry Jones, *The Working Faith of the Social Reformer* (1910), 23–4.
[92] MacCunn, *Political Philosophy of Burke*, 1–5.   [93] Ibid., 44.
[94] Ibid., 68.   [95] Ibid., 14–15.   [96] Ibid., 70.

who not only avows a passionate theistic creed, but applies this creed with such assiduity that neither his conservative faith nor his conservative fear can be adequately understood apart from it?'[97] To Burke, 'the attempted secularization of history and politics was nothing less than a conspiracy to denationalize the nation and to dehumanize the race.'[98] Shifting his focus to contemporary Britain, MacCunn said that he 'cannot disagree' with Burke's 'plea' to ally citizenship with a broad Christian faith and, while some had sought to replace religion with 'the Nation' and 'Humanity', these were all part of an indivisible whole in Burke.[99] Pragmatic outcomes were of course highly valued by Burke, but still they were tightly controlled by a set of fundamental a priori principles which could, in 1913, be safely described as a political philosophy.

MacCunn stated emphatically that Burke's political philosophy was not utilitarian. It was a misnomer, we are told, to construe Burke's work in this light, since 'the greatest happiness of the people' in Burke is quite different from Bentham's numerical conception.[100] Here is the explanation for Burke's non-elective conception of representation: it was 'the Whig theory of political trusteeship'. MacCunn stated that this catered for an elite 'public' of 400,000 men who were represented by their MPs, peers, and the monarch in the mixed constitution, alternatively described as 'Virtual Representation'.[101] It was based on a belief in the fundamental inequality of men, though it could still coexist with deeply held moral sympathies for mankind as a whole. In this respect, Burke was aligned with other 'Conservatives of genius' such as Johnson, Walter Scott, and the later Wordsworth.[102] Here lay the basis of Burke's political thought: 'Burke's theory of government, be its value what it may, had its foundations deeply laid in his conception of a people, and in the profoundly conservative principles deduced therefrom.'[103] Undemocratic, aristocratic Whiggism was still, however, very different from a monarchical Toryism. Thus, MacCunn explained that Burke's love of defending the constitution made him 'by far the greatest of conservatives' without being a 'worshipper of Kings'.[104] As stated earlier, a 'Whig' aversion to a now antiquated royal prerogative coupled with dislike of constitutional change became a way of expressing a form of constitutional conservatism that was polemically useful to Unionists, a group which now included a large number of Whigs.

---

[97] Ibid., 85.   [98] Ibid., 143.
[99] Ibid., 132, 136, 140–1. For similar sentiments, see W. B. Morris, 'Edmund Burke and the Revolution', *DR* (July 1900), 71–7. Interestingly, MacCunn on Burke's religion is inserted as a chapter between contributions by Conor Cruise O'Brien and Irving Babbitt in Daniel E. Ritchie, *Edmund Burke: Appraisals and Applications* (1990).
[100] MacCunn, *Political Philosophy of Burke*, 49.   [101] Ibid., 165.
[102] Ibid., 172.   [103] Ibid., 189.   [104] Ibid., 150–1.

MacCunn therefore modernized Burke's political philosophy for his Edwardian readers. Burke's 'impossible conservatism' (i.e. of a constitution and society which had in fact been fundamentally altered beyond the limits he held permissible) could be modified in light of experience since his day. Firstly, one must read Burke in conjunction with the conscious desire that existed from the mid-nineteenth century to produce new schemes of political legislation. Secondly, in the light of the continuing constitutional crisis post-1909, MacCunn instructed his readers to remember that government exists to administer in a just and efficient way, rather than to broker constitutional reforms.[105] In this way Burke's 'reformism' was portrayed as being administrative rather than constitutional. It is here that MacCunn's disappointment with Burke is most palpable. As a Liberal, MacCunn acknowledged the debt of Idealism to Burke's knowledge, imagination, experience, and religious feeling. But he regretted that Burke could not imagine a future ideal of constitutional and social progress. Burke was not organic *enough*: his aristocratic bias blinded him to the inevitability of democracy: 'Its strength lies in its insistence, so eloquent, so convincing, on the unity of the whole: the weakness is that the unity is not complete.'[106] Thus:

> The result is that we find in Burke's writings the presence of two things and the absence of a third. We find an unfaltering faith in the presence of a 'Divine tactic' in the lives of men and nations. We find also an *apologia* such as has never been equalled, for the existing social and political system as it has come to be by the long toil of successive generations. What we do not find, and are fain to wish for, and most of all from a thinker to whom the happiness of the people was always paramount, is some encouragement for the hope that the 'stupendous Wisdom' which has done so much in the past, and even till now, will not fail to operate in the varieties of untried being through which the State, even the democratic State, must pass in the vicissitudes and adventures of the future.[107]

MacCunn's work was avowedly Idealist, but his reviewers revealed that by 1913 the idea of Burke the theorist was generally established in learned society. They all, whether in disciplinary journals or more popular print media, acknowledged that MacCunn's task had been to outline Burke's fundamental theories and their relation to modern political ideas, and many were content to approve and relay MacCunn's exposition of Burke's consistent political 'doctrine', as for example in the *Spectator* and the *American Political Science Review*.[108] The philosopher G. C. Field

---

[105] Ibid., 179–80. [106] Ibid., 218, 230. [107] Ibid., 271–2.
[108] *Spectator* (10 May 1913), 23–4; James W. Gardner, 'The Political Philosophy of Burke', *American Political Science Review* (May 1914), 316–18. Gardner noted that both

(1887–1955), at the time Lecturer in Ethics and Politics at Manchester, was particularly laudatory in his review for the *International Journal of Ethics*.[109] His analysis of Burke's 'conservative' contribution to political thought was highly recommended to students and general readers alike by the *Daily Telegraph*.[110] MacCunn's submergence of Whiggism into conservatism was upheld in the *Athenaeum*, which noted that Burke's 'belief in the divine right of the English Constitution of 1688 was the basis of his conservatism'.[111] J. E. Creighton (1861–1924), an American philosopher at Cornell whose early influences included Kant, Bradley, and Bosanquet, accepted MacCunn's recommendation of Burke as a theological political theorist, but rejected Morley's 1879 claim that Burke would appeal to modern thought in 1913: again, because he was not organic (i.e. democratic) enough.[112] MacCunn's book was seen as a clear, scholarly, and reputable condensation of Burke the Whig statesman into the originator of a political philosophy of 'conservatism'. It brought together the most prominent strands and themes of Burke criticism since the mid-1860s, and was read favourably by reviewers in Britain and the United States.

POLITICAL CONSERVATISM

Burke's reception history at this time also has a more directly political dimension. It is bound up with the broader development of Tory, Conservative, and Unionist thought, as well as the history of the political party itself. Although earlier writers, from Disraeli to W. H. Mallock, had made sporadic attempts at developing a historically and intellectually grounded C/conservatism, the energy expended on this task after 1885 was unprecedented. But it should be remembered that this argument sets up Burke as the primary *founder* of 'modern conservatism'. This does not mean that Burke became the chief or sole intellectual crutch for everyone to the right of the Gladstonian Liberals. In fact, for those who were actively engaged in the construction of new historical genealogies Burke had varying levels of appeal. One could, for example, accept Burke as C/conservatism's founder

---

Graham and MacCunn had provided systematic accounts of Burke's thought as a unified theory, though overall he preferred Graham's more 'brilliant and informing analysis' (p. 316).

[109] G. C. Field, 'The Political Philosophy of Burke', *International Journal of Ethics* (Apr. 1914), 373.
[110] *Daily Telegraph* (28 Mar. 1913), 16.
[111] 'The Political Philosophy of Burke', *Athenaeum* (29 Mar. 1913), 356.
[112] [J. E. Creighton], 'The Political Philosophy of Burke', *Philosophical Review* (Sept. 1913), 558–9.

or greatest thinker while upholding Disraelian 'Tory Democracy' as more polemically useful. Moreover, there was a great deal of Conservative and Unionist politics and thought which simply stood outside of this discussion. Work on the Primrose League, diverse incarnations of working-class Conservatism, and debates over Tariff Reform, for example, has demonstrated the complex coalitions which make up democratic political parties and traditions.[113] Indeed, an important strand of twentieth-century 'modern conservatism' has insisted on its non-ideological basis,[114] and it would be foolish to ignore the fact that political abstractions had limited appeal even though, in linguistic terms, the increasing appropriation of terms such as political theory and philosophy was a significant development at the time. Even so, the Conservative Unionist reception of Burke between 1885 and 1914 was dramatically different from that in the preceding decades of the nineteenth century.

Hence, it became crucial for Conservative Unionists to see Burke as an intellectual ancestor. This happened, broadly, in two ways. First, he was taken up as a guide to political prudence. The historiography of Conservative thought in this period reflects a division between 'negative' and 'constructive' approaches. For example, Stanley Baldwin, in a 1933 speech, stated that the Conservatives could always win with Disraelian Conservatism, but not if they 'sagged into the old negative habit'.[115] Ewen Green, alongside many other political historians, traces a long tradition of 'Conservative statism' through Randolph Churchill, Disraeli and Young England, Bolingbroke, and Shaftesbury. This particular brand of statism, Green asserts, proposed an organic conception of the relationship between individuals and the state, according to values of reciprocal obligation and duty, which was of particular importance for social reform and issues such as housing, education, poor law reform, and health.[116] The memory of Disraeli was particularly powerful, and was representative of 'rational reform' rather than 'reaction'. 'Disraelian conservatism' is contrasted with 'the old negative habit' of staunch reaction and maintenance of the status quo: Green accuses Lord Salisbury of 'pessimistic quietism'.[117] Elsewhere, M. W. Taylor draws a line between 'individualist' and

---

[113] For example, Green, *Crisis of Conservatism*; Pugh, *Tories and the People*; Francis and Zweininger-Bargielowska, *Conservatives and British Society*.
[114] Vincent, *Modern Political Ideologies*, 55.
[115] Philip Williamson, *Stanley Baldwin: Conservative Leadership and National Values* (1999), 223.
[116] Green, *Crisis of Conservatism*, 286–7.
[117] Green, 'Radical Conservatism', 690.

'collectivist' Unionists.[118] These categories are, no doubt, helpful in delineating between very obvious intellectual differences and practical approaches to policy.

Still the term 'maintenance' ('maintenance of the status quo') was fluid. As Salisbury himself stated in 1883, 'the object of our party is not, and ought not to be, simply to keep things as they are'.[119] For many Conservative Unionists, maintenance had an active meaning—that is, it was a constructive process in itself. One could argue that this was merely rhetoric for masking a reactionary position. But in any case, the adoption of an active conception of maintenance had important consequences for Burke's aphorisms, drawn from *Reflections*, that 'a state without the means of some change is without the means of its conservation' and, again, 'I would not exclude alteration neither; but even when I changed, it should be to preserve.'[120] Macaulay had coined a similar phrase during the debates on the 1832 Reform Act: 'Reform, that you may preserve' (on this, see 'English Constitutionalism' in Chapter 2), while later historians of the Conservative party discovered a similar principle in Peel's Tamworth Manifesto.[121] At the turn of the twentieth century, however, this general sentiment of conservative reform was now recognized as Burke's intellectual property and quoted with enthusiasm by many Conservative Unionists.[122] It was Burke who represented the political middle way between the excesses of inaction and construction.

Secondly, in almost all of the written constructions of 'New C/conservatism' the birth of modern political parties and thought was dated from the French Revolution, and this was of course deeply indebted to Burke. Nineteenth-century political thought was effectively recast as a reaction to events in France, or rather 'the principles of 1789' (liberty, equality, fraternity—the 'three-fanged serpent'[123]), instead of being based around an indigenous English constitutional agenda. Of course, alternative histories could be found. Another favourite analogy among Unionists

---

[118] Taylor, *Men versus the State*, 264.
[119] Quoted in Richard Shannon, *The Age of Salisbury, 1881–1902* (1996), 51.
[120] *WSEB*, viii. 72, 292.
[121] On Peel and Tamworth, see G. Kitson Clark, *Peel and the Conservative Party* (1929), 208–14. Here Kitson Clark made perhaps the earliest attempt to link Peel and the Conservative party, though still there was no claim that Peel was the founder of modern Conservatism. Instead he accepted 'that Peel may have...possibly followed Conservative principles that did not stand the test of usefulness of time' (p. xiv).
[122] 'He is...idolized by Conservatives that do not utterly disregard progress and by Liberals whose motto is "Hasten slowly"': 'Edmund Burke at Beaconsfield', *Speaker* (16 July 1898), 72–3.
[123] D. H. Lawrence to Bertrand Russell (19 July 1915), *Letters of D. H. Lawrence*, eds. J. T. Boulton et al. (1979–2000), ii. 366.

was between Liberals and seventeenth-century Puritans: anti-national, unimaginative, enemies to culture, who favoured the application of cold, hard logic to political problems.[124] But the predominant view was that the central ideas which framed the nineteenth century—hence *modern* conservatism—were articulated in response to the cataclysmic political and social changes in France. In 1897, for example, Arthur Baumann declared that the '*causa causans* of modern Toryism' lay with the French Revolution and with Burke, rather than 'passive' Pitt. For this reason Baumann, barrister, City director, Conservative MP, and later editor of the *Saturday Review* (1917–21), argued against a consistent Tory tradition.[125] Like MacCunn, his background was Scottish-Balliol and, like MacCunn, Baumann linked Burke to Conservatism because it was eighteenth-century Whiggism, not Toryism, which sought to conserve the status quo. The French Revolution united all would-be 'Conservatives', meaning Burke the Whig could give 'to the creed of Conservatism its highest form of expression'.[126] The *Saturday Review* noted that this was still a comparatively recent development for Conservative Unionists in 1899:

> It used to be the fashion forty years ago to sneer at Burke as a madman and incendiary. But if there is anyone who can now read the 'Reflections on the Revolution in France' by the light of the world's experience with modern democracy, without being impressed by the almost superhuman wisdom of the writer, the obscurity is not in Burke's intellect but his own.[127]

That same year, the Liberal Unionist historian Goldwin Smith also maintained that political parties had formed themselves anew around the 'burning question' of the Revolution.[128] The Tory *Blackwood's Magazine* likewise asserted that the Revolution had crystallized emerging political ideas, and Burke's 'disposition to preserve, and an ability to improve' expressed the 'Tory ideal'.[129] The result of explicitly tracing the Conservative party back to Burke and the French Revolution was that a tradition

---

[124] See Timothy Lang, *The Victorians and the Stuart Heritage* (1995).
[125] 'Baumann, Arthur Anthony', *Who Was Who* (2014), at <http://www.ukwhoswho.com/>.
[126] A. A. Baumann, 'An Apology for Unprincipled Toryism', *FR* (Oct. 1897), 621. Baumann first expressed his view that Conservatism was essentially 'Anti-Jacobinism' in 'The Truth about Tory Democracy', *NR* (Mar. 1887), 1–10. He repeated his assertions of Conservatism's Whig heritage in 'The Demise of the Tory Party', *SR* (19 Dec. 1903), 755–6. For similar sentiments by different contributors, see William Barry, 'Edmund Burke, Statesman and Prophet', *NR* (Jan. 1898), 775; Lord Selborne, 'Thoughts about Party', *CR* (Jan. 1887), 5–7; [Anon.], 'Mr. Pitt', *SR* (31 Dec. 1898), 874–5.
[127] [Anon.], 'The Story of the Nations: Modern England before the Reform Bill', *SR* (14 Jan. 1899), 54.
[128] Godwin Smith, *The United Kingdom: A Political History* (1899), ii. 275.
[129] [Anon.], 'The Tory Future', *BM* (Feb. 1900), 188. See also T. E. Kebbel, 'The Sentiment of Chivalry', *Macmillan's* (Aug. 1897), 300–3.

was created which had little connection with party history as understood earlier in the nineteenth century, or with whatever later scholarship has recovered.[130] It was, nevertheless, a powerful reimagining that has had significant staying power.

Unionist attempts to reshape party identity around the Revolution were replicated in Liberal outlets. Thus, Fox became the father of Liberalism, as distinct from Whiggism;[131] ideas of nationality and democracy were traced back to 'French principles'—presumably liberty, equality, and fraternity—which blossomed in 1789;[132] and Burke continued to be set in opposition to Rousseau[133] and Thomas Paine.[134] Though this latter point was not a particularly original intellectual venture, it nonetheless stressed a dualism which divided the Revolution into political binaries with strong connections to the political present. The Liberal *Speaker* declared, in 1895, that Burke and Paine represented both sides of a great two-party struggle.[135] Edwardian Liberals, such as Herbert Paul and J. M. Robertson, repeated Unionist assertions that the Revolution 'crystallizes' Burke's ideas which became 'more Conservative than ever'.[136] Henceforth (it was accepted) one can trace 'modern English Conservatism... in its typical form'.[137] This was a bipartisan development which more or less explicitly invalidated nineteenth-century Whig/Tory constitutional divisions in favour of newly constructed genealogies based upon historic reactions to the French Revolution, using Burke as an intellectual and political centrepiece.[138]

Even so, modern literature on the Conservative party has also established the heterogeneity of the discussions of what 'new' Conservatism was, and it is easy to see why it would be impossible to claim Burke as any

[130] Compare, for example, Sack, *From Jacobite to Conservative*.
[131] A. C. Forster Boulton, 'Liberalism and the Empire', *WR* (May 1899), 488.
[132] P. J. Macdonell, 'Historic Basis of Liberalism', in F. W. Hirst and J. S. Phillimore, eds., *Essays on Liberalism, by Six Oxford Men* (1897), 269–70; C. B. Roylance Kent, *The English Radicals* (1899), 82, 436–7; T. M. Kettle, 'The Philosophy of Politics' (1906), 9; [Anon.], 'Fifty Years of English Literature', *Academy* (21 Dec. 1912), 792–3.
[133] Malcolm MacColl, 'Lord Acton's Letters to Mary Gladstone', *FR* (June 1904), 998; Edmund Gosse, 'Rousseau in England in the Nineteenth Century', *FR* (July 1912), 22–38.
[134] Fisher, *The Republican Tradition in Europe*, 142–3. Cf. p. 89: 'what Burke said in 1790 the conservatives of Europe have believed ever since'.
[135] [Anon.], 'Rights of Man', *Speaker* (19 Jan. 1895), 78.
[136] Herbert Paul, *Life of Froude* (1905), 240.
[137] J. M. Robertson, *The Meaning of Liberalism* (1912), 16. Robertson had previously described the English Revolution of Charles I (not 1688) as the hinge of English political thought: 'England Before and Since the French Revolution', *Our Corner* (May 1888), 267–80.
[138] Duncan Bell also notes the emerging association at this time of the late eighteenth century with the creation of 'liberalism': *Reordering the World: Essays on Liberalism and Empire* (2016), pp. 74–7.

kind of exclusive agent in shaping it. Consider, for example, the question of what Unionists should be called, and the names which various writers and politicians appropriated. The 'irrational' importance of names, songs, and colours to political parties, aside from reasoned principles, was recognized most notably by Graham Wallas' *Human Nature and Politics* (1908).[139] For many Conservative Unionists, 'Tory' and 'Toryism' were preferable to 'Conservative' and 'Conservatism'—although again there were no agreed definitions on what these terms actually meant. Toryism could mean 'Parson and Squire' to one writer, and democratic paternalism to another. Conservatism, on the other hand, could be conceived in defensive or constructive 'maintenance' terms, and even as outright theft of Whig/Liberal policy. Peel was frequently seen to be guilty of the latter apostasy in this period.[140] Strangely, many of the specifically 'Tory' writers who mourned a lost golden age before Whig or Liberal Unionist influence on the party, also went on to quote or reference Burke, and this is no doubt a significant indication of Burke's established position at the head of C/conservative intellectual and political traditions. Edwardian Unionists were fully engaged in a process of intellectual and political regeneration: the early twentieth century saw numerous publications concerned with the perceived intellectual drought within the party. Alfred Milner (1854–1925), Lord Hugh Cecil (1869–1956), Harry Roberts (1871–1946), F. E. Smith (1872–1930), Leo Amery (1873–1955), T. E. Hulme (1883–1917), Keith Feiling (1884–1977), and Geoffrey Butler (1887–1929), among many others, all produced examinations of Toryism and/or Conservatism, depending on authorial preference.[141] Burke was not the only beneficiary of this process of re-examination, but he was a principal beneficiary, and insofar as Conservatism could be defined in historical and intellectual terms, probably *the* principal beneficiary.

Smith's *Toryism* (1903) was one of the first attempts to establish Burke as the head of a modern Conservative tradition. Smith, a rising star of the legal profession and MP for Walton from 1906, sought to represent the spectrum of political thought within his party's history through an

---

[139] Graham Wallas, *Human Nature in Politics* (1908).
[140] F. E. Smith, for instance, sneered at Peel's 'whiggism' in *Toryism* (p. 14). Similarly, Lord Rosebery saw Peel as a Liberal: *Lord Randolph Churchill* (1906), 122. See also Boyd Hilton, 'Peel: A Reappraisal', *HJ*, 22 (1979), 585–6.
[141] Cecil, *Conservatism*; Butler, *Tory Tradition*; Smith, *Toryism*; F. E. Smith, *Unionist Policy and Other Essays* (1912); Leo Amery, *Union and Strength* (1912); T. E. Hulme, 'A Tory Philosophy' [1912], in *The Collected Writings of T. E. Hulme*, ed. Karen Csengeri (1994); Harry Roberts, *Constructive Conservatism*, intro. Leo Amery (1913); Alfred Milner, *The Nation and the Empire* (1914); Keith Feiling, *Tory Democracy* (1914).

anthology of extracts from speeches and writings. It was, like Baumann's, a history which recognized that hitherto there had been no coherent and logical body of Tory doctrine. A product of University College, Liverpool and Wadham College, Oxford, Smith's awareness of the different schools within the party proper was a long-standing feature of his thought, and he himself was comfortable both as a self-styled progressive modern Conservative in the Unionist Social Reform Committee and as a die-hard (during the constitutional crisis of 1909–14).[142] *Toryism* did, however, identify three embedded 'ground ideas': loyalty to the crown; devotion to the church; and the 'necessity of subordination', that is, social hierarchy and inequality.[143] On Burke, Smith admitted his Whiggism as Baumann had, but insisted that the loyalty, chivalry, and opposition to parliamentary reform found in Burke's French writings 'inspired almost all that is noblest in the Toryism of later days'.[144] The Revolution found him a 'Conservative Whig and left him a high Tory'.[145] Smith, who consciously uses the term 'Toryism' (rather than Conservatism) ends his introduction: 'Burke, it has been seen, had become the corner-piece of the Tory building.'[146] *Toryism* was well received and the reviews collaborated in the blurring of the lines between Whigs and Tories. The *Spectator*, for instance, emphasized that Whigs and Tories, though different parties, valued similar traits in a more longstanding 'Conservatism' of order, law, and tradition; Liberalism, in contrast, preferred progress, enthusiasm, and freedom of individuality.[147]

Smith was clever—prescient perhaps—but he was not yet 'respectable' or orthodox. So it was not until the rejection of the 1909 budget by the Lords and the subsequent threat to the veto power of the Upper Chamber that Conservative Unionist writing gained its full momentum. It is here that Burke was most systematically welcomed into the Conservative fold, and this shift can be noted even at the level of the party leadership. As previously discussed (Chapter 5), Salisbury demonstrated no interest in Burke as a model or guide for his Conservative principles. This want of interest was equally true of his nephew, Arthur Balfour, who in 1911—the year in which he was replaced as leader by Andrew Bonar Law—can be found stating that Burke was neither a Liberal nor a Conservative.[148]

---

[142] Smith, *Unionist Policy*, 5.
[143] Smith, *Toryism*, i–iii. This publication receives scant mention in John Campbell's otherwise substantial biography: *F. E. Smith, First Earl of Birkenhead* (1983).
[144] Smith, *Toryism*, xlviii.   [145] Ibid., lix.
[146] Ibid., lxiv. Smith would later give a centenary address on Burke at TCD: 'Burke's Place in History', *Manchester Guardian* (12 Dec. 1928), 4.
[147] 'Toryism', *Spectator* (30 Jan. 1904), 187; 'Toryism', *Irish Times* (4 Feb. 1904), 7; 'Toryism', *Speaker* (20 Feb. 1904), 499–500.
[148] *Hansard*, 21 Feb. 1911, vol. 21, c.1756.

Given Balfour's background as a moral sciences student at Cambridge and his later philosophical work, the possible reasons behind this statement are worth explaining. His interests were more abstract and academic than most other prominent Conservatives, being purely philosophical and scientific. In *Theism and Humanism* (1915), he reflected that he had gravitated towards moral sciences because of his desire to 'discover what I ought to think about the world and why'. But, to Balfour, this was a rather different intellectual enterprise than studying past thinkers such as Burke: 'For the history of speculation I cared not a jot. Dead systems seemed to me of no more interest than abandoned fashions. My business was with the groundwork of that scientific knowledge whose recent developments had so profoundly moved mankind.'[149] His philosophical preferences, meanwhile, led to a deep criticism of Idealism—despite his personal friendship with another philosopher-politician, the Liberal and Idealist Richard Haldane (1856–1928).[150] So, intellectually at least, there is very little common ground between Balfour and the philosophically-minded admirers of Burke, ranging from the histories and biographies of John Morley and Leslie Stephen, to the Idealism of MacCunn, Ritchie, and Jones—and this may explain why Balfour would not have looked to an earlier thinker such as Burke as a model for present and future principles of Conservatism.

In contrast, Bonar Law's speech to the 1911 party conference—by then as leader of the opposition—outlined his definition of 'conservatism' with reference to Burke. This was a noteworthy move for a notoriously 'unintellectual' party leader and it is even more remarkable that he takes Burke as his guide: 'A disposition to preserve, and an ability to improve, taken together, would be my standard of a statesman.' According to Bonar Law's biographer, he frequently repeated this aphorism precisely because it came so close to enunciating his own political principles.[151] Even more remarkable, however, is the evidence that Bonar Law was subsequently joined by a number of Unionists who expressed their 'Conservatism' through Burke.

The first of these is the political essayist Arthur Baumann, who appeared earlier in this chapter. The constitutional crisis explains why he saw Burke as the most relevant 'Tory' hero in 1912 as he had not in 1897. In both years he posed the same question: who should be the patron saint of Toryism? Bolingbroke or Burke? Pitt or Peel? Disraeli or Salisbury? In 1897, though 'Burkeism' was the 'only systematic body of Conservative

---

[149] Arthur Balfour, *Theism and Humanism* (1915), 137.
[150] J. D. Root, 'The Philosophical and Religious Thought of Arthur James Balfour (1848–1930)', *JBS*, 19 (1980), 137.
[151] R. Q. Adams, *Bonar Law* (1999), 70.

doctrine that has ever been presented to the world', at this date he nonetheless supposed that the defensive 'anti-revolutionary Toryism of Burke' was dead; and he promoted instead the cause of constructive Conservatism with Disraeli serving as the model for injecting 'Socialism' (factory, workshop, and housing acts) into Toryism. This was predicated on the assumption that the threat of 'Jacobinism' (i.e. 'Irish Separatism') was minimal—which in 1897 was not unreasonable—although Baumann, who used 'Toryism' and 'Conservatism' synonymously, did not rule out a return to defensive Toryism should such forces rear their head again.[152] When in 1912 it became clear that such forces had returned, with British politics in turmoil after the 1911 Parliament Act, a recent wave of strike action, and the revival of Irish Home Rule as a realistic political prospect, it is no surprise to find that Baumann returned to Burke:

> The genius of Burke seated the Tories in power for forty years. The writings of Burke contain the most complete body of Conservative doctrine, expressed in the most perfect language that has ever been given to the world. The question is whether a Tory revival, in the sense of recurrence to the Conservatism of Burke, is possible... The greater part of Burke's philosophy, like all classical work, is detachable from the circumstances of the time... and might have been produced in the atmosphere of Mr. Lloyd George quite as well as in that of Santerre... The national mind *must* return to the mind of Burke sooner or later, because it is the only view of politics possible to men who are not mad and who are able and allowed to reason. But in order to lead the nation back to the paths of sanity and safety the Conservative party must be Conservative in principles and practice.[153]

Baumann pleaded for a little 'plain, old-fashioned, common-sense Conservatism': the restoration of the constitution, the defence of the empire, and support for the liberty of the individual and the rights of property.[154] Baumann's thought, which stressed the fluidity of Tory and Conservative traditions, was a straightforward separation of negative 'Burkean Conservatism' and positive, Disraelian, 'Tory Socialism'. This is distinctive: there is little sense of the 'reform to preserve' organic Burke in this reading, which can perhaps be explained by Baumann's strong anti-democratic views, especially concerning women's suffrage. He stopped short of describing Disraeli as a 'Tory Democrat', for instance, because this

---

[152] Baumann, 'Apology for Unprincipled Toryism', 622–5. Baumann was against Tariff Reform schemes until after the war, when he deemed 'peaceful' free trade as impossible.
[153] A. A. Baumann, 'Is a Tory Revival Possible?', *FR* (Feb. 1912), 219–21. In his fourth letter on a *Regicide Peace* [1795], Burke accused the Jacobin Antoine Joseph Santerre of ordering military drummers to drown out Louis XVI's final speech. See *WSEB*, ix. 111–12.
[154] Ibid., 224.

implied something quite different from the 'state regulation of industry' suggested by his preferred label of 'Tory Socialist'. He also regretted, in 1914, that Disraeli had not divined the long-term consequences of the 1867 Reform Act.[155] Indeed it was the defensive Burke, over thirty years after his 1897 article, who remained Baumann's anti-democratic hero in his *Burke: The Founder of Conservatism* (1929). However, it comes as no surprise to find that this title had been used long before, by our next author, Lord Hugh Cecil.

Cecil, the youngest son of Lord Salisbury, is an altogether more prominent figure. Prior to 1912, he had established himself as one of the most prominent of Edwardian Conservatives and an articulate critic of his cousin Arthur Balfour's leadership. MP for Greenwich from 1895 and for Oxford University from 1906, Cecil's unbending High-Church Anglicanism on the 1902 Education Act, and criticism of Chamberlain's Tariff Reform scheme, won him and his allies (including Smith and the young Winston Churchill) the nickname 'Hughligans'.[156] Like his friend Smith, Cecil looked back to Burke during the early Edwardian period. In a Bristol speech of 1904, for example, Cecil defended the view that a member sat in parliament to 'use his own judgement' and not to defend specific party policies.[157] His discussion of 'Conservatism' can be dated from April 1905, when Cecil addressed his Greenwich constituents in a fight against an 'official' Tariff Reform candidate standing against him. He argued that Conservatism, which he loyally supported, was not to be confused with protectionism.[158] The following October, Cecil spoke at a crowded meeting of the Glasgow Parliamentary Debating Union on Conservatism again. Here he differentiated between the Conservatism associated with the political party, and the 'general temperament' of Conservatism as a 'school of thought', which could be held by anyone and was certainly not found in all Conservative MPs—Tariff Reform was, in this interpretation, unnecessary reform.[159] In its coverage of Cecil's speech, the *Speaker* likened Cecil's detestation of Chamberlain to his father's of Disraeli.[160]

---

[155] Baumann claimed that Tories realized that they cannot 'reach Conservatism by diving deeper and deeper into the proletariat'. 'Bye-Products of Disraeli', *SR* (10 Jan. 1914), 44–5. Cf. 'Was Disraeli a Democrat?', *FR* (Jan. 1918), 71–9.

[156] Richard A. Rempel, 'Lord Hugh Cecil's Parliamentary Career, 1900–1914: Promise Unfulfilled', *JBS*, 11 (1972), 104–30; William S. Rodner, 'Conservatism, Resistance and Lord Hugh Cecil', *HPT*, 9 (1988), 529–51.

[157] 'Lord Hugh Cecil at Bristol', *The Times* (30 Apr. 1904), 8.

[158] 'Lord H. Cecil at Greenwich', *The Times* (8 Apr. 1905), 6.

[159] 'Lord H. Cecil on Conservatism', *The Times* (14 Oct. 1905), 10.

[160] 'Lord H. Cecil on Conservatism', *Speaker* (21 Oct. 1905), 53–4. D. J. Dutton goes beyond personal animosity to argue that there was a general feeling of distrust of Liberal Unionists by their Conservative allies well into the Edwardian period, based around fear

As Salisbury's son, Cecil held a remarkable Conservative pedigree but his High Churchmanship and staunch independence from the party whip were seen as problematic. He was not, however, without supporters, though at this date they were of a narrower kind. Thus, in 1909, Wilfrid Ward (1856–1916), an English Catholic writing in the *Dublin Review*, applied the 'principles of Burke' to Cecil's arguments regarding the toleration of 'free-fooders' and held Cecil up as the embodiment of Burke's notion of a principled representative.[161] Similarly, in 1910, M. G. Glazebrook, canon of Ely, invoked Burke when supporting Cecil's arguments for re-punctuation in the Lord's Prayer.[162]

Cecil's original motivation for separating Conservative thought and the party proper derived from his increasing sense of alienation at what he perceived as 'official' Unionist acceptance of Tariff Reform. To Cecil this was simply not Conservatism. Chamberlain retired in 1906, however, and the second stimulus for Cecil to systematize and disseminate his views grew out of the constitutional crisis. It was Burke, Cecil argued in a speech of November 1909 (published in 1910), who had pointed out that 'the insistence on equality by the French revolutionary leaders was in fact a preparation for despotism; and what is true in 1790 is always true.'[163] It was also from 1910 that he began quoting Burke more frequently with regard to Home Rule. Cecil cited the Gladstonian favourite, Burke on conciliation with America ('whose authority on such a question will be admitted to be decisive'), to argue that the Irish already had self-government: that is, they had representation in the 'Imperial Parliament' (in contrast to the Thirteen Colonies).[164] He repeated this point in the Commons in 1911.[165] His principal text *Conservatism* (1912) was then written and published with a popular audience in mind, and appeared as part of the Home University Library series—despite Cecil's recognized erudition, *Conservatism* was not an elite text. Central to its argument was

---

that the LUs were a 'clique' attempting to take over the party through bureaucratic 'efficiency': 'The Unionist Party and Social Policy, 1906–1914', *HJ*, 24 (1981), 875.

[161] Wilfrid Ward, 'Politics and Party', *Dublin Review* (July 1909), 36–58, also discussed in *The Times* (30 July 1909), 9.

[162] M. G. Glazebrook, 'The Repunctuation of the Lord's Prayer,' *The Times* (19 July 1910), 6. The controversy occurred over the issue of whether a comma should be placed after the word 'done'.

[163] Lord Hugh Cecil, *Liberty and Authority* (1910), 55.

[164] Lord Hugh Cecil, 'Home Rule and Imperial Federation', *The Times* (28 Oct. 1910), 8.

[165] *Hansard*, 15 Feb. 1911, vol. 21, cc.1089–90. Ian Malcolm (1868–1944), Conservative MP for Croyden and a 'Hughligan', also referenced Burke in this sitting after predicting a 'great revolution': ibid., c.1069. Balfour cited Burke a week later: 21 Feb. 1911, vol. 21, c.1756, and F. E. Smith enlisted Burke again the following day: 22 Feb. 1911, vol. 21, c.1945.

the connection between Burke and both intellectual and political Conservatism, and it devoted an entire chapter to Burke as 'the founder of conservatism'.

Cecil began by distinguishing between the tenets of the Conservative party and the 'natural conservatism' which is a disposition of the human mind. They were not one and the same, even if 'modern Conservatism', or 'the Conservatism of the Conservative Party', arose from and was dependent on the 'natural conservatism' found 'in almost every human mind'.[166] For Cecil, Conservatism consisted of three elements: Toryism, or the reverence for religion and authority; natural conservatism, the distrust of the unknown and love of the familiar; and imperialism, a feeling for the unity and greatness of Britain.[167] However, despite these very widely defined roots, Conservatism did not come into existence until the French Revolution. Before 1790 (the publication date of Burke's *Reflections*), there was nothing resembling a 'Conservative doctrine'.[168] When it emerged, this doctrine was composed of support for Church and King; for order and the status quo; and concern for the greatness and safety of England. Therefore:

> In Burke Conservatism found its first and perhaps its greatest teacher, who poured forth with extraordinary rhetorical power the language of an anti-revolutionary faith, and gave to the Conservative movement the dignity of a philosophical creed and the fervour of a religious crusade... Burke is commonly regarded as a Whig and Pitt as a Tory, but this is really a serious misapprehension. Burke was a conservative all his life.[169]

Again, the importance of the French Revolution in ideological and party terms is stressed, and Burke's Whiggishness is turned into conservatism, and thence Conservatism. Given the historical origin of Conservatism in the combat against Jacobinism, it followed that the 'true division of English parties' would relate to the principles of 1789. 'Men' were now either Jacobins or Burkeans.[170] Socialists and 'new' Liberals made up the former, Unionists the latter.

To Cecil, Burke's thought was of lasting and current importance. He identified six themes in *Reflections* which 'permanently underlie Conservative thought'. These were: the importance of religion and the value of its recognition by the state; the hatred of injustice to individuals committed in the course of political and social reform; an attack on the revolutionary

---

[166] Cecil, *Conservatism*, 8.   [167] Ibid., 8, 244.   [168] Ibid., 39.
[169] Ibid., 40. For similar sentiments, see [Anon.], 'Fifty Years of English Literature', *Academy*, 792–3.
[170] Cecil, *Conservatism*, 44, 248.

conception of equality which suppressed the reality and necessity of rank and distinctions; the sanctity of private property and its necessity to the well-being of society; the idea that human society is an organism, of which much is mysterious; and therefore, finally, the importance of continuity with the historical past and of making any change as gradual and with as slight dislocation as possible.[171] In this way Burke was reduced to a six-point Conservative political theory. Unsurprisingly given his churchmanship, Cecil went on to assert: 'This sense that the state is a mysterious organism may be almost called the keynote of Burke's political philosophy.'[172] Throughout the book, Cecil goes back repeatedly to Conservatism's opposition to Revolutionary principles as the foundation for the twin beliefs in religion and property.[173] The religious basis of Conservatism gave rise to a sense of revulsion against injustice, and therefore explained the logic of Conservative social reform, which would be conducted in a more scrupulous fashion than that of Liberals or Socialists.[174] Likewise, in order to maintain the constitution, Cecil argued in favour of bipartisan Lords reform, suggesting a preservation scheme which would allow for change in keeping with the existing character and traditions of the second chamber.[175] This was, no doubt, an active form of 'maintenance'. Cecil concluded by stating that, though Conservatism opposed Liberalism and Socialism in practical politics, it was not directly antagonistic to either as 'a system of political thought'. Instead, it occupied a position 'between the old-fashioned individualist Liberalism of the early nineteenth century and the authoritative methods of the socialist movement'.[176] Still, in their attitude to property and the constitution, Land-Leaguers and Home Rulers were Jacobins.[177]

Cecil's work was eagerly received. The philosopher C. D. Broad (1887–1971), then assistant to the Professor of Logic at St Andrews, stated in the *International Journal of Ethics* that *Conservatism* was considered an 'event' at the time due to the 'general paucity of literature on the history and character of British conservatism'. Broad wrote the fullest critique of Cecil's exposition of Conservatism, although he ignored all of its 'historical claims' (including those made for Burke) and focused on

[171] Ibid., 48. [172] Ibid., 54. [173] Ibid., 114, 118.
[174] Ibid., 198. This drew on a long tradition of High Church social concern, stretching back to the Oxford Movement. For its origins, see Simon Skinner, *Tractarians and the 'Condition of England': The Social and Political Thought of the Oxford Movement* (2004).
[175] Cecil, *Conservatism*, 233.
[176] Ibid., 246–7. K. Swart argues that the term 'individualism' was rarely used before the 1870s as a description of a political ideology synonymous with the supposedly 'classical' liberalism of 'philosophic Radicalism': Swart, 'Individualism in the Mid-Nineteenth Century', *JHI*, 13 (1962), 77–90.
[177] Ibid., 241.

Cecil's abstract arguments, such as his defence of property. Broad concluded that the book was 'interesting' and 'ingenious', though 'very questionable'.[178] The *Athenaeum* and the *English Review* also noted the value and interest of Cecil's book, as 'philosophical conservatism is for some inexplicable reason less defined than philosophic liberalism'. The *English Review* accused Cecil's Conservatism of leading to political quietism, which it believed was an 'impossible' standpoint and saw his appeal to temperament over theory as harmful to his own position.[179] In contrast, Baumann, in the *Fortnightly Review*, stressed the 'classical' nature of Burke's work which allowed it to be abstracted from its context and ensured its practical relevance.[180] Baumann and the *Review of Reviews* disputed Cecil's claim that Burke lacked the 'imperialist' component of the triple compound of Conservatism, citing Burke's extensive colonial writing as evidence. (The unspoken thought here was probably that, if only Burke had been listened to, America might still be part of the Empire; it would certainly have been difficult to enlist the prosecutor of Warren Hastings as a jingoistic imperialist.) Both reviewers, however, affirmed that Conservatism was a consequence of the French Revolution.[181] The problem of political theory arose again, however, in the *Saturday Review*. The *Saturday* criticized both Cecil and Baumann for their attempts at theorizing practical politics.[182] This was hardly glowing praise. Indeed, the idea of 'conservative political philosophy' continued to be much more contested than that of liberalism or socialism, and Cecil's unconventional parliamentary behaviour put him out of favour with many.[183] Silences are, however, important: none of the reviews disagreed with Cecil's assertion that the founder of 'modern conservatism' was a Whig named Edmund Burke.

Cecil's rebelliousness demonstrates that Conservative Unionism really was a broad church. It is important to note, therefore, that not all Conservative and/or Tory tracts from the late Edwardian period placed Burke at their centre. A correspondent to the *Saturday Review* in November 1910 protested that 'You really cannot be intending to go on with this Burke business', and rejected the notion that Burke could ever be used to

---

[178] C. D. Broad, 'Lord Hugh Cecil's Conservatism', *International Journal of Ethics* (July 1913), 396.
[179] 'Conservatism', *English Review* (July 1912), 668–9; 'Home University Library of Modern Knowledge', *Athenaeum* (4 May 1912), 502.
[180] A. A. Baumann, 'Lord Hugh Cecil on Conservatism', *FR* (July 1912), 39–52. Cf. Cecil, *Conservatism*, 62.
[181] 'Lord Hugh Cecil's Conservatism', *Review of Reviews* (July 1912), 108–9.
[182] 'Conservatism', *SR* (27 July 1912), 115–16.
[183] Rodner, 'Conservatism, Resistance, and Lord Hugh Cecil', 537.

support a Tory party intent on social reform.[184] Likewise, in 1913, Arthur Boutwood's *National Revival: A Restatement of Tory Principles*, introduced by the leader of the 'die-hard' peers Lord Willoughby de Broke, was no Burkean manifesto. De Broke, now conventionally regarded as a reactionary, had a philosophical slant to his thought and later collaborated with Anthony Mario Ludovici, one of Britain's most extreme right-wing writers (who also wrote on Burke in the 1920s), on theories of Tory revivalism.[185] His introduction stated that 'duty must be the starting point of political thought', since it was duty that differentiated Tory social reform from that of the Socialists and Radicals. The Tory test for reform proposals of institutions and laws was, de Broke explained, a maxim taken from Burke: will it maintain and improve the best aspects of British character?[186] Burke was also invoked to stress the intrinsically religious aspect of Toryism once more.[187] In Boutwood's text, however, Burke is never mentioned. Boutwood, a 'middle-brow' autodidact of the Home University series, was a Conservative Idealist: his reading of Hegel and Green informed his organic, pragmatic, undemocratic ideal of 'Constructive Toryism' which would both conserve and reform.[188] While his text may sound Burkean in light of the scholarship drawn on in this chapter, it is important to note that Boutwood does not—like so many Unionists and Liberal Idealists—cite Burke.

Likewise, Keith Feiling's *Toryism: A Political Dialogue* (1913) asserted the need for a Tory 'creed' of positive, rather than negative, beliefs. F. E. Smith provided the introduction, in which he described Disraeli as the recognized 'inspired fount of Tory wisdom'.[189] Meanwhile Feiling regretted that the 'extreme Whig' position was being taken by Conservatives against Revolutionary Liberalism. 'Franklin', the leading character in the dialogue, stated: 'I should say [Burke was] a converted Whig. The doctrines that the converted Whigs have brought into the Tory Party are its greatest danger.'[190] *Toryism* shows that Feiling's attitude to Burke was confused at best, as Burke was simultaneously canonized as a 'great Tory'. Thus: 'you must have always noticed that all the great Tory writers, Burke

---

[184] B. R. Carter, 'Burke-ing the Issue', *SR* (5 Nov. 1910), 581–2.
[185] Dan Stone, 'Ludovici, Anthony Mario', *ODNB* (2004); 'The Extremes of Englishness: The Exceptional Ideology of Antony Mario Ludovici', *Journal of Political Ideologies*, 4 (1999), 191–218; Anthony M. Ludovici, *A Defence of Conservatism, a Further Text-book for Tories* (1927).
[186] Arthur Boutwood, *National Revival, a Restatement of Tory Principles* (1913), ix–x.
[187] Ibid., xix.
[188] For Boutwood, see Green, *Ideologies of Conservatism*, 46–56; Greenleaf, *The British Political Tradition*, ii. 233–4.
[189] Keith Feiling, *Toryism: A Political Dialogue* (1913), ix.
[190] Ibid., 39.

or Bolingbroke or Coleridge, make affection of the people for the government and their institutions the sure sign of national health'.[191] Later, Franklin stated that God was 'engraved' on all Tories in the government of men—a list which included Aristotle alongside Burke and Disraeli.[192] Moreover, the text is littered with direct quotations from Burke's works. For instance, the statement: 'Two things we must do for this country and the same for Toryism—find the true base of our ancient polity and then broaden it to suit our new needs' was supported by a footnote to Burke's maxim, from *Reflections*, that 'a State without the means of some change is without the means of its conservation'.[193] So despite—or even because of—his resistance to Burke, Feiling demonstrated the extent to which Burke's thought had permeated contemporary Unionist thinking, however messily.

The final text to be considered is Geoffrey Butler's *The Tory Tradition: Bolingbroke, Burke, Disraeli, Salisbury* (1914). Butler, a Cambridge historian and fellow of Corpus Christi College, was a member of an academic dynasty: his nephew was R. A. Butler, and his work on Burke in fact goes back to the notes of his uncle, Henry Montagu Butler (1833–1918), a classicist who, as Headmaster of Harrow, Dean of Gloucester, and Master of Trinity College, Cambridge, had stood at the pinnacle of the educational and religious establishment.[194] Alongside Cecil, Montagu Butler had been a member of the bipartisan Synthetic Society which aimed to produce a philosophical basis for religious belief.[195] His son and Geoffrey's cousin, the historian J. R. M. Butler, described his father as: 'A Peelite by tradition, a conservative Liberal by conviction, he passed gradually to liberal Conservatism, Gladstone's conversion to Home Rule and his failure to save Gordon proving important turning-points.' He added that 'the names of Chatham, Burke, Pitt... Canning, Peel, Palmerston and Bright were at all times on his lips'. Montagu Butler had not, however, been a democrat: Burke was his 'great master'.[196] Though a Conservative, he had been an enthusiastic advocate of women's colleges and the Workers' Educational Association, and this was reflected in his collection of lectures, *Ten Great and Good Men* (1909), which begins with an 1895 address on Burke to the London University Extension Society. Claiming to offer no criticism of the sort made by Lecky or Morley, he

---

[191] Ibid., 142. [192] Ibid., 50.
[193] Ibid., 16.
[194] Butler, *Tory Tradition*, 13.
[195] W. C. Lubenow, 'Synthetic Society (act. 1896–1909)', *ODNB* (2004).
[196] J. R. M. Butler, *Henry Montagu Butler: Master of Trinity College, Cambridge, 1886–1918* (1925), 94; Michael Bentley, 'Liberal Toryism in the Twentieth-Century', *TRHS*, 4, 6th ser. (1994), 187–8.

confessed that Burke was, and always had been, his favourite author: returned to again and again, copied out, and memorized.[197] The volume (which also included school, university, and extension lectures on Canning, Wesley, Pitt, Bright, General Gordon, Thomas Arnold, Thomas Erskine, and Lord Shaftesbury) demonstrated the upstanding moral character of these characters. They do not contain explicitly political criticism.

In contrast, Geoffrey Butler's *Tory Tradition* was a political tract for the times. First delivered as a series of lectures at the University of Pennsylvania, his tradition was made up of four protagonists. Bolingbroke was the great Tory party leader, with both destructive and constructive abilities. Burke was the most profound Tory 'political philosopher'.[198] Disraeli, 'the greatest of all Tories', combined romantic imagination with pragmatic political skill; his ideal was a national Toryism, with an enfranchised people and a Patriot King, which could effectively ward off factional interests and garner the support of the working classes.[199] Lord Salisbury was held up as a great conciliatory diplomat: quietly confident, with a historical approach to addressing oppression which was an 'active weapon' (and not a 'passive accomplishment').[200] Each had left his legacy to modern Tories. The similarities between the four, however loose, such as the 'literary qualities' shared by Bolingbroke, Burke, and Disraeli, were stressed throughout as a means of tying together the canon.

As with other Unionist texts on Burke, Butler—though stating Burke's overall consistency—argued for the unique importance of the French Revolution in bringing out the Conservatism of his thought. This therefore made it possible to disregard the British, Indian, and American portions of Burke's work. To leave out the rest, and to talk alone of the French writings alone, was to do what was 'most useful' in a systematic study of the growth of Tory doctrine.[201] Burke's 'doctrine' (according to Butler) of the organic, as opposed to the mechanical, conception of society, was 'the fundamental doctrine of all Toryism'.[202] Burke also shared the 'Tory disbelief' in infinite individual capabilities and trust in inherited methods of government. He was 'almost the only English political philosopher who rejected the *a priori* method'.[203] Furthermore, Butler agreed with Burke that individuals owed a duty to the organism

---

[197] H. M. Butler, *Ten Great and Good Men* (1909), 2. In 1959–60 J. R. M. Butler arranged for an edition of Burke's works to be gifted to Harrow in memory of his father: Trinity College, Cambridge (J. R. M. Butler Papers), JRMB/B/10. The Butler Papers also contain a much earlier (privately published) speech of Montagu Butler's on Burke very similar to that contained in *Great and Good Men*: H. M. Butler, *The Character of Edmund Burke* (1854), JRMB/M3/8/1.
[198] Butler, *Tory Tradition*, 23, 103.   [199] Ibid., 60–7.
[200] Ibid., 116.   [201] Ibid., 33.   [202] Ibid., 36.   [203] Ibid., 38.

which made their personality and that this duty should be expressed through organizations and institutions.[204] Burke was therefore presented as an essential modern guide:

> The Tory must draw upon the wisdom of our Fathers, he must select and he must reinterpret their sacred principles in a language understood of the people. There must be a Renaissance, a Reformation, a Reception of unexampled brilliance and of unparalleled effect... 'Back to Burke', 'An open Burke'. He must be the Bible of a pure and reformed Conservatism, which alone can oust the misguided if generous proposals of the modern Radicals, and meet and solve the problems which have given those proposals motive force.[205]

The Tory Tradition was well received. The *Athenaeum* was congratulatory in its review and regretted that the English had been apt to forget the 'constructive side of Toryism'.[206] The *Daily Telegraph*, noting that Butler's aim was to 'clear up some possible doubts as to the purposes of the Conservative party', similarly stated that *The Tory Tradition* 'illustrates his theory that Toryism has constructive as well as negative functions to perform'.[207] Unlike Cecil and his inflammatory parliamentary antics, Butler was no doubt a less divisive figure, both inside and outside the party proper, and he had a considerable academic pedigree. His work may have promoted a major about-turn by the *Saturday Review*, which had been previously critical of Tory and Liberal attempts to talk about Burke's 'political philosophy' but now celebrated Butler's work. It emphasized that the text was especially instructive as to the contemporary relevance of Burke, though it questioned the appropriateness of the label 'Tory'. In reality, the *Saturday* suggested that there could be no doubt: Burke must be labelled as a firm 'Conservative'.[208]

CONCLUSION

At the turn of the twentieth century, Burke was a more visible figure in all senses of the term. Material commemorations, including statues and memorials in Belfast, Bristol, and Bath, nearly doubled within a six-year period and added to the existing monuments in Westminster Hall, Dublin, and Beaconsfield.[209] At a political level, the debates over Irish

---

[204] Ibid., 39–40.   [205] Ibid., 59.
[206] 'Political Thought', *Athenaeum* (26 Dec. 1914), 666.
[207] 'Notes and Reviews', *Daily Telegraph* (6 Nov. 1914), 4.
[208] 'The Tory Tradition', *SR* (16 Jan. 1915), 64–5.
[209] Statues of Burke can be found in St Stephen's Hall, Westminster (1858); outside TCD (1868); and on Colston Avenue, Bristol (1894). A series of stained glass windows

Home Rule had made Burke's writings a living force, but his lack of clear 'disciples' meant that at first his legacy was freely available and ripe for adoption. When the political dust settled, however, the 'spirit' of Burke was eventually seen to be embodied best of all in the Liberal Unionists who resurrected an anti-Jacobin vocabulary and styled themselves as old Whigs defending both the constitution and the liberty of an endangered religious group. By 1893, their Conservative allies felt comfortable quoting Burke's previously Gladstonian American speeches. But this did not happen in a vacuum: the intellectual climate, as Morley foresaw in 1879, was ripe for an interpretation of Burke's oeuvre which stressed the organic, historical, and developmental nature of his thought. Moreover, this was increasingly framed in more philosophical terminology: doctrine, theory, and political philosophy. This general tendency can be seen in the Liberals Graham, Keynes, and MacCunn, and in Burke's Conservative appropriators Baumann, Smith, Cecil, and Butler. The example of MacCunn, in particular, highlights the contribution of Idealism to the creation of organic conservatism. Thus, Burke's heyday as an organic historicist thinker also led to his abstraction from his original historical context.

As a philosophy of 'conservatism' Burke's thought was centred round one main event: the French Revolution. The Revolution was a significant moment in modern history which was increasingly seen to generate historical, political, and literary consequences as its actions and thought reverberated around the Western world. In one sense the Revolution ceased to be threatening: the wave of Western European revolutions (1848–9) had expired and even then Britain had been left untouched. But in another sense the revolution was closer to home; the enemy was now within. At the *fin de siècle*, fears of national degeneration and the loss of Britain's leading global status to Germany and the USA led to attacks on Jewish immigrants; the urban working classes; the New Woman; and Socialists.[210] Much of the derogatory language generated towards Home-Rulers, Gladstonian Liberals, Socialists, and Labourites framed these people as destructive Jacobins. Hence it was that modern constructions of 'conservatism' and 'liberalism' after 1885 were routinely traced back to the French Revolution. Even the language of natural rights resurfaced in the writings of Herbert Spencer, Ritchie, and other Idealists. Going back to the French Revolution (rather than, say, the English Civil War,

---

were installed in the Linen Hall Library, Belfast in 1892, featuring Burke. A memorial (1898) was added to an existing brass tablet (1862) in St Mary and All Saints Church, Beaconsfield, and a plaque was unveiled in Bath in 1908 by the US Ambassador Whitelaw Reid: *American and English Essays* (1914), ii. 73–4.

[210] Sally Ledger and Scott McCracken, eds., *Cultural Politics at the Fin de Siècle* (1995).

or 1688) necessitated the smoothing over of uncomfortable historical realities, and it is perhaps unnecessary to state how much staying power this interpretation has had. In particular, Burke's Whig identity was incorporated into newly constructed categories of 'C/conservatism', summarized as opposition to the principles of 1789, as fears of English Jacobins attacking property, religion, and the constitution came to life. This process of incorporation was helped, of course, by the fact that many former Whigs were now allied politically with Conservatives in the Unionist party. Yet, simultaneously, one can see the continuing centrality of constitutional maintenance—from the House of Lords to the Act of Union—to Conservative thought and the party proper; and this provided a link to the agenda that had dominated politics before 1885.

Yet an unresolved contradiction in both the 'theoretical' and political discussions of Burke and C/conservatism remains. On the one hand, Burke symbolized a more positive, historically informed organic C/conservatism, which would reform—within boundaries—so as to preserve national values and institutions. He was a 'political philosopher' who valued outcomes over abstract principles. Thus, the idea of 'maintenance' of the constitution, property, and 'religion' could have an active, constructive meaning. On the other hand, Burke was seen as intellectual ammunition: a defensive weapon against democratic British Jacobins who would radically reform the constitution. The result is not conceptually clear-cut, but then neither Burke's works nor British political debate had ever been theoretically rigorous. In short, Burke was used to symbolize different approaches—positive and negative—depending on what the specific situation required.

The overall result was that Burke, a Whig statesman cherished in the mid-nineteenth century more for his powers of rhetoric than his principles, was increasingly regarded as a great Conservative and/or Tory philosopher across the political spectrum in a way that was quite novel. By 1914 there was widespread agreement that the intellectual and political traditions of an organic historicist 'C/conservatism' had come into being in 1790 with the publication of Burke's *Reflections*. In reality, however, both British Conservatism and conservatism, as significant bodies of thought, came into being in the years 1885 to 1914—and it was this which raised Burke into the canonical position he still enjoys as 'the founder of modern conservatism'. What remains to be seen, then, is how this high-cultural, intellectual, and political rendering of Burke became a commonplace at a non-elite level. It is essential, therefore, to now address the ways in which Burke's writings and thought were taught and learnt in schools, universities, and by autodidacts.

7

Learning Conservatism

Burke in Education, c.1880–1914

In 1897, the centenary of Burke's death, N. W. Sibley proclaimed in the *Westminster Review*: 'we are living in an age of renaissance as far as Burke is concerned'. 'Perhaps,' Sibley continued, 'in order to understand the present renaissance of Burke's philosophy, it is only necessary to suppose that he is more attentively studied than in Lord Macaulay's day.'[1] This chapter therefore elaborates on *how* Burke was studied from the 1880s and the links this had to contemporary intellectual and political movements. At university level, Burke was of particular interest to philosophical Idealists, English literature professors and students, and a generation of historians who taught increasingly modern courses, particularly in the civic colleges and universities. Topics such as the French Revolution, the historical roots of literary Romanticism, and late eighteenth-century British history opened up a curriculum which lectured on Burke, examined answers on Burke, and set texts by him. These courses were taught as day classes to matriculated undergraduates, as single courses and evening classes to adult learners, and as university extension courses. Burke also became a regular feature in schools and for Indian Civil Service (ICS) examinations. At school, affordable textbooks of Burke's works were printed from 1890, and girls and boys began to study his American speeches and *Reflections on the Revolution in France*. Indeed, the late nineteenth-century publishing revolution in cheap editions generally made Burke much more accessible to readers inside and outside of institutional education of all ages, genders, localities, and social classes at a time when the lower classes were finally beginning to have the leisure time and disposable income which made reading increasingly common.[2]

---

[1] N. W. Sibley, 'Edmund Burke', *WR* (Nov. 1897), 497–8.
[2] Richard Altick, *The English Common Reader: A Social History of the Mass Reading Public, 1800–1900* (1957).

An important theme in this chapter, as in the last, is the diffusion and enactment of Idealist philosophy. Though Burke was not an Idealist or a moral philosopher of any kind, his organic historicism was nonetheless highly attractive to many Idealists—particularly those who had studied at Balliol and went on from Oxford to teach at the new civic institutions and universities across the country, and as far afield as India. Peter Gordon and John White explain that Idealists laid much stress on education because, on the one hand, institutional education was a practical way of ensuring self-realization for the common good, and at the same time mediating between the individual and the state. Even here, however, universities, schools, and evening classes were only segments of an educational experience which also recognized the didactic role played by churches, families, and factories.[3] These Idealist social and educational aims combined with an intellectual commitment to developmental, organic, and philosophical approaches to the humanities and social sciences in institutions beyond Oxbridge and the public schools, such as university extension and working men's colleges.[4]

Thus, the Idealists in this chapter are of the second generation. Though tutored by Benjamin Jowett, T. H. Green, and Edward Caird, they were not purists who simply reiterated the gospel of Green's *Prolegomena*. Each cultivated their own interests in philosophy, history, and literature while retaining distinctive Idealist traits, evident in their friendships, families, and academic communities, and in intellectual and extra-mural pursuits. For example, Charles Edwin Vaughan (1854–1922), a younger cousin of Green's and 'idolized' at Balliol, had a similar effect as a young tutor at Clifton College, Bristol, where his pupils included Andrew George Little (1863–1945), future Professor of History at Cardiff. Bored with the classical curriculum at Clifton, Vaughan modernized the content of his teaching and published textbooks on Burke—he had a lifelong interest in political philosophy. Vaughan later obtained chairs in English Literature at Cardiff (1889–98), Newcastle (1899–1904), and Leeds (1904–13) and spent the final years of his life in Manchester seeking to reassert Rousseau's

---

[3] Peter Gordon and John White, *Philosophers as Educational Reformers: The Influence of Idealism on British Educational Thought and Practice* (1979). R. G. Collingwood stated in *An Autobiography* (1939) that Green sent out into public life 'a stream of ex-pupils who carried with them the conviction that philosophy ... was an important thing, and their vocation was to put it into practice.... Through this effect on the minds of its pupils, the philosophy of Green's school might be found, from 1880 to about 1910, penetrating and fertilizing every part of the national life' (p. 17).
[4] Laurence Goldman, *Dons and Workers: Oxford and Adult Education since 1850* (1995), 51–6.

place within the history of political thought.[5] Here he worked alongside his Balliol contemporary T. F. Tout (1855–1929), Professor of Medieval and Modern History at Manchester (1890–1925) and a dedicated social worker, who established Manchester as a centre of medieval scholarship, yet spent increasing amounts of time teaching modern subjects, including Burke's works, to meet the demand of his northern undergraduates.[6] Tout had previously taught Burke at Lampeter with his and Vaughan's old friend and colleague Hugh Walker (1855–1939), a Snell exhibitioner at Balliol, Mayor of Lampeter, and Professor of English Literature.[7] Vaughan, Tout, and Walker, among others, shared an intellectual interest in the history, development, and unity of thought and all became educators in the newly founded civic institutions, teaching evening classes alongside day students. Green himself had supported Oxford graduates who went on to enter 'into the educational life of the cities'.[8] Meanwhile, the history of political ideas, whether pursued in English or historical studies, was the perfect subject to elaborate a developmental, inclusive, and philosophical academic method. Burke's specific appeal lay in the perception of his organic and historicist *theory* of the state which simultaneously emphasized the importance of the locality, the 'little platoon', as a stepping-stone towards wider integration within the nation.[9]

A second theme is the preponderance of courses concerned with the French Revolution, especially in newer universities and subjects. The French Revolution as an academic subject of course is much wider than Burke, but still it led straight into Burke: *Reflections* had long since been canonized as the most important and eloquent anti-revolutionary British response to the Revolution and to the thought of Rousseau. Idealists in particular attempted to rehabilitate Rousseau's thought, particularly that concerning education and the 'general will'.[10] Beyond Idealism, English Literature, insofar as it was not a linguistic study, had a firm historical

---

[5] F. M. Powicke, *Modern Historians and the Study of History: Essays and Papers* (1955), 24. Vaughan's absence from the *ODNB* is a major omission.

[6] F. M. Powicke, 'Memoir', in T. F. Tout, *The Collected Papers of Thomas Frederick Tout, with a Memoir and Bibliography* (1932–4), i. 10–11.

[7] Walker's extraordinarily inclusive account of 'literature' considered science and history alongside fiction and poetry: Hugh Walker, *The Literature of the Victorian Era* (1910; repr. 1913).

[8] T. H. Green, 'Lecture on the Grading of Secondary Schools', in *Works of T. H. Green*, ed. R. L. Nettleship (1888), iii. 409–10, cited in Goldman, *Dons and Workers*, 53.

[9] For the broader appeal of the history of political thought, see Collini, *Public Moralists*, 248–9.

[10] The Idealist interest in Rousseau was noted in Harris, 'Political Thought and the Welfare State', 126. Harris suggests that the appeal of Rousseau for Idealists derived from 'collectivist' (rather than 'Socialist') stress on intensity in civic life and zeal for the welfare of the community.

grounding and studies of Romanticism involved teaching the Revolution and Burke. Generational change meant that the French Revolution went from being a 'dangerous' subject to William Stubbs in 1876, to a topic increasingly studied, discussed, and examined in schools, universities, and extension lectures.[11] Notable professors such as Edward Dowden, Professor of English Literature at Trinity College, Dublin, and Lord Acton, Regius Professor of Modern History at Cambridge, delivered and published their lectures on the Revolution. Lecturers at newly founded universities and extension centres were equally if not more important as pioneers of new subjects and disciplines to cater for a burgeoning demand from an increasing number of students outside of the ancient universities.[12] This was not, of course, an esoteric intellectual bubble. Following the centenary of the Revolution in 1889, a wealth of popular culture—theatre, popular histories, historical novels, biographies, and translations of autobiographies—can be found covering the 1789–1815 period.[13] Alongside medieval and early modern English history, Burke became a feature of eighteenth-century English constitutional history and also an influential participant in world affairs, including America, India, and France. In intellectual terms, however, it is clear that it was the French Revolution, rather than the American, which was considered to be the most cataclysmic and significant in relation to its impact on British thought at the time and since.

The increasing study of Burke was thanks to several converging movements and developments: in publishing and technology; in philosophical thought; in the disposable income and leisure time of greater portions of the population; and in education movements for men and women at all levels. It was also a turning point in the history of Burke's reputation: the promotion of Burke and the eighteenth century by Morley, Lecky, and Stephen and Matthew Arnold from the mid-1860s fed into his establishment as a relevant contemporary political thinker following the Home Rule

---

[11] Cited in Ian Small, 'Introduction', in Ceri Crossley and Ian Small, eds., *The French Revolution and British Culture* (1989), xiv.

[12] William Whyte, *Redbrick: A Social and Architectural History of Britain's Civic Universities* (2015), 127–30, 146.

[13] Billie Melman, *The Culture of History: English Uses of the Past, 1800–1953* (2006), 249. Melman counts 254 novels in 1914, of which 141 focus on the 1789–1814 period (113 on impact on Britain). For non-fiction examples, see Hilaire Belloc's, *Danton* (1899); *Robespierre* (1901); *Marie Antoinette* (1909); and *The French Revolution* (1911). The full lists are documented in Ernest Baker's, *History in Fiction* (1907); and *A Guide to Historical Fiction* (1914). Hatchards released a special catalogue of titles on the period 1789–1815: 'Napoleon and his Time: A Collection of Standard Books in Fine Secondhand Condition' (1908). G. K. Fortescue also documented the 'vivid and growing interest of writers and readers who pursue the history of the French Revolution' in 'The French Revolution in Contemporary Literature', *QR* (Apr. 1913), 353.

debates. This was combined with a widespread acceptance of the association of Burke with the historical, organic, and developmental thought so central to the late Victorian period. Between 1886 and 1914 Burke became thought of as 'conservative', and thus it is necessary to examine how he was presented to his ever-expanding student audience: how did they learn what Burke stood for? When, if ever, did students start to be taught an abstract, 'conservative' Burke in the classroom and the lecture hall? What did 'conservative' in these texts signify? It required more than gentlemanly scholarship for Burke to become a figure of popular caricature, the 'founder of conservatism'. The process needed teachers, lecturers, tutors, and textbooks to promulgate broadly similar analyses. Of course, this was not a mechanical indoctrination, but the increasing consistency of Burke's role and thought within education is a vital part in the circulation of his thought as politically and intellectually C/conservative.

This chapter considers the adoption of Burke in educational texts and institutions at a variety of levels. The first section examines the secondary school level, and the second focuses on Burke in university curricula. The final section details autodidact readers, extension courses, the ICS examinations, and the proliferation of cheap editions. In all cases, the teaching of Burke was reflective of contemporary intellectual, political, and generational shifts in emphasis and preoccupations. Education is close to politics, but it is not politics. Thus Burke's transformation into a 'C/conservative' became increasingly prominent in textbooks and examinations throughout the Edwardian period, which corresponds with the texts discussed in Chapter 6. The study of Burke, however, was also a productive intellectual process in itself. The transformative role of teaching and learning about Burke fed into, as well as from, the construction of Burke's reputation in this period.

AT SCHOOL

Successful expansion of higher education was (and is) necessarily connected with the growth and development of school education. This problem was identified in the early years of Owens College, Manchester in the 1850s: school education as it stood was not, for most, a sufficient precursor to university learning.[14] The Education Acts of 1870, 1891, and 1902 were seminal in providing free primary education and the first public

---

[14] D. J. Palmer, *The Rise of English Studies* (1965), 57.

provision for secondary education, though much of the material concerned with teaching Burke has been found in the experiences of middle- and upper-class boys and girls at private and public schools. Critical examination of the history and literature studied in schools is vital because it is here that a growing number of students, many of whom did not go on to university, were introduced to texts, authors, and time periods at a relatively shallow or simple analytical level. School-texts laid the foundation for future studies, if undertaken. Burke was studied more frequently as his work was abridged and annotated in textbooks for higher-level pupils—usually in the Fifth or Sixth Form. Dorothea Beale (1831–1906), Headmistress of Cheltenham Ladies' College from 1858 until her death, suffered from the widespread problem of lack of school or cheap editions in her early days as a schoolmistress. Unless texts were privately printed, the only way to study specific texts was to buy the complete works of an author.[15] Demand for school texts began to be met by publishers from the mid-century and, in particular, by the university presses at Oxford (the Clarendon series, 1866) and Cambridge (the Pitt series, 1875). By 1887 Low's Educational Catalogue listed 280 school editions of English literature, exclusive of Shakespeare.[16] The most successful school books, including those on Burke, were generally written by Oxbridge graduates who pursued careers in a variety of educational institutions.[17] Promoted as scholarly, these editions explicitly engaged with commentaries on Burke's thought, especially those by Morley and Lecky, and newer publications central to the late Victorian and Edwardian presentation of Burke, including those of Graham and MacCunn.

A debate about 'usefulness' surrounded the teaching of Burke throughout schools and universities. This was tied to a particular attitude towards education: that history and literature should teach broader moral and political lessons. Closely related to this was the argument most frequently associated with J. R. Seeley (1834–95), from his 1870 inaugural lecture as Regius Professor of Modern History at Cambridge, that the study of modern history and literature, inclusive of Burke, was a 'school of statesmanship'.[18] John Morley had been championing Burke's unique status in supplying a political education since his earliest publications, and repeated himself once again in his 1887 address to the London University Extension Society:

---

[15] F. Cecily Steadman, *In the Days of Miss Beale: A Study of her Work and Influence* (1931), 43; Kate Flint, *The Woman Reader, 1837–1914* (1995), 128.
[16] Palmer, *Rise of English Studies*, 50.   [17] Ibid., 49.
[18] J. R. Seeley, 'The Teaching of Politics', *Lectures and Essays* (1870), 296. For Seeley's approval of Burke see (in the same volume): 'Milton's Political Opinions', 93–4; 'Elementary Principles in Art', 171; 'English in Schools', 242.

We should still have everything to learn from the author's treatment; the vigorous grasp of masses of compressed detail, the wide illumination from great principles of human experience, the strong and masculine feeling for the two great political ends of Justice and Freedom, the large and generous interpretation of expediency, the morality, the vision, the noble temper.

To the advanced Liberal and Home Ruler Morley, it was in the American speeches in which he found 'the most perfect manual in all literature for the study of great affairs, whether for the purpose of knowledge or action'.[19] Morley was speaking on this occasion in favour of the study of literature as a serious academic subject, a campaign of which he was, alongside Leslie Stephen and John Churton Collins, a vocal supporter.[20] Collins (1848–1908), another former student of Green's and an assertive extension lecturer who fought for a literary, rather than philological or linguistic, English chair at Oxford, argued in 1891 that Burke should be studied alongside Cicero as a way of linking modern classics with the ancient.[21] Collins echoed Morley, whom he admired, and Seeley by claiming Burke's usefulness for politicians and political philosophers. He should therefore be central to the Indian Civil Service examinations (which we will return to later): the study of Burke's speeches was not, unlike the Saxon witenagemot, 'merely' antiquarian.[22] Burke was invoked in all instances as a prime example of how a more modern and 'literary' liberal education could benefit students and society as a whole.

Burke was therefore recommended for providing schoolboys with a political education not deemed necessary for girls. Despite this, Burke was taught in girls' schools as English Literature: a subject seen as particularly valuable in girls' schools, though gendered assumptions again pervaded perceptions of appropriate reading.[23] Beale, for example, was criticized by

[19] John Morley, *On the Study of Literature: Annual Address to Students of the London Society for the Extension of University Teaching* (1887), 33–6. For a wonderful account of a female reader taking up Morley's challenge to read more Burke, see Elsa D'sterre-Keeling, 'A Woman on Books', *The Women's Penny Paper* (23 Aug. 1890), 519.
[20] Leslie Stephen, 'The Study of English Literature' [1887], in Albert F. Blaisdell, ed., *The Study of English Literature: Three Essays* (Boston, 1902); Anthony Kearney, 'Leslie Stephen and the English Studies Debate, 1886–87', *History of Education Society Bulletin*, 43 (1989), 41–57. Blaisdell's book also included Morley's lecture, indicative of the transatlantic influence of both of these men.
[21] John Churton Collins, *The Study of English Literature: A Plea for its Recognition and Organization at the Universities* (1891), 133. Churton Collins was awarded an English chair at Birmingham in 1905: Goldman, *Dons and Workers*, 71.
[22] John Churton Collins, 'The New Scheme for the Indian Civil Service Examinations', *CR* (June 1891), 845. Collins, praising Morley's earlier works, later published *Voltaire, Montesquieu and Rousseau in England* (1908), which charted the various degrees of English influence on the three French thinkers.
[23] History was also considered to be especially appropriate, and both subjects were widely taught before 1880: Christina de Bellaigue, *Educating Women: Schooling and Identity in England and France, 1800–1867* (2007), 174–6.

the *Academy* in 1898 for her prescribed texts, and suggested instead that girls would prefer R. L. Stevenson's *Travels with a Donkey* to Milton's *Areopagitica* and Burke's speeches.[24] But Beale, a former student of F. D. Maurice at Queen's College, London, held a different conception of usefulness: as a deeply religious woman, she saw individual education and development as a duty to God which would, simultaneously, bring the student closer to him. An additional, more practical, concern was which authors and texts were set for examinations: girls and boys studied 'modern classics', Burke included. An 1883 Oxford Junior exam, for instance, asked students to name and describe chief works by Chaucer, Spenser, Milton, or Burke.[25] Similarly, Florence Low, a critic of exam-focused teaching, claimed much later in a 1906 number of the *Nineteenth Century*: 'The ordinary girl of eighteen leaves school with a knowledge of probably two or three Shakespeare plays, a Chaucer story, one book of the Faerie Queen, perhaps a volume of Burke, and some of Scott's poems.'[26] For Burke to be placed alongside, if not equal to, Chaucer and Shakespeare in a short canon of English literature is a remarkable moment in his reception history—indicating real elite canonical status. However, this kind of study was not possible until the publication of the first textbooks of Burke's works in the 1890s.

The production of school editions of Burke dates from Francis Guy Selby's (1852–1927) edition of *Reflections* (1890), last reissued in 1930.[27] After matriculating at Wadham College, Oxford in the 1870s, Selby went on to become a Professor of Logic and Moral Philosophy in India at Deccan College, Poona and a Fellow of the University of Bombay.[28] In 1895, he issued a textbook of Burke's collected American speeches, reprinted by Macmillan (London and New York) in 1912 and 1954, and *Thoughts on the Cause of the Present Discontents* in 1902.[29] Selby respected Morley's work on Burke, which was acknowledged in a preface,[30] but in contrast to Morley's historical and biographical approach Selby's

---

[24] Quoted in Flint, *The Woman Reader*, 68.
[25] F. W. Levander, *Questions on History and Geography set at the Matriculation Examinations of the Oxford and Cambridge Examination Papers in English History, 1881 to 1890* (1891). For the growing importance of examinations in girls' schools from the 1860s, see de Bellaigue, *Educating Women*, 182.
[26] Florence Low, 'The Reading of the Modern Girl', *NC* (1906), 285, cited in Flint, *The Woman Reader*, 160.
[27] Edmund Burke, *Reflections on the Revolution in France*, ed. F. G. Selby (1890).
[28] 'Selby, Francis Guy', *Who Was Who* (2014).
[29] Edmund Burke, *Thoughts on the Cause of the Present Discontents*, ed. F. G. Selby (1902). Selby also published school books with Macmillan targeted specifically at Indian students learning 'Western thought': see, for example, his Francis Bacon, *Bacon's Essays* (1889).
[30] Ibid., preface.

critique of Burke's thought in his introductory notes was coloured by his philosophical background. These notes were intended to direct teachers and pupils towards Burke's 'Philosophy of Politics' as found most explicitly in *Reflections*: 'never again, perhaps, will whatever is good in Conservatism be so thoughtfully or so attractively set forth'.[31] Again, the French Revolution proved decisive: 'It is a philosophic conservatism, more intensely conservative than it otherwise would have been, owing to his horror of the acts of the Assembly, and his fear that they might be imitated elsewhere.'[32] Indeed, Selby's interest in Burke was never historical, and when introducing the Macmillan edition of Burke's American speeches he instructed his (presumed male) student readers not to go to Burke for history, but for an approach to politics.[33] The *Spectator* was particularly impressed by Selby's ability to produce an unusually complete character of Burke in only 70 pages of introduction—tacitly agreeing with the views it contained.[34] To his many readers, Selby construed Burke's thought—his 'philosophy of politics'—as 'conservatism' which was stimulated by the events of 1789. Selby's editions were also set for English undergraduates at Manchester from 1908 by C. H. Herford (1853–1931), Professor of English Literature.[35]

C. E. Vaughan similarly produced abridged school editions of *Reflections* for students aged sixteen to eighteen in 1892, reprinted in 1893 and 1906. His textbook of Burke's American speeches was published the following year with reprints in 1898, 1904, 1907, and 1914.[36] The texts were produced for Perceval's Education Works and, by way of comparison, other abridged editions at the same level included More's *Utopia* and Macaulay's *History of England*. The *Spectator* again approved of Vaughan's school books, and stated that Burke was 'for obvious reasons an excellent subject for higher forms, as giving them a view of the political aspects of history'.[37] Though the American speeches received more reissues, for Vaughan *Reflections* was the critical text. He stressed the

---

[31] Burke, *Reflections*, ed. F. G. Selby, xiv.
[32] Ibid., xxxiv.
[33] Edmund Burke, *Burke's Speech on Conciliation with America*, ed. F. G. Selby (1895). This text was last reissued in the US by Greenwood Press, Westport, CT in 1974.
[34] 'School-books', *Spectator* (25 July 1891), 26–7.
[35] *Victoria University of Manchester Calendars* (1908–14).
[36] Edmund Burke, *Selections from Burke's Reflections on the French Revolution*, ed. C. E. Vaughan (1892); Edmund Burke, *Burke's Speeches on America*, ed. C. E. Vaughan (1893).
[37] 'Of English Classics Selected and Annotated for Purposes of Education' *Spectator* (23 Sept. 1893), 24.

importance of *Reflections* because, firstly, of Burke's eloquent and exquisite style—Vaughan would go on to be Professor of English Literature—and, secondly, because it was 'the work of a great political thinker on the most important political movement recorded in history'.[38] His pupils also noticed this insistence in his schoolteaching at Clifton.[39] Here again the French Revolution was positioned as the seminal moment in the shaping of nineteenth-century British thought and literature which gave Burke, and specifically *Reflections*, a foundational status. Vaughan's only schoolbooks are on Burke and he continued to teach and publish on the intellectual history and political philosophy of Burke, Rousseau, Romanticism, and the Revolution throughout his professorships (to be discussed below). That said, as his scholarship on Rousseau suggests, Vaughan was a Liberal Idealist and was no 'Burkean C/conservative' himself.

Following the first creation of a system of local education authority-funded secondary education in 1902, the above texts were reissued alongside newer texts attempting to capitalize on a mushrooming market. Macmillan's 1899 student edition of Burke's American speeches, by an American English teacher, went through ten reprints in a decade,[40] but it was *Reflections* which attracted the most instructive editorial comment on Burke's overall political thought. For instance, W. H. D. Rouse, a graduate of Christ's College, Cambridge and Headmaster of Rugby and the Perse Schools, released Burke's American speeches as part of Blackie's School Texts in 1906, providing only a very short biographical introduction with few notes.[41] Presumably in an age when the United States was becoming an increasingly large part of Britain's cultural horizons and family connections, what Burke had to say was in some sense self-evident. By contrast, the history of France and the Revolution was given much firmer direction. F. J. C. Hearnshaw (1869–1946), then Professor of History at University College, Southampton, released an edition of the first of Burke's *Letters on a Regicide Peace* in 1906, which stated that when Burke left Parliament in 1794 and his followers accepted office under Pitt, 'the new "Conservative" party had its origin'.[42]

---

[38] Burke, *Selections from Burke's Reflections*, ed. C. E. Vaughan, vii.
[39] Andrew Little, 'Memoir', in C. E. Vaughan, *Studies in the History of Political Philosophy Before and After Rousseau* (1925), i. xiv.
[40] Edmund Burke, *Burke's Speech on Conciliation with America*, ed. Sidney Carleton Newsom (1909).
[41] Edmund Burke, *Edmund Burke's Speeches on America*, ed. W. H. D. Rouse [Blackie's School Texts] (1906). See also Edmund Burke, *Burke's Speeches on America*, eds., A. J. F. Collins and F. J. C. Hearnshaw [University Tutorial Series] (1913).
[42] Edmund Burke, *On the Proposed Peace with the Regicide Directory of France: Letter I*, ed. F. J. C. Hearnshaw (1906), xviii. Hearnshaw later became Professor of Modern History at Durham (1910–12), and of Medieval History at King's College London (1913–34). He

Another edition of *Reflections* for the 'University Tutorial Series' was published in 1910 by Henry Packwood Adams, a Cambridge graduate, whose notes were lifted directly from Hearnshaw's edition of *Regicide Peace*, including the quote cited above.[43] Again, in 1910 the Revd. A. J. Grieve produced an edition of *Reflections* for Dent's series of 'English Texts for Schools'. Grieve was educated variously at Aberystwyth, Mansfield College, Oxford, and Berlin and was an experienced schoolteacher who went on to hold numerous academic posts in theology and ecclesiastical history in India and across Britain.[44] Unusually, therefore, his introduction placed Burke within a European intellectual movement and stressed the importance of Burke to anti-Hegelian historicist thinkers such as Savigny. Grieve's commentary was forceful: Burke held his 'commanding place in English thought' because he challenged the primacy of individual reason and argued, on the contrary, that 'society is an organic whole in which each mind is a particular growth, conditioned by the rest, and incapable of fully living if it detaches itself from the rest'. Grieve explained that this was why Burke placed such value on custom and tradition and attacked the assertion of individual abstract rights over society, a view which again reflects the growing association of Burke with organic thought.[45] In 1911, J. H. Boardman, a teacher and educational writer, published *Reflections* with an introduction, notes, and appendices for both students and a general readership in the 'Normal Tutorial Series'.[46] They all served the same function—that of an introduction—for a variety of different audiences.

School editions of *Reflections* became more prescriptive from 1910. This climaxed in the edition produced by Walter Alison Phillips (1864–1950), a diplomatic historian and the first Lecky Professor of Modern History at TCD, and his wife Catherine Beatrice Phillips, an accomplished linguist and translator of several historical works, for the

---

later published *Burke's Speeches on America*, eds. A. J. F. Collins and F. J. C. Hearnshaw (1913) for the University Tutorial Series, citing Graham and Morley's works.

[43] Edmund Burke, *Reflections on the Revolution in France*, ed. H. P. Adams [University Tutorial Series] (1910; 2nd edn 1927), xvii. He later produced *The French Revolution* (1914); *The Life and Writings of Giambattista Vico* (1935); and *Karl Marx in his Early Writings* (1940).
[44] 'Grieve, Revd. Alexander James', *Who Was Who* (2014).
[45] Edmund Burke, *Reflections on the Revolution in France, with a Letter to a Member of the National Assembly and Thoughts on French Affairs*, ed. A. J. Grieve [Dent's English Texts for Schools] (1910), x.
[46] Edmund Burke, *Reflections on the Revolution in France*, ed. J. H. Boardman [Normal Tutorial Series] (1911).

'Pitt Press Series' at Cambridge University Press in 1914.[47] In 1913, the same series had made a fairly unusual choice of printing a school book of the *Present Discontents* which included only uncontroversial historical notes by the relatively unknown W. Murison.[48] In contrast the Phillipses, and in particular Catherine Phillips who is credited with much of the writing, had a polemical mission: 'Fox was the champion of the new Liberalism, Burke of the principle which was to develop into Conservatism... some of Burke's views tended to take a Tory colour.'[49] The Phillipses established Burke's consistency of thought as follows: 'From the first Burke was alive to the perils of that hazy Liberalism which was ready to approve of democratic principles in theory without realizing what would be the result were they carried out to their full logical consequences.'[50] They finished by quoting G. P. Gooch's 1904 contribution to the *Cambridge Modern History*: '[*Reflections*] "is not only the greatest exposition of the philosophic basis of conservatism ever written, but a declaration of the principles of evolution, continuity, and solidarity which must hold their place in all sound political thinking."'[51] In this case both the text and the identity of the authors suggest quite clearly that the increasing confidence of exposition within school books of Burke's 'conservative' political thought is a reflection of his enhanced cultural and political status after 1910.

Taken overall, however, Burke's editors represented a variety of points of view—the Phillipses would have had little time for Vaughan's learned researches into Rousseau—and it cannot be assumed that the ways in which Burke (or any author) was taught and prescribed were taken on without question: these texts were read and taught by individuals with their own interests and preoccupations. Introductions and text were consumed and criticized in a multitude of ways, just as there were different levels of sophistication and intellectual engagement at work. Certainly, disagreement as to Burke's modern political label continued through the twentieth century and so the process was not one of simple indoctrination through late Victorian and Edwardian schooling. Canonized with Shakespeare and Milton, however, Burke evidently appealed to students and teachers. Moreover, published 'model' exam answers can go some way to

---

[47] T. G. Otte, 'Phillips, Walter Alison', *ODNB* (2004).
[48] Edmund Burke, *Thoughts on the Cause of the Present Discontents*, ed. W. Murison [Pitt Press Series] (1913).
[49] Edmund Burke, *Reflections on the Revolution in France*, eds. W. A. Phillips and C. B. Phillips [Pitt Press Series] (1913), xxvii.
[50] Ibid.
[51] Ibid., xlvii; G. P. Gooch, 'Europe and the French Revolution', *Cambridge Modern History* (1902–12), viii. 757.

ascertaining uncontroversial high-scoring student responses. Thus, one historical matriculation question at the University of London in 1904 (set by A. F. Pollard) was: 'Compare Burke's attitude towards the American and French Revolutions.' The model answer, written by Hearnshaw and J. W. Horrocks[52] began:

> Burke's political theories were essentially conservative, though he held that these should be applied in a spirit of moderate liberalism. He loved order, revered the past, believed in a limited monarchy, and had little sympathy with attempts to tamper with ancient institutions, but he favoured the removal, as far as possible, of defects of abuses which hindered their smooth working. In his attitude to both the American and French Revolutions he was guided by the same principles, and the fact that he appeared to be more liberal in one case than the other arose from the differences between the problems presented by the movements themselves. While Americans resisted the arbitrary exercise of authority, the French revolted against all authority whatsoever.[53]

Hearnshaw and Horrock's model answer was an explicit statement of Burke's 'conservative' 'political theory', and it is worth noting that Hearnshaw was himself a Conservative.[54] The model answer gave a direction to Burke's thinking, without degenerating into a party political affirmation.

Burke was taught because he had a contemporary relevance in addition to his historical status as a politician and eloquent writer. Many of the tutors teaching and writing textbooks and exams followed and engaged in contemporary debates, literatures, and uses of Burke in scholarship. By 1921, the Newbolt report by the Board of Education, *The Teaching of English in England*, recognized Burke as an established part of an informal but effective national curriculum, though it still assumed that his appeal was largely to boys rather than girls. The report also insisted on the intellectual rigour involved in mastering 'the political philosophy of Burke' and is suggestive of what school students had been taught to do with Burke's writings up to that point: to identify components of a political philosophy within a historical context. This philosophy was undoubtedly promoted as being, by the Edwardian period, a philosophy of conservatism.[55]

---

[52] Horrocks was perhaps a student of Hearnshaw's in 1904; he was subsequently appointed as a lecturer in History at Southampton in 1914. Both were thanked by James Tait in *British Borough Charters, 1216–1307* (1923).
[53] University Tutorial Series, *Matriculation Model Answers: Modern & English History, being the London University Matriculation Papers in English History from January 1896 to June 1902, and in Modern History of September 1902 to January 1904* (1904).
[54] F. J. C. Hearnshaw, *Conservatism in England: An Analytical, Historical, and Political Survey* (1933).
[55] *'The Teaching of English in England': Report of the Departmental Committee Appointed by the President of the Board of Education to Inquire into the Position of English in the Educational System of England* (1921), 180, 184, 203, 207.

AT UNIVERSITY

From the 1880s Burke became a much more prominent feature of History and English Literature degree courses across the country. Lord Acton and Edward Dowden were two notable figures who lectured on the French Revolution and, in turn, on Burke.[56] This is not to say that new topics superseded the study of English language, Shakespeare, or the predominant medieval and early modern English constitutional history.[57] History had, however, been founded as a separate degree in Oxford and Cambridge relatively recently (1872–3) and, as with any discipline, History papers were vulnerable to changing interests in progressive generations. It is possible to chart a growing curiosity in the eighteenth and nineteenth centuries, in which Revolutionary France and America became central turning points in British, European, and World history. Attention from English Literature as much as History focused on the French Revolution and its impact on British politics, literature, and thought. No doubt this was in part down to the labours of men such as Leslie Stephen, John Morley, and W. E. H. Lecky, who had written to critical acclaim on the value and importance of the eighteenth century to the nineteenth from the 1860s. The relative proximity of the eighteenth century to the modern day may also explain its appeal to the non-Oxbridge constituency attending the new civic universities and colleges across the country from the 1880s. Burke became increasingly prominent in the syllabuses of these universities and colleges, notably as set reading on British relations with America and France.

It would be wrong to suppose that Burke was completely absent from university courses before the Home Rule debates catapulted his name into political debates. On the contrary, it would seem as if the critical recovery carried out by Morley, the Stephens, Arnold, and Lecky was beginning to bear fruit by the 1880s. At Cambridge in 1884, for example, Burke featured in both the Moral Sciences[58] and Modern Languages tripos examination papers. The former included two Modern Ethical and

---

[56] For Dowden see pp. 63–4, 86, 167–9 in this volume.

[57] This earlier predominance can be very succinctly seen in the following volume which features no questions beyond the early eighteenth century: F. W. Levander, *Questions on History and Geography set at the Matriculation Examinations of the University of London, 1844–1886*, 2nd edn (1886).

[58] The Moral Sciences tripos was established in 1848 as an honours option, but could not confer a degree. Through the mid-Victorian period the tripos was criticized for its perceived breadth of unscholarly (i.e. non-classical or mathematical) content. Reforms in 1867 removed its historical and jurisprudence components and introduced political philosophy. By 1870–80, Moral Sciences was attracting first-class students including William

Political Philosophy papers totalling sixteen questions. These two papers asked three questions on Burke, including: 'Compare the views of Burke on the English Revolution [i.e. 1688], the French Revolution and (if you like) on the Revolt of the American Colonies.' The remaining questions asked students to state and criticize Burke's views on representation and prescription. In the English component of the Modern Languages tripos two special papers were examined: one on Chaucer, the other on Burke's *Present Discontents* and American speeches. The paper set five questions which asked for factual as well as analytical answers, for instance: 'Give the dates of Burke's birth and death, of his... *Present Discontents*, and of his Two Speeches on America. Name some other of his works. How would you describe his political opinions? Mention some of the merits for which his works are remarkable.' The other questions call for definitions of terms such as 'King's Men' and 'the Double Cabinet'; awareness of historical context such as the consequences of the repeal of the Stamp Act; and some appreciation of earlier political thought cited by Burke—Plato's *Republic*, More's *Utopia*, and Harrington's *Oceana*.[59] Both papers implicitly ask questions relating to the consistency of his thought and are suggestive of the theoretical emphasis attributed to Cambridge (*contra* Oxford) in this period.[60] However, English exams for women at Oxford for the same year ask almost identical questions about the thought contained in *Present Discontents*.[61] So students at Cambridge *and* Oxford in 1884 were studying Burke's thought in historical context because he was considered an important and eloquent writer and politician; but the great expansion of Burke in university education was, in 1884, still in its infancy.

The most notable lecture series dates from the mid-1890s. Lord Acton (1832–1902) became Regius Professor of Modern History at Cambridge in 1895 and lectured on the French Revolution until 1899. Acton had read and admired Burke from an early age, though, as we have seen, was not himself a 'Burkean'. Here it should be noted that while Acton was not entirely untypical of the literary world, his cosmopolitan, Catholic education meant that, despite his high reputation, he was less representative of English thought than his popularity may lead one to believe. Even Acton's crowded lectures on the Revolution were an example of his deviation from

---

Cunningham, F. W. Maitland, and J. N. Keynes. It was usually examined by Seeley and Henry Sidgwick: D. A. Winstanley, *Later Victorian Cambridge* (1947), 187–9.

[59] *Cambridge University Calendar for the Year 1884* (1884), 462, 464, 474.
[60] Peter Slee, *Learning and a Liberal Education: The Study of Modern History in the Universities of Oxford, Cambridge, and Manchester, 1800–1914* (1986), 126.
[61] *Oxford University Examinations for Women: Papers of the Examinations held in December 1883, and June 1884* (1884), 63.

tradition, as he refrained from overt political and educational asides.[62] Similarly, while it had become a relative commonplace in educated circles, following the work of Morley and Lecky, to view Burke as a consistent thinker, Acton still maintained that his writings on the French Revolution marked a clear break in Burke's thought just as he had done when writing to Lecky in 1882.[63] In his inaugural lecture in 1895, he declared the question of Burke's consistency one of the central questions of modern history.[64] Burke was promoted in these lectures as a political thinker who transformed from being 'as revolutionary as Washington' to 'the most strenuous and violent of conservatives'.[65] It is a sign of Acton's scholarly individualism that in 1895 he could describe Burke as 'the best of Liberals and the purest of revolutionary statesmen'.[66] Despite Acton's unorthodox interpretation of Burke's thought in relation to British and Irish scholarship, he remained influential both in Cambridge and wider literary society. His alignment of *Reflections* with 'conservative' thought was well-diffused: not only were his lectures on the French Revolution (and Burke) published—thus ensuring a wider audience—but the Revolution became a special subject in the Cambridge historical tripos alongside Acton's lectures. The lectures were therefore listened to, studied, revised, and examined.[67]

Beyond the ancient universities, the shift in subjects and periods taught at university level was inextricably connected to the new civic institutions. The increasing popularity of Burke's works blossomed through the establishment of historicist English Literature as a subject to be studied along strictly historical lines. This was true for Dowden at TCD, and in the newer, smaller institutions where History and English were often linked, and the study of literature was conducted with reference to contextual historical study. University (1826) and King's Colleges (1829), London had been early pioneers in creating English and History professorships, though degrees were not actually offered until much later (1896 for History).[68] Thus Henry Morley (1822–94), Professor of English Literature at University College London (UCL) between 1865 and 1889,

---

[62] Ben-Israel, *English Historians on the French Revolution*, 246.
[63] Lecky, *Memoir of the Rt. Hon. W. E. H. Lecky*, 162–3.
[64] Lord Acton, 'Inaugural Lecture on the Study of History' [1895], *Lectures on Modern History* (1906), 48. For a review acknowledging Acton's debt to Burke, see [Anon], 'Lord Acton's Lectures on Modern History', *ER*, (Apr. 1907), 273–98.
[65] Lord Acton, *Lectures on the French Revolution*, eds. J. N. Figgis and R. V. Laurence (1910), 27.
[66] Ibid., 204.   [67] Roland Hill, *Lord Acton* (2000), 383.
[68] A. F. Pollard states the unpopularity of the University of London history degree (sixteen passes 1896–1901) in *Factors in Modern History* [1907] (1932), 234–47. These figures rose to 186 (BA) and thirty-seven (MA) between 1904 and 1911 (p. 254). See also

lectured on topics such as 'The Effects of the French Revolution on English Literature'.[69] Similarly, A. J. Scott (1805–66) established a historicist approach to English Literature at King's before his appointment as the first principal of Owens College, Manchester in 1851.[70] English Literature was promoted as a suitable subject by F. D. Maurice and Charles Kingsley upon opening Queen's College, which Morley lectured at, in 1858, as Dowden did at the Alexandra College for women in Dublin in the 1860s.[71]

Oxbridge was particularly hostile to the literary study of English, with many tutors and graduates deeming the 'dilettante' literary subject unworthy of degree status.[72] F. W. H. Myers, a Cambridge classicist, asked in the *Pall Mall Gazette*: 'should anything so easy and so agreeable as the reading, say, of Burke and Macaulay, be classed as serious work at all?'[73] English was of course eventually founded as an independent degree in both Oxford (1894) and Cambridge (1917), and many of those who would later produce historically sensitive English Literature courses came from Oxford 'Greats' degrees, such as Oliver Elton and A. C. Bradley at Liverpool, and Churton Collins.[74] Yet the English course at Oxford, for instance, remained attractive primarily to female students, and this was further entrenched by a perceived lack of competent teaching staff in the older (male) colleges.[75] In contrast, the civic universities and colleges aimed to attract a non-Oxbridge constituency primarily without the classical training which was still required in the ancient universities. While at Oxbridge English, and even to an extent history, remained inferior to classics and mathematics, students at the civic universities, male and female, increasingly flocked to the popular subjects of English literature, history, and economics. Subjects and set texts were therefore not simply imposed, but responded to the demands and interests of students. Moreover, the civic universities needed to stay afloat, and it was also in their financial interest to attract as many paying students as

---

Alan Bacon, 'English Literature Becomes a University Subject: King's College, London as Pioneer', *VS*, 29 (1986), 591–612.

[69] H. S. Solly, *Life of Henry Morley* (1898), 293–4.
[70] Palmer, *Rise of English* Studies, 26.
[71] Ibid., 38; Jo McMurty, *English Language, English Literature: The Creation of an Academic Discipline* (1985), 100.
[72] D. J. Palmer, 'English', in M. G. Brock and M. C. Curthoys, eds., *The History of the University of Oxford: Volume VII, Part 2* (2000), 401–2.
[73] F. W. H. Myers, 'English at the Universities', *Pall Mall Gazette* (27 Nov. 1886), 1–2. Myers (1843–1901) was a poet, classicist, schools inspector, philologist, advocate of women's higher education, and a founder of the Society for Psychical Research.
[74] Palmer, *Rise of English Studies*, 64.   [75] Palmer, 'English', 405.

possible.⁷⁶ Mass education did, however, provoke concern about reading material, and there was a conscious desire to cultivate a taste for new canons of English literature which were being constructed.⁷⁷ That Burke's texts, usually *Reflections* and the American speeches, were included regularly is indicative of their canonical status in period-relevant literary and historical bibliographies, and also of the level of student engagement the texts generated.

Women and men were now attending lectures and matriculating at the numerous civic institutions across the country. Whereas in 1860 undergraduates in England numbered 3,300 of which 2,500 were at Oxbridge, by 1900 the total had ballooned to 17,000 of which 6,000 were at Oxbridge.⁷⁸ Burke was often a feature of courses at these institutions, whether in English Literature degrees at Leeds, History at Manchester, or evening classes in Political Philosophy at Liverpool. The Victoria University, which united three civic colleges—Manchester (1880), Liverpool (1884), and Leeds (1887)—while freeing them from a London-imposed curriculum, is of particular interest. The northern colleges were, of course, not unique in their study of Burke.⁷⁹ Nonetheless, the development of the Victoria University colleges into three independent institutions (from 1903) as, concurrently, Burke's reputation as a 'conservative' thinker became widely entrenched, provides a unique case study of curriculum development.

The Victoria University calendars for the three northern colleges—Manchester and Leeds in particular—provide voluminous evidence of the ways in which Burke was included in civic university-level studies. Examination questions in English literature and modern history frequently called for answers and essays involving Burke on the American and French Revolutions; the historical causes of the Romantic Movement in literature; views on late eighteenth-century Ireland; and expositions and

---

⁷⁶ D. R. Jones, *The Origins of Civic Universities: Manchester, Leeds, and Liverpool* (1988), 3, 135, 156. Whyte, *Redbrick*, however, presents a more nuanced view of this subject (p. 139).

⁷⁷ For an example of this at a broader cultural level, see John Kijinski, 'John Morley's "English Men of Letters" Series and the Politics of Reading', *VS*, 34 (1991), 205–25.

⁷⁸ A. J. Engel, *From Clergyman to Don: The Rise of the Academic Profession in 19th-Century Oxford* (1983), 92–6. It should however be stressed that these figures are somewhat loose, to say nothing of the differences in the intensity and demands of student life in different institutions and courses: compare Whyte, *Redbrick*, 146 for a slightly different figure for Oxbridge (7,000 out of the 17,000 total) in 1914.

⁷⁹ *Calendar of the University College of Wales, Aberystwyth* (1885). An 1887 study of the Oxford history syllabus shows that a number of Burke's texts were included in the 1714–1815 and 1760–1848 portions of the history of England: Paul Frédéricq, *The Study of History in England and Scotland* (1887), 39.

comparisons of specific texts by Burke.[80] These questions directly and indirectly expect student engagement with Burke's 'ideas' and texts in their answers. For Liverpool and Manchester, the 1886 English examinations featured the first explicit question on Burke's writings and, with the Gladstonian Liberal James Bryce as examiner, History questions on late eighteenth-century Ireland.[81] The Victoria University Colleges frequently shared examiners, who included Walter Raleigh, a pupil of Henry Morley who was appointed to the new chair of English Literature at Oxford in 1904, for English Literature (1889–1900), and J. M. Mackay for History (1884–1914). Burke was never a set author in Philosophy degrees in the Victoria Colleges yet, in 1896–7, MacCunn, Professor of Philosophy at University College, Liverpool and author of *The Political Philosophy of Burke* (1913), delivered a set of evening classes on 'Political Philosophy', the second of which was entitled 'Burke: the Conservative Whig'.[82] The course was, needless to say, a chronological history of political thought which began in the mid-eighteenth century, rather than of timeless abstract concepts. Liverpool gained its university charter in 1903 and the new Professor of English Literature, Oliver Elton, re-introduced Burke, generally *Reflections* or the American speeches, in reading lists and examinations after a short absence.[83] In Manchester, 1903 was also the first year a direct question on Burke appeared in an entrance examination for History under Mackay.[84] In sum, university calendars give us an idea of the context behind A. F. Pollard's 1904 call, as newly founded Professor of Constitutional History at UCL, for historians to look 'as much to the discoveries of Joseph Priestley as to the speeches of Edmund Burke', suggesting an oversupply of the latter.[85]

The increasingly extensive study of Burke can be traced in the University of Leeds following the granting of its charter in 1904.[86] Between the appointment of A. J. Grant, a popular extension lecturer, as Professor of Modern Literature and History in 1896, and the final year of Leeds' membership of the Victoria University in 1903, his student numbers had doubled to over 800.[87] The style and substance of his subsequent

---

[80] *University College, Liverpool Calendar* (1896), 55, 239.
[81] The English question asked: 'Connect together by a brief biographical sketch the principal speeches and political writings of Burke, and dwell upon the qualities which they have in common.' *Victoria University Calendar* (1886), cxxx.
[82] *University College, Liverpool Calendar* (1896), 213–14.
[83] Ibid. (1903), 297.   [84] *Victoria University of Manchester Calendar* (1904).
[85] Pollard, *Factors in Modern History*, 251.
[86] *University of Leeds Calendar* (1904–16).
[87] A. N. Shimmin, *The University of Leeds: The First Half Century* (1954), 1–23; A. J. Taylor, 'History at Leeds, 1877–1974: The Evolution of a Discipline', *Northern History*, 10 (1975), 141–64. Grant is also notable for publishing one of the first histories of modern historiography: A. J. Grant, *English Historians* (1906).

courses are therefore particularly interesting as representative of an attractive and accessible study of history, literature, and ideas in which Burke became an annual feature of different examinations. For example: the first (1904) independent English History exam called for a restatement of Burke's opinion on American independence; a 1905 scholarship question paper, examined by Grant and G. M. Young, listed five short titles as the basis of an open essay, one of which was from Burke (from *Reflections*): 'the age of chivalry is dead'. Burke was not, obviously, a part of the outlines of medieval or early modern constitutional history which were very much present, yet more modern special subjects were added to the Honours and MA programmes under Grant and Alice Margaret Cooke (one of the earliest female academic appointments and who had also taught at Manchester). From 1906, a course on 'Europe, 1789–1904' became a regular option and another, 'English History, 1760–1815', from 1910. Two 'History of Political Theory' papers were cultivated: the first studied the transition, as Maine had done, 'from ancient law to social contract', while the second covered the political thought of the French Revolution, including Rousseau, and was taught consistently up to and during the First World War. Further scholarship examinations asked questions about the influence of theorists on the French Revolution and, in particular, how the theories of Rousseau influenced the course of the Revolution. The established status of Burke's *Reflections* as an influential political and historical text in the question papers at Leeds (as elsewhere) would have generated an expectation of its inclusion. The special papers were also widely available as single courses to adult learners, pointing to an expanded and diversified 'student body'. The weight placed on the history of political theory at Leeds was formalized in 1907 as it became a component of the History syllabus, with J. N. Figgis, a student of Acton, becoming an Honorary Lecturer in the History of Political Theory from 1913.[88] Leeds, like many other universities, retained English constitutional history up to the present day while developing cosmopolitan, European, and theoretical 'special papers'. Burke was included in historical studies which largely centred round the turning point of 1789.

This European, historical, and philosophical interest is similarly perceptible in English Literature degrees at Leeds under Vaughan, Professor of English Literature from 1904, and Frederick Moorman (1879–1918), who held a German doctorate. Both tutors also took evening classes modelled on their undergraduate teaching of canonical writers—Shakespeare, Spenser, Burke—and periods, such as Elizabethan drama and Romanticism. Burke's

---

[88] 'Political Theory' also appeared in the Political Economy degree from 1910 with a paper on 'The Natures and Duties of the State and the Basis of Citizenship'.

writings on America and France became regular set texts in alternating English papers from 1907 through to the outbreak of the Great War. The texts selected were usually the American speeches on taxation and conciliation and *Reflections*, but occasionally one of the *Letters on a Regicide Peace* for Honours and MA students.[89] Vaughan's historicism can be seen in his creation of a postgraduate English course on relations between England and France in the eighteenth century. Indeed, during his time at Leeds Vaughan's interest in political philosophy and continental thought, particularly from France, was evident in his published works on histories of literature, such as *The Romantic Revolt* (1907), as well in his edition of Rousseau's collected writings.[90] Throughout his career Vaughan sought to reintegrate Rousseau within the history of political philosophy, and Burke was clearly a long-standing interest alongside French thought and the French Revolution.[91] Although English Literature did not have a paper in political theory, it nonetheless fostered the study of the history of political ideas and those associated with the French Revolution in particular.

The situation at independent Manchester from 1904 was remarkably similar under Tout and James Tait (1863–1944), Professor of Ancient and Medieval History. Modern history was extended to 1901, and constitutional history to Gladstone. The same was true of English Literature under C. H. Herford, a Cambridge classicist who had also studied in Berlin: alongside ancient, medieval, and early modern constitutional history papers and outlines of Shakespeare, Chaucer, and Milton, there were increasingly more modern, more cosmopolitan, and more theoretical 'special subjects'. A set text for the ordinary BA in English Literature was Morley's *Burke* (1879). The study of political thought, especially Rousseau, gained frequency across English and History—even Philosophy set an unprecedented 'Political Philosophy' paper in 1910. Frequent examinations, including those for scholarships, asked questions about Burke's

[89] *University of Leeds Calendar* (1907–16).
[90] C. E. Vaughan, *The Romantic Revolt* (1907); *The Political Writings of Rousseau* (1915). Richard Bourke argues that Vaughan's thesis in *Romantic Revolt*—which positioned Burke as a seminal figure in the progression from individualism and social contract theory towards a conception of political community—was a major influence on Alfred Cobban's influential *Edmund Burke and the Revolt against the Eighteenth Century* (1929), in which Burke became a hero of irrational Romanticism: 'Burke, Enlightenment and Romanticism', in Dwan and Insole, *Cambridge Companion to Edmund Burke* (2012), 28–9.
[91] Vaughan, *Studies in the History of Political Philosophy Before and After Rousseau*. The text features an extensive introduction in which Rousseau's thought was presented as a combination of the historical with the abstract method; it also criticizes Burke's abandonment of his own historical method in the *Reflections*, though it was still a passionate 'masterpiece of speculative genius' (p. 85). Cf. Vaughan, *Political Writings of Rousseau*, i. 113–14; Barker, *Political Thought from 1848–1914*, 217–21.

political thought in relation to English politics and Revolutionary France in History and English Literature papers.[92] Tout had in fact been teaching 1789–1832 as a 'special period' since his post at Lampeter.[93] His most suggestive examination paper on Burke was a three-part 'Modern History' examination from 1910 on the period 1714–1815. In question one, candidates were required to comment on five short quotes taken from primary sources, two of which were from *Present Discontents* (the others being quotes from Pitt's speeches and the 1713 Treaty of Utrecht). Students were then required to attempt at least one question from each of the sections A, B, and C (maximum six). Part A covered the earlier eighteenth century, but Parts B and C read as follows:

B.

5. Contrast and comment upon the ideas of Bolingbroke and Burke with regard to party government.
6. 'The true contest is between the electors of the Kingdom and the Crown; the Crown is acting by an instrumental House of Commons.' Is this a true interpretation of the political situation in 1770?
7. Account for Burke's apparent failure as a practical politician.
8. Show from his statements in 'Thoughts on the Causes of the Present Discontents' and 'Reflections on the Revolution in France' how far Burke sympathized with democracy.

C.

9. Compare the attitudes of Burke and the younger Pitt towards the French Revolution.
10. How far and for what reasons did the French Revolution excite sympathy in England?
11. Explain the reasons given by Pitt to the House of Commons for making war upon France in 1793.

---

[92] *Victoria University of Manchester Calendars* (1904–14).
[93] St David's College, Lampeter, *Calendar for the Year 1885* (1885). Hugh Walker took all English Literature classes: the special authors studied for 'outlines of English Literature' were Shakespeare, Chaucer, Milton, and Burke (examiner for history and English: C. H. Firth). Both taught philosophy classes in political economy (Tout) and Logic (Walker). Likewise, in 1890 Tout's 'English History II' paper (examiner: W. H. Hutton) from Stuarts to 1848 Revolutions asked candidates to explain Burke's thought on the American and French Revolutions. St David's College, Lampeter: *Calendar for the Year 1890*, lxv.

12. 'The younger Pitt was the creator of the modern Tory party.' Discuss this statement.[94]

High-scoring answers to question 5 would have established Burke as a modern political thinker on party government; 6 is a quote from *Present Discontents*; question 7 hinted at Burke's essentially philosophical and essayistic qualities in the context of the practical failure of the Rockingham and Foxite Whigs (not to mention his temper); question 8 called for an assessment of Burke's consistency as an anti-democratic political thinker; questions 9 through 11 would have established Burke as the loudest opponent of Revolutionary France and advocate of war; and question 12, in light of the previous seven questions, might appear to be demanding a rebuttal. What the paper shows is that, in trying to construe English history in this period, Burke became a central thread. He united the minutiae of high politics with the broad vistas supplied by political ideas. It was a vision that would be challenged by the systematic high-political and anti-intellectual approach laid down by Lewis Namier after 1929, just as, after the Great War and Bolshevik Revolution, France in 1789 was no longer the last word in modern European history.

AUTODIDACTICISM

Reading and learning, of course, continued beyond institutional education. This section, in focusing on further education, examines (in turn) the relevant content of the Indian Civil Service (ICS) curriculum, university extension lectures, and cheap editions of Burke's texts.

Examinations for the Indian Civil Service were prepared for and undertaken both inside and outside of universities. The first exam sat was the competitive examination, designed by Macaulay in the 1850s, which covered a broad range of topics, including jurisprudence, languages, history, and literature. Those selected spent a further academic year studying for the final examination, which generally featured more specific questions on Indian history, geography, languages, and law.[95] After reforms in 1891–2 the maximum age at application was raised from

---

[94] *Victoria University of Manchester Calendar* (1910), ccxlvi–ccxlvii. The 1910 London exam also increased the number of questions on Burke: University of London, *School Examinations: Matriculation Standard and Higher Standard* (1907–17), 12.

[95] For more detailed studies of the ICS, see Bradford Spangenberg, 'The Problem of Recruitment for the Indian Civil Service during the Late-Nineteenth Century', *Journal of Asian Studies*, 30 (1971), 341–60; C. J. Dewey, 'The Education of a Ruling Caste: The Indian Civil Service in the Era of Competitive Examination', *EHR*, 88 (1973), 262–85; C. J. Dewey, *Anglo-Indian Attitudes: The Mind of the Civil Service* (1993); Takehiko

nineteen to twenty-three, and many more Oxbridge university graduates—the long-desired 'gentleman-scholars'—began to apply. The ICS examiners were usually drawn from British universities and thus the exams again reflected prevailing intellectual trends and contemporary concerns. Burke featured in both sets of papers: the competitive exam for the general reasons given above (useful, eloquent, influential) and the final exam because of his involvement in the controversy over Fox's India Bill in 1783, and his attempted impeachment of Warren Hastings as Governor-General (1788–95). Questions on the character and actions of Hastings were not entirely absent from school or university courses either, but they are unsurprisingly more prominent in the ICS examinations—particularly in the annual final examinations, as can be seen in the published scripts from 1896 to 1916.[96] Examples include: 'Comment on the statement: "If Burke did not convict the man, he overthrew the system"' [1901] and 'Describe the course of the impeachment of Warren Hastings and the attitude towards him of prominent statesmen of the day. Specify the chief counts of the indictment. On how many of them was a verdict actually given?' [1912]. Other topics included James Mill's *History of British India*, Macaulay on Indian education, and Lords Clive and Cornwallis.

These examinations are, of course, central to comprehending how Burke was studied by hopeful graduate civil servants. Yet, the specific discussion of Burke's attitude towards India in the final examinations was inevitably a more particular one: compared to questions on America and France, Indian questions were less obviously related to historic and current British political and constitutional thought and were, as such, less controversial. As previous chapters have illustrated, Burke's compassion for the oppressed in British India was well established and widely praised. But on the more particular question—like that of 1912 above—on whether the actions of Hastings were justifiable, Burke was open to criticism. Fitzjames Stephen's *Nuncomar and Impey* (1885), which drew on extensive legal studies as well as his own Indian experience in order to defend the actions of Hastings against both Burke and Macaulay, had obtained widespread scholarly pre-eminence and was accepted by most commentators between 1885 and 1945.[97]

Honda, 'Indian Civil Servants, 1892–1937: An Age of Transition', DPhil thesis, University of Oxford, 1996.

[96] Civil Service Commission, *Final Examination of Candidates Selected in [1896–1916] for the Civil Service of India, September [1898–1917]* (1897–1917). For later published competitive examinations, see Civil Service Commission, *Competitive Examination for the Indian Civil Service, held in India* (1922–7).

[97] Edwards, 'Macaulay's Warren Hastings', in Carnall and Nicholson, *Impeachment of Warren Hastings*, 129–35; Young, *Victorian Eighteenth Century*, 6–7. For contemporary

Beyond the walls of the universities, public lectures, including extension lectures, increasingly brought higher education to the general public. From 1885, university extension courses began to take off: the *University Extension Journal* claimed in 1891 that the figures had more than doubled in three years, from sixty-five courses with 5,662 entries in 1887, to 130 courses with 12,923 entries in 1890.[98] Two reports by the Oxford *Committee of Delegates for Local Examinations* claimed that about a quarter of attendees in the 1880s and 1890s were drawn from the working classes: it is estimated that over three thousand, out of a total of thirteen thousand students in 1887–8, were artisans, and in 1892–3 over five thousand 'workmen' attended lectures out of over twenty thousand students.[99] Moreover, the Oxford and Cambridge extension lectures of Oxford and Cambridge were not the only available options: the popularity of self-education was reflected in the published 'successes' of non-institutional students who undertook correspondence-only courses. For instance, the University of London's Correspondence College between 1887 and 1893 recorded 2,637 'pass' students and, by 1901, its northern equivalent boasted of 15,000 successful pass students.[100] In content, the oral university extension lectures, though frequently criticized for failing to attract adequate numbers of working-class attendees, were similar in their subject matter to the courses in the new civic universities.[101] Popular courses included botany, Shakespeare, and eighteenth- and nineteenth-century English literature and history. One of the most popular topics was, again, the French Revolution.

The most popular recorded extension course in December 1890 was thus that of S. R. Gardiner—an early modern historian—on the French Revolution, with over 200 students at Whitechapel. Alongside this were two further lectures on the Revolution period by Churton Collins: one on Byron and Wordsworth and another more obviously literary course entitled 'The Age of Burke', consisting of historical outlines of late eighteenth-century writers such as Burke, Johnson, and Goldsmith. It was attended, according to the *University Extension Journal*, almost

---

examples, see Lecky, 'The Empire: its Value and Growth' [1893] in *Historical and Political Essays*, 49–50; Goldwin Smith, *The United Kingdom: a Political History* (1899), ii. 417.

[98] 'Annual Meeting of the London Society', *University Extension Journal* (1 Mar. 1891), 34.
[99] Goldman, *Dons and Workers*, 80.
[100] University Tutorial Series/University Correspondence College, *Model Answers: English History and Geography, being the London University Matriculation Papers in English History and Geography from June 1888 to Jan 1894* (1894); *Northern Matriculation Guide: The Universities of Manchester, Liverpool, Leeds, Sheffield* (1901).
[101] Bernard Jennings, *Albert Mansbridge: The Life and Work of the Founder of the WEA* (2002), 22.

exclusively by women—another indication that Burke's appeal stretched beyond future statesmen.[102] The following February, one course on the Revolution was attended by 200 in the afternoon and 130 in the evening, with eighty-six essays submitted and 108 registering as students. Similarly, we find in 1891, Collins' 'Age of Burke' was being delivered at Potter's Bar; W. A. S. Hewins (1865–1931), the imperialist who became the first Director of the London School of Economics in 1895 and, later, a Conservative MP, led a course on 'Pitt, Fox, Burke' at Bacup; and various other lecturers taught the French Revolution in Nottingham, Pendleton, Plymouth, Exeter, Exmouth, Warminster, Hitchin, Beckenham, and Caterham.[103] The Fabian 'new' Liberal Graham Wallas gave Oxford extension lectures on the growth of English institutions (1891–5) and set Burke's *Present Discontents* as reading; even though the lecture itself discussed Burke and Paine.[104] This kind of activity was a bipartisan interest: Liberals and Unionists alike delivered popular courses on the Revolution and the Revolutionary 'influence' on British politics and literature.

One lecturer, the Revd. J. E. Symes (1847–1921), published a history of the French Revolution for the University Extension Series in 1892 (2nd edn 1904). As Principal (1890–1912) and Professor of English Literature (1881–96) at University College, Nottingham, he complemented the popular extension lectures with an easily comprehensible textbook, which provides us with a way into Symes' own teaching as well as what he saw as the core of many of the extension lectures listed above. Thus, Burke's *Reflections* and Morley's *Voltaire* and *Rousseau* were set as further reading, though the book itself is written at a substantially lower analytical level. As in the school editions, this had implications for Symes' explanations of political theories. Burke was presented in very basic language as someone who had 'studied history and knew how powerful traditions and customs were'. Likewise, when explaining the response of Burke to the Revolution—and thus the categorization of his thought, Symes stated: 'in the main the Whigs were just as conservative as Tories'.[105] In a text evidently striving for simplicity, Burke the Whig was quite easily transformed into a 'conservative' political thinker by Symes, a Home-Ruler, former Cambridge Apostle, and liberal churchman.[106] The commentaries

---

[102] 'Lent Term Lectures', *University Extension Journal* (1 Dec. 1890), 133, 137.
[103] 'Lent Term Lectures', *University Extension Journal* (15 Feb. 1891), 20–7.
[104] Graham Wallas, 'Syllabus of a Course of Lectures on the Growth of English Institutions in Town and Country: or, the English Citizen, Past and Present' (1894), 11.
[105] J. E. Symes, *The French Revolution* (1892), 44, 88.
[106] Lubenow, *The Cambridge Apostles, 1820–1914*, 308; A. W. Coats, 'John Elliotson Symes, Henry George, and Academic Freedom in Nottingham During the 1880s', *British and American Essays* (1993), ii. 291–306.

by Liberals and Unionists presented essentially the same Burke: a 'conservative' Whig, a Unionist. Meanwhile the popular interest in the Revolution inevitably led to more people reading Burke independently, and specifically Burke's *Reflections*.

It is significant therefore that there was a corresponding outpouring of popular availability of Burke's speeches, letters, and writings, as 'elite' discussion ran in parallel with the publication of numerous cheap editions from 1886.[107] There was both a perceived autodidact market among the lower-middle and working classes and a top-down interest in the promotion of literary and historical canons. Burke was included in a range of publishers' edited series—to name a few: Henry Morley's Universal Library, Methuen's Standard Library, Bell's English Classics, John Long's Carlton Classics, and Nelson's 6*d*. Classics. On top of the mainstream editions, which ranged in price from 1*d*. to 6*d*., were several independent contributions by little known authors. Many of the cheap editions printed in full an ample selection of Burke's work: *On the Sublime and Beautiful*;[108] *Present Discontents*;[109] the speeches on America;[110] *Reflections*;[111] and the *Letters on a Regicide Peace*.[112] Additional volumes were released which were made up of thematic or chronological abridgements and covered a broader range of topics in one volume, including India, Britain, America, and France.[113] The most simple and accessible

---

[107] Earlier editions were fewer in number, though there was a populist Irish imitator of Arnold's *Irish Affairs*: Edmund Burke, *Thoughts on the Cause of the Present Discontents*, ed. Vincent Scully (1882); Edmund Burke, *Edmund Burke: On Conciliation with America, and Two Letters to Gentlemen of Bristol on Trade with Ireland*, ed. Vincent Scully (1882).

[108] Edmund Burke, *On the Sublime and Beautiful*, ed. Henry Morley [Cassell's National Library] (1887).

[109] Edmund Burke, *Thoughts on the Cause of the Present Discontents and Observations on a Late State of the Nation* [Routledge New Universal Library] (1906).

[110] Edmund Burke, *Two Speeches on Conciliation with America and Two Letters on Irish Questions*, ed. Henry Morley (1886); Edmund Burke, *Speeches on America by Edmund Burke*, ed. C. B. Hawkins [Dent's Temple Classics] (1906); Edmund Burke, *Burke's Speeches and Letters on American Affairs*, ed. Hugh Law [Everyman Oratory Series] (1908); repr. 1911, 1915; Edmund Burke, *Burke's Speech on Conciliation with America*, ed. John Morrison [Bell's English Classics] (1912); Edmund Burke, *Burke's Speeches on America*, ed. F. A. Cavanagh [Bell's Annotated Classics] (1915).

[111] Edmund Burke, *Reflections on the Revolution in France*, ed. George Sampson [Scott Library] (1900; 2nd edn 1905); Edmund Burke, *Selected Works of Edmund Burke, vol. I: Reflections on the French Revolution*, ed. Sidney Lee [Methuen's 6*d*. Standard Library] (1905); Edmund Burke, *Reflections on the Revolution in France, with a Letter to a Member of the National Assembly*, ed. A. J. Grieve [Everyman] (1910); Edmund Burke, *Reflections on the Revolution in France*, ed. H. P. Adams [University Tutorial Series] (1910).

[112] Edmund Burke, *Burke's Regicide Peace*, ed. H. G. Keene [Bell's English Classics] (1893).

[113] Edmund Burke, *Forgotten Truths, Selections from the Speeches and Writings of the Rt. Hon. Edmund Burke*, ed. T. Dundas Pillans (1898); *Selections from Edmund Burke*, ed. Bliss

books contained snippets and aphorisms, some just a few lines long, never stretching to more than a page or two. Such distillations of Burke's wisdom were devoid of any refined context and were structured quite randomly around subtitles such as 'rational liberty', 'the lessons of history', and 'possessions';[114] one (from 1886) had the explicit purpose of furnishing a set of abstract non-partisan principles from Burke.[115] Many other authors were given similar treatment, although it was the latter category of 'chewed-up' pre-digested aphoristic literature which received the most scathing criticism, including from Dowden.[116]

The production of cheaper texts was significant for autodidact readers from the lower-middle and working classes, particularly for those who could not afford the five or six shillings to attend extension lectures. As the work of Altick, Sheila Rowbotham, and Jonathan Rose has demonstrated, it is important to take the idea of the earnest working-class autodidact reader seriously, even if precise measurement of its significance is difficult.[117] For the lower middle classes, Altick proposes that, whereas in 1850–1 83,300 families could be placed in the £150–£400 annual income bracket, in 1879–80 there were 285,100 such families. At the same time, average income in lower-middle-class families rose from £90 in 1851 to £110 in 1881. Yet the sharply falling prices of the period 1874–96 affected everyone, and an average family's real income rose by seventy to eighty per cent in fifty years. Greater disposable income—even just a few pennies a week—provided publishing houses with the impetus to source cheaper materials and printing mechanisms: the implementation of which lead to the commission of cheap 'classics' series, peaking in 1906 with Dent's 'Everyman' series. The Chandos Classics series alone reported sales of 3.5 million between 1868 and 1884.[118] Henry Morley produced extensive series of Universal Classics and Cassell's editions from 1885

Perry (1908); Edmund Burke, *Edmund Burke: Selections from his Political Writings and Speeches*, ed. J[ohn]. B[uchan]. [Nelson's 6*d*. Classics] (1911).

[114] Edmund Burke, *Selections from the Speeches and Writings of Edmund Burke*, ed. Hannaford Bennett [Carlton Classics] (1907); Edmund Burke, *Maxims and Reflections of Edmund Burke*, ed. F. W. Rafferty [Series for Busy Readers] (1909).

[115] Edmund Burke, *The Wisdom of Burke: Extracts from his Speeches and Writings*, ed. E. A. Pankhurst (1886), v–vi.

[116] Edward Dowden, 'Hopes and Fears for Literature', *FR* (Feb. 1889), 166–83; J. Edwards, 'The Literature of Snippets', *SR* (15, 22, 29 Apr. 1899), 455–56, 497, 529.

[117] Jonathan Rose, *The Intellectual Life of the British Working Classes* (2001); Sheila Rowbotham, 'Travellers in a Strange Country: Responses of Working Class Students to the University Extension Movement, 1873–1910', *History Workshop Journal*, 12 (1981), 62–95. Recent scholarship is increasingly addressing this issue: see, for example, Aruna Krishnamurthy, ed., *The Working-Class Intellectual in Eighteenth- and Nineteenth-Century Britain* (2009).

[118] Altick, *English Common Reader*, 306.

which were distributed weekly over the next five years to subscribers (between 50,000 and 100,000), with the aim of providing 'good' books at affordable prices.[119] These books were no doubt shared with friends and family too.[120] However, it is much more difficult, as Rose has argued, to establish how these books—and indeed any books—were read and received.[121] As with school books, these texts were intended to provoke critical analysis and higher thought in their readers as much as to admire elegant prose or fiction styles; hence their intrinsic value over shilling shockers or penny dreadfuls. We cannot assume that audiences read Burke, or other canonical authors, and their editors with unadulterated sympathy and reverence. Nor was the reader guaranteed to enjoy reading the 'classic' author in question, or be interested enough to pursue further reading or discussion.

With reader agency in mind, as with textbooks the analysis of editors' introductions to cheap editions is our best guide. For texts which may have been the first work by an author the reader had encountered, introductions were no doubt crucial in conveying succinct and relevant information. Thus, while many editors did simply provide biographical and/or historical context,[122] others were more suggestive, primarily through potted interpretations of Burke's political thought. For example, Henry George Keene, an ex-Indian Civil Servant, prefaced his 1893 edition of the first two letters of *Regicide Peace* by criticizing Morley for placing Burke's 1791 *Appeal* as the last of his sane utterances, and claimed Burke for 'conservative reform'.[123] In 1898, T. Dundas Pillans attempted to claim Burke for anti-socialist Liberals like himself, and was commended by the *Academy* for popularizing Burke's 'fine apophthegms'.[124] Like Keene, George Sampson's 1900 edition of *Reflections* (2nd edn 1905) argued that *Regicide Peace* was wrongly belittled because 'the political thought is reactionary'.[125] By 1910, Burke had captured the attention of the Unionist and future Governor-General of Canada, John Buchan (1875–1940), who declared that although Burke was 'in no sense a

---

[119] Solly, *Life of Henry Morley*, 356–7.
[120] Flora Thompson memorably remarked: 'Modern writers who speak of the booklessness of the poor at that time must mean books as possessions; there were always books to borrow.' 'On Her Majesty's Service', *Candleford Green* (1943).
[121] Jonathan Rose, 'Re-reading the English Common Reader: a Preface to the History of Audiences', *JHI*, 53 (1992), 47–70.
[122] For examples, see Burke, *Speeches on America*, ed. Hawkins; *Burke's Speech on Conciliation with America*, ed. Morrison; *Speech on Conciliation with America*, ed. Selby; Edmund Burke, *Burke's Speeches on America*, ed. A. J. F. Collins and F. J. C. Hearnshaw (1913).
[123] *Burke's Regicide Peace*, ed. Keene, xii.
[124] 'Forgotten Truths', *Academy* (23 July 1898), 80.
[125] Burke, *Reflections on the Revolution*, ed. Sampson, xxii.

Tory', nonetheless 'he founded Conservatism by his insistence upon the historical method of treating state policy, and by his distinction between reform and innovation'.[126] Likewise, in 1912, John Morrison (who by comparison with Buchan is completely unknown) stated that Burke, though a Whig in name, 'was from the very outset thoroughly Conservative at heart. He had a profound reluctance to interfere with what appeared to be the natural growth of communities and institutions... Burke, the great political philosopher is also the great apostle of common-sense in politics.'[127] Again, Burke was consistently presented as a C/conservative in a pithy and accessible way. Though historical and biographical introductions were relatively neutral, the editions prefaced by consistent and assertive expositions surely offer some guidance for assessment of the readily available analyses of Burke's thought to a majority of readers who did not have the money, time, and/or inclination to read the complete works of Burke.

CONCLUSION

Taken together, the school textbooks, cheap editions, and university syllabuses of the late Victorian and Edwardian period were a vital part of the process which constructed Burke as the founder of conservatism and, crucially, disseminated it. But while it is essential to allow for reader agency, the similarities between the various forms of analysis in this period are striking nonetheless. While nearly all of the texts provided biographical and historical introductions, many also included explicit critical discussion of Burke's 'C/conservative' political thought. It was a two-way process: education was reflective of contemporary preoccupations as much as it furthered and circulated them. Transformations in education, publishing, leisure time, and disposable income meant that children and adults were able to learn about the literary and historical status of Burke's writing and thought. Though Burke was not an Idealist, educators—and specifically Idealist educators—were drawn to the teaching of Burke for his organic but 'philosophical' thought, and to the history of great ideas more generally. Within universities, History and historically-based English Literature departments were of significant importance in disseminating Burke's thought and, though he would never become part of a pure Philosophy syllabus, significant tutors, from Seeley to Dowden to Tout and Vaughan, looked to him as a philosopher of politics. The breadth of English Literature as a discipline at this time, in conception and execution, was

---

[126] *Edmund Burke: Selections from his Political Writings*, ed. Buchan, iii.
[127] *Burke's Speech on Conciliation with America*, ed. Morrison, xv.

extensive and placed immense importance on prose non-fiction alongside poetry, prose fiction, and drama.

Ultimately, it was the French Revolution (and therefore *Reflections*) which formed the basis of many of the 'modern' subjects in history and literature. The Revolution captured the imagination of popular audiences as readers and lecture attendees; of new higher education students, male and female; and of many of the tutors themselves. The Revolution provided a way of approaching British history from a different angle: how had it influenced British political and intellectual history? How had events in France affected the course of English literature? This was Revolutionary study for the British, by the British—but that does not detract from its conceptual importance. The French Revolution became the turning point of modern history, literature, and political thought. The consequences of this for Burke were significant. *Present Discontents* and the American and Indian works *were* read and studied. He was placed in canons of English literature alongside Shakespeare and Chaucer, and also alongside medieval and early modern constitutional history. In contemporary history and literature, *Reflections* was promoted as an extremely eloquent and influential British response to the Revolution. Moreover, it provided the key to understanding Burke's political philosophy of 'conservatism'. Crystallized by events in France, his pre-existing anti-democratic, religious, and traditional Whig principles were sharpened into a political philosophy of 'conservatism' which transcended historical constitutional party divisions. As we have seen, from 1886 this exposition was utilized more and more in scholarly studies and, in the Edwardian period, by political Conservatives and Unionists. But it was also circulated, studied, digested, and—in many instances—simplified, through a complicated and extensive educational network.

8
Epilogue

Between 1830 and 1914 a dramatic transformation in Burke's reputation occurred. He became established, in Britain, as one of the principal founders of conservatism. His newly outlined political philosophy provided nourishment for political Conservatism and Unionism at a time when it was desperately seeking new ideas, inspiration, and intellectual cohesion. It is also evident that, by 1914, all of the criteria of the framework listed at the beginning of this book had been achieved. By the early 1880s, it is possible to identify broad cross-party agreement that Burke *was* an important political thinker with a distinctive, consistent, body of political thought. His vaguely defined 'political thought' was then increasingly worked into a systematic theory of 'conservatism' from the 1890s. The Home Rule debates made Burke's writings directly relevant to contemporary political problems. The efforts of the Liberal Unionists during the ensuing battle over his legacy ensured that he was first assimilated into Liberal Unionism, and by default became a close ally of the Conservative Unionists. By the Edwardian period, and particularly following the constitutional crisis which followed the introduction of Lloyd George's 'People's Budget' in 1909, Burke's work, name, and legacy were adopted enthusiastically by a considerable number of political Conservative Unionists who identified themselves as Burke's intellectual heirs in works that were read and reviewed around the world—including North America. Indeed, texts such as those by Dowden and Butler were first delivered as lecture series at Princeton and Pennsylvania, respectively. 'Mr Burke' the adventuring 'dinner-bell' was no more.

Burke had, furthermore, become a literary classic, raised up high with the elite of English literature—Shakespeare, Chaucer, Milton—in a canon which at this time placed a great deal more emphasis on non-fiction than today. As a result, selections from his political writings were available for as little as a penny at a time when literacy, leisure time, and disposable income were on the increase. This meant that his political thought was readily accessible for autodidacts of all classes, promoted as much for its stylistic merits as its theory of politics and statesmanship. Considering that today's commonplace understanding of Burke is very much that of a C/conservative thinker—and our task has been to understand how this happened—it is extremely significant that a plain-English version of 'Burkean C/conservatism' became the established method of introducing learners to Burke by the Edwardian period. It is worth stressing here, therefore, the interdependence of these contexts—political, literary, educational, intellectual—since all played their part in shaping and consolidating the interpretation of Burke as C/conservative which still holds sway to this day.

Though this is the end of our story, this was the beginning of a new period in Burke's reception history. This book has shown how a distilled political theory was gradually extracted from his corpus and de-contextualized accordingly. It was a trend which continued into the twentieth century—not just in Britain, but also in America. To G. M. Young, therefore, in his *Victorian Essays* of 1962, 'the true English tradition' which 'the radicals had done their best to sever' was 'the tradition of Burke'.[1] This is not to say that writers ignored or obscured Burke's Irish or Whig identities, but that these details became less central in explaining and interpreting his thought: Burke was instead recruited in bestsellers like Russell Kirk's *The Conservative Mind* (1953) as a champion of 'moral intuition' over positivistic and consequentialist standards of right.[2] The magnitude of this trend towards de-contextualization became evident when, at last, the purely empirical study of eighteenth-century politics began to reverse this trend. Frank O'Gorman's analytical narrative history of the Rockingham Whigs, for example, warned against exaggerating Burke's role within the Newcastle-Rockingham party as compared to that of Rockingham himself.[3] At the same time, the psychological slant of Isaac Kramnick's *The Rage of Edmund Burke* (1977)—which opens with the memorable line, 'Edmund Burke was an angry man'—used quite different methods to argue for the importance of personality and experience in driving past thought and action by focusing on Burke's correspondence.[4] This was then reinforced as the notion of the 'separate kingdoms' or 'four nations' of the British Isles has become a focus of attention since the 1970s. As the continued unity of Britain has been questioned in the political sphere, historians have also increasingly stressed the unique historical experiences of England, Wales, Scotland, and Ireland;

---

[1] G. M. Young, 'The Greatest Victorian', *Victorian Essays* (1962), 128.
[2] Maciag, *Burke in America*, 192.
[3] Frank O'Gorman, *The Rise of Party in England: The Rockingham Whigs 1760–1782* (1975).
[4] Kramnick, *The Rage of Edmund Burke*.

emphasizing the need for British history to be pluralistic, and less Anglocentric—that is, not equating British and (at least in Burke's case as an English MP) Irish history and identity with the history of England and Englishness.[5] From Conor Cruise O'Brien and Luke Gibbons, to Ian McBride in the recent *Cambridge Companion to Burke*, historians and critics have consequently sought to put the Irishness back into Burke studies.[6] As Michel Fuchs argues, Ireland was not just a *factor* to consider when investigating Burke's thought, but an 'all-pervading existential structure'.[7] Together, this literature is indicative of a broader historiographical shift towards the local and the biographical in analyses of Burke.[8]

There has, in addition, been a corresponding historical interrogation of Burke's purported 'conservatism' by historians of political thought. J. G. A. Pocock offered preliminary observations on the variety of sources from which Burke's thought was drawn, and which made him difficult to fit into a single political tradition.[9] More recently, Richard Bourke has reintegrated Burke's thought with its historical contexts—political, imperial, and intellectual—in order to gain a more sophisticated understanding of his political thought far beyond that of 'Burkean conservatism'.[10] David Bromwich has similarly argued, in *The Intellectual Life of Edmund Burke*, that 'no serious historian would repeat the commonplace that Burke was the father of modern conservatism'.[11] Indeed, the detailed scholarship of Bourke and Bromwich absolutely demonstrates the inadequacy of such a label as 'conservative' as an explanation and as a tool for situating Burke's thought both intellectually and historically; though what impact these weighty tomes will have on the way he is presented to larger general audiences is yet to be seen.

---

[5] For example, Raphael Samuel's 'Four Nations History', in *Island Stories: Unravelling Britain*, ed. Alison Light (1998).
[6] Conor Cruise O'Brien, *The Great Melody: A Thematic Biography of Edmund Burke* (1992); Luke Gibbons, *Edmund Burke and Ireland: Aesthetics, Politics and the Colonial Sublime* (2003); Ian McBride, 'Burke and Ireland', in Dwan and Insole, *Cambridge Companion to Edmund Burke* (2012), 181–94.
[7] Fuchs, *Edmund Burke, Ireland and the Fashioning of the Self*, 312.
[8] F. P. Lock, *Edmund Burke* (2008–9); Lambert, *Edmund Burke of Beaconsfield*.
[9] J. G. A. Pocock, 'Burke and the Ancient Constitution: a Problem in the History of Ideas', in *Politics, Language, and Time: Essays on Political Thought and History* (1971); 'The Political Economy of Burke's Analysis of the French Revolution', in *Virtue, Commerce, and History: Essays on Political Thought and History, Chiefly in the Eighteenth Century* (1985).
[10] Richard Bourke, 'Edmund Burke and the Politics of Conquest', *Modern Intellectual History*, 4 (2007), 403–32; 'Party, Parliament and Conquest in Newly Ascribed Burke Manuscripts', *HJ*, 55 (2012), 619–52; *Empire and Revolution: The Political Life of Edmund Burke* (2015); 'War Edmund Burke ein Konservativer? Notizen zum Begriff des Konservatismus', *Leviathan*, 44 (2016), 65–96.
[11] David Bromwich, *The Intellectual Life of Edmund Burke: From the Sublime and Beautiful to American Independence* (2014), 19.

Burke also continued to have what might be called an 'anti-history'. In the mid-twentieth century, his position as a serious thinker was damaged by Namierite historians whose criticism of Burke as a 'political charlatan' is reminiscent of his earliest Radical detractors.[12] Nevertheless, he retained his status as a proto-Romantic anti-revolutionary figure who upheld the virtues of religious faith and reverence of the historical past, and who therefore inspired the 'revolt against the eighteenth century'.[13] And while the bulk of attention has come from the Conservative end of the political spectrum, he has not been completely abandoned by the Left, though they tend to prefer his Irish, Indian, and American writings. This should not be surprising: Burke's appeal as a classic, canonical political writer is of course very wide, and commentators such as David Marquand and the Marxists Terry Eagleton and C. B. Macpherson have sporadically claimed inspiration.[14] His fervent criticism of Warren Hastings and British treatment of Indian subjects has also boosted his standing among postcolonial theorists,[15] though the extent to which Burke's criticism of the British in India was intended to preserve rather than destroy the empire is a question worth considering. Finally, the early to mid-twentieth century witnessed the refinement and consolidation of another influential strand of C/conservatism: that of One Nation Conservatism, primarily based upon a romanticized Disraelian legend.[16] A 'One Nation' approach promoting limited social reform and cross-class harmony was not necessarily opposed to a 'Burkean' one (especially an 'organic, reformist' version), nor did it dislocate him from his 'foundational' position. But it is suggestive of which Conservative 'heroes' are deemed appropriate for different contexts, and which threads have been woven together at particular times in order to offer inspiration, guidance, and legitimacy. That said, it is always helpful to have the 'founder of modern conservatism' tucked up one's sleeve—even Margaret Thatcher can be found quoting Burke on 'little platoons'.[17]

---

[12] For a concise account, see James Smyth, 'Lewis Namier, Herbert Butterfield and Edmund Burke', *Journal of Eighteenth Century Studies*, 35 (2012), 381–4.

[13] Cobban, *Edmund Burke and the Revolt against the Eighteenth Century* (1929; 2nd edn 1960).

[14] David Marquand, 'My Hero: Edmund Burke', *The Guardian* (11 Sept. 2010); Terry Eagleton, 'Saving Burke from the Tories', *New Statesman* (4 July 1997), 32–3; C. B. Macpherson, *Burke* (1980); Isaac Kramnick, 'The Left and Edmund Burke', *Political Theory*, 11 (1983), 189–214.

[15] Uday Singh Mehta, *Liberalism and Empire: A Study in Nineteenth-Century British Liberal Thought* (1999).

[16] Williamson, *Stanley Baldwin*, 131–2, 149, 179, 223; Green, *Crisis of Conservatism*, 286–7.

[17] Margaret Thatcher, 'Speech to Scottish Conservative Party Conference, 12 May 1990', Margaret Thatcher Foundation: http://www.margaretthatcher.org/document/108087.

All the same, despite hostile criticism, historiographical revisionism, and the consolidation of further strands of C/conservatism, Burke is still most commonly promoted as the 'founder of conservatism'. He remains caricatured as the originator of a limited but distinctive political philosophy deeply integrated with the British Conservative Party. As a label and a theory of politics it has stuck: utilized by politicians, intellectuals, and academics, and taught to students around the world every year. Burke remains an attractive icon globally because of the worldwide importance of the events on which his work provides a comment: a Disraeli or a Peel could never have the same appeal as the eloquent defender of American freedom or the most notorious critic of the French Revolution. His history is bigger than C/conservatism, though this has provided a crucial (because simple) method of interpretation. No doubt Burke's reputation will go through many further adaptations and reinterpretations. What this book has shown, however, is how, when, and why this intellectual and political reputation was first established in Britain. It is the history of Burke's transformation from Whig to C/conservative, but it is also a vital insight into the development of British Conservatism and conservatism—as traditions and bodies of thought—which chose to place Burke at their head.

Bibliography

1. MANUSCRIPTS

King's College, Cambridge: J. M. Keynes Papers.
Trinity College, Cambridge: J. R. M. Butler Papers; miscellaneous letters from Leslie Stephen and Henry Sidgwick.

2. ONLINE RESOURCES

19th Century UK Periodicals <http://gale.cengage.co.uk/product-highlights/history/19th-century-uk-periodicals-parts-1-and-2.aspx>.
Blake, R., 'Disraeli and Gladstone: Opposing Forces', *BBC History Online* (2011) <http://www.bbc.co.uk/history/british/victorians/disraeli_gladstone_01.shtml>.
British Newspapers 1600–1950 <http://gdc.gale.com/products/19th-century-british-library-newspapers-part-i-and-part-ii/>.
Dictionary of Irish Biography <http://dib.cambridge.org>.
Edmund Burke Institute <http://www.edmundburkeinstitute.org/edmundburke.htm>.
Hansard <http://hansard.millbanksystems.com>.
JSTOR Nineteenth Century Pamphlets Online <http://www.jstor.com>.
Marquand, D., 'My Hero: Edmund Burke', *The Guardian* (11 Sept. 2010), <http://www.theguardian.com/books/2010/sep/11/edmund-burke-hero-david-marquand>.
Oxford Dictionary of National Biography <http://www.oxforddnb.com>.
ProQuest British Periodicals <http://search.proquest.com/britishperiodicals>.
Thatcher, M., 'Speech to Scottish Conservative Party Conference, 12 May 1990', *Margaret Thatcher Foundation* <http://www.margaretthatcher.org/document/108087>.
The Spectator Archive <http://archive.spectator.co.uk>.
The Telegraph Historical Archive <http://gale.cengage.co.uk/home/telegraph-archive.aspx>.
The Times Digital Archive <http://find.galegroup.com/ttda/>.
Who Was Who <http://www.ukwhoswho.com/>.

3. PRINTED PRIMARY SOURCES

(i) Anonymous Short Reviews, Reports, and Notices
Academy
'Burke' (16 July 1898), pp. 64–5.
'English Political Philosophy' (16 Dec. 1899), pp. 720–1.
'Fifty Years of English Literature' (21 Dec. 1912), pp. 792–3.
'Forgotten Truths' (23 July 1898), p. 80.
'School-books' (23 Oct. 1875), p. 426.

Athenaeum
'Edmund Burke: A Historical Sketch' (30 Nov. 1867), p. 723.
'English Men of Letters—Burke' (13 Sept. 1879), pp. 334–6.
'English Political Philosophy from Hobbes to Maine' (2 Dec. 1899), p. 754.
'History of the Life and Times of Edmund Burke' (22 Dec. 1860), pp. 866–7.
'Home University Library of Modern Knowledge' (4 May 1912), p. 502.
'Lectures on the Life, Writings, and Times of Edmund Burke' (29 Aug. 1868), pp. 265–6.
'Life and Times of Edmund Burke' (20 Feb. 1858), pp. 236–8.
'Life of the Right Honourable Edmund Burke' (17 Feb. 1855), pp. 195–7.
'Political Thought' (26 Dec. 1914), p. 666.
'The Political Philosophy of Burke' (29 Mar. 1913), p. 356.

British Quarterly Review
'English Men of Letters—Burke' (Oct. 1879), pp. 488–90.
'History of the Life and Times of Edmund Burke' (July 1858), pp. 232–3.

Christian Remembrancer
'History of the Life and Times of Edmund Burke' (Oct. 1861), pp. 297–318.

The Critic
'History of the Life and Times of Edmund Burke' (31 July 1858), pp. 428–9.
'Life of Disraeli' (1 Feb. 1854), pp. 68–70.

Daily Telegraph [London]
['An Old Liberal'], 'A National Party' (5 Jan. 1891), p. 5.
'French Recollections of Mr. Gladstone' (26 May 1898), p. 10.
'History of the Life and Times of Edmund Burke' (4 Mar. 1858), p. 2.
'Notes and Reviews' (6 Nov. 1914), p. 4.
'The Political Philosophy of Burke' (28 Mar. 1913), p. 16.

Dublin Review
'Lectures on the Life, Writings, and Times of Edmund Burke' (Oct. 1868), pp. 563–7.

English Review
'Conservatism' (July 1912), pp. 668–9.

Examiner
'Edmund Burke: A Historical Sketch' (30 Nov. 1867), p. 757.
'History of the Life and Times of Edmund Burke' (2 Mar. 1861), p. 133.
'How Burke Would Have Governed Ireland' (2 Jan. 1869), p. 1.
'Notes on Books' (24 Oct. 1874), p. 1166.

Geographical Journal
'Obituary: Edward John Payne' (Feb. 1905), pp. 224–5.

Irish Times
'Toryism' (4 Feb. 1904), p. 7.

Leader
'Edmund Burke' (13 Feb. 1858), p. 160.

London Journal
'Burke and Goldsmith' (1 May 1868), p. 392.

Manchester Guardian
'Burke's Place in History' (12 Dec. 1928), p. 4.

New Monthly Magazine
'Macknight's Life and Times of Burke' (Apr. 1858), pp. 420–8.

New Quarterly Review
'History of the Life and Times of Edmund Burke' (Jan. 1861), pp. 38–47.

North British Review
'History of the Life and Times of Edmund Burke' (Nov. 1861), pp. 445–79.

The Penny Magazine of the Society for the Diffusion of Useful Knowledge
'Local Recollections of Great Men: Burke', 10 (1841), pp.129–31.

Review of Reviews
'Lord Hugh Cecil's Conservatism' (July 1912), pp. 108–9.

Saturday Review
'Conservatism' (27 July 1912), pp. 115–16.
'English Political Philosophy' (20 Jan. 1900), pp. 83–4.
'Morley's Life of Burke' (16 Aug. 1879), pp. 208–9.
'Mr. Morley on Burke' (9 Nov. 1867), pp. 605–6.
'Mr. Pitt' (31 Dec. 1898), pp. 874–5.
'The Tory Tradition' (16 Jan. 1915), pp. 64–5.

Scottish Review
'Macknight's Life of Burke' (July 1861), pp. 204–19.

Speaker
'Burke's Reverence for Order' (5 Aug. 1899), pp. 126–7.
'Edmund Burke at Beaconsfield' (16 July 1898), pp. 72–3.
'Lord H. Cecil on Conservatism' (21 Oct. 1905), pp. 53–4.
'Rights of Man' (19 Jan. 1895), p. 78.
'The Second Reading' (8 Apr. 1893), pp. 386–7.
'Toryism' (20 Feb. 1904), pp. 499–500.

Spectator
'Of English Classics Selected and Annotated for Purposes of Education' (23 Sept. 1893), pp. 8–9.
'School-books' (25 July 1891), pp. 26–7.
'The Duke of Argyll's Speech' (20 July 1889), pp. 8–9.
'The Political Philosophy of Burke' (10 May 1913), pp. 23–4.
'Toryism' (30 Jan. 1904), pp. 35–6.

The Times
'Election Intelligence' (5 Dec. 1904), p. 6.
'Extension Students at Oxford' (2 Aug. 1897), p. 8.
'Lord H. Cecil at Greenwich' (8 Apr. 1905), p. 6.
'Lord H. Cecil on Conservatism' (14 Oct. 1905), p. 10.
'Lord Hugh Cecil at Bristol' (30 Apr. 1904), p. 8.
'Lord Randolph Churchill in Rossendale' (13 July 1893), p. 12.
'Lord Rosebery at Leeds' (10 Oct. 1888), p. 10.
'Mr. Asquith in Berwerkshire' (28 Mar. 1894), p. 4.
'Mr. Chamberlain and Mr. Matthews at Birmingham' (18 Aug. 1892), p. 4.
'Mr. Chamberlain and the Birmingham Association' (22 Apr. 1886), p. 10.
'Mr. Chamberlain at Greenwich' (1 Aug. 1889), p. 6.
'Sir G. Trevelyan at Sunderland' (13 Dec. 1887), p. 10.
'The Government of Ireland' (15 Apr. 1886), pp. 6–7.
'The Government of Ireland Bill' (11 May 1886), p. 8.
'The National Radical Union' (2 June 1887), pp. 6–7.

University Extension Journal
'Annual Meeting of the London Society' (1 Mar. 1891), p. 34.
'Lent Term Lectures' (1 Dec. 1890), p. 137.
'Lent Term Lectures' (15 Feb. 1891), pp. 26–7.
'List of Candidates to whom Certificates are Awarded' (15 Feb. 1891), pp. 21–5.
'London Local Centres' (1 Dec. 1890), pp. 132–3.

(ii) Articles, including longer and/or autographed reviews
[Abraham, G. W.], 'The Works and Correspondence of the Right Hon. Edmund Burke', *DR* (Mar. 1853), pp. 68–104.
[Acton, J. D.], 'History of the Life and Times of Edmund Burke', *Rambler* (Apr. 1858), pp. 268–73.
[Addison, J.], 'Monday, June 25', *The Freeholder* (25 June 1716), pp. 256–7.
[Anon.], 'Church and State', *WR* (July 1868), pp. 151–83.
[Anon.], 'Earl Grey on Reform', *NR* (Apr. 1858), pp. 424–43.
[Anon.], 'Home Affairs: A National Party', *FR* (July 1887), pp. 140–51.
[Anon.], 'Lord Acton's Lectures on Modern History', *ER* (Apr. 1907), pp. 273–98.
[Anon.], 'Lord Hartington', *WR* (Apr. 1887), pp. 929–39.
[Anon.], 'Prior's Life of Burke', *British Critic* (Nov. 1824), pp. 521–33.

[Anon.], 'Sir Robert Peel and His Policy', *WR* (July 1852), pp. 205–46.
[Anon.], 'The Decline and Fall of Whiggery', *Fraser's Magazine* (Oct. 1864), pp. 395–406.
[Anon.], 'The Duke of Devonshire and the Liberal Unionist Party', *QR* (Jan. 1912), pp. 558–80.
[Anon.], 'The Expansion of England', *QR* (July 1884), pp. 134–61.
[Anon.], 'The Irish Church Measure', *North British Review* (July 1869), pp. 568–601.
[Anon.], 'The Maecenas of the Whigs', *SR* (18 Nov. 1905), pp. 657–68.
[Anon.], 'The Orange Prosecutions', *SR* (14 Sept. 1867), pp. 333–4.
[Anon.], 'The Party Future', *BM* (Nov. 1896), pp. 715–24.
[Anon.], 'The Story of the Nations: Modern England before the Reform Bill', *SR* (14 Jan. 1899), pp. 54–5.
[Anon.], 'The Tory Future', *BM* (Feb. 1900), pp. 182–93.
['Anti-Jacobin'], 'Mr. Burke and the Separatists', *The Times* (17 Dec. 1887), p. 9.
Duke of Argyll, 'Mr. Canning on the Irish Question', *The Times* (23 June 1886), p. 10.
Arnold, M., 'The Zenith of Conservatism', *NC* (Jan. 1887), pp. 148–64.
[Arnold, T.], 'The Church of England', *ER* (Sept. 1826), pp. 490–513.
Arnold-Forster, H. O., 'An English View of Irish Secession', *Political Science Quarterly*, 4 (1889), pp. 66–103.
[Bagehot, W.], 'The Character of Sir Robert Peel', *NR* (July 1856), pp. 146–74.
[Bagehot, W.], 'William Pitt', *NR* (July 1861), pp. 197–228.
Ball, S., 'English Political Philosophy', *International Journal of Ethics* (July 1900), pp. 520–5.
Barry, W., 'Edmund Burke, Statesman and Prophet', *NR* (Jan. 1898), pp. 762–78.
Baumann, A. A., 'An Apology for Unprincipled Toryism', *FR* (Oct. 1897), pp. 617–25.
Baumann, A. A., 'Bye-Products of Disraeli', *SR* (10 Jan. 1914), pp. 44–5.
Baumann, A. A., 'Is a Tory Revival Possible?', *FR* (Feb. 1912), pp. 217–25.
Baumann, A. A., 'Lord Hugh Cecil on Conservatism', *FR* (July 1912), pp. 39–52.
Baumann, A. A., 'The Demise of the Tory Party', *SR* (19 Dec. 1903), pp. 755–6.
Baumann, A. A., 'The Truth about Tory Democracy', *NR* (Mar. 1887), pp. 1–10.
Baumann, A. A., 'Was Disraeli a Democrat?', *FR* (Jan. 1918), pp. 71–9.
Birrell, A., 'Edmund Burke', *CR* (July 1886), pp. 27–43.
Brady, W. M., 'The Irish Establishment under Papal and Protestant Princes', *CR* (Sept. 1868), pp. 1–36.
Broad, C. D., 'Lord Hugh Cecil's Conservatism', *International Journal of Ethics* (July 1913), pp. 396–418.
Bryce, J., 'Goldwin Smith', *North American Review* (Apr. 1914), pp. 513–27.
[Burrows, M.], 'Burke; Select Works', *QR* (Oct. 1878), pp. 331–61.
Carter, B. R., 'Burke-ing the Issue', *SR* (5 Nov. 1910), pp. 581–2.
Cecil, H., 'Home Rule and Imperial Federation', *The Times* (28 Oct. 1910), p. 8.
Collins, J. C., 'The New Scheme for the Indian Civil Service Examinations', *CR* (June 1891), pp. 836–51.

Courthope, W. J., 'A Conservative View: Prophecy and Politics', *NR* (June 1886), pp. 475–86.
[Creighton, J. E.], 'The Political Philosophy of Burke', *Philosophical Review* (Sept. 1913), pp. 558–9.
[Lord Crewe], 'The Disintegration of the Opposition', *The Times* (1 Nov. 1900), p. 10.
Dicey, A. V., 'New Jacobinism and Old Morality', *CR* (Apr. 1888), pp. 475–502.
Dicey, A. V., 'The Protest of Irish Protestantism', *CR* (July 1892), pp. 1–15.
[Dickinson, G. L.], 'Recent Political Theory and Practice', *QR* (Oct. 1900), pp. 359–80.
Dowden, E., 'Coleridge as a Poet', *FR* (Sept. 1889), 342–66.
Dowden, E., 'Hopes and Fears for Literature', *FR* (Feb. 1889), pp. 166–83.
D'sterre-Keeling, E., 'A Woman on Books', *Women's Penny Paper* (23 Aug. 1890), p. 519.
Edwards, J., 'The Literature of Snippets', *SR* (15, 22, 29 Apr. 1899), pp. 455–6.
Escott, T. H. S., 'Mr. Gladstone and Mr. Chamberlain', *WR* (July 1894), pp. 15–21.
de Fellenberg Montgomery, H., 'Burke and Gladstone', *The Times* (16 June 1886), p. 7.
Field, G. C., 'The Political Philosophy of Burke', *International Journal of Ethics* (Apr. 1914), p. 373.
[Figgis, J. N.], 'Gierke's Political Theories of the Middle Ages', *Athenaeum* (2 Feb. 1901), 133–4.
Forster Boulton, A. C., 'Liberalism and the Empire', *WR* (May 1899), pp. 486–91.
Fortescue, G. K., 'The French Revolution in Contemporary Literature', *QR* (Apr. 1913), pp. 353–71.
[Freeman, E. A.], 'The Conquest and the Conqueror', *The Theologian and Ecclesiastic* (Oct. 1848), pp. 197–211 and 261–77.
Froude, J. A., 'Mr. Disraeli's Letters of Runnymede', *Fraser's Magazine* (Aug. 1874), pp. 254–68.
Gardner, J. W., 'The Political Philosophy of Burke', *American Political Science Review* (May 1914), pp. 316–18.
Giddings, F. H., 'History of the New World Called America', *Political Science Quarterly* (Dec. 1893), pp. 733–6.
Glazebrook, M. G., 'The Repunctuation of the Lord's Prayer', *The Times* (19 July 1910), p. 6.
Gosse, E., 'Rousseau in England in the Nineteenth Century', *FR* (July 1912), pp. 22–38.
[Green, J. R.], 'Freeman's Growth of the English Constitution', *SR* (4 May 1872), pp. 573–5.
Harrison, F., 'A Rejoinder to the Duke of Argyll', *CR* (Feb. 1889), pp. 301–16.
['H. B.'], 'English Political Philosophy', *Speaker* (16 Dec. 1899), pp. 289–90.
[Jennings, L. J.], 'Mr. Gladstone and Ireland', *QR* (July 1886), pp. 257–88.
Kebbel, T. E., 'Is the Party System Breaking Up?', *NC* (Mar. 1899), pp. 502–11.
[Kebbel, T. E.], 'Mr. Lecky and George III', *FR* (July 1882), pp. 41–59.

Kebbel, T. E., 'Party Prospects', *NC* (Feb. 1890), pp. 312–26.
Kebbel, T. E., 'The Sentiment of Chivalry', *Macmillan's* (Aug. 1897), pp. 299–306.
Kettle, T. M., 'Home Rule and Antiquarianism', *Academy* (14 Oct. 1911), pp. 466–7.
Lilly, W. S., 'Illiberal Liberalism', *FR* (Nov. 1895), pp. 641–61.
MacColl, M., 'Lord Acton's Letters to Mary Gladstone', *FR* (June 1904), pp. 996–1010.
Mackintosh, A., 'Lord Morley as a Man of Letters', *The Bookman* (Jan. 1913), pp. 203–8.
[Maginn, W.], 'On the Chances of the Reconstruction of the Tory Party: Sketch of the History of Parties from the Revolution to Burke', *Fraser's Magazine* (Feb. 1833), pp. 223–30.
Marriott, W. T., 'Lectures on the Life, Writings, and Times of Edmund Burke', *FR* (Dec. 1868), pp. 699–701.
Mason, O. T., 'Review: History of the New World Called America', *American Anthropologist* (Jan. 1900), pp. 170–2.
Mill, J. S., 'Periodical Literature', *WR* (Apr. 1824), pp. 505–51.
[M. M. M.], 'Letter', *Gentleman's Magazine* (May 1830), pp. 412–15.
Lord Monteagle, 'The New Irish Policy', *NC* (June 1897), pp. 1016–22.
Morgan, G. O., 'The Evolution of Liberal Unionism', *CR* (Aug. 1893), pp. 299–308.
Morley, J., 'A Few Words on French Revolutionary Models', *NC* (Mar. 1888), pp. 468–80.
Morley, J., 'A New Calendar of Great Men', *NC* (Feb. 1892), pp. 312–28.
Morley, J., 'A Word with Some Critics', *FR* (Oct. 1879), pp. 577–84.
Morley, J., 'Home and Foreign Affairs', *FR* (Sept. 1876), pp. 395–408.
Morley, J., 'The Government of Ireland', *NC* (Jan. 1887), pp. 19–39.
Morris, W. B., 'Edmund Burke and the Revolution', *DR* (July 1900), pp. 69–94.
Mundella, A. J., 'Mr. Gladstone and Burke', *The Times* (14 Dec. 1886), p. 10.
Myers, F. W. H., 'English at the Universities', *Pall Mall Gazette* (27 Nov. 1886), pp. 1–2.
Partridge, J. A., 'Ireland and the Empire', *WR* (July 1889), pp. 449–69.
Payne, E. J., 'Letters, Speeches, and Tracts on Irish Affairs', *Academy* (9 July 1881), p. 22.
Payne, E. J., 'Mr. Morley on Burke', *Academy* (18 Oct. 1879), p. 287.
Pease, A., 'The Constitutional Course', *The Times* (14 June 1886), p. 4.
Read, C., 'English Political Philosophy', *Economic Journal* (Mar. 1900), pp. 83–5.
Robertson, J. M., 'England Before and Since the French Revolution', *Our Corner* (May 1888), pp. 267–80.
Russell, F., 'Review: History of the New World Called America', *American Historical Review* (July 1901), pp. 796–9.
Seeley, J. R., 'History and Politics', *Macmillan's* (Oct. 1879), pp. 449–58.
Seeley, J. R., 'The Impartial Study of Politics', *CR* (July 1888), pp. 53–65.
Lord Selborne, 'Thoughts about Party', *CR* (Jan. 1887), pp. 5–7.
Sibley, N. W., 'Edmund Burke', *WR* (Nov. 1897), pp. 496–509.
Smith, G., 'Burke', *Cornhill* (July 1896), pp. 17–29.
Smith, G., 'Reform the House of Lords!', *CR* (Apr. 1897), pp. 511–16.

Smith, G., 'The Fallacy of Irish History', *FR* (Jan. 1884), pp. 37–49.
[Stephen, J. F.], 'Buckle's Theory of Civilization in England', *ER* (July 1861), pp. 183–211.
[Stephen, J. F.], 'Burke on Popular Representation', *SR* (23 Sept. 1865), pp. 394–6.
[Stephen, J. F.], 'Burke on the English Constitution', *SR* (28 Dec. 1867), pp. 815–17.
[Stephen, J. F.], 'Edmund Burke', *SR* (10 Apr. 1858), pp. 372–3.
[Stephen, J. F.], 'Liberalism', *Cornhill* (Jan. 1862), pp. 70–83.
Stephen, L., 'An Attempted Philosophy of History', *FR* (May 1880), pp. 672–95.
Stephen, L., 'Thomas Paine', *FR* (Aug. 1893), pp. 267–81.
Stewart, John L., 'Introduction to the History of the Science of Politics', *Annals of the American Academy of Political and Social Science*, 1 (Jan. 1891), 505–7.
Walker, H., 'The Right Hon. W. E. Hartpole Lecky', *Good Words* (Dec. 1899), pp. 114–19.
Ward, W., 'Politics and Party', *DR* (July 1909), pp. 25–58.
Winsor, J., 'Review: History of the New World Called America', *EHR* (Apr. 1893), pp. 346–51.

(iii) Editions of Edmund Burke's Works
Burke: Select Works, ed. E. J. Payne, 3 vols (Oxford, 1874–8).
Burke's Regicide Peace, ed. H. G. Keene (London, 1893).
Burke's Speech on Conciliation with America, ed. F. G. Selby (London, 1895).
Burke's Speech on Conciliation with America, ed. John Morrison (London, 1912).
Burke's Speech on Conciliation with America, ed. Sidney Carleton Newsom (London, 1909).
Burke's Speeches and Letters on American Affairs, ed. Hugh Law (London, 1908).
Burke's Speeches on America, ed. F. A. Cavanagh (London, 1915).
Burke's Speeches on America, eds. A. J. F. Collins and F. J. C. Hearnshaw (London, 1913).
Burke's Speeches on America, ed. C. E. Vaughan (London, 1893).
Correspondence of the Rt. Hon. Edmund Burke, eds. C. W. W. Fitzwilliam and R. Bourke, 4 vols (London, 1844).
Edmund Burke: On Conciliation with America, and Two Letters to Gentlemen of Bristol on Trade with Ireland, ed. Vincent Scully (Dublin, 1882).
Edmund Burke: Selections from his Political Writings and Speeches, ed. J[ohn]. B[uchan]. (London, 1911).
Edmund Burke's Speeches on America, ed. W. H. D. Rouse (London, 1906).
Forgotten Truths, Selections from the Speeches and Writings of the Rt. Hon. Edmund Burke, ed. T. Dundas Pillans (London, 1898).
Irish Affairs, ed. Matthew Arnold (London, 1881).
Maxims and Reflections of Edmund Burke, ed. F. W. Rafferty (London, 1909).
On the Proposed Peace with the Regicide Directory of France: Letter I, ed. F. J. C. Hearnshaw (London, 1906).
On the Sublime and Beautiful, ed. Henry Morley (London, 1887).
Opinions on Reform, by Edmund Burke, ed. T. H. Burke (London, 1831).

Reflections on the Revolution in France, ed. H. P. Adams (London, 1910).
Reflections on the Revolution in France, ed. J. H. Boardman (London, 1911).
Reflections on the Revolution in France, ed. J. C. D. Clark (Stanford, 2001).
Reflections on the Revolution in France, eds. W. A. Phillips and C. B. Phillips (Cambridge, 1913).
Reflections on the Revolution in France, ed. J. G. A. Pocock (Indianapolis, 1987).
Reflections on the Revolution in France, ed. George Sampson (London, 1900).
Reflections on the Revolution in France, ed. F. G. Selby (London, 1890).
Reflections on the Revolution in France, with a Letter to a Member of the National Assembly and Thoughts on French Affairs, ed. A. J. Grieve (London, 1910).
Selected Works of Edmund Burke, vol I: Reflections on the French Revolution, ed. Sidney Lee (London, 1905).
Selections from Burke's Reflections on the French Revolution, ed. C. E. Vaughan (London, 1892).
Selections from Edmund Burke, ed. Bliss Perry (London, 1908).
Selections from the Speeches and Writings of Edmund Burke, ed. Hannaford Bennett (London, 1907).
The Speeches of the Rt. Hon. Edmund Burke, with Memoir and Historical Introduction, ed. James Burke (Dublin, 1854).
Speeches on America by Edmund Burke, ed. C. B. Hawkins (London, 1906).
The Wisdom of Burke: Extracts from his Speeches and Writings, ed. E. A. Pankhurst (London, 1886).
The Works of Edmund Burke, eds. W. King and F. Laurence, 16 vols (London, 1803–27).
The Works of the Rt. Hon. Edmund Burke, ed. H. G. Bohn, 9 vols (London, 1854).
The Works of the Rt. Hon. Edmund Burke [Bell's], 6 vols (London, 1868–72).
The Works of the Rt. Hon. Edmund Burke [J. C. Nimmo], 12 vols (London, 1887).
The Works of the Rt. Hon. Edmund Burke, eds. H. Wills and F. W. Rafferty, 6 vols (London, 1906–7).
Thoughts on the Cause of the Present Discontents, ed. W. Murison (Cambridge, 1913).
Thoughts on the Cause of the Present Discontents, ed. F. G. Selby (London, 1902).
Thoughts on the Cause of the Present Discontents, ed. Vincent Scully (Dublin, 1882).
Thoughts on the Cause of the Present Discontents and Observations on a Late State of the Nation (London, 1906).
Two Speeches on Conciliation with America and Two Letters on Irish Questions, ed. Henry Morley (London, 1886).
Writings and Speeches of Edmund Burke, eds. Paul Langford and Leslie Mitchell, 8 vols (Oxford, 1981–2000).

(iv) Pamphlets

[Anon.], 'A Few Extracts from the Works and Speeches of Edmund Burke, in support of the case of present policy of the Liberal Party towards Ireland' (London, 1887).

[Anon.], 'From Liberal Ulster to England' (London, 1886).
[Anon.], 'Junius Proved to be Burke, with an Outline of his Biography' (London, 1826).
[Anon.], 'Lord Hartington's Address' (London, 1886).
[Anon.], 'Scheme for a Reform of Parliament, by an Ex-MP and a Tory' (London, 1858).
[Anon.], 'Speech Delivered by the Rt. Hon. Joseph Chamberlain, M.P. to the Members of the Liberal Union Club, at Willis' Rooms, June 14 1887' (London, 1887).
[Anon.], 'The Constitution as it is or Democracy?' (London, 1837).
[Anon.], 'The Inherent Evils of all State Governments Demonstrated; being a reprint of Edmund Burke's celebrated Essay entitled "A Vindication of Natural Society" with notes' (London, 1858).
Baxter, R. D., 'English Parties and Conservatism' (London, 1870).
Butler, J., 'The Constitution Violated' (Edinburgh, 1871).
Cobden, R., '1793 and 1853, in Three Letters' (London, 1853).
Cooper, C., 'Upon Party' (London, 1850).
Earl of Derby, 'The Irish Question' (London, 1886).
Ewing, T. J., 'Mr. Gladstone and Ireland; or, Lord Salisbury and the Orange Faction' (London, 1886).
de Fellenberg Montgomery, H., 'Gladstone and Burke' (London, 1886).
Fox, J. A., 'From Galilee to Gweedore, a Drama with a Purpose' (London, 1889).
Gore, M., 'Reply to Sir John Walsh's Pamphlet, Entitled "The Present Balance of Parties"' (London, 1832).
Hamilton, A. H. A., 'The Past and Present Schisms of the Liberal Party: A Historical Parallel' (Oxford, 1888).
Harvey, E., 'A Summary of Irish Grievances, still existing in 1886; with some Remarks on Home Rule' (London, 1886).
Hatchards, 'Napoleon and his Time: A Collection of Standard Books in Fine Secondhand Condition' (London, 1908).
Hobhouse, A., 'Liberals and the New Conservatism' (Manchester, 1880).
Hollowell, J. H., 'Ireland: The Story of Her Wrongs, and a Plea for her Rights' (Nottingham, 1886).
Jones, H., 'Wales and its Prospects' (Wrexham, 1890).
Kettle, T. M., 'The Philosophy of Politics' (Dublin, 1906).
[Lecky, W. E. H.], 'Grattan's Parliament: a Letter by Mr. W. E. H. Lecky, addressed to the Editor of the Times, June 7 1886' (London, 1887).
Leech, H. J., 'Henry Grattan: A Lecture, delivered at the Manchester Liberal Club, Oct. 8 1886' (London, 1886).
MacColl, M., 'Reasons for Home Rule' (London, 1886).
Mahaffy, G., 'The Attitude of Irish Churchmen in the Present Political Crisis' (Dublin, 1886).
Plainspoken, P., 'Short Notes on a Long Chapter of Mr. Gladstone's Autobiography, reprinted from John Bull' (London, 1868).

[Prior, J.], 'The Remonstrance of a Tory to the Right Hon. Robert Peel' (London, 1827).
['Radical'], 'How Ireland Flourished under Home Rule 100 Years Ago' (London, 1884).
Sharman, C. H., 'Twelve Reasons Why I am a Conservative' (London, 1887).
Smith, J. G., 'Home Rule in Ireland, the Colonies, and the United States. An Address Delivered in the College Division, Glasgow, 17 Dec. 1886' (London, 1889).
[Thompson, C.], 'Observations upon Parliamentary Pledges by Candidates to their Constituents' (London, 1837).
Wade, J., 'A Political Dictionary: or Pocket Companion, Chiefly for the Use of Members of Parliament, Whigs, Tories, Loyalists, Magistrates, Clergymen, Half-Pay Officers, Worshipful Aldermen and Reviewers; Being an Illustration and Commentary on all Words, Phrases, and Proper Names, in the Vocabulary of Corruption' (London, 1821).
Wallas, G., 'Syllabus of a Course of Lectures on the Growth of English Institutions in Town and Country: or, the English Citizen, Past and Present' (London, 1894).
Wileman, W., 'Rome Rule in Ireland, the Facts of the Case Plainly Stated: Opinions of Eminent Men' (London, 1886).
Willans, J. W., 'Grattan's Parliament: What Led up to it; What it was; What it did; and How it Fell' (London, 1887).
Willis, W., 'Edmund Burke: The Story of His Life, a lecture delivered at Beaconsfield 5th December 1888' (London, 1889).

(v) Books and Monographs

Abbey, C. J. and J. H. Overton, *The English Church in the Eighteenth Century*, 2 vols (London, 1878).
Lord Acton, *Essays on Church and State*, ed. Douglas Woodruff (London, 1952).
Lord Acton, *Lectures on Modern History* (London, 1906).
Lord Acton, *Lectures on the French Revolution*, eds. J. N. Figgis and R. V. Laurence (London, 1910).
Lord Acton, *The History of Freedom and Other Essays*, eds. J. N. Figgis and J. V. Laurence (London, 1907).
Adams, H. P., *Karl Marx in his Early Writings* (London, 1940).
Adams, H. P., *The French Revolution* (London, 1914).
Adams, H. P., *The Life and Writings of Giambattista Vico* (London, 1935).
Alison, A., *Essays Political, Historical, and Miscellaneous*, 3 vols (Edinburgh, 1850).
Amery, L., *Union and Strength* (London, 1912).
Amos, S., *Fifty Years of the English Constitution, 1830–1880* (London, 1880).
Amos, S., *The Science of Politics*, 2nd edn (London, 1883).
Anderson, R., *Sidelights on the Home Rule Movement* (London, 1906).
Duke of Argyll, *Irish Nationalism: An Appeal to History* (London, 1893).

Arnold, M., *A French Eton, or Middle Class Education and the State* (London, 1864).
Arnold, M., *Essays in Criticism* (London, 1965).
Arnold, M., *Last Essays on Church and Religion* (London, 1903).
Arnold, M., *Irish Essays* (London, 1882).
Arnold, M., *On Home Rule for Ireland: Two Letters to The Times* (London, 1891).
Arnold, M., *On the Study of Celtic Literature* (London, 1877).
Arnold, M., *The Letters of Matthew Arnold*, ed. Cecil Y. Lang, 6 vols (Charlottesville and London, 1996–2002).
Arnold, T., *Introductory Lectures on Modern History*, 4th edn (London, 1849).
Austin, J., *A Plea for the Constitution* (London, 1859).
Bacon, F., *Bacon's Essays*, ed. F. G. Selby (London, 1889).
Bagehot, W., *Literary Studies: Volume One* (London, 1920).
Bagehot, W., *The English Constitution* (London, 1867).
Baker, E. A., *A Guide to Historical Fiction* (London, 1914).
Baker, E. A., *History in Fiction*, 2 vols (London, 1907).
Balfour, A. J., *Theism and Humanism* (London, 1915).
Barker, E., *Political Thought from 1848–1914* (London, 1915).
Baumann, A. A., *Burke: The Founder of Conservatism* (London, 1929).
Belloc, H., *Danton* (London, 1899).
Belloc, H., *Marie Antoinette* (London, 1909).
Belloc, H., *Robespierre* (London, 1901).
Belloc, H., *The French Revolution* (London, 1911).
Birrell, A., *Obiter Dicta: Second Series* (London, 1887).
Bisset, R., *The Life of Edmund Burke, Comprehending an Impartial Account of his Literary and Political Efforts and a Sketch of the Conduct and Character of his most Eminent Associates, Coadjutors, and Opponents*, 2 vols (London, 1798).
Boutwood, A., *National Revival, a Restatement of Tory Principles* (London, 1913).
Brewer, J. S., *English Studies, or Essays: English Literature and History* (London, 1881).
Brodrick, G. C., 'The Utilitarian Argument Against Reform', in *Essays on Reform* (London, 1867).
Brougham, H., *Government without Whigs* (London, 1830).
Brougham, H., *Historical Sketches of Statesmen who flourished in the Time of George III; to which are added, remarks on party*, 3 vols (London, 1845).
Brown, I., *English Political Theory* (London, 1920).
Bryce, J., ed., *Handbook of Home Rule*, 2nd edn (London, 1887).
Buckle, H. T., *History of Civilization in England*, 2 vols (London, 1857–61).
Burrows, M., *Imperial England* (London, 1880).
Butler, G., *The Tory Tradition: Bolingbroke, Burke, Disraeli, Salisbury* (London, 1914).
Butler, H. M., *Ten Great and Good Men* (London, 1909).
Butler, J. R. M., *Henry Montagu Butler: Master of Trinity College, Cambridge, 1886–1918* (London, 1925).

Canning, G., *Speeches of the Rt. Hon. George Canning delivered on Public Occasions in Liverpool* (London, 1825).
Lord Hugh Cecil, *Conservatism* (London, 1912).
Lord Hugh Cecil, *Liberty and Authority* (London, 1910).
Charley, W. T., *The Crusade against the Constitution: An Historical Vindication of the House of Lords* (London, 1895).
Coleridge, S. T., *The Collected Works of Samuel Taylor Coleridge*, eds. Kathleen Coburn et al., 16 vols (1969–2002).
Collins, J. C., *The Study of English Literature: A Plea for its Recognition and Organization at the Universities* (London, 1891).
Collins, J. C., *Voltaire, Montesquieu and Rousseau in England* (London, 1908).
Congreve, R., *Essays Political, Social, and Religious and Historical Lectures*, 3 vols (London, 1874–1900).
Congreve, R., *International Policy* (London, 1866).
Cornewall Lewis, G., *An Essay on the Influence of Authority in Matters of Opinion*, 2nd edn (London, 1875).
Cornewall Lewis, G., *Essays on the Administrations of Great Britain, from 1783 to 1830* (London, 1864).
Cornewall Lewis, G., *Letters of George Cornewall Lewis*, ed. Gilbert Frankland (London, 1870).
Creasy, E. S., *The Rise and Progress of the English Constitution*, 3rd edn (London, 1856).
Creasy, E. S., *The Rise and Progress of the English Constitution*, 4th edn (London, 1858).
Creasy, E. S., *The Text-Book of the Constitution: Magna Charta, the Petition of Right, and the Bill of Rights* (London, 1848).
Creighton, M., *The English National Character* (London, 1896).
Croly, G., *A Memoir of the Rt. Hon. Edmund Burke*, 2 vols (Edinburgh and London, 1840).
Dicey, A. V., *A Fool's Paradise: being a Constitutionalist's Criticism of the Home Rule Bill of 1912* (London, 1913).
Dicey, A. V., *A Leap in the Dark, or, our New Constitution* (London, 1893; 2nd edn, 1911).
Dicey, A. V., *England's Case against Home Rule* (London, 1886).
Dicey, A. V., *Lectures on the Relation between Law and Public Opinion in England during the Nineteenth Century* (London, 1905).
Dicey, A. V., *Unionist Delusions* (London, 1887).
Dicey, A. V., *Why England Maintains the Union* (London, 1887).
Dickens, C., *Hard Times* (London, 1854).
Disraeli, B., *Benjamin Disraeli Letters*, eds. M. G. Weibe and Mary S. Millar, 9 vols (Toronto, 2004).
Disraeli, B., *Coningsby; or, the New Generation* (London, 1844).
Disraeli, B., *Endymion* (London, 1880).
Disraeli, B., *Sybil; or, the Two Nations* (London, 1845).
Disraeli, B., *Vindication of the English Constitution, in a Letter to a Noble and Learned Lord* (London, 1835).

Dowden, E., *Letters of Edward Dowden and his Correspondents*, eds. Elizabeth and Hilda Dowden (London, 1914).
Dowden, E., *New Studies in Literature* (London, 1895).
Dowden, E., *Studies in Literature, 1789–1877* (London, 1878).
Dowden, E., *The French Revolution and English Literature* (London, 1897).
Dundas Pillans, T., *Edmund Burke: Apostle of Justice and Liberty* (London, 1905).
Eliot, G., *Middlemarch* (London, 1874).
Erskine May, T., *Democracy in Europe: A History*, 2 vols (London, 1877).
Erskine May, T., *The Constitutional History of England: From the Accession of George the Third*, 3 vols (London, 1912 edn).
Feiling, K., *Tory Democracy* (London, 1914).
Feiling, K., *Toryism: A Political Dialogue* (London, 1913).
Figgis, J. N., *The Value of Historical Study* (Kettering, 1896).
Fisher, H. A. L., *The Republican Tradition in Europe* (London, 1911).
Frédéricq, P., *The Study of History in England and Scotland* (Baltimore, 1887).
Froude, J. A., *The English in Ireland in the Eighteenth Century*, 3 vols (London, 1872–4).
Gladstone, W. E., *A Chapter of Autobiography* (London, 1868).
Gladstone, W. E., *Correspondence on Church and Religion of W. E. Gladstone*, ed. D. C. Lathbury, 2 vols (London, 1910).
Gladstone, W. E., *Gleanings of Past Years, 1843–1878*, 7 vols (London, 1879).
Gladstone, W. E., *Special Aspects of the Irish Question: A Series of Reflections in and since 1886* (London, 1892).
Gladstone, W. E., *The Gladstone Diaries*, eds. M. R. D. Foot and H. C. G. Matthew, 14 vols (Oxford, 1968–1996).
Gladstone, W. E., *The Vatican Decrees in their Bearing on Civil Allegiance: A Political Expostulation* (London, 1874).
Gooch, G. P., 'Europe and the French Revolution', *Cambridge Modern History*, 14 vols (Cambridge, 1902–12).
Graham, W., *English Political Philosophy, from Hobbes to Maine* (London, 1899).
Graham, W., *Idealism: An Essay Metaphysical and Critical* (London, 1892).
Graham, W., *The Creed of Science* (London, 1881).
Grant, A. J., *English Historians* (London, 1906).
Green, J. R., *A Short History of the English People* (London, 1874).
Hallam, A. H., 'Burke', *Gallery of Portraits; with memoirs*, 7 vols (London, 1833–7).
Hallam, H., *Constitutional History of England, from the Accession of Henry VII to the Death of George II*, 2 vols (London, 1827).
Hare, T., *The Election of Representatives, Parliamentary and Municipal*, 3rd edn (London, 1865).
Hazlitt, W., *Political Essays* (London, 1819).
Hearnshaw, F. J. C., *Conservatism in England: An Analytical, Historical, and Political Survey* (London, 1933).

Hearnshaw, F. J. C., *Some Memories of an Elderly Man* (West Kirby, 2001).
Hirst, F. W. and J. S. Phillimore, eds., *Essays on Liberalism, by Six Oxford Men* (London, 1897).
Holland, B., *Life of the Duke of Devonshire, 1833–1908*, 2 vols (London, 1911).
Holland, H. R. V., *Further Memoirs of the Whig Party, 1807–1821*, ed. Lord Stavordale (London, 1905).
Holland, H. R. V., *Memoirs of the Whig Party*, ed. H. E. Holland, 2 vols (London, 1852–4).
Hulme, T. E., *The Collected Writings of T. E. Hulme*, ed. Karen Csengeri (Oxford, 1994).
Jones, H., *Idealism as a Practical Creed* (Glasgow, 1909).
Jones, H., *The Working Faith of the Social Reformer* (London, 1910).
Kebbel, T. E., *A History of Toryism, from the Accession of Mr. Pitt in Power in 1783, to the Death of Lord Beaconsfield in 1881* (London, 1886).
Kebbel, T. E., *Essays upon History and Politics* (London, 1864).
Lawrence, D. H., *The Letters of D. H. Lawrence*, eds. J. T. Boulton et al., 8 vols (Cambridge, 1979–2000).
Lecky, E. van D., *A Memoir of the Rt. Hon. W. E. H. Lecky* (London, 1909).
Lecky, W. E. H., *Historical and Political Essays*, new edn (London, 1910).
Lecky, W. E. H., *History of England in the Eighteenth Century*, 8 vols (London, 1878–90).
Lecky, W. E. H., *History of Ireland in the Eighteenth Century*, 5 vols (London, 1892).
Lecky, W. E. H., *History of the Rise and Influence of the Spirit of Rationalism in Europe* (London, 1865).
Lecky, W. E. H., *The Leaders of Public Opinion in Ireland*, new edn, 2 vols (London, 1861; 1903).
Lecky, W. E. H., *The Political Value of History* (London, 1892).
Lever, C., *Cornelious O'Dowd upon Men, Women, and Things in General* (Edinburgh, 1865).
Loftus, P., *The Conservative Party and the Future: A Programme for Tory Democracy* (London, 1912).
Ludovici, A. M., *A Defence of Conservatism, a Further Text-book for Tories* (London, 1927).
Macaulay, T. B., *Critical and Historical Essays*, 2 vols (London, 1907).
Macaulay, T. B., *History of England, from the Accession of James II*, 5 vols (London, 1858–61).
Macaulay, T. B., *Journals of Thomas Babington Macaulay*, ed. William Thomas, 5 vols (London, 2008).
Macaulay, T. B., *Lays of Ancient Rome, Essays and Poems* (London, 1910).
Macaulay, T. B., *Speeches of T. B. Macaulay* (London, 1853).
MacCunn, J., *Liverpool Addresses on the Ethics of Social Work* (Liverpool and London, 1911).
MacCunn, J., *Six Radical Thinkers* (London, 1907).

MacCunn, J., *The Ethics of Citizenship*, 6th edn (Glasgow, 1922).
MacCunn, J., *The Political Philosophy of Burke* (London, 1913).
McDonnell Bodkin, M., *Grattan's Parliament: Before and After* (London, 1912).
Mackintosh, J., *Dissertation on the Progress of Ethical Philosophy* (Edinburgh, 1830).
Mackintosh, J., *Memoirs of the Life of the Rt. Hon. Sir James Mackintosh*, ed. R. J. Mackintosh, 2 vols (London, 1835).
Macknight, T., *History of the Life and Times of Edmund Burke*, 3 vols (London, 1858–60).
Macknight, T., *Life of Lord Bolingbroke* (London, 1863).
Macknight, T., *Political Progress of the Nineteenth Century*, ed. C. C. Osborne (London, 1905).
[Macknight, T.], *The Rt. Hon. Benjamin Disraeli: A Literary and Political Biography* (London, 1854).
Macknight, T., *Ulster as it is: or, Twenty-Eight Years' Experience as an Irish Editor*, 2 vols (London, 1896).
Lord Macmillian, *Two Ways of Thinking* (Cambridge, 1934).
M'Cormick, C., *Memoirs of the Rt. Hon. Edmund Burke; or, an Impartial Review of his Private Life, His Publick Conduct, his Speeches in Parliament, &c.* (London, 1797).
Madden, D. O., *The Age of Pitt and Fox* (London, 1846).
Lord Mahon, *History of England from the Peace of Utrecht to the Peace of Versailles, 1713–83*, 3rd edn, 7 vols (London, 1853).
Maitland, F. W., *Life and Letters of Leslie Stephen* (London, 1906).
Marx, K. and F. Engels, *Collected Works*, 50 vols (London, 1996).
Massey, W., *A History of England during the Reign of George III*, 4 vols (London, 1865).
Maurice, F. D., *Kingdom of Christ: or, Hints to a Quaker respecting the Principles, Constitution and Ordinances of the Catholic Church*, 2nd edn, 2 vols (London, 1842).
Maurice, F. D., *Moral and Metaphysical Philosophy*, new edn, 2 vols (London, 1872).
Maurice, F. D., *The Friendship of Books and Other Lectures*, ed. Thomas Hughes (London, 1874).
Mazzini, G., *The Duties of Man* (London, 1862).
Mill, J. S., *A System of Logic*, 2 vols (London, 1843).
Mill, J. S., *Collected Works of John Stuart Mill*, ed. J. M. Robson, 33 vols (London, 1979).
Milner, A., *The Nation and the Empire* (London, 1914).
Montgomery, R., *Edmund Burke: being First Principles selected from his Writings, with an Introductory Essay* (London, 1853).
Monypenny, W. and Buckle, G., *Life of Benjamin Disraeli*, 6 vols (London, 1910–20).
Moore, T., *Life of the Rt. Hon. Richard Sheridan*, 3rd edn (London, 1825).
Morley, J., *Burke* (London, 1879).
Morley, J., *Edmund Burke: A Historical Study* (London, 1867).
Morley, J., *Life of Gladstone*, 3 vols (London, 1903).

Morley, J., *Life of Richard Cobden*, new edn (London, 1895).
Morley, J., *Notes on Politics and History* (London, 1914).
Morley, J., *On Compromise* (London, 1874).
Morley, J., *On the Study of Literature: Annual Address to Students of the London Society for the Extension of University Teaching* (London, 1887).
Morley, J., *Oracles on Man and Government* (London, 1923).
Morley, J., *Recollections*, 2 vols (London, 1917).
Morley, J., *Rousseau*, 2 vols (London, 1873).
Muirhead, J. H., *The Service of the State: Four Lectures on the Political Teaching of T. H. Green* (London, 1908).
Napier, J., *Edmund Burke: A Lecture, Delivered before the Dublin YMCA* (Dublin, 1862).
Nash, T. A., *Life of Lord Westbury*, 2 vols (London, 1888).
Oldfield, T. B. H., *The Representative History of Great Britain and Ireland*, 6 vols (London, 1816).
Paine, T., *Rights of Man*, 2nd edn (London, 1791).
Pankhurst, E. A., *Edmund Burke: A Study of his Life and Character* (London, 1886).
Pattison, M., 'Tendencies of Religious Thought in England, 1688–1750', in *Essays and Reviews* (London, 1860).
Paul, H., *The Life of Froude* (London, 1905).
Pease, A. E., *Elections and Recollections* (London, 1932).
Peel, R., *Speeches of the Late Rt. Hon. Sir Robert Peel*, 4 vols (London, 1853).
Pollard, A. F., *Factors in Modern History* (London, 1932).
Pollock, F., *Introduction to the Science of Politics* (London, 1890).
Powicke, F. M., *Modern Historians and the Study of History: Essays and Papers* (London, 1955).
Prior, J., *Memoir of the Life and Character of the Rt. Hon. Edmund Burke*, 2nd edn, 2 vols (London, 1826).
Prior, J., *Memoir of the Life and Character of the Rt. Hon. Edmund Burke*, 5th edn (London, 1854).
Read, C., *The Cabinet of Irish Literature*, 4 vols (Glasgow, 1879).
Reid, W., *American and English Essays*, 2 vols (London, 1914).
Ritchie, D. G., *Darwin and Hegel* (London, 1893).
Ritchie, D. G., *Natural Rights*, 2nd edn (London, 1903).
Ritchie, D. G., *The Principles of State Interference: Four Essays on the Political Philosophy of Mr Herbert Spencer, J. S. Mill, and T. H. Green* (London, 1891).
Roberts, H., *Constructive Conservatism*, intro. L. S. Amery (London, 1913).
Robertson, J. B., *Lectures on the Life, Writings, and Times of Edmund Burke* (Dublin, 1868).
Robertson, J. B., *Public Lectures on Ancient and Modern History, Delivered before the Catholic University of Ireland* (London, 1859).
Robertson, J. M., *The Meaning of Liberalism* (London, 1912).
Lord Rosebery, *Appreciations and Addresses*, ed. Charles Geake (London, 1899).
Lord Rosebery, *Life of Pitt* (London, 1891).

Lord Rosebery, *Lord Randolph Churchill* (London, 1906).
Lord Rosebery, *Miscellanies, Literary and Historical*, 2 vols (London, 1921).
Roylance Kent, C. B., *The English Radicals* (London, 1899).
Lord John Russell, *An Essay on the History of the English Government and Constitution: from the Reign of Henry VII to the Present Time*, 2nd edn (London, 1823).
Lord John Russell, *Life and Times of Charles James Fox*, 3 vols (London, 1859–66).
Lord John Russell, *Memorials and Correspondence of Charles James Fox*, 4 vols (London, 1853–7).
Seeley, J. R., *Lectures and Essays* (London, 1870).
Lord Selborne, *Memorials, part II: Personal and Political, 1865–1895* (London, 1898).
Sidgwick, H., *Miscellaneous Essays and Addresses*, eds. E. M. and A. Sidgwick (London, 1904).
Smith, F. E., *Toryism* (London, 1903).
Smith, F. E., *Unionist Policy and Other Essays* (London, 1912).
Smith, G., *Burke on Party* (London, 1905).
Smith, G., *Essays on Questions of the Day, Political and Social* (London and New York, 1894).
Smith, G., *Irish History and Irish Character* (London, 1861).
Smith, G., *The Schism in the Anglo-Saxon Race* (New York, 1887).
Smith, G., *The United Kingdom: A Political History*, 2 vols (London, 1899).
Smith, G., *Three English Statesmen: A Course of Lectures on the Political History of England* (London, 1868).
Smyth, W., *Lectures on History: On the French Revolution* (London, 1840).
Smyth, W., *Lectures on Modern History* (London, 1840).
Solly, H. S., *Life of Henry Morley* (London, 1898).
Stanley, A. P., *The Life and Correspondence of Thomas Arnold*, 2 vols (London, 1844).
Stephen, J. F., *Horae Sabbaticae*, 3 vols (London, 1892).
Stephen, J. F., *Liberty, Equality, Fraternity* (London, 1873).
Stephen, J. F., *The Story of Nuncomar and the Impeachment of Sir Elijah Impey*, 2 vols (London, 1885).
Stephen, L., *English Literature and Society in the Eighteenth Century* (London, 1904).
Stephen, L., *History of English Thought in the Eighteenth Century*, 2 vols (London, 1876).
Stephen, L., *Hours in a Library*, 3 vols (London, 1874; new edn, 1892).
Stephen, L., *Life of James Fitzjames Stephen* (London, 1895).
Stephen, L., *Social Rights and Duties*, 2 vols (Cambridge, 1896; 2011).
Stephen, L., *The English Utilitarians*, 3 vols (London, 1900).
Stephen, L., *The Playground of Europe* (London, 1871).
Stephen, L., 'The Study of English Literature', in Albert F. Blaisdell, ed., *The Study of English Literature: Three Essays* (Boston, 1902).
Stopford Green, A., *Irish Nationality* (London, 1908).

Swift MacNeill, J. G., *What I Have Seen and Heard* (London, 1925).
Symes, J. E., *The French Revolution* (London, 1892).
Tait, J., *British Borough Charters, 1216–1307* (Manchester, 1923).
Thelwall, J., *The Rights of Nature against the Usurpations of Establishments* (London, 1796).
Thorold Rogers, J. E., *Historical Gleanings: A Series of Sketches* (London, 1869).
Tone, W., *Writings of Theobald Wolfe Tone*, eds. T. W. Moody, and R. B. McDowell, 3 vols (Oxford, 1998–2007).
Tout, T. F., *The Collected Papers of Thomas Frederick Tout, with a Memoir and Bibliography*, 3 vols (Manchester, 1932–4).
Toynbee, A., *Lectures on the Industrial Revolution in England* (London, 1884).
Trollope, A., *The Eustace Diamonds* (London, 1872).
Vaughan, C. E., *Studies in the History of Political Philosophy Before and After Rousseau*, 2 vols (Manchester, 1925).
Vaughan, C. E., *The Political Writings of Rousseau*, 2 vols (Cambridge, 1915).
Vaughan, C. E., *The Romantic Revolt* (Edinburgh and London, 1907).
Walker, H., *The Literature of the Victorian Era* (Cambridge, 1910).
Wallas, G., *Human Nature in Politics* (London, 1908).
Walpole, S., *Life of Lord John Russell*, 2 vols (London, 1889).
Wingrove Cooke, G., *A History of Party, from the Rise of Whig and Tory Factions in the Reign of Charles II to the Passing of the Reform Bill* (London, 1836–7).
Wollstonecraft, M., *A Vindication of the Rights of Men*, 2nd edn (London, 1790).
Wordsworth, W., *The Prelude: The Four Texts (1798, 1799, 1805, 1850)*, ed. Jonathan Wordsworth (London, 2004).
Yeats, W. B., *The Collected Letters of W. B. Yeats*, eds. John Kelly and Ronald Schuchnard, 4 vols (Oxford, 1986–).
Yeats, W. B., *The Collected Works of W. B. Yeats*, eds. W. H. O'Donnell and D. N. Archibald, 14 vols (Basingstoke, 2002).

(vi) Miscellaneous Reports and Calendars

Calendar of the University College of Wales, Aberystwyth (Manchester, 1885).
Cambridge University Calendar for the Year 1884 (Cambridge, 1884).
Civil Service Commission, *Competitive Examination for the Indian Civil Service, held in India* (London, 1922–7).
Civil Service Commission, *Final Examination of Candidates Selected in [1896–1916] for the Civil Service of India, September [1898–1917]* (London, 1897–1917).
Levander, F. W., *Questions on History and Geography set at the Matriculation Examinations of the Oxford and Cambridge Examination Papers in English History, 1881 to 1890* (London, 1891).
Levander, F. W., *Questions on History and Geography set at the Matriculation Examinations of the University of London, 1844–1886*, 2nd edn (London, 1886).
Northern Matriculation Guide: The Universities of Manchester, Liverpool, Leeds, Sheffield (London, 1901).

Oxford University Examination for Women: Papers of the Examinations held in December 1883, and June 1884 (Oxford and London, 1884).

St David's College, Lampeter, *Calendar for the Year 1885* (Lampeter and London, 1885).

St David's College, Lampeter, *Calendar for the Year 1890* (Lampeter and London, 1890).

'*The Teaching of English in England*': *Report of the Departmental Committee Appointed by the President of the Board of Education to Inquire into the Position of English in the Educational System of England* (London, 1921).

University of Leeds Calendar (Leeds, 1904–16).

Victoria University Calendar (Manchester, 1886).

Victoria University of Manchester Calendars (Manchester, 1904–14).

University College, Liverpool Calendar (Liverpool, 1896 and 1903).

University of London, *School Examinations: Matriculation Standard and Higher Standard* (London, 1907–17).

University of Oxford Palmerston Club, *Rules and List of Members* (Oxford, 1891).

University Tutorial Series, *Matriculation Model Answers: Modern & English History, being the London University Matriculation Papers in English History from January 1896 to June 1902, and in Modern History of September 1902 to January 1904* (London, 1904).

University Tutorial Series/University Correspondence College, *Model Answers: English History and Geography, being the London University Matriculation Papers in English History and Geography from June 1888 to Jan 1894* (London, 1894).

4. PRINTED SECONDARY SOURCES

Adams, R. Q., *Bonar Law* (London, 1999).

Adcock, R., M. Bevir, and S. C. Stimson, eds., *Modern Political Science: Anglo American Exchanges since 1880* (Princeton and Oxford, 2007).

Altick, R., *The English Common Reader: A Social History of the Mass Reading Public, 1800–1900* (Chicago, 1957).

Anderson, R. D., 'University History Teaching, National Identity and Unionism in Scotland, 1862–1914', *Scottish Historical Review*, 91 (2012), pp. 1–41.

Annan, N., *Leslie Stephen: The Godless Victorian* (London, 1984).

Arnold, M., *Edmund Burke on Irish Affairs*, ed. C. C. O'Brien (London, 1988).

Auchmuty, J. J., *Lecky: A Biographical and Critical Essay* (Dublin and London, 1945).

Bacon, A., 'English Literature Becomes a University Subject: King's College, London as Pioneer', *VS*, 29 (1986), pp. 591–612.

Bayly, C. and E. Biagini, *Giuseppe Mazzini and the Globalisation of Democratic Nationalism, 1830–1920* (Oxford, 2008).

Beales, D., 'Edmund Burke and the Monasteries of France', *HJ*, 48 (2005), pp. 415–36.

Bebbington, D., *The Mind of Gladstone: Religion, Homer and Politics* (Oxford, 2004).

Bell, B., 'Beyond the Death of the Author: Matthew Arnold's Two Audiences, 1888–1930', *Book History*, 3 (2000), pp. 155–65.
Bell, D., *Reordering the World: Essays on Liberalism and Empire* (Princeton, 2016).
Ben-Israel, H., *English Historians on the French Revolution* (Cambridge, 1968).
Bennett, S., 'Catholic Emancipation, the "Quarterly Review", and Britain's Constitutional Revolution', *VS*, 12 (Mar. 1969), pp. 283–304.
Bentley, M., 'Liberal Toryism in the Twentieth-Century', *TRHS* 4, 6th ser. (1994), pp. 177–201.
Bentley, M., *Lord Salisbury's World: Conservative Environments in Late-Victorian Britain* (Cambridge, 2001).
Bentley, M., *The Climax of Liberal Politics: British Liberalism in Theory and Practice, 1868–1918* (London, 1987).
Bevir, M., 'A History of Modern Pluralism', in M. Bevir, ed., *Modern Pluralism: Anglo-American Exchanges since 1880* (Cambridge, 2012).
Bevir, M., 'On Tradition', *Humanitas*, 8 (2000), pp. 28–53.
Bevir, M., *The Making of British Socialism* (Princeton and Oxford, 2011).
Bew, P., *Ireland: The Politics of Enmity* (Oxford, 2009).
Biagini, E., *Liberty, Retrenchment and Reform: Popular Liberalism in the Age of Gladstone, 1860–1880* (Cambridge, 2004).
Bicknell, J. W., 'Leslie Stephen's *English Thought in the Eighteenth Century*: A Tract for the Times', *VS*, 6 (1962), pp. 103–20.
Blake, A., 'Writing from the Outside In: Charles Lever', in Neil McCaw, ed., *Writing Irishness in Nineteenth-Century British Culture* (Aldershot, 2004).
Blanning, T., *The Romantic Revolution* (London, 2011).
Boucher, D. and A. Vincent, *British Idealism and Political Theory* (Edinburgh, 2000).
Bourke, R., 'Burke, Enlightenment and Romanticism', in David Dwan and Christopher Insole, eds., *The Cambridge Companion to Edmund Burke* (Cambridge, 2012).
Bourke, R., 'Edmund Burke and the Politics of Conquest', *Modern Intellectual History*, 4 (2007), pp. 403–32.
Bourke, R., 'Party, Parliament and Conquest in Newly Ascribed Burke Manuscripts', *HJ*, 55 (2012), pp. 619–52.
Bourke, R., *Empire and Revolution: The Political Life of Edmund Burke* (Princeton, 2015).
Bourke, R., 'War Edmund Burke ein Konservativer? Notizen zum Begriff des Konservatismus', *Leviathan*, 44 (2016), pp. 65–96.
Bowra, M., *The Romantic Imagination* (Oxford, 1961).
Bromwich, D., *The Intellectual Life of Edmund Burke: From the Sublime and Beautiful to American Independence* (Cambridge, MA, 2014).
Browne, S. H., *Edmund Burke and the Discourse of Virtue* (Tuscaloosa, and London, 1993).
Brundage, A. and R. A. Cosgrove, *The Great Tradition: Constitutional History and National Identity in Britain and the United States, 1870–1960* (Stanford, 2007).

Burns, A. and J. Innes, eds., *Rethinking the Age of Reform: Britain 1780–1850* (Cambridge, 2003).
Burrow, J. W., *A History of Histories: Epics, Chronicles, Romances and Inquiries from Herodotus and Thucydides to the Twentieth Century* (London, 2007).
Burrow, J. W., *A Liberal Descent: Victorian Historians and the English Past* (Cambridge, 1983).
Burrow, J. W., *Evolution and Society: A Study in Victorian Social Thought* (Cambridge, 1966).
Burrow, J. W., *Whigs and Liberals: Continuity and Change in English Political Thought* (Oxford, 1988).
Campbell, J., *F. E. Smith, First Earl of Birkenhead* (London, 1983).
Canavan, F., *Edmund Burke: Prescription and Providence* (Durham, NC, 1987).
Canavan, F., *The Political Economy of Edmund Burke: The Role of Property in his Thought* (New York, 1995).
Canavan, F., *The Political Reason of Edmund Burke* (Cambridge, 1960).
Cannadine, D., 'The Context, Performance and Meaning of Ritual: The British Monarchy and the "Invention of Tradition", *c.*1820–1977', in Eric Hobsbawm and Terence Ranger, eds., *The Invention of Tradition* (Cambridge, 1983).
Catch, J. R., 'Edward John Payne: Victorian Gambist', *Galpin Society Journal*, 50 (Mar. 1997), pp. 127–35.
Cawood, I., *The Liberal Unionist Party* (London, 2012).
Cecily Steadman, F., *In the Days of Miss Beale: A Study of her Work and Influence* (London, 1931).
Chancellor, V. E., *History for their Masters. Opinion in the English History Textbook: 1800–1914* (Bath, 1970).
Clarke, P., *Liberals and Social Democrats* (Cambridge, 1981).
Coats, A. W., 'John Elliotson Symes, Henry George, and Academic Freedom in Nottingham During the 1880s', *British and American Essays*, 2 vols (London and New York, 1993).
Cobban, A., *Edmund Burke and the Revolt against the Eighteenth Century: A Study of the Political Thinking of Burke, Wordsworth, Coleridge and Southey* (London, 1929).
Colaiaco, J. A., *James Fitzjames Stephen and the Crisis of Victorian Thought* (London, 1983).
Collingwood, R. G., *An Autobiography* (London, 1939).
Collini, S., 'Idealism and "Cambridge Idealism"', *HJ*, 18 (1975), pp. 171–7.
Collini, S., 'Manly Fellows: Fawcett, Stephen, and the Liberal Temper', in Laurence Goldman, ed., *The Blind Victorian: Henry Fawcett and British Liberalism* (Cambridge, 1989).
Collini, S., *Public Moralists: Political Thought and Intellectual Life in Britain, 1860–1930* (Oxford, 1991).
Collini, S., D. Winch, and J. Burrow, *That Noble Science of Politics: A Study in Nineteenth-Century Intellectual History* (Cambridge, 1983).
Collini, S., 'The Idea of "Character" in Victorian Political Thought', *TRHS*, 5th ser., 35 (1985), pp. 29–50.

Collini, S., 'The Ordinary Experience of Civilized Life', in Bart Schultz, ed., *Essays on Henry Sidgwick* (Cambridge, 2002).
Coniff, J., *The Useful Cobbler: Edmund Burke and the Politics of Progress* (London, 1994).
Copeland, T. W., 'The Reputation of Edmund Burke', *JBS*, 1 (1962), 78–90.
Craig, D. M., 'Advanced Conservative Liberalism: Party and Principle in Trollope's Parliamentary Novels', *Victorian Literature and Culture*, 38 (2010), pp. 355–71.
Craig, D. M., 'Democracy and "National Character"', *HEI*, 29 (2003), pp. 493–501.
Craig, D. M., *Robert Southey and Romantic Apostasy: Political Argument in Britain, 1780–1840* (Woodbridge, 2007).
Craig, D. M., 'Statesmanship', in David Craig and James Thompson, eds., *Languages of Politics in Nineteenth-Century Britain* (Basingstoke, 2013).
Crossley, C. and I. Small, eds., *The French Revolution and British Culture* (Oxford, 1989).
Curtis, L. P., *Anglo-Saxon and Celts: A Study of Anti-Irish Prejudice in Victorian England* (Bridgeport, CT, 1968).
de Bellaigue, C., *Educating Women: Schooling and Identity in England and France, 1800–1867* (Oxford, 2007).
de Nie, M., 'Britannia's Sick Sister: Irish Identity and the British Press, 1798–1882', in Neil McCaw, ed., *Writing Irishness in Nineteenth-Century British Culture* (Aldershot, 2004).
Deane, S., 'Freedom Betrayed: Acton, Burke and Ireland', *Irish Review*, 30 (2003), pp. 13–35.
Deane, S., 'Lord Acton and Edmund Burke', *JHI*, 33 (1972), pp. 325–35.
den Otter, S., '"*Thinking in Communities*": Late Nineteenth-Century Liberals, Idealists and the Retrieval of Community', *Parliamentary History*, 16 (1997), pp. 67–84.
Dewey, C. J., *Anglo-Indian Attitudes: The Mind of the Civil Service* (London, 1993).
Dewey, C. J., '"Cambridge Idealism": Utilitarian Revisionists in Late Nineteenth-Century Cambridge', *HJ*, 17 (1974), pp. 63–78.
Dewey, C. J., 'The Education of a Ruling Caste: The Indian Civil Service in the Era of Competitive Examination', *EHR*, 88 (1973), pp. 262–85.
Donlan, S. P., 'Burke on Law and Legal Theory', in David Dwan and Christopher Insole, eds., *The Cambridge Companion to Edmund Burke* (Cambridge, 2012).
Dutton, D. J., 'The Unionist Party and Social Policy 1906–1914', *HJ*, 24 (1981), pp. 871–84.
Dwan, D. and C. Insole, eds., *The Cambridge Companion to Edmund Burke* (Cambridge, 2012).
Eagleton, T., *Figures of Dissent* (London, 2003).
Eagleton, T., 'Saving Burke from the Tories', *New Statesman* (4 July 1997), pp. 32–3.
Eccleshall, R., *English Conservatism since the Restoration* (London, 1990).

Edwards, O. D., 'Macaulay's Warren Hastings', in Geoffrey Carnall and Colin Nicholson, eds., *The Impeachment of Warren Hastings* (Edinburgh, 1989).
Ellegård, A., *The Readership of the Periodical Press in Mid-Victorian Britain* (Göteborg, 1957).
Emami, Z. and P. Olsen, *Engendering Economics* (London, 2004).
Engel, A. J., *From Clergyman to Don: The Rise of the Academic Profession in 19th-Century Oxford* (Oxford, 1983).
Finkelstein, D., 'Selling Blackwood's Magazine, 1817–1834', in Robert Morrison and Daniel S. Roberts, eds., *Romanticism and Blackwood's Magazine: 'An Unprecedented Phenomenon'* (Basingstoke, 2013).
Flint, K., *The Woman Reader, 1837–1914* (Oxford, 1995).
Foster, R. F., *Paddy and Mr Punch: Connections in English and Irish History* (London, 1993).
Foster, R. F., *W. B. Yeats: A Life*, 2 vols (Oxford, 1997).
Francis, M. and J. Morrow, *History of English Political Thought in the Nineteenth Century* (London, 1994).
Francis, M. and I. Zweininger-Bargielowska, eds., *The Conservatives and British Society* (Cardiff, 1996).
Freeden, M., *The New Liberalism: An Ideology of Social Reform* (Oxford, 1978).
Fuchs, M., *Edmund Burke, Ireland and the Fashioning of the Self* (Oxford, 1996).
Gandy, C. I., 'A Bibliographical Survey of Writings on Edmund Burke, 1945–75', *British Studies Monitor*, 8 (1978), pp. 3–21.
Gasquet, F. A., ed., *Lord Acton and His Circle* (London, 1906).
Ghosh, P., 'Gladstone and Peel', in P. Ghosh and L. Goldman, eds., *Politics and Culture in Victorian Britain: Essays in Memory of Colin Matthew* (Oxford, 2006), pp. 43–73.
Ghosh, P., 'Macaulay and the Heritage of the Enlightenment', *EHR*, 112, (1997), pp. 358–95.
Gibbons, L., *Edmund Burke and Ireland: Aesthetics, Politics and the Colonial Sublime* (Cambridge, 2003).
Gilley, S., 'English Attitudes to the Irish in England, 1780–1900', in C. Holmes, ed., *Immigrants and Minorities in British Society* (London, 1978).
Gilmartin, K., *Writing Against Revolution: Literary Conservatism in Britain, 1790–1832* (Cambridge, 2007).
Goldman, L., *Dons and Workers: Oxford and Adult Education since 1850* (Oxford, 1995).
Gordon, P. and J. White, *Philosophers as Educational Reformers: The Influence of Idealism on British Educational Thought and Practice* (London, 1979).
Green, E. H. H., *Ideologies of Conservatism: Conservative Political Ideas in the Twentieth Century* (Oxford, 2002).
Green, E. H. H., 'Radical Conservatism: The Electoral Genesis of Tariff Reform', *HJ*, 28 (1985), pp. 667–92.
Green, E. H. H., *The Crisis of Conservatism: The Politics, Economics and Ideology of the British Conservative Party, 1880–1914* (London and New York, 1995).

Green, J. A., 'Friedrich Gentz's Translation of Burke's Reflections', *HJ*, 57 (Sept. 2014), pp. 639–59.
Greenleaf, W. H., *The British Political Tradition*, 3 vols (London, 1983).
Hall, M., *Political Traditions and UK Politics* (Basingstoke, 2011).
Hall, W. E., *Dialogues in the Margin: A Study of the Dublin University Magazine* (Gerrards Cross, 2000).
Hamer, D., *John Morley: Liberal Intellectual in Politics* (Oxford, 1968).
Hammond, J. L., *Gladstone and the Irish Nation* (London, 1938; 1964).
Hampsher-Monk, I., 'Edmund Burke in the Tory World', in Jeremy Black, ed., *The Tory World* (London, 2016), 91–2.
Harris, J., 'Political Thought and the Welfare State, 1870–1940: An Intellectual Framework for British Social Policy', *Past and Present*, 135 (1994), pp. 116–41.
Harris, J., *Private Lives, Public Spirit: A Social History of Britain, 1870–1914* (Oxford, 1993).
Harvie, C., 'Ideology and Home Rule: James Bryce, A. V. Dicey, and Ireland, 1880–1887', *EHR*, 359 (1976), pp. 298–314.
Harvie, C., *The Lights of Liberalism: University Liberals and the Challenge of Democracy, 1860–1886* (London, 1976).
Hawkins, A., '"Parliamentary Government" and Victorian Political Parties c.1830–1880', *EHR*, 104 (1989), pp. 638–69.
Hawkins, A., *Victorian Political Culture: 'Habits of Heart and Mind'* (Oxford, 2015).
Hayek, F. A., *New Studies in Philosophy, Politics, Economics and the History of Ideas* (London, 1978).
Helburn, S., 'Burke and Keynes', in B. W. Bateman and J. B. Davis, eds., *Keynes and Philosophy: Essays on the Origin of Keynes' Thought* (Aldershot, 1991).
Hill, R., *Lord Acton* (New Haven, 2000).
Hilton, B. 'Peel: A Reappraisal', *HJ*, 22 (1979), pp. 585–614.
Himmelfarb, G., 'The American Revolution in the Political Theory of Lord Acton', *Journal of Modern History*, 21 (1949), pp. 293–312.
Hobsbawm, E., 'Mass-Producing Traditions: Europe, 1870-1914', in Eric Hobsbawm and Terence Ranger, eds., *The Invention of Tradition* (Cambridge, 1983).
Hobsbawm, E. and T. Ranger, eds., *The Invention of Tradition* (Cambridge, 1983).
Honderich, T., *Conservatism: Burke, Nozick, Bush, Blair?* (London, 2005).
Jackson, A., *Ireland, 1798–2008* (Oxford, 2010).
Jackson, D., *Popular Opposition to Irish Home Rule in Edwardian Britain* (Liverpool, 2009).
Jackson, P., *Morley of Blackburn: A Literary and Political Biography of John Morley* (Madison, 2012).
Jarrells, A., 'Tales of the Colonies: Blackwood's, Provincialism, and British Interests Abroad', in Robert Morrison and Daniel S. Roberts, eds., *Romanticism and Blackwood's Magazine: 'An Unprecedented Phenomenon'* (Basingstoke, 2013).
Jennings, B., *Albert Mansbridge: The Life and Work of the Founder of the WEA* (Leeds, 2002).
Jones, D. R., *The Origins of Civic Universities: Manchester, Leeds, and Liverpool* (London, 1988).

Jones, E., 'Drew Maciag: Edmund Burke in America', *History*, 99 (Apr. 2014), 399–41.
Jones, H. S., 'Education for Citizenship in Great Britain, c.1880–1944: The Renewal of a Civic Tradition', in Inge Botteri, Elena Riva, and Adolfo Scotto di Luzio, eds., *Fare il cittadino. La formazione di un nuovo soggetto sociale nell'Europa tra XIX et XXI secolo* (Soveria Mannelli, 2012).
Jones, H. S., *Intellect and Character in Victorian Britain: Mark Pattison and the Invention of the Don* (Cambridge, 2007).
Jones, H. S., 'John Stuart Mill as Moralist', *JHI*, 53 (1992), pp. 287–308.
Jones, H. S., 'The Idea of the National in Victorian Political Thought', *EJPT*, 5 (2006), pp. 12–21.
Jones, H. S., *Victorian Political Thought* (Basingstoke, 2000).
Kadish, A., *Apostle Arnold: The Life and Death of Arnold Toynbee* (Durham, NC, 1986).
Kearney, A., 'Leslie Stephen and the English Studies Debate, 1886–87', *History of Education Society Bulletin* 43 (1989), pp. 41–7.
Kent, C., *Brains and Numbers: Elitism, Comtism, and Democracy in Mid-Victorian England* (Toronto, 1978).
Kijinski, J., 'John Morley's "English Men of Letters" Series and the Politics of Reading', *VS*, 34 (1991), pp. 205–25.
Kirby, J., *Historians and the Church of England: Religion and Historical Scholarship, 1870–1920* (Oxford, 2016).
Kirk, R., *The Conservative Mind* (London, 1954).
Kirk, R., 'The Foreboding Conservatism of Stephen', *Western Political Quarterly*, 5 (Dec. 1952), pp. 563–77.
Kitson Clark, G., *Peel and the Conservative Party* (London, 1929).
Koss, S. E., *John Morley and the India Office, 1905–1910* (New Haven, 1969).
Kramnick, I., 'The Left and Edmund Burke', *Political Theory*, 11 (1983), pp. 189–214.
Kramnick, I., *The Rage of Edmund Burke: Portrait of an Ambivalent Conservative* (New York, 1977).
Krishnamurthy, A., ed., *The Working-Class Intellectual in Eighteenth- and Nineteenth-Century Britain* (Farnham, 2009).
Lambert, E. R., *Edmund Burke of Beaconsfield* (Newark and London, 2003).
Lang, T., *The Victorians and the Stuart Heritage* (Cambridge, 1995).
Laprade, W. T., 'Edmund Burke: An Adventure in Reputation', *Journal of Modern History*, 32 (1960), pp. 321–32.
Lawrence, J., 'Class and Gender in the Making of Urban Toryism' *EHR*, 428 (1993), pp. 629–52.
Ledger, S. and S. McCracken, eds., *Cultural Politics at the Fin de Siècle* (Cambridge, 1995).
Lightman, B., 'The Creed of Science and its Critics', in Martin Hewitt, ed., *The Victorian World* (London, 2012).
Lippincott, B. E., 'James Fitzjames Stephen: Critic of Democracy', *Economica*, 33 (Aug. 1931), pp. 296–307.

Lippincott, B. E., *Victorian Critics of Democracy* (London, 1938).
Livingston, J. C., 'The Religious Creed and Criticism of Sir James Fitzjames Stephen', *VS*, 17 (1974), pp. 279–300.
Lock, F. P., *Burke's Reflections on the Revolution in France* (London, 1985).
Lock, F. P., *Edmund Burke*, 2 vols (Oxford, 2008–9).
Loughlin, J., *Gladstone and the Ulster Question, 1882–1893* (Dublin, 1986).
Lubenow, W. C., *The Cambridge Apostles, 1820–1914: Liberalism, Imagination, and Friendship in British Intellectual and Professional Life* (Cambridge, 1998).
McBride, I., 'Burke and Ireland', in David Dwan and Christopher Insole, eds., *The Cambridge Companion to Edmund Burke* (Cambridge, 2012).
McCartney, D., *W. E. H. Lecky: Historian and Politician, 1838–1903* (Dublin, 1994).
Machin, G. I. T., *Politics and the Churches in Great Britain, 1832–68* (Oxford, 1977).
Maciag, D., *Edmund Burke in America: The Contested Career of the Father of Modern Conservatism* (New York, 2013).
McMurty, J., *English Language, English Literature: The Creation of an Academic Discipline* (Hamden, CT., 1985).
Macpherson, C. B., *Burke* (Oxford, 1980).
Mahoney, C. H., 'Women's Education, Edward Dowden, and the University Curriculum in English Literature: An Unlikely Progression', in Margaret Kelleher and James H. Murphy, eds., *Gender Perspectives in Nineteenth-Century Ireland* (Dublin, 1997).
Mandler, P., ' "Race" and "Nation" in Mid-Victorian Thought', in Stefan Collini, Richard Whatmore, and Brian Young, eds., *History, Religion, Culture: British Intellectual History, 1750–1950* (Cambridge, 2000).
Mandler, P., *The English National Character: The History of an Idea from Edmund Burke to Tony Blair* (New Haven, 2006).
Marsh, P., *The Discipline of Popular Government: Lord Salisbury's Domestic Statecraft, 1881–1902* (Hassocks, 1978).
Marsh, P., *Joseph Chamberlain: Entrepreneur in Politics* (New Haven, 1994).
Matthew, H. C. G., *Gladstone, 1809–1898* (Oxford, 1997).
Matthew, H., R. McKibbin, and J. Kay, 'The Franchise Factor and the Rise of Labour', *EHR*, 91 (1976), pp. 723–52.
Maume, P., 'Burke in Belfast: Thomas Macknight, Gladstone and Liberal Unionism', in D. G. Boyce and Alan O'Day, eds., *Gladstone and Ireland: Politics, Religion and Nationality in the Victorian Age* (London, 2010).
Mehta, U. S., *Liberalism and Empire: A Study in Nineteenth-Century British Liberal Thought* (Chicago, 1999).
Melman, B., *The Culture of History: English Uses of the Past, 1800–1953* (Oxford, 2006).
Mitchell, R., *Picturing the Past: English History in Text and Image 1830–1870* (Oxford, 2000).
Mitchie, M., *An Enlightenment Tory in Victorian Scotland: The Career of Sir Archibald Alison* (Montreal, 1997).

Morrow, J., *Coleridge's Political Thought* (Basingstoke, 1990).
Nally, C., *Envisioning Ireland: W. B. Yeats' Occult Nationalism* (Oxford, 2010).
Neill, E., 'Conceptions of Citizenship in Twentieth-Century Britain', *Twentieth Century British History*, 17 (2006), pp. 424–38.
Neill, E., 'Evolutionary Theory and British Idealism: The Case of D. G. Ritchie', *History of European Ideas*, 29 (2003), pp. 313–38.
Norman, J., *Edmund Burke: Philosopher, Politician, Prophet* (London, 2013).
O'Brien, C. C., 'Setting People on Thinking: Burke's Legacy in the Debate on Irish Affairs', in Ian Crowe, ed., *Edmund Burke: His Life and Legacy* (Dublin, 1997).
O'Brien, C. C., *The Great Melody: A Thematic Biography of Edmund Burke* (London, 1992).
O'Gorman, F., *British Conservatism from Burke to Thatcher* (London and New York, 1986).
O'Gorman, F., *Edmund Burke: His Political Philosophy* (London, 1973).
O'Gorman, F., *The Rise of Party in England: The Rockingham Whigs 1760–1782* (London, 1975).
O'Keeffe, D., *Edmund Burke* (New York, 2010).
Palmer, D. J., 'English', in M. G. Brock and M. C. Curthoys, eds., *The History of the University of Oxford: Volume VII, Part 2* (Oxford, 2000).
Palmer, D. J., *The Rise of English Studies* (Oxford, 1965).
Parker, J., 'The Dragon and The Raven: Saxons, Danes and the Problem of Defining National Character in Victorian England', *European Journal of English Studies*, 13 (2009), pp. 257–73.
Parry, J. P., *Democracy and Religion: Gladstone and the Liberal Party, 1867–1875* (Cambridge, 1986).
Parry, J. P., 'Disraeli and England', *HJ*, 43 (2000), pp. 699–728.
Parry, J. P., 'The Impact of Napoleon III on British Politics, 1851–1880', *TRHS*, 6th ser., 11 (2001), pp. 147–75.
Parry, J. P., *The Politics of Patriotism: English Liberty, National Identity, and Europe, 1830–1886* (Cambridge, 2006).
Parry, J. P., *The Rise and Fall of Liberal Government in Victorian Britain* (New Haven and London, 1993).
Parsons, F. D., *Thomas Hare and Political Representation in Victorian Britain* (London, 2009).
Paz, D. G., 'Anti-Catholicism, Anti-Irish Stereotyping, and Anti-Celtic Racism in Mid-Victorian Working-Class Periodicals', *Albion*, 18 (1986), pp. 601–16.
Paz, D. G., *Popular Anti-Catholicism in Mid-Victorian England* (Stanford, 1992).
Pereiro, J., 'The Reformation and the Principles of the English Constitution in Disraeli's "Young England" Novels', *Bulletin of the John Rylands Library*, 90 (2014), pp. 323–43.
Pickering, M., *Auguste Comte: An Intellectual Biography*, 3 vols (Cambridge, 2009).
Pilling, N., 'Lecky and Dicey: English and Irish Histories', *Éire-Ireland*, 16 (1981), pp. 43–56.
Pinto-Duschinsky, M., *The Political Thought of Lord Salisbury, 1858–1868* (London, 1967).

Pocock, J. G. A., *Politics, Language, and Time: Essays on Political Thought and History* (Chicago and London, 1971).

Pocock, J. G. A., *Virtue, Commerce and History: Essays on Political Thought and History, Chiefly in the Eighteenth Century* (Cambridge, 1985).

Portsmouth, R., *John Wilson Croker: Irish Ideas and the Invention of Modern Conservatism, 1800–1835* (Dublin, 2010).

Preece, R., 'Edmund Burke and his European Reception', *The Eighteenth Century*, 21 (1980), pp. 255–73.

Pugh, M., *Lloyd George* (London, 1988).

Pugh, M., *The Tories and the People, 1880–1935* (Oxford, 1985).

Readman, P., 'The Place of the Past in English Culture, c.1890–1914', *Past and Present*, 186 (2005), pp. 147–99.

Rempel, R. A., 'Lord Hugh Cecil's Parliamentary Career, 1900–1914: Promise Unfulfilled', *JBS*, 11 (1972), pp. 104–30.

Ritchie, D. E., 'Burke's Influence on the Imagination of Walter Bagehot', *Modern Age* (Fall 1989), pp. 324–8.

Ritchie, D. E., *Edmund Burke: Appraisals and Applications* (New Brunswick and London, 1990).

Roach, J., 'Liberalism and the Victorian Intelligentsia', *HJ*, 8 (1957), pp. 71–88.

Roberts, A., *Salisbury: Victorian Titan* (London, 1999).

Robin, C., *The Reactionary Mind: Conservatism from Edmund Burke to Sarah Palin* (Oxford, 2011).

Robinson, N. K., *Edmund Burke: A Life in Caricature* (New Haven and London, 1996).

Rodner, W. S., 'Conservatism, Resistance and Lord Hugh Cecil', *HPT*, 9 (1988), pp. 529–51.

Rogers, E., '1688 and 1888: Victorian Society and the Bicentenary of the Glorious Revolution', *JBS*, 50 (2011), pp. 892–916.

Romani, R., 'British Views on Irish National Character, 1800–1846: An Intellectual History', *HEI*, 23 (1998), pp. 193–219.

Romani, R., *National Character and Public Spirit in Britain and France, 1750–1914* (Cambridge, 2004).

Root, J. D., 'The Philosophical and Religious Thought of Arthur James Balfour (1848–1930)', *JBS*, 19 (1980), pp. 120–41.

Rose, J., 'Re-reading the English Common Reader: A Preface to the History of Audiences', *JHI*, 53 (1992), pp. 47–70.

Rose, J., *The Intellectual Life of the British Working Classes* (New Haven and London, 2001).

Rowbotham, S., 'Travellers in a Strange Country: Responses of Working Class Students to the University Extension Movement, 1873–1910', *History Workshop Journal*, 12 (1981), pp. 62–95.

Sack, J. J., 'Edmund Burke and the Conservative Party', in Ian Crowe, ed., *Edmund Burke: His Life and Legacy* (Dublin, 1997).

Sack, J. J., *From Jacobite to Conservative: Reaction and Orthodoxy in Britain, c.1760–1832* (Cambridge, 1993).

Sack, J. J., 'The Memory of Pitt and the Memory of Burke: English Conservatism Confronts its Past, 1806–1829', *HJ*, 30 (1987), pp. 623–40.

Samuel, R., *Island Stories: Unravelling Britain*, ed. Alison Light (London, 1998).

Saunders, R., *Democracy and the Vote in British Politics, 1848–1867: The Making of the Second Reform Act* (Farnham, 2011).

Saunders, R., 'Parliament and People: The British Constitution in the Long Nineteenth Century', *Journal of Modern European History*, 6 (2008), 72–87.

Schultz, B., *Henry Sidgwick—Eye of the Universe: An Intellectual Biography* (Cambridge, 2004).

Semmel, B., 'H. T. Buckle: The Liberal Faith and the Science of History', *British Journal of Sociology*, 27 (1976), pp. 370–86.

Shannon, R., *The Age of Salisbury, 1881–1902* (London, 1996).

Shields, A., *The Irish Conservative Party, 1852–1868: Land, Politics, and Religion* (Dublin, 2007).

Shimmin, A. N., *The University of Leeds: The First Half Century* (Cambridge, 1954).

Skidelsky, R., *John Maynard Keynes*, 3 vols (London, 1983–2001).

Skinner, S., 'Religion', in David Craig and James Thompson, eds., *Languages of Politics in Nineteenth-Century Britain* (Basingstoke, 2013).

Skinner, S., *Tractarians and the 'Condition of England': The Social and Political Thought of the Oxford Movement* (Oxford, 2004).

Slee, P. R. H., *Learning and a Liberal Education: The Study of Modern History in the Universities of Oxford, Cambridge, and Manchester, 1800–1914* (Manchester, 1986).

Smith, R. J., *The Gothic Bequest: Medieval Institutions in British Thought, 1688–1863* (Cambridge, 1987).

Smyth, J., 'Lewis Namier, Herbert Butterfield and Edmund Burke', *Journal of Eighteenth Century Studies*, 35 (2012), pp. 381–9.

Spangenberg, B., 'The Problem of Recruitment for the Indian Civil Service during the Late-Nineteenth Century', *Journal of Asian Studies*, 30 (1971), pp. 341–60.

Spence, J., 'Isaac Butt, Irish Nationality and the Conditional Defence of the Union, 1833–70', in D. G. Boyce and Alan O'Day, eds., *Defenders of the Union: A Survey of British and Irish Unionism since 1801* (London, 2001).

Stanlis, P., *Edmund Burke and the Natural Law* (Ann Arbor, 1958).

Stanlis, P., 'Edmund Burke in the Twentieth Century', in P. Stanlis, ed., *The Relevance of Edmund Burke* (New York, 1964).

Stapleton, J., *Englishness and the Study of Politics: The Social and Political Thought of Ernest Barker* (Cambridge, 2006).

Stapleton, J., 'James Fitzjames Stephen: Liberalism, Patriotism, and English Liberty', *VS*, 41 (1998), pp. 243–63.

Steele, G. R., *Keynes and Hayek* (London, 2002).

Stewart, R., *The Foundation of the Conservative Party, 1830–1867* (London, 1978).

Stone, D., 'The Extremes of Englishness: The Exceptional Ideology of Antony Mario Ludovici', *Journal of Political Ideologies*, 4 (1999), pp. 191–218.

Sutcliffe, M. P., *Victorian Radicals and Italian Democrats* (London, 2014).

Swart, K., 'Individualism in the Mid-Nineteenth Century', *JHI*, 13 (1962), pp. 77–90.
Taylor, A. J., 'History at Leeds, 1877–1974: The Evolution of a Discipline', *Northern History*, 10 (1975), pp. 141–64.
Taylor, M. W., *Men versus the State: Herbert Spencer and Late Victorian Individualism* (Oxford, 1992).
Taylor, R., *Lord Salisbury* (London, 1975).
Thomas, W., *The Quarrel of Macaulay and Croker: Politics and History in an Age of Reform* (Oxford, 2000).
Thompson, F., *Candleford Green* (London, 1943).
Tomko, M., *British Romanticism and the Catholic Question: Religion, History and National Identity, 1778–1829* (Basingstoke, 2011).
Torchiana, D. T., *W. B. Yeats and Georgian Ireland* (Washington, DC, 1992).
Tosh, J., 'Gentlemanly Politeness and Manly Simplicity in Victorian England', *TRHS*, 6th ser., 12 (2002), pp. 455–72.
Trevor-Roper, H., 'The Invention of a Tradition: The Highland Tradition of Scotland', in Eric Hobsbawm and Terence Ranger, eds., *The Invention of Tradition* (Cambridge, 1983).
Varouxakis, G., 'National Character in John Stuart Mill's Thought', *HEI*, 24 (1998), pp. 375–91.
Varouxakis, G., '"Patriotism", "Cosmopolitanism", and "Humanity" in Victorian Political Thought', *EJPT*, 5 (2006), pp. 100–18.
Varouxakis, G., *Victorian Political Thought on France and the French* (Basingstoke, 2002).
Vincent, A., *Modern Political Ideologies*, 3rd edn (Oxford, 2010).
Von Arx, J. P., *Progress and Pessimism: Religion, Politics, and History in Late Nineteenth-Century Britain* (Cambridge, MA, 1985).
Wallace, E., *Goldwin Smith: Victorian Liberal* (Toronto, 1957).
Wallace, N., 'Matthew Arnold, Edmund Burke, and Irish Reconciliation', *Prose Studies: History, Theory, Criticism*, 34 (2012), pp. 197–223.
Watson, G., *The English Ideology: Studies in the Language of Victorian Politics* (London, 1973).
Wheeler, M., *The Old Enemies: Catholic and Protestant in Nineteenth-Century English Culture* (Cambridge, 2006).
White, H. O., *Edward Dowden, 1843–1913: An Address Delivered in the Chapel of Trinity College, Dublin* (Dublin, 1943).
Whyte, W., *Redbrick: A Social and Architectural History of Britain's Civic Universities* (Oxford, 2015).
Williams, R., 'The Organic Society', in D. E. Ritchie, ed., *Edmund Burke: Appraisals and Applications* (New Brunswick and London, 1990).
Williamson, P., 'Review: Ideologies of Conservatism', *EHR*, 475 (Feb 2003), pp. 270–1.
Williamson, P., *Stanley Baldwin: Conservative Leadership and National Values* (Cambridge, 1999).

Wilson, J., 'The Silence of Empire: Imperialism and Empire', in David Craig and James Thompson, eds., *Languages of Politics in Nineteenth-Century Britain* (Basingstoke, 2013).
Winstanley, D. A., *Later Victorian Cambridge* (Cambridge, 1947).
Wolffe, J., *God and Greater Britain: Religion and National Life in Britain and Ireland, 1843–1945* (London, 1994).
Wolffe, J., *The Protestant Crusade in Great Britain, 1829–1860* (Oxford, 1991).
Wright, T. R., *The Religion of Humanity: the Impact of Comtean Positivism on Victorian Britain* (Cambridge, 1986).
Yeats, W. B., 'Samhaim' [1904], in Georgie Yeats, ed., *Explorations* (London, 1962).
Young, B. W., *The Victorian Eighteenth Century* (Oxford, 2007).
Young, G. M., 'The Greatest Victorian', *Victorian Essays* (Oxford, 1962).
Zink, D. D., *Leslie Stephen* (New York, 1972).

5. THESES

Green, J. A., 'Edmund Burke's German Readers at the End of Enlightenment, 1790–1815' (PhD thesis, University of Cambridge, 2017).
Honda, T., 'Indian Civil Servants, 1892–1937: An Age of Transition' (DPhil thesis, University of Oxford, 1996).
McCarthy, J. P., 'Gladstone's Irish Questions: An Historical Approach, 1830–1886' (DPhil thesis, University of Oxford, 2010).
Peters, J. N., 'Anti-Socialism in British Politics c.1900–22: The Emergence of a Counter-Ideology' (DPhil thesis, University of Oxford, 1992).
Pilling, N., 'The Reception of the Major Works of W. E. H. Lecky, 1865–1896' (MPhil thesis, University College, London, 1978).
Sidney, H. Z., 'Inventing Burke: Edmund Burke and the Conservative Party, 1790–1918', (MA thesis, City University of New York, 2014).
Spence, J., 'The Philosophy of Irish Toryism, 1833–1852' (PhD thesis, University of London, 1991).

6. RADIO SOURCES

McElvoy, A., 'Conservatism: The Grand Tour', first broadcast on BBC Radio 4, Sept. 2013.

Index

Act of Union (1801) 196
  and Burke 128, 131, 134, 142
  and the Home Rule Bill (1886) 115–16, 124–5, 136, 140
Acton, Lord 200
  on Burke's Catholicism 45–6, 51–2
  on Burke's consistency 29, 37, 212
  on the French Revolution 211–12
Alison, Archibald 38
Althorp, John Charles, 3rd Earl 33
America, *see* United States
Amery, Leo 182
Amos, Sheldon 26–7
Anti-Catholicism:
  and Irishness 44, 47–8, 137–8
  and nonconformity 142
  at the *fin de siècle* 52, 80
  'Rome Rule', fears of 119, 120, 136
  see also Catholic emancipation; Catholicism; Penal Code, the
Argyll, Duke of 136, 138–9
Arnold, Matthew 79, 82, 85, 91–2, 113
  'Essay on the Function of Criticism' 64–5, 96 n. 79
  and Irish Home Rule 118–19, 121, 128 n. 52, 135, 136, 140–1
  his Liberalism 5, 118
  influence of 66 n. 43, 200, 210
  Irish Affairs 13, 114, 115, 116, 118
  on church establishment 49–50
  On the Study of Celtic Literature 65–6, 118
  recollection of Disraeli on Burke 43
Arnold, Thomas 85, 193
  influence of 106, 108
  on church establishment 49–50
Asquith, H. H. 152
autodidacticism 219, 223–6
  access to books 224–5
  Burke, cheap editions of 13, 223–4, 225–6
  evening classes 215
  Home University Library 187
  see also education; Indian Civil Service; university extension

Bagehot, Walter 16–17, 39
Balfour, Arthur James 152–3, 183–4, 186
Ball, Sidney 171
Barker, Ernest 167, 169
Baumann, A. A. 180, 184–6, 190, 195
Beale, Dorothea 202, 203–4
Beesly, E. S. 83–4
Bentham, Jeremy 86, 156, 169
  and late-nineteenth century utilitarianism 162
  compared to Burke 21, 63–4, 69, 89, 102–3, 175
  criticism of 171
  see also utilitarianism
Birrell, Augustine 45, 56, 70–2, 77
Blackwood's Magazine 36 n. 94, 54, 180
Bolingbroke, Henry St John, 1st Viscount 184
  and Disraeli 41–2
  his Toryism 170, 173, 178, 191–2, 193
  in education 218
Bonar Law, Andrew 183, 184
Boutwood, Arthur 191
Bradlaugh, Charles 101, 151
Brewer, J. S. 37, 42
Bright, John 121, 149, 192, 193
British Constitution, the, *see* constitutionalism, English
British Idealism, *see* Idealism
Broad, C. D. 189
Brodrick, George 26–7
Brougham, Henry, 1st baron 29–30, 83 n. 7, 98
Bryce, James 51, 120–1, 215
Buchan, John 225–6
Buckle, Henry Thomas 90, 98, 104
  on Burke's madness 30, 75–6, 81–2
Burke, Edmund, aspects of his thought:
  as political theory 163–4, 168–77
  as providential 97, 104, 168–9
  bipartisanship 53–4
  consistency 81, 96–7, 98, 102, 130, 143, 163–5, 165, 209, 212
  empiricism 96–8, 103–4
  imagination 68
  imperialism 190
  'little platoons' 161, 199, 232
  prophecy 60
  providence 97, 104
  virtual representation 175
  wisdom 59–67, 81

Burke, Edmund, his conservatism 103, 105–7, 110, 113, 156, 163–4
 as maintenance of institutions 101, 105, 170–1, 173
 as organicist 167, 176–7
 as religious 168–9, 173, 175
 in Cold War context 3–4, 230
 in education 205, 208–9, 218–19, 225–6
 in modern scholarship 1–2, 231
Burke, Edmund, his Conservatism 157, 208–9, 225–6
 as 'Liberal Conservatism' 96, 209
 after Home Rule 154–5
 and Lord Salisbury 143–4
 and the French Revolution 179–81
 in broader Conservative tradition 177–9, 181–2
 in Conservative texts 182–94
Burke, Edmund, life and personal character:
 his 'madness' 1, 29, 73–8
 his modern appeal 232–3
 his moral character 82, 107–12
 literary reputation 52–5, 63, 67, 71, 74, 77, 94
 material commemorations of 194
 potted biography of 2–3
Burke, Edmund, works of:
 Abridgement of English History 20
 American speeches on conciliation and taxation (1774–5) 2, 12, 81, 95
  and Burke's challenge to rights of taxation 103
  and Burke's foresight 60
  as a textbook 204–5, 206
  as English literature 215
  Conservative use of 153, 187
  in education 203, 211, 214, 217, 223
  in the 1832 reform debates 33
  in the argument against Home Rule 137, 143, 153–4
  in the argument for Home Rule 115, 122–4, 129, 130, 132, 153–4
 Appeal from the New to the Old Whigs 12, 77, 96, 100, 146, 148–9, 164–5, 170, 225
 Bristol speeches (1774–80) 24–5, 124, 126, 143, 150, 152, 153, 186
 cheap editions 13, 223–6
 collected works 12
 correspondence 12
 Indian writings and speeches 2, 12, 70, 118–19
 Irish letters and speeches 117–18, 122–4, 139

 Letters on a Regicide Peace 12, 74, 95, 101, 147–8, 206, 217, 223, 225
 Letter to a Noble Lord 74, 77
 On the Origins of the Sublime and Beautiful 2, 12, 74, 223
 Thoughts and Details on Scarcity 12, 42
 Thoughts on the Cause of the Present Discontents 2, 12, 81, 95
  and party government 23, 28–30, 60, 150
  and royal prerogative 28–29, 34, 37
  as a textbook 204, 208
  Disraeli on 41–2
  in education 211, 218–19, 222, 223, 227
 Reflections on the Revolution in France 8, 12, 33, 81, 95
  and church establishment 50, 51
  and constitutionalism 19, 20, 27, 28, 29, 52
  and Liberal Unionism 142–3
  and liberty 136
  and the study of the French Revolution 199, 212, 214, 216–18, 223, 227
  and 'the historical method' 174
  as C/conservative 37 n. 97, 106, 107, 179, 180, 188, 192, 196, 225–6
  as English literature 215
  as political thought 96, 99, 101, 168, 170
  as a textbook 197, 204–8
  criticism of 78
  immediate influence of 64, 74
  on France 60
 Sketch of a Negro Code 70
 Vindication of Natural Society 2, 12
Burke, Thomas Haviland 34
Burrows, Montagu 54, 112
Butler, Geoffrey 159, 182, 192, 195
 The Tory Tradition 193–4
Butler, Henry Montagu 192
Butler, J. R. M. 192
Butler, Josephine 16
Butler, R. A. 192
Butt, Isaac 117

Caird, Edward 161, 173, 198
Cambridge, University of 87, 192, 200, 202, 211
 student numbers 214
 see also education; university extension
Canada 115
Canning, George 32, 192, 193
 his Toryism 13, 18, 35

Index

Carpenter, Bishop William Boyd 114, 153
Catholic emancipation 25, 35–7, 38, 50, 73
 Burke's support of 43, 45, 51
 see also anti-Catholicism; Catholicism
Catholicism 43–4, 132
 and Burke's political thought 45–8, 51, 91
 Burke's attitude towards 37, 43–9, 55, 110, 126
 Burke's perceived 43–4, 48, 58, 78, 92
 see also anti-Catholicism; Catholic emancipation
Cecil, Lord Hugh 4 n. 12, 159, 182, 194, 195
 Conservatism 143–4, 187–90
 Hughligans 186–7
Chamberlain, Joseph 140, 141, 152, 186, 187
 Burke, use of 133–4, 142, 148–9
Childers, Hugh 125–6
Christian Socialism 14, 26, 65
 see also Liberal Anglicanism
Churchill, Lord Randolph 153, 178
Churchill, Winston 186
Church establishment 14, 43, 106, 147
 and Burke 49–52, 104–5, 117–18, 173
 Church of England 50–1
 Church of Ireland 38, 51, 132
 disestablishment of the Irish Church 14, 48–9, 117–18, 121
 Thirty-Nine Articles 104
 see also Penal Code, the
Cicero 54, 100, 203
civic universities 212–18
 see also Leeds, University of; Liverpool, University of; Manchester, University of; Victoria University, the
Cobbett, William 31
Cobden, Richard 75 n. 79, 149
Coleridge, S. T. 49, 85
 compared to Burke 50, 68 n. 49, 106, 191–2
 on Burke 60, 68, 72–3
Collins, John Churton 203, 221–2
Comte, Auguste 86, 89, 90
 see also Positivism, English
Congreve, Richard 84
 see also Positivism, English
conservatism:
 and inequality 18, 170, 183
 and organicism 189, 193–4
 and property 170, 173, 185, 189, 190, 196

and religion 183, 189, 191, 196
 as separate from Conservatism 186–90
Conservative party 24
 and Burke's madness 76–7
 and Home Rule 117, 143–4
 and royal prerogative 23–4, 37, 170–1, 175
 and the constitution 18–19
 and the search for new ideas 177–82
 Burke, use of 81, 136, 151–3
 Liberal Unionists, impact of 140, 145, 148–50, 154, 159
 'One Nation Conservatism' 232
 'Tory Democracy' and social reform 178, 185–6, 191
 see also conservatism; Disraeli, Benjamin; Liberal Unionism; Peel, Sir Robert; Toryism
constitutionalism, English 6, 16–17, 42
 and Burke 28, 40, 67, 101–2, 106, 142, 176
 and Home Rule 123, 128, 141, 142, 154
 and philosophic radicalism 64
 'catholic' constitutionalism 46, 52
 constitutional crisis (1909–14) 157–8, 185, 195–6
 constitutional politics after 1885 157–9
 criticism of unicameral government 144
 'paper constitutions' 99
 party government 22–3
 see also Glorious Revolution (1688); parliamentary reform; parliamentary sovereignty
Cooke, George Wingrove 35
Cornewall Lewis, George 20, 60
Cornhill Magazine 87
Creasy, E. S. 27
Creighton, Mandell 22
Croker, John Wilson 13
 use of Burke 33, 35–6, 38
Croly, George 13, 22–4, 35–7, 38

Dale, R. W. 141–2
Derby, Edward, 14th earl of 153
Dicey, A. V. 6 n. 17, 114, 123, 133 n. 71, 144
 and Liberal Unionism 135, 143, 147–8, 151
 his utilitarianism 89, 162
 on Burke 143, 147–8, 151
 on Lecky 119–20
 on parliamentary sovereignty 115

Disraeli, Benjamin, 1st earl of
    Beaconsfield 8, 14, 18, 153,
    177, 186
  and 'Conservative statism' 178, 232
  compared to Burke 42 n. 123,
    184–6, 233
  on Burke 38, 39–43, 54, 63
  posthumous reception 191, 192, 193,
    232–3
Dowden, Edward 82, 86, 135, 174
  and English literature 212–13, 224
  interest in the French Revolution 210
  on Burke 63–4, 167–9
Dublin University Magazine 117

Edinburgh Review 30, 57
education:
  evening classes 215
  examinations 208–9, 210–11, 214–15,
    216, 217–19
  Newbolt report (1921) 209
  of women and girls 202, 203–4
  'school of statesmanship' 202–3
  school text-books 202, 204–9
  university education 161, 164
  see also autodidacticism; English
    literature, study of; history, study
    of; Indian Civil Service
Eliot, George 67
Empire, British:
  and Burke 110–11, 126, 132, 190
  and education 198, 204
  and Irish Home Rule 124, 129,
    135, 141
  and the ethics of empire 110
  in high politics 159
  see also Indian Civil Service; Hastings,
    Warren
empiricism 89, 90, 98, 103–4, 112
  political expediency 94, 96–7
  see also utilitarianism
Engels, Friedrich 59
English literature, study of 197
  and Idealism 198–9
  and university extension 221–2
  as historical 199–200
  at school 203–4
  at university 212–14, 216–17
  see also education; Romanticism
Englishness 56–8
  and antipathy to thought 65–6, 118
  and Burke's 'madness' 73–4
  and empiricism 102, 112
  and political wisdom 63–4, 69
  see also Irishness; national character

Europe:
  reception of Burke 7–8, 46–7, 91,
    100–1, 107
  revolutions (1848–9) 92
Everyman's Classics, *see* Burke, Edmund,
  works of: cheap editions

Feiling, Keith 182, 191–2
Figgis, J. N. 166, 216
Fortnightly Review 14, 87–8, 90
Fox, Charles James 71, 93, 137, 172
  1783 India Bill 220
  as a 'Liberal' 181, 208
  compared to Burke 2, 109, 130
  in education 222
  in Home Rule debates 145–7,
    150–1, 153
  on Burke 74–5
Fox, Henry 70–1
French Revolution (1789) 2, 51, 90, 97,
    99–100
  and English literature 167–8
  and liberty 32
  and party politics 24, 29–30, 41,
    144–8, 150, 179–81
  and Positivism 84, 85
  impact on Burke's state of mind 68,
    74–5
  impact on Burke's thought 64–5, 71,
    101, 205, 206
  importance in British politics
    34–5, 137
  in education 21, 197, 210, 221–3, 227
  Peel's interest in 38
  see also Burke, Edmund, works of:
    Reflections; Jacobinism;
    Romanticism
Froude, J. A. 48, 80

Gardiner, S. R. 221
Gaelic Revival Movement 78–80, 133
Gladstone, W. E. 150, 151, 152
  Burke, early reading of 29
  criticism of 137, 138, 146
  Home Rule, conversion to 82, 91,
    115, 192
  Home Rule, use of Burke in support
    of 114, 116, 121, 122–34
  influence of Burke on 8, 122–3, 143
  on Burke and disestablishment
    48–9
  on Burke and the 1832 Reform Act
    32, 34
  on Lecky 120
  praise of 14

Glasgow, University of 161
Glorious Revolution (1688–9) 20 n. 19,
    181 n. 137, 195–6
  and Burke 26–8, 45, 163, 166, 177
  criticism of 46, 51
  see also constitutionalism, English
Godwin, William 63–4, 84, 156
Graham, William 64, 174, 177 n. 108, 195
  English Political Philosophy 169–71, 173
  influence of 202
Grant, A. J. 215–16
Grattan, Henry 38, 115, 119, 130,
    132, 151
'Grattan's Parliament'
    (1782–1800) 115–16, 120
  and Burke 122, 134, 153
  as an argument for Home Rule 124,
    128 n. 54, 130–2
  in Liberal Unionist arguments 136,
    138–40
Green, Alice Stopford 132
Green, J. R. 96, 132
  on Burke's conservatism 105
  on Burke's constitutionalism 21, 26
  on Burke's philosophy of politics 69, 73
Green, T. H. 51, 90
  influence of 161–2, 173, 191, 198–9
Grieve, A. J. 207

Hallam, A. H. 29, 122
Hallam, Henry 16, 57
Hartington, Spencer Cavendish, marquess
    of (later 8th duke of Devonshire):
  and Home Rule 117 n. 10, 140, 146
  compared to Burke 149–50, 154
  compared to Gladstone 136, 137,
    144 n. 115
  on Burke 140 n. 95
Hastings, Warren 2, 31
  and Macaulay 31–2, 89
  and postcolonialism 232
  impeachment trial 12, 76, 78, 105, 110,
    111, 190
  in ICS examinations 220
  mainstream opinion of 61, 220
Harcourt, Sir William Vernon
    40, 114
  Burke, use of 131–2, 145–6, 151
Hare, Thomas 23, 25–6
Harrison, Frederic 83–4
Hazlitt, William 30–1, 53
Hearnshaw, F. J. C 206–7
Hegel, G. W. F. 46
Herford, C. H. 205, 217
Hewins, W. A. S. 222

historicism 46, 83–4, 85, 101
  and Home Rule 123–4
  Burke's 21, 102, 174, 208
  Burke's, in European context 207
  see also historical method, the
historical method, the 160,
    163 n. 29, 171
  and Idealism 166
  as providing a link between Burke and
    Henry Maine 167
  Burke as father of 103, 163,
    164–6
  Burke's abandonment of 217 n. 91
  see also historicism
history of political thought, the 164,
    198–9, 215, 216
History, study of 200
  at school 203
  at university 212–13, 214–15, 216,
    217–19
Holland, Henry, 3rd Baron 30, 74–5
Home Rule (Irish) 89, 91,
    114–55, 195
  political aftermath 157
  see also Act of Union; Grattan's
    Parliament
Home Rule (Welsh) 166
Hulme, T. E. 182
Hutton, R. H. 123
Huxley, T. H. 135, 137–8, 141

Idealism 62, 90, 108, 173
  and Burke 161–2, 166–7, 226
  and education 198–9
  and the history of thought 169,
    198–9
  link to conservatism 195
India 35, 76
  Fox's India Bill (1783) 220
  see also Burke, Edmund, works of: Indian
    writings and speeches; Empire,
    British; Hastings, Warren; Indian
    Civil Service
Indian Civil Service 197, 203
  examinations 219–20
Ireland 6, 8, 13–14, 34–6
  see also Act of Union; Grattan's
    Parliament; Home Rule; Penal
    Code, the
Irishness 56–8, 74, 230–1
  and political aptitude 62–3, 121
  Burke's 'Irish' traits 66–7, 68, 69–70,
    77–8
  see also Englishness; Gaelic Revival
    Movement; national character

Jacobinism:
  and Communism 3
  and Home Rule 120, 145–7, 189,
  and the constitutional crisis (1909–14) 158, 180 n. 126, 185, 188, 195–6
  see also French Revolution
James, Henry 148–9, 152
Jones, Henry 166, 174, 184

Kebbel, T. E. 120 n. 23, 158
  on Burke 24, 76–7, 149–50
  on Conservatism 18–19, 39, 149–50, 180 n. 129
Keynes, John Maynard 171–3, 174, 195
King, Walter 12
King's College, London 14

Lampeter, St David's College 218
Lawrence, French 3, 12, 131
Lecky, W. E. H. 82, 91, 168
  his Irish writings 119–20, 121, 128
  his Liberal Unionism 114, 135, 136–7, 138, 146, 152
  his thought 5, 85, 104
  influence of 3–4, 200, 210, 212
  on Burke's conception of liberty 32
  on Burke's Conservatism 52
  on Burke's intellect 73
Leeds, University of 214
  and the teaching of Burke 215–17
Lever, Charles 66
Liberal Anglicanism 49–51, 85, 106–7, 108–9
  and Idealism 175
Liberalism 144–52, 183
  and constitutionalism 17–18
  and progress 89
  and the French Revolution 181, 191
  'civil and religious liberty' 17, 116–17, 127, 135–7, 138, 151
  New Liberalism 159, 188
  see also Liberal Unionism; Liberal Party; Whiggism; Whig Party
Liberal party:
  and Home Rule 114–17, 121, 125, 127, 134, 146
  and parliamentary reform 17–18, 32–4, 77
  see also Gladstone, W. E.; Liberal Unionism; Liberalism; Whiggism; Whig Party
Liberal Unionism 116–17, 120, 135–6, 144–52, 154–5
  and Burke 114, 121, 136–43, 154–5, 169

  and Catholicism 126
  and parliamentary sovereignty 115
  and the Conservative party 159
  as 'Old Whiggism' 145–52
  see also Gladstone, W. E.; Liberalism; Liberalism; Whiggism; Whig Party
liberty:
  American 124
  and Burke 31–2, 69–70, 93, 101, 111
  and Liberal Unionism 135–7, 151
  and the French Revolution 145, 179, 181
  and Whig-Liberals 34, 117, 127
  coercion 124, 126, 128
  constitutional liberty 16–17, 21–2, 101, 130
  individual 185
  tyranny of the majority 135–6, 137–8, 154, 195
Little, Andrew George 198
Liverpool, University of 161
  and the teaching of Burke 215
  University College, Liverpool 183
London, University of 209, 214
  Correspondence College 221
  see also University College, London
Lowe, Robert 49
Ludovici, A. M. 191

Macaulay, T. B. 16, 147, 163 n. 28
  and Warren Hastings 32, 89, 220
  commentary on 197
  his similarity to Burke 6, 8, 28, 103, 179
  in education 205, 213
  on Burke's literary qualities 53, 74
  on Burke's politics 1, 30, 72
MacCunn, John 3, 108, 180, 195
  as an educator 215
  his Idealism 161–2, 166, 184
  influence of 202
  The Political Philosophy of Burke 15, 173–7
Mackintosh, James 33, 57, 75 n. 79, 165
Macknight, Thomas:
  biography of 14
  Burke, defence of 25, 32, 76
  Burke, praise of 45, 53–4, 69, 70
  criticism of 77, 93–4
  on Burke's thought 63, 65
  on Disraeli 42
  on Home Rule 131, 137–8
  Whig party, criticism of 30
Maine, Henry 88, 133
  compared to Burke 164, 167
  in university education 216

Maitland, F. W. 6
Mallet, J. L. 21
Mallock, W. H. 177
Manchester, University of 113
  and the teaching of Burke 215, 217–19
  history, teaching of 199
  Owen's College 201, 213
Manners, Lord John 144
Marx, Karl 59
Maurice, F. D. 26, 79, 108
  influence of 204
  on Burke and national churches 49–51
  on Burke's Irishness 65–6
  on English literature 213
May, Thomas Erskine 27
Maynooth College 36, 123
Mazzini, Giuseppe 108–9, 173
Mill, John Stuart 10, 90, 91
  compared to Burke 64, 169
  influence of 14, 84–5, 86, 87, 162
  on Burke 73 n. 72, 84
  System of Logic 75, 87, 107
Milner, Alfred 182
Monteagle, Thomas Spring Rice, 2nd baron 141
Montgomery, Robert 20
Monypenny, W. F. 40
Morley, Henry 212–13, 215
  Henry Morley's Universal Library 223, 224–5
Morley, John 82, 195
  biography 14–15
  contemporary reception 113
  criticism of 168–9, 172, 177, 225
  his thought 17, 83–7, 90–2, 104, 109
  in educational contexts 200, 202, 210, 212, 217, 222
  on Burke 156, 160, 184
  and free thought 104
  and liberty 32
  as C/conservative 105–6
  compared to Disraeli 42–3
  criticism of 111
  his consistency 69, 98–100
  his ethics 109–110
  his importance as a thinker 95, 108, 112
  his passion 72
  his utilitarianism 82, 164
  his value to students 202–3
  his wisdom 62, 63
  on Home Rule 117, 122, 128, 133–4, 140, 145
Muirhead, J. H. 162

Napier, Joseph 45, 77–8, 94–5
national character 56–8, 118
  'Four Nations' history 230–1
  see also Englishness; Irishness
natural law 4, 169
natural rights 166, 195
  and Burke 21, 99, 101, 170
Newman, J. H. 46
Nonconformity 141–2, 157–8

Oldfield, T. B. H. 74
organicism 91
  and conservatism 189, 193–4
  and constitutionalism 6, 27
  and democracy 176–7
  and Idealism 166–7
  Burke's 85, 102, 112, 166–7, 185, 207
  evolutionary thinking 90, 101, 102, 105, 106, 161
  in European context 207
  organic metaphors 160–1
  see also historicism
Oxford, University of 14, 87, 211
  Balliol College 51, 161
  Palmerston Club 173 n. 87
  Snell exhibition 161
  student numbers 214
  see also education, university extension

Paine, Thomas 71, 165, 181
  in education 222
Parker-Smith, James 152
parliament:
  political representation 24–6, 33
parliamentary reform:
  1832 Reform Act 32–4, 42, 158
  1867 Reform Act 42, 82, 186
  1884–5 Reform Acts 157
  Burke's opposition to 39, 42, 71–2, 76, 97, 111
  see also constitutionalism, English
parliamentary sovereignty 115, 141
  see also constitutionalism, English; Dicey, A. V.; Irish Home Rule; Liberal Unionism
Parnell, Charles Stewart 56, 131 n. 62
  see also Home Rule (Irish)
Pattison, Mark 86
Paul, Herbert 181
Payne, Edward John 82, 102
  Burke: Select Works 12, 95–6, 112–13
  criticism of Buckle 75–6
  on Burke's thought 100–1, 104, 107

Peel, Sir Robert 35–6, 53, 145, 184, 192
  his Conservatism 19, 41, 179
  compared to Burke 39, 233
  on Burke 38–9, 43, 49, 54
Peelites 14, 192
Penal Code, the 122
  Burke's criticism of 48, 123, 128, 136, 143
  basis of Burke's criticism of 45, 60
  see also church establishment; Home Rule
Phillips, Catherine Beatrice 207–8
Phillips, Walter Alison 207–8
Pitt, William (the Younger) 72, 131, 134, 145, 149, 153, 184, 192–3
  as 'C/conservative' 35, 36, 93–4, 188, 206
  compared to Burke 34, 36, 40–2, 93–4, 180, 188
  in education 218, 222
Pittites 61, 71
Playfair, Lyon 127–8
political traditions 9–11
Pollard, A. F. 209, 215
Pollock, Fredrick 164–5, 167
Positivism, English 83
  influence of 14, 90, 91, 106
  on Burke 84–5, 112
  see also Auguste Comte
Prendergast, J. P. 120
Primrose League, the 178
Prior, Sir James 12–13, 62, 65, 66, 71, 92
  on Burke's Catholicism 44
  on Burke's Irish qualities 69–70, 79
  on Burke's support of Catholic relief 36

Quarterly Review 171
Queen's College, Belfast 64

Redmond, John 125, 151–2
Reform Acts, *see* parliamentary reform
representative government, *see* Burke, Edmund, works of: Bristol speeches; parliament, political representation
rights of man, *see* natural rights
Ritchie, D. G. 162, 184, 195
  on Burke 166, 167
Robertson, J. B. 91–2
  on Burke's constitutionalism 46–7
Robertson, J. M. 181
Romanticism 167–8
  in education 187, 199–200, 206, 216–17

see also Coleridge, S. T.; English literature
Rousseau, J. J. 198–9, 206, 208, 217
  compared to Burke 21, 165, 170, 181
  'general will' 163, 199
  in education 216
Rosebery, Lord 134, 148
Russell, Lord John 83 n. 7, 96, 151
  on Burke and party government 23, 29
  on Burke's inconsistency 30, 32–3, 74–5

Salisbury, Robert Cecil, 3rd marquess 140, 153, 184, 187
  and Burke 136, 143–4, 183
  his Conservatism 178–9, 193
Saturday Review 88
  on Burke 98–9, 106, 171, 180, 190–1, 194
Savigny, F. K. 46, 164, 207
Seeley, J. R. 106, 202–3, 226
Selborne, Roundell Palmer, 1st earl 147
Selby, Francis Guy 204–5
Shaw Lefevre, George 129
Sidgwick, Henry 16, 54, 89, 107, 156
  his utilitarianism 162–3
Sieyès, Abbé 21
Smith, F. E. 159, 186, 195
  on Disraeli 191
  Toryism 182–3
Smith, Goldwin 158, 180
  his Liberal Unionism 121, 135
  Irish History and Irish Character 120–1
  on Burke's Irishness 67, 77–8
  on the 'Catholicism' of Burke's thought 47–8, 80
Smyth, William 21
socialism 101
  fears of 157, 188, 195
Southey, Robert 68
Spencer, Herbert 166, 171, 195
Stanhope, Arthur, 6th earl 61, 71
Stanley, A. P. 50
Stephen, James Fitzjames 82
  his thought 5, 87–90, 107, 135
  influence of 3–4, 210
  on Burke 95–8, 104, 112–13, 168, 174
  on Warren Hastings 111, 220
Stephen, Leslie 82, 135, 156, 184
  and Positivism 83–4
  criticism of Burke 103, 105, 111
  his interest in Burke 85–6, 91–2
  his thought 87–8, 89–90, 104, 107–8
  influence of 3–4, 200, 202, 210
  on Burke's historicism 102, 165–6

on Burke's thought 95, 102–3, 109, 112–13
on the study of English literature 203
Stubbs, Bishop William 6
Swift MacNeill, J. G. 131
Symes, J. E. 222–3

Tariff Reform 178, 186, 187
Thatcher, Margaret 232
Thelwall, John 68
Thring, Henry, 1st baron 129–30
Tone, Wolfe 117
Toryism 18
  as part of Conservatism 188
  as preferable to C/conservative 41–2, 180, 182–3, 191–3
  Burke's 37, 184–5, 191, 194
  compared to Whiggism 175
  Irish Toryism 35
  see also conservatism, Conservative Party; Tory party
Tory party 170–1
  see also Bolingbroke, Lord; conservatism, Conservative party; Pitt, William; Toryism
Tout, T. F. 199, 217–18, 226
Trevelyan, George 147, 148
Trinity College, Dublin 49, 58, 73, 119, 200, 207, 212
Trollope, Anthony 67
Tyndall, John 135

United States 58 n. 10, 93, 229
  British texts, reception of 101 n. 106, 121 n. 26
  Butler's *The Tory Tradition*, reception of 193
  Cold War, Burke reception during 3–4, 8, 230
  MacCunn's *Political Philosophy of Burke*, reception of 176–7
  Morley on Burke, reception of 99 n. 95, 113
  Pollock's *Introduction to the Science of Politics*, reception of 165
  Revolution, American 31, 33, 60, 69, 97, 103, 115
  Stephen's *History of English Thought*, reception of 102 n. 111
  US ambassadors and Burke 195 n. 209
  see also Burke, Edmund: American Speeches

University College, London 212–13
  see also London, University of
university education, see education
university extension 202, 221–3
  see also education
utilitarianism 82–3, 102
  Burke's divergence from 63–4
  Burke's (in long 19thc) 103–4, 106, 112, 172–3
  Burke's (modern) 4, 85
  criticism of 171
  late-Victorian 162–3
  see also Jeremy Bentham; J. S. Mill; Henry Sidgwick

Vaughan, Charles Edwin 108, 198–9
  his school text-books 205–6
  his university teaching 216–17
  The Romantic Revolt 217
  on Burke 226
  on Rousseau 217
Victoria University, the 214
  see also civic universities; Leeds, University of; Liverpool, University of; Manchester, University of

Wade, John 31
Walker, Hugh 62–3, 199, 218 n. 93
Wallas, Graham 182, 222
Willoughby de Broke, Richard Verney, 19th baron 191
Windham, William 3
Whiggism 130, 136, 144–51
  as 'conservatism' 105–6, 123, 177, 183, 188, 196, 222, 226–7
  Burke's 41, 130, 136, 144, 175
  see also Liberal Unionism; Liberalism; Burke, Edmund: conservatism; Whig Party
Whig Party:
  aristocratic exclusiveness 77
  Holland House 71, 85
  constitution, view of the 17–18
  on Burke's legacy to party 28–30, 41, 81, 130
  see also Fox, Charles James; Liberal Unionism; Liberalism; Russell, Lord John; Whiggism
Wodehouse, Edmond 138
Wollstonecraft, Mary 59, 74
Wordsworth, William 68, 175, 221

Yeats, W. B. 78–80